UPDIKE

UPDIKE

AMERICA'S MAN OF LETTERS

WILLIAM H. PRITCHARD

STEERFORTH PRESS
SOUTH ROYALTON, VERMONT

For information about permission to reproduce
selections from this book, write to:
Steerforth Press l.c.
PO Box 70, South Royalton, Vermont 05068

LIBRARY OF CONGRESS CATALOGING-IN-PUBLICATION DATA

Pritchard, William H.
    Updike : America's man of letters / William H. Pritchard.
    p. cm.
    Includes bibliographical references (p.) and index.
    ISBN 1-58642-002-X (alk. paper)
    1. Updike, John — Criticism and interpretation. I. Title.

PS 3571.P4 Z83 2000
813'.54—dc21

                                        00-033835

FIRST EDITION

Once more, to Marietta

CONTENTS

ACKNOWLEDGMENTS

A few years back I wrote the subject of this book to ask how he would feel about my undertaking such a project. His reply, prompt and courteous as ever, was something to the effect of blessings on it as long as it wasn't a biography. So I have tried not to bother him with questions about either his life or his writings. The main encourager, supporter, and obliging reader chapter by chapter has been Warner Berthoff, whose knowledge of American and other literature is prodigious, and whose particular admiration of Updike's work has set a standard of appreciation for me. I should like also to thank Rand Richards Cooper and Lawrence Douglas, who read the completed manuscript and made useful suggestions. Thanks also to Harvard University's Houghton Library, where I consulted Updike's early unpublished novel *Home* and where I was overwhelmed by the decades' worth of manuscripts and letters that, someday, a biographer will need to consult.

As always, Amherst College, especially Dean of Faculty Lisa Raskin, has been hospitable toward funding incidental expenses. The Amherst College Library's archives contain, by the gift of Jack W. C. Hagstrom, a large collection of Updike's works in the original and in translations, which I have perused with interest. For help with various technological matters I'm indebted to Susan Raymond-Fic, Julie Howland, and Laura Moser. My editor, Alan Lelchuk, has been an ideal one, whose real criticisms have I hope made this a better book.

CHRONOLOGY

1932 John Hoyer Updike born March 18 in Reading, Pennsylvania; grows up in Shillington with parents and maternal grandparents.

1945 Family moves to farmhouse in Plowville, eleven miles away, where Updike's mother was born.

1950 Graduates as co-valedictorian from Shillington High School; enters Harvard University in the fall.

1953 Marries Mary Pennington, a fine arts major at Radcliffe; editor of *Harvard Lampoon*.

1954 Graduates from Harvard summa cum laude in English, thesis on Robert Herrick.

1954–5 Spends year at the Ruskin School of Drawing and Fine Arts, Oxford; joins staff of the *New Yorker* in fall of 1955; first child Elizabeth born.

1957 Son David born. Moves to Ipswich, Massachusetts; completes a novel, *Home*, which he does not attempt to publish.

1958 *The Carpentered Hen, And Other Tame Creatures* (poems).

1959 Son Michael born; *The Same Door* (stories) and *The Poorhouse Fair* (novel) published.

1960   Daughter Miranda born; *Rabbit, Run* (novel).

1962   *Pigeon Feathers* (stories).

1963   *The Centaur* (novel), wins National Book Award; *Telephone Poles* (poems).

1964   *Olinger Stories;* travels to Eastern Europe for State Department; elected to National Institute of Arts and Letters.

1965   *Of the Farm* (novel); *Assorted Prose.*

1966   *The Music School* (stories).

1968   *Couples* (novel).

1968–9 Lives with family in London; *Midpoint* (poems).

1970   *Bech: A Book* (stories).

1971   *Rabbit Redux* (novel).

1972   Father dies; *Museums and Women* (stories).

1973   Fulbright lectureship in Africa.

1974   *Buchanan Dying* (play); separates from wife, lives in Boston.

1975   *A Month of Sundays* (novel); *Picked-Up Pieces* (prose).

1976   *Marry Me* (novel); divorced; moves to Georgetown, Massachusetts; elected to Academy of Arts and Letters.

1977   Marries Martha Bernhard; *Tossing and Turning* (poems).

1978   *The Coup* (novel).

1979   *Too Far to Go: The Maples Stories; Problems* (stories).

1981   *Rabbit Is Rich* (novel); wins Pulitzer prize, American Book Award, and National Book Critics' Circle Award.

1982   *Bech Is Back* (stories); moves to Beverly Farms, Massachusetts.

1983   *Hugging the Shore* (prose); National Book Critics' Circle Award for criticism.

1984   *The Witches of Eastwick* (novel).

1985   *Facing Nature* (poems).

1986   *Roger's Version* (novel).

1987   *Trust Me* (stories).

1988   *S* (novel).

1989   *Self-Consciousness* (memoirs); *Just Looking* (art criticism); mother dies.

1990   *Rabbit at Rest* (novel); receives Pulitzer prize, National Book Critics' Circle Award.

1991   *Odd Jobs* (prose).

1992   *Memories of the Ford Administration* (novel).

1993   *Collected Poems: 1953–1993.*

1994   *Brazil* (novel); *The Afterlife* (stories).

1995   *Rabbit Angstrom: A Tetralogy* (Everyman's Library).

1996   *In the Beauty of the Lilies* (novel); *Golf Dreams* (prose).

1997   *Toward the End of Time* (novel).

1998   *Bech at Bay* (stories).

1999   *More Matter* (prose).

2000   *Gertrude and Claudius* (novel); *Licks of Love* (stories).

INTRODUCTION
THE MAN OF LETTERS

In the fall of 1997, at the time John Updike's novel *Toward the End of Time* was published, the New York *Observer* featured a page headlined "Twilight of the Phallocrats," consisting of pieces by the critic Sven Birkerts and the novelist David Foster Wallace about the current state of American fiction. That state was not good insofar as it concerned what Birkerts called "our giants, our arts-bemedaled senior male novelists." He was referring to Updike, Philip Roth, Norman Mailer, and Saul Bellow, whose recent novels were "manifestly second-rate" yet who were not "getting called onto the carpet for it." Birkerts suggested that these eminent writers would be well advised to yield their crowns to a younger generation of "brothers," novelists such as Don DeLillo, Thomas Pynchon, Robert Stone, and John Edgar Wideman, who had their eyes on politics and society, the "larger world" Updike and his contemporaries, in their obsessive preoccupation with the self, were neglecting. Wallace took a similar line in more abusive terms, declaring that readers under age forty — particularly female ones — had no time for what he termed the G.M.N.s (Great Male Novelists) and disliked Updike in particular. *Toward the End of Time* was a prime example of what these novelists shared — "their radical self-absorption and their uncritical celebration of this self-absorption both in themselves and in their characters."

This is aggressive, knockabout polemic of the emperor-has-no-clothes variety, and for both Birkerts and Wallace narcissism or "self-absorption" is an evil, simply and wholly a failure of moral imagination. I am not concerned to defend the other senior male novelists from this charge, and I bring it up at the beginning of this book about a literary career not to dismiss it but to see whether such absorption might be instead the mark of aesthetic power. From his earliest work, Updike's engagement with himself — with a man living a life — has been paramount and unabashed. There are and have been critics of his work for whom that concern, that engagement with a self, is not enough; who believe that something larger and more important has been neglected, is lacking. I am not of their number, since — forty-five years or so after it began — Updike's literary career seems to me exemplary and inspiring, one that has yielded up book after book full of artistic, human satisfaction. These introductory pages aim to situate him as a man of letters in relation to some American predecessors; also to situate myself as a critic of his work.

Although he had published short stories and poems, along with various humorous squibs, in high-school magazines, in the newspaper of his home city Reading, Pennsylvania, and prolifically in the *Harvard Lampoon* (which he also edited), Updike's national career as a writer began in 1954, when the *New Yorker* published his story "Friends from Philadelphia." In that magazine the same year appeared "Duet, with Muffled Brake Drums," a poem about the fateful day when Mr. Rolls met Mr. Royce. The poem, accepted the month Updike graduated from Harvard, would open his first collection of verse, *The Carpentered Hen, And Other Tame Creatures*, published by Harper in 1958. A year later "Friends from Philadelphia" would similarly open his first collection of stories, *The Same Door*, which — along with his novel *The Poorhouse Fair*, also published in 1959 — inaugurated a lifetime association with the firm of Alfred Knopf. In his twenty-eighth year, then, Updike had published books in the three major genres he would continue to exploit, with steadily expanding brilliance and authority, in fifty books. In the closing years of the 1950s, a literary career had been launched which over the next four decades would realize itself centrally in these three forms, but also in the steady work of reviewing and criticism, both of literature and painting; in memoirs; and in resourceful commentary on his own work — the stuff of many interviews and prefaces.

Now, four decades after his burst upon the scene, Updike has presented us with his fifth collection of prose essays and criticism (sixth, if you count the art pieces in *Just Looking*): *More Matter* comprises nine hundred pages of wide-ranging reflections on writers, on writing, and on America as he has perceived it for sixty-eight years. The range is from grand matters of state ("The State of the Union, as of March 1992") to trivia like suntanning or Lana Turner, all of them made interesting by the writer's sensibility and treatment. Overall, *More Matter*, in its terminal place at the millennium, makes a strong case for this writer as our preeminent man of letters. In suggesting what that phrase may mean, I quote some useful words of Denis Donoghue about an earlier collection of Updike's prose, *Hugging the Shore*.[1] The old-fashioned-sounding phrase *man of letters*, Donoghue wrote, referred "not to writers who regularly review books but to those who take the occasion of reviewing to reflect on the intellectual and moral issues that beset us." The man of letters, he went on, "admires knowledge but isn't intimidated by experts or disabled by the probability that in any particular area of knowledge he must yield to them in the end." He relies, said Donoghue, "upon nothing more than a cultivated intelligence and assiduous reading."

Updike's role in American letters has been performed by three major predecessors: Nathaniel Hawthorne, William Dean Howells, and Edmund Wilson. It is true that Hawthorne and Howells were principally novelists; Wilson a critic and essayist. But each was a writer with many strings to his bow, committed to speaking with conviction, wit, and authority about the intellectual and moral condition of his native land. By setting Updike in relation to these writers, rather than to our three most famous expatriate men of letters — Henry James, Ezra Pound, and T. S. Eliot — I have in mind a common sense he shares with the "American" triumvirate. Like them, he mainly stayed home, thinking it his primary task to give us reports and bulletins on American manners. He may have decided, as did his predecessors, that it does not make sense for an American writer to take up permanent residence in England, France, or Italy. But another "sense" Updike shares with Hawthorne, Howells, and Wilson is a social, ironic one: his invitation to the reader, often a humorous one, is to join in acts of human and artistic measuring that hospitably include us, rather than holding us off at arm's length as the great modernists (James in his late novels, Eliot in *The Waste Land*, Pound in "Mauberley" and *The Cantos*) often do.

To illustrate: Hawthorne's fiction is full of extravagance, of tall tales, of characters behaving in the most improbable, melodramatic, deranged ways. Yet the novels, and especially the stories in which these characters live, are subject to an unillusioned and reassuring narrative voice of sensible, even comic, social judgment. Edmund Wilson's appeal throughout his work is to the generally intelligent reader, unencumbered by theories or distorting ideologies; yet those readers are asked to be wholly immoderate and extreme in their appetite for reading novels, histories, politics, religion. All we have to do to succeed, that is, is become as voracious as Wilson himself and devote our entire lives to reading everything, not just American but world writing. As for Howells — to my mind Updike's single most inescapable analogue — here is a writer, most grievously neglected today, who spent his literary life making the best case he could for the vitality and interest of American life and letters. Yet he is too often remembered, and dismissed, as the source of an infamous pronouncement about how our writers perforce deal with the "smiling aspects" of life. From where Howells stood over a century ago, in *Criticism and Fiction*, there were no Dostoyevskian tribulations available in America: not even — in his witty example — the rigors of a winter in Duluth, Minnesota, would qualify. Analogously we might recall a moment in *Rabbit at Rest* when Updike's hero, having successfully impersonated Uncle Sam in a Fourth of July parade in his Pennsylvania hometown, declares "that all in all this is the happiest fucking country the world has ever seen." For a moment at least, the unsmiling aspects of life in these United States have been triumphantly, even belligerently, disregarded.

Unlike Hawthorne's or Wilson's, Howells's career displays the perfect balance of literary modes: there are the poems, written early, and promising in their delicacy of observation; there are, early and late, the novels; there are dramatic compositions and many travel books; there are a number of delightful and important literary reminiscences, appearing at intervals over the career; there are the memoirs of childhood, especially *A Boy's Town*, in which small-town midwestern life in the last century is lovingly rendered. And there is Howells the literary editor and critic. In *Criticism and Fiction* he pays tribute to what he calls "the realist writer," of which he considers himself an instance:

> In life he finds nothing insignificant; all tells for destiny and character, nothing that God has made is contemptible. He cannot look upon human life and declare this thing or that unworthy of notice, any more than the scientist can declare a fact of the material world beneath the dignity of his inquiry. He feels in every nerve the equality of things and the unity of man.

This democratic gesture is peculiarly American and manifests the spirit with which, in his first nonfiction essay in autobiography, Updike describes his own project as a writer. In "The Dogwood Tree: A Boyhood" *(Assorted Prose)* he tells us that as a young man he saw art, whether drawing or writing, "as a method of riding a thin pencil line out of Shillington" (the small Pennsylvania town where he grew up) "into an infinity of unseen and even unborn hearts," and that he pictured this infinity as "radiant." The radiance had to do, at least in part, with the solidity of the world's body:

> Blankness is not emptiness; we may skate upon an intense radiance we do not see because we see nothing else. And in fact there is a color, a quiet but tireless goodness that things at rest, like a brick wall or a small stone, seem to affirm. A wordless reassurance these things are pressing to give. An hallucination? To transcribe middleness with all its grits, bumps, and anonymities, in its fullness of satisfaction and mystery: is it

possible or, in view of the suffering that violently colors the
periphery and that at all moments threatens to move into the
center, worth doing?

We scarcely credit him when he follows with the disclaimer,
"Possibly not," since such transcribings of the world's body are what
have so tirelessly occupied him in his writing career since "The
Dogwood Tree." He has never deviated from his conviction that we
were put in this world to give praise and to pay attention.

In "The Dogwood Tree" Updike invokes Goethe, who tells us "to
be wary of our youthful wishes, for in maturity we are apt to get
them." The sage also warned that being a man of letters is an incurable disease, and doubtless Thomas Mann, Goethe's successor in that
line, would have agreed, since in "Goethe's Career as a Man of
Letters" Mann connects the incurable nature of the ailment with
Goethe's capacity for wonder, and claims that his productivity was
closely bound up with what Mann calls his "positive genius for admiration" (*admirare:* to wonder at). This capacity is also at the root of
Updike's endeavor, having everything to do with the affirming tone
he takes toward things, a tone that has annoyed competitors for the
American-man-of-letters sweepstakes. (Gore Vidal, for instance,
wrote a long and disparaging review of Updike's In the Beauty of the
Lilies and of his "patriotic" attitude toward America generally.[2])
Rather than saying No, in Thunder as Herman Melville perceived
Hawthorne to have done, Updike, in the eyes of more than one
critic, has said Yes, in Sunshine to American phenomena on which
they would prefer to cast a much colder eye. For example: Updike
attends church, refused to condemn American involvement in the
Vietnam War, and has even confessed satisfaction with Bill Clinton
as president (he has later qualified that). Furthermore he is a highly
successful writer with no literary agent, has stayed with one publisher
throughout his career, and seems never to stop smiling. His many
books, published at a rate of more than one per year, show no traces
of agonized spiritual travail; they don't, in W. B. Yeats's words, suggest "beauty born out of its own despair / Nor blear-eyed wisdom out

of midnight oil." Instead it seems all casual elegance, effortless, an act performed with no hands, revealing first and last — in Robert Frost's words — "what a *hell* of a good time I had writing it."

At any rate it's undeniable that Updike's capacity for admiration, for paying unstinting attention to the things of this world, is at the center of his strengths as an artist. Philip Roth once remarked, with self-deprecating humor, that he'd just read *Rabbit Is Rich* and that Updike "knows so much, about golf, about porn, about kids, about America. I don't know anything about anything."[3] A list of subjects Updike is interested in and conversant with would include the following: the graphic arts, in particular drawing and painting; journalism and the mechanics of printing and newspaper life; geographical, topological, and botanical lore about the landscape of eastern Pennsylvania and the Massachusetts coast north and south of Boston; theological and philosophical inquiry, especially as it involves Protestant "crisis" thinkers from the nineteenth century and beyond; popular song lyrics listened to on the radio and celebrated in his own light verse. He possesses the inclination and ability to find out how things work, as well as what sort of work has preceded us — as revealed in natural history, the evolution of species, the world's progress since prehistoric time (see George Caldwell's lecture in *The Centaur*). There is a fascination generally with scientific, cosmological theories, especially "popular" ones, of the universe's origins and its possible extinction. No writer is more intelligently acquainted with the details of plumbing, with how the frame of a house is constructed, how its boards fit together. Being put on earth to notice things, to give praise, carries with it the obligation to fathom the depths and dimensions of the nonhuman world that supports us. In the short sketch "Plumbing" (*Museums and Women*), as the plumber indicates a finely made joint in the man's cellar, the man thinks, "He knows my plumbing; I merely own it. . . . We think we are what we think and see when in truth we are upright bags of tripe. We think we have bought living space and a view when in truth we have bought a maze, a history, an archeology of pipes and cut-ins and traps and valves." Exploring the maze, this history, can add up to a lifework of writing, and the very homeliness of such materials is an incitement to Updike's writerly ability to transform them into radiance, as in some lines from his poem "The Melancholy of Storm Windows":

> In need of paint, they heave
> up from the cellar and back down again
> like a species of cloud,
> shedding a snow of flakes and grime.
> They rotate heavy in our hands; the screwdriver
> stiffly twirls; the Windex swipes evaporate
> in air ominous of coming worse
> or, at winter's end, of Easter entombment,
> of cobwebbed storage among belittling ants
> while the grasshopper world above basks.
>
> Stacked, they savor of the crypt,
> of the unvisitable nook
> and the stinking pipe, irreparable.

What are the challenges and hazards that confront the writer of a critical book about this phenomenon? First perhaps is the man's fearsome articulateness, at all moments, on all subjects, in all forms. An amusing example of how his powers in this regard can overbear and frustrate aspiring novelists occurs in Nicholson Baker's *U&I*, when Baker remembers watching a documentary on Updike in which,

> in one scene, as the camera follows his climb up a ladder at his mother's house to put up or take down some storm windows, in the midst of this tricky physical act, he tosses down to us some startlingly lucid little felicity, something about "These small yearly duties which blah blah blah," and I was stunned to recognize that in Updike we were dealing with a man so naturally verbal that he could write his fucking memoirs *on a ladder!*

Baker's book, while advertising itself as a "true story" of his obsession with Updike, is also the best book on the writer that has appeared. The others have been written by academics quite properly concerned with describing and analyzing their subject's oeuvre; Baker's wholly unacademic gambit is to put himself front and center, as he treats us to a display, from the opening chapter on, of his decision to write about his hero. So *U&I* is a book rich enough to make any critic of Updike hesitate. A related cause for hesitation is that Updike's interviews and his many introductions to his own books, as they are reprinted, have resulted in a dauntingly impressive body of commentary. One is of course rightly wary about trusting an author on the nature and quality of his own work; still, Updike's self-commentary seems notably dispassionate, full of sound and untendentious judgments.

But there is a further, more individual challenge to the attempt on my part to speak disinterestedly about this writer's achievement, to give it what Matthew Arnold in "The Study of Poetry" called a "real estimate" rather than one that is primarily historical or primarily personal. In speaking of the dangers of succumbing to a merely "personal" estimate of a writer Arnold wrote as follows:

> a poet or a poem may count to us on grounds personal to ourselves. Our personal affinities, likings, and circumstances, have great power to sway our estimate of this or that poet's work, and to make us attach more importance to it as poetry than in itself it really possesses, because to us it is, or has been, of high importance. Here . . . we over-rate the object of our interest, and apply to it a language of praise which is quite exaggerated.

To what extent can a non-novelist professional critic like myself presume to speak truly about a contemporary writer, the stuff of whose work is, to a large extent, the stuff of his — my — own American life in the second half of this century? Even though this is an age, as the phrase goes, of identity politics, it may still be that with writers such as, say, George Herbert or Jane Austen, someone addressing the task of writing about either would not need to begin by producing his credentials or confessing her limitations. He or she would not, at least arguably, need to mention biographical data, gender, sexual preference, religious belief or lack of it before setting out to write a clear-headed, useful book about Herbert's poetry or Austen's novels. Is it any different when we are dealing with a contemporary writer? Probably so, inasmuch as there are intelligent, serious readers of fiction who do *not* spend time reading Updike, indeed find him uncongenial, trivial, "narcissistic," male-chauvinist. The case is significantly different from that of Herbert or Austen — or James Joyce. There may, that is, be card-carrying academics who dislike Herbert's lyrics or find Austen's novels dull, or who think *Ulysses* is a fraud, but I don't know any willing to make such confessions. Is it not, however, the case that considerations of gender, race, and politics *are* important constituents of one's sense of what's important or not so important in contemporary fiction? Can one imagine a lively argument among three readers about artistic superiority when the first's notion of a great work is Toni Morrison's *Beloved*, while for the second it is Pynchon's *Mason & Dixon,* and for the third Updike's *Rabbit at Rest?* Most likely these readers would politely or rudely go their ways rather than attempt to persuade each other of their favorite's preeminence.

It is time, then, to unpack my bag and declare the circumstances in my own life that might make for a sympathetic reading of Updike's work. I was born in 1932, eight months after he was, into a world which, as he puts it in "The Dogwood Tree," was "made tranquil by two invisible catastrophes: the Depression and World War II." I grew up in Johnson City, New York, a small industrial town of twenty thousand inhabitants (an "incorporated village" officially), located just north of the New York–Pennsylvania state line, some 150 miles north of Updike's Shillington. My equivalent, in a neighboring large city, to his Reading was Binghamton, three miles away, which contained the record stores and movie houses I frequented. Like Updike, though not as an only child, I had the benefit of parents convinced of my giftedness and — especially in my mother's case — actively bent on seeing those gifts develop, insofar as encouragement, sometimes vigorously applied, could do so. (Updike has left ample written testimony to the centrality of his mother's influence.) His gifts were literary and pictorial ("riding a thin pencil line out of Shillington"); my own were literary and, to an even greater extent, musical. Updike lived with his parents and maternal grandparents for thirteen years in a house on Shillington's Philadelphia Avenue, then in a sandstone farmhouse ten miles into the country beyond Shillington. My earliest years were spent in a house shared with my paternal grandmother and aunts; when I was four my parents built their own house, but were joined some years afterward by the grandmother and aunts who built a house three doors away. Like Updike's father Wesley, who taught mathematics in the Shillington high school, my mother was a public-school music teacher; my father, a lawyer, became president of the Johnson City board of education. There was never a thought in our family, as I presume there wasn't in Updike's, of sending the son to any place other than public school in preparation for college.

Updike has written eloquently about his twin afflictions of psoriasis and stammering; the closest I can come to that is the eczema that from infancy visited my skin periodically. His list of the three "great secret things" of boyhood — sex, religion, and art — were likewise the ones that counted most for me. The sex was mostly a matter of fantasizing, the religion was low-church Episcopalian, as compared to Updike's Lutheran upbringing. We were equally children of the radio and the movies, the former providing a hit parade of popular songs to be drawn on forever, the latter giving us a weekly infusion of Hollywood heroics (admission: eleven cents) as observed in the gods and goddesses of the silver screen. Updike remembers his mother saying that, in his boyhood, they were "poor," but that feeling doesn't come through strongly in his writing, and I doubt he quite believed it. My parents worked hard and unstintingly to put themselves in an economic bracket they thought of as middle, even upper-middle class. Finally, to draw a curtain over this doubtless unseemly display, we were both high-school valedictorians, were admitted to prestigious schools of higher education (both of us turned down by Princeton, he went to Harvard, I to Amherst). We were married in our early twenties, to Radcliffe girls who gave us children young — four in his case, three in mine.

My purpose in listing these circumstantial similarities is not to claim that I am therefore the ideal person to write convincingly about and judge accurately Updike's work. Indeed the opposite might be more plausibly maintained, especially with Arnold's warning about the personal estimate in mind: that such "identification" between critic and subject makes the necessary detachment unlikely if not impossible to achieve; any comparisons with other writers are weighted in advance, and in Updike's favor. Yet it's also the case that an excursus into autobiography is not something I've engaged in when writing about other literary subjects, nor do "the times" command it any more than they ever did. Rather, the impulse comes unbidden, is prompted by no clear motive or design. It comes, I'm convinced, from some sense of affinity, deep, not quite explicable, with a writer whose vision of things seemed immensely attractive to me — also a writer, but one who has never produced a novel, short story, or "serious" poem. A recent book of my essays was titled *Talking Back to Emily Dickinson*. With Updike, I find that impulse to talk back strong and persistent; and so I have followed it.

Comparison and analysis, says T. S. Eliot, are the critic's tools. This means that, prior to any question of valuing and weighing, we must engage with the writer's pages, paragraphs, and sentences — with, in Updike's case, the famous style that has, from the beginning of his career, received mixed reviews. Nicholson Baker's obsession, a competitive one, is with Updike the writer of sentences as he makes them up either on or off a ladder. Whether or not he will be judged to have written a masterwork, one single book that unquestionably qualifies for such an accolade, he has given us, from the beginning to now, sentences unsurpassed in their witty, rhythmic, intelligently turned and tuned performance (along with, now and then, some outrageous ones, the fruit of over-reaching). Accumulated after four decades, they make up a writer whose claim to genius is located in the small (the particular paragraph or sentence) and the large (the production of these sentences throughout a career). In my judgment, more than sufficient attention has already been paid by critics of Updike to something other than his writing: to themes, to religious significances and existential questionings, to their subject's attitudes toward women, toward sex, toward politics. We see a similar focus on "content," on thematic socio-political concerns, in university and college English classrooms directed by teachers who claim their main concern is with language, but may really be interested in something they think more significant. No one would claim these matters unimportant in judging a writer, but it's likely that by focusing concern elsewhere they may usurp the place of art. In other words, the particular novel or short story is treated as a vehicle for conveying ideas to be applauded or deplored, rather than as the very thing to be experienced for itself. And if you don't think — as an early critic of Updike, Norman Podhoretz, did not — that his work contained any ideas worth talking about, then "style" can be treated as a substitute for having something to say. In either case, for the critic who admires or who disparages Updike's "content," the style, the sentences can be ignored or dismissed. This is unfortunate.

Mention of the academy reminds us that Updike, more than his contemporaries Bellow and Roth, has — except for a single summer teaching a writing course at Harvard — stayed away from it, perhaps sensing how hostile it was and would increasingly become to the kind of generalist aspirations his life as a writer has embodied. It wouldn't be overstating, I think, to say that we begin a new millennium in which the very *idea* of a life in letters, or of a passionate, "general" reader across fields, is virtually extinct. We hear talk on all sides about the balkanization, the professionalizing of academic instruction, in "English" as in other disciplines. In the preface to the second edition of John Gross's authoritative survey, *The Rise and Fall of the Man of Letters*, Gross writes, somewhat bitterly, about the kind of closed shop the academy has become, departments of literature now consisting wholly of various specialists doing their own thing while getting along with their colleagues in one way or another. Updike's assumption that, in these late days, one can write and talk about writing to an audience that is homogenous, even "universal," is a throwback to what some might feel was a bad old time of exclusion and hierarchical assumptions. And indeed, in that sense Updike, like Edmund Wilson before him, is such a throwback, perhaps to an idea whose time may have come around again.

I should want to say of him what he once wrote about Vladimir Nabokov (in *Assorted Prose*), whom he called "the best writer of English prose at present holding American citizenship, the only writer . . . whose books, considered as a whole, give the happy impression of an *oeuvre*, of a continuous task carried forward variously, of a solid personality, of a plenitude of gifts exploited knowingly."[4] The *only* American writer? (I speak now of Updike.) One thinks immediately of those other aging males, of Philip Roth in particular, whose sequence of astonishing novels over the past decade — *Operation Shylock, Sabbath's Theater, American Pastoral, I Married a Communist, The Human Stain* — may outdistance the fiction Updike has given us in the years since *Rabbit at Rest*. But it is as the supremely gifted *novelist* that Roth strikes us almost entirely. Except for his two memoirs, he has chosen not to perform his "continuous task" as a writer on a number of fronts, confining himself to the novel. Thus his books, distinguished as they are, add up to an identity somewhat different from that of the man of letters who knowingly exploits "a plenitude of gifts." Then there is Bellow, who has given us major fiction, three or four matchless novels; and Mailer, whose cultural commentary from the 1960s and 1970s is unparalleled in bite and brilliance. There may be no need to insist upon Updike's preeminence in this very impressive company. But his continuous task of writing has added up to nothing less than the unfolding of a self, over a career of books. And, *contra* those who talk about narcissism, the unfolding of that self has been also the unfolding of a society and a nation — America in the second half of our century.

A note on what this book is and is not. It is not a biography. On the face of it Updike has had a richly successful and productive life, has performed admirably as a spokesman for the American literary world, has traveled for the government, been interviewed almost to death, yet mainly kept himself away from the vulgarities of talk-show revelations and displays. But such events pale in interest when put next to his writings, products of all those hours sitting at the desk with pencil or typewriter or computer. From time to time I point to facts in the life that seem to parallel or even help to account for certain moments in the writing; yet I presume the reader to be mainly interested in that writing, and I would be pleased if he or she were moved to put down my book and substitute for it one of the subject's stories or poems. With a corpus so large as his, certain omissions had to be made in order to keep the treatment from being headlong. Thus I have omitted from consideration the books for children and have said nothing about his energetic reviews of paintings, exhibitions, photography, and other visual matters. (The handsomely designed *Just Looking* contains representative examples of his writing about art.) I have restricted commentary to the first of three books of stories about Henry Bech and have mentioned only in passing his most recent book of prose essays and criticism, *More Matter*. Ignored also, except for brief reference, is his play, *Buchanan Dying*. Otherwise I have attempted to say something, more or less, about all the books. Endnotes have been kept to a minimum.

As with my earlier accounts of the literary careers of Wyndham Lewis or Robert Frost or Randall Jarrell, my practice here has been to take chronology seriously by using it to tell a story of Updike's progress from one book to the next. In doing so I have had to rehearse matters of plot or location or character — after all, what reader is so familiar with the work as to remember clearly each piece of it? But such rehearsal is done only to facilitate the discussion of artistic value. There have been a number of solid books on Updike, most recently James A. Schiff's *John Updike Revisited,* in the Twayne United States Authors Series. I distinguish myself from most previous commentators by saying that I am not mainly an interpreter of literature; that is, I am less interested in telling someone else what the novel or poem means, what its "significance" is, than in suggesting what the experience of reading it is like, and how that experience is a vital one. In a classroom this approach means plenty of reading aloud in the attempt to focus on the literary performance before us. In print the task becomes more difficult, since with the absence of vocal emphasis the text is harder to bring to life. That doesn't make the attempt any less necessary. For despite all the fuss, positive and negative, about Updike's style (in fact he has many styles), there is something even more elemental than that to acknowledge and account for in his writing. Let us call it, for want of a better term, "voice," meaning by that what the novelist E. L. Lonoff in Philip Roth's *The Ghost Writer* meant when he spoke of "something that begins at around the back of the knees and reaches well above the head." Updike's voice is unique in American letters, and this book is written in response to that uniqueness.

ONE
FIRST FRUITS
The Carpentered Hen • The Poorhouse Fair • The Same Door

Updike's first three published volumes — a book of poems, a novel, and a collection of stories — were written over a five-year period, 1954–9, although he reached back into the *Harvard Lampoon* for two poems published in 1953. Each of these books received respectful, "positive" notices, but their collective impact was minor compared to that of a predecessor like Salinger (*The Catcher in the Rye,* 1951) or of his contemporary Philip Roth, who made his debut in 1959 with the prizewinning *Goodbye, Columbus.* Updike's earliest books didn't set out, so it seems, to make major claims for themselves: full of style, they might well be called "stylish," a word with just the hint of a reservation about it. The poems, almost entirely light verse, are undeniably clever, but then — so the reservation says — perhaps too clever, merely cute. The novel, in its determination to avoid the autobiographical sprawl of a first book, is compact, elusive, often oblique in its presentation. The stories present graceful, unfervid renderings of people in very much less than extreme circumstances — in a high-school classroom, at the dentist, on a New York City bus, or returning to see old classmates at a high-school party.

With hindsight and knowledge of the forty-year career of books about to unfold, however, we can say that Updike's first three showed a writer who was concerned to demonstrate more than one string to his bow. Although the strings have intimate relations with one another, individually they exhibit different sides of an inclination and temperament. *The Carpentered Hen* (*"And Other Tame Creatures"* is the subtitle) exhibits Updike the "gagster," as he once called himself: the cartoonist in print, the former *Lampoon* editor whose specialty, he tells us in an interview, was Chinese jokes in which children at a birthday party sing "Happy Birthday, Tu Yu," or "coolies" listening to a labor agitator ask one another, "Why *shouldn't* we work for coolie wages?" In the stories from *The Same Door* the gagster is subdued; a single character is observed in relation to other characters and placed by an ironic narration whose voice is quieter, woven into a subtler texture. By contrast with these straightforward ways of address to a reader, the narrative of *The Poorhouse Fair* is impersonal, almost disembodied, fully caught up in the elaborate patterns of image and perception that inform the novel's sentences. In the spirit of Holden Caulfield's formulation in *The Catcher in the Rye*, one might (if one were Holden, certainly) phone up the light-verse writer or the author of the stories for an animated conversation, but one would not be at all inclined to dial the creator of the novel.

It may be too easy to credit Updike with supreme canniness in distributing his three earliest eggs in baskets distinct from one another, yet together they stake out a claim for a writer who fancied himself, from the beginning, at least a triple threat. In their different ways each book avoids falling into the blatantly autobiographical plea of an "I"-dominated young man making his debut. Updike declares himself, but does so by also keeping a lot back. In one of his letters Robert Frost speaks satisfiedly of having a "strong box" of poems he's written but not yet published; "I have myself all in a strong box where I can unfold as a personality at discretion," he wrote. Updike might be said to have "had" himself this way as well, though he didn't bother to boast about it. These books called forth words from reviewers that would stick to him throughout his career: elegance, charm, wit, gracefulness, verbal talent — the stuff that made up "a writer's writer." This is of course a dangerous thing to be called, perhaps especially when one is starting out, for it is but a step away from the suggestion, first made by Norman Podhoretz in 1964, that one has nothing to say. A writer's writer deals in words rather than things, art rather than life; his art shows itself ostentatiously as embroidery, astutely stitched but cloying in its richness. "Clever" quickly modulates into too clever, merely clever, clever at the expense of worthier things for a writer to be. What such predictable and not very imaginative responses ignore — or simply aren't able to conceive — is the boldness that lies in unrepentantly making language a display of self, rather than hiding that self behind more modest appearances. The young Updike inhabited his lines and sentences in ways that were audacious, provocative, extravagant. If, from the beginning, he was a writer's writer, that makes him all the more difficult to come to terms with — after all, the poet's poet, Edmund Spenser, still presents a problem for readers.

The Carpentered Hen

It may seem odd to launch an account of Updike's career as man of letters with his early light verse. But he has noted, in the preface to *Collected Poems* (1993), that this way of "cartooning with words" first got him into print, in the work for his hometown papers and the *Harvard Lampoon* that preceded his first published volume. In retrospect Updike's way of dividing his light verse from his "poems" was intended to say that the poems derived from the "real (the given, the substantial) world," while light verse "took its spark from language" and came "from the man-made world of information — books, newspapers, words, signs." He did not attempt to conceal light verse's derivation from verbal sources; many of the poems in *The Carpentered Hen* have as epigraph a line picked out of a newspaper, a magazine, a sign in a bus. "Youth's Progress," for example, was sparked by some words from *Life* magazine that occurred, doubtless, in one of its reports of goings-on in American colleges: "Dick Schneider of Wisconsin . . . was elected 'Greek God' for an interfraternity ball." Updike duly celebrates the lad in three stanzas:

> When I was born, my mother taped my ears
> So they lay flat. When I had aged ten years,

My teeth were firmly braced and much improved.
Two years went by; my tonsils were removed.

At fourteen, I began to comb my hair
A fancy way. Though nothing much was there,
I shaved my upper lip — next year, my chin.
At seventeen, the freckles left my skin.

Just turned nineteen, a nicely molded lad,
I said goodbye to Sis and Mother; Dad
Drove me to Wisconsin and set me loose.
At twenty-one, I was elected Zeus.

The low-key, modest, and rather toneless account by the young man of how he was shaped into divinity exists only to usher in that closing apotheosis, locked into placed by strongly rhymed couplets (the difference to the eye of "loose" and "Zeus" is also part of the fun). Doubtless Updike could have provided an accompanying graphic cartoon, but the words do well enough on their own.

Kingsley Amis, who chose and edited *The New Oxford Book of English Light Verse*, wrote a valuable introduction to it in which he called light verse altogether literary and artificial, a kind of performance that caters to certain expectations in its audience. Its task is to emphasize "manners, social forms, amusements, fashion (from millinery to philosophy), topicality, even gossip," and to treat these matters always in "a bright, perspicuous style." One of the ways Amis distinguished light from what he called "high" verse is that in the latter, as with a concert pianist, a wrong note here or there was permissible; with light verse, the writer — like a juggler — must not drop a plate. This caveat applies to the tight prosodic control necessary to good light verse, and the one spot where "Youth's Progress" strikes a slightly wrong note is its penultimate line ("Dad drove me to Wisconsin and set me loose"), where the extra syllable causes a falter in the middle — hardly as notable, though, as a juggler's plate dropping.

In his 1982 foreword to the reissued *Carpentered Hen*, Updike noted that many of the poems were written during the year he spent, after graduating from Harvard, on a fellowship in Oxford at the Ruskin School of Art, and that the details triggering the poems — such as the line from *Life* about Dick Schneider's deification — took on quaintness from an overseas perspective. In the same foreword he locates his endeavors in a tradition that latterly included such American light-versers as E. B. White, Phyllis McGinley, and Morris Bishop. Today's reader may well find those names stone dead, along with the poems they produced; but in the 1950s and a way beyond, the light-verse industry enjoyed a relative boom. Books by its practitioners were reviewed in the *New York Times Book Review*, the general sense being that, in the age of Eliot and Wallace Stevens, it was an excellent alternative to high modernism. For that very reason I remember setting myself resolutely against light verse and its advocates, making sure I did not find in their productions the "superior amusement" T. S. Eliot said was poetry. Looked back on from forty years, Updike's light verse appeals partly because of its period furniture: poems, for instance, about what Debbie Reynolds and Eddie Fisher did on their whirlwind honeymoon, or a *Life* article about the tribulations of the starlet Kim Novak. But sometimes a mere word is enough to strike off a sequence that builds in surprise and delight — as happens in "To an Usherette":

> Ah, come with me,
> *Petite chérie,*
> And we shall rather happy be.
> I know a modest luncheonette
> Where, for a little, one can get
> A choplet, baby lima beans,
> And, segmented, two tangerines.
>
> *Le coup de grâce*
> My pretty lass,
> Will be a demi-demitasse
> Within a serviette conveyed
> By weazened waiters, underpaid,

> Who mincingly might grant us spoons
> While a combo tinkles trivial tunes.
>
> Ah, with me come,
> My mini-*femme*
> And I shall say I love you some.[1]

This homage to the diminutive is a perfect instance of what its creator, in the same foreword, called light verse's "hyperordering of language through alliteration, rhyme, and pun." It was a "way of dealing with the universe," he said, that partook of high spirits. For the
reader, as well as, doubtless, the writer, such an exercise generates a
purely literary pleasure that has in it a strong element of admiration
— of wondering at the spirited facility brought to bear on the usherette and her related items.

Updike observed that it was around 1964, after the Kennedy
assassination, when he found the market for light verse drying up.
Although he didn't himself cease to write it, the practice became
more and more occasional for him — an exception rather than the
rule of his poetry composition. It is also of interest that these early
evidences of high spirits were thrown off by a sensibility which, at
its opposite end, concerned itself with thoughts about God, immor-
tality, the soul. The composer of light-verse squibs was also a man
whose reading in Kierkegaard, Karl Barth, and other soul-doctors
was no disinterested game but one played for ultimate stakes.

The Poorhouse Fair

When Updike and his family returned in 1955 from the year at
Oxford, they settled in New York City, he having been hired by
Katharine White to provide "Talk of the Town" columns and other
contributions to the *New Yorker*. Sometime in 1956 he completed a
draft of a six-hundred-page novel titled *Home*, but decided against
further revising it and gave his attention instead to the poems and
stories he was writing and publishing in the magazine. In 1957, with
a second child on the way, he and Mary decided to move to New
England, his determination being to function as a self-employed,

self-supporting writer. The decision may have helped to concentrate composition of a relatively short novel, very different in focus and narration from the abandoned one; at any rate, *The Poorhouse Fair* was written in three months after the move to Ipswich, Massachusetts. When Harper Brothers, which had brought out *The Carpentered Hen*, expressed dissatisfaction with the novel's ending, Updike changed publishers to Alfred Knopf, beginning — when Knopf published *The Poorhouse Fair* in 1959 — the mutually gratifying association that has endured ever since.

By far the most interesting commentary on *The Poorhouse Fair* came from its author twenty years after the writing of the book when, in an introduction to the 1977 edition, he provided a rationale for its futuristic setting and named a few books and writers instrumental to its conception. The novel had its roots, he tells us, in a 1957 visit to Shillington in which he inspected the site of the former County Home, a yellow "poorhouse" at the end of the street where he had lived. He decided to write a novel in celebration of the fairs held at that institution during his childhood, and in conceiving the book's central figure, a ninety-four-year-old inmate named John Hook, he would pay tribute to his recently deceased maternal grandfather, John Hoyer. The novel's time is set roughly twenty years hence, not really a long jump ahead compared to other examples of the futuristic genre. Orwell's *1984* had been in Updike's mind: there is, in *The Poorhouse Fair*, a disposition of countries reminiscent of the tripartite division in Orwell's totalitarian world. But in Updike's novel, *totalitarian* is hardly the adjective for the benignly intended administration of Conner, the prefect whose attempts to preside efficiently and thoughtfully over the old people's declining years go awry.

More important than Orwell's novel for the literary texture of *The Poorhouse Fair* were the examples of two other English writers: H. G. Wells's science fiction classic "The Time Machine," and a not very well-known futuristic novel by a writer Updike would more than once admire in print: Henry Green's *Concluding* (1948). Both writers are invoked in the 1977 introduction for their stylistic distinctiveness:

singling out the "superb and dreadful poetry" of "The Time Machine," Updike names an aspect of Wells's work that is typically ignored by critics concerned with themes and ideas. With Henry Green, Updike admits to appropriating from *Concluding* an "embarrassing" number of particulars; he acknowledges also the influence of Green's "wilfully impressionist style" by quoting from the opening paragraph of *Concluding,* then following it with early sentences from *The Poorhouse Fair.* It's hard to see why the extremely mannered English writer held so much attraction for the American, but it is useful to be directed, at the novel's outset, to the way typical sentences from *The Poorhouse Fair* conduct themselves:

> In the cool wash of early sun the individual strands of osier compounding the chairs stood out sharply; arched like separate serpents springing up and turning again into the knit of the wickerwork. An unusual glint of metal pierced the lenient wall of Hook's eyes and struck into his brain, which urged his body closer, to inspect. Onto the left arm of the chair that was customarily his in the row that lined the men's porch the authorities had fixed a metal tab, perhaps one inch by two, bearing MR, printed, plus, in ink, his latter name.

This is both cool and arresting, by not nudging us into an easily remembered impression — as who should say, oh yes, I've noticed how, in wickerwork, strands of osier arched like serpents spring up — but inviting us to recognize the poet's eye as Emerson named it at the beginning of *Nature:* "There is a property in the horizon which no man has but he whose eye can integrate all the parts, that is, the poet." Such seeing is some way beyond our ordinary, finite procedures.

   Thus one understands why a stylist like the *New Yorker* jazz critic, Whitney Balliett, should have written an admiring review of *The Poorhouse Fair.*[2] Balliett praised Updike's prose as "tight but never brittle . . . breaded with simile and metaphor," also his "tough, hounding selectivity of materials," an especial characteristic of poetry. Such a prose was like what Balliett was writing so well in his descriptions of a cornet solo by Bix Beiderbecke or one of Sid Catlett's drum riffs. Hook's discovery of the metal tags Conner has had placed on the inmates' chairs — a trivial example, but one that quickly establishes the kind of officious care (for their own good) being provided them — is negotiated in a language Hook himself, like the rest of us, would not employ, as in the detail of the metallic glint piercing "the lenient wall of Hook's eyes," thus urging his body closer. Such language has its hand in making the book feel strangely remote, and Balliett himself mentioned that he never thought of either "liking" or "disliking" it. Its remoteness is part of our relation even to the main character, Hook, who again sees with a poet's eye as he looks eastward over farm plains to the New Jersey hills:

> Despite the low orange sun, still wet from its dawning, crescents of mist like the webs of tent caterpillars adhered in the crotches of the hills. Preternaturally sensitive within its limits, his vision made out the patterned spheres of an orchard on the nearest blue rise, seven miles off.

Hook goes on seeing the landscape, through a long paragraph, and even though he's been familiar with it for a long time, his perceptions are surely extraordinary ones for a ninety-four-year-old ("webs of tent caterpillars adhered in the crotches of the hills"). But we acknowledge Updike's writerly hand in all this: as with the verbal high jinks of his light verse, this novel's prose calls attention to itself and makes a demand on readers some were — and are — unwilling to meet.

The disposition of narrative action in *The Poorhouse Fair* is as coolly detached as the behavior of individual sentences. Its 185 pages are divided into three untitled sections, which are subdivided into forty parts, separated one from another by extra space. There are no chapters: we move from one character's perspective to another's, and as the book proceeds the cross-referencing becomes intricate, often pleasurable. What happens is always tame, never the stuff of tragedy, nothing that would be amiss in a novel by Howells. We are told of the physical appearance of quilts, readied for sale at the fair; what to do with a half-dead cat that suddenly materializes; a trip to the infirmary by an inmate with an inflamed ear; a parakeet on the loose; a delivery truck that knocks down part of the poorhouse's surrounding wall as it attempts to deliver soft drinks for the festivities. These less-than-momentous events are presented in a narrative voice devoid of anything, it seems, but the obligation to set them down clearly, distinctly, and with nuance. So in those rare moments when the voice deepens and moves inward — mainly when Hook is the focus — the narrative temperature makes a pronounced rise. For a moment we glimpse a different kind of book.

Here is Hook, having been confronted with some frank sentiments about death by one of the female inmates he's been conversing with, and now attempting to regain his composure:

> Her speaking so plainly of death stirred the uglier humors in him. In the mid-mornings of days he usually felt that he would persist, on this earth, forever; that all the countless others, his daughter and son among them, who had vanished, had done so out of carelessness; that if like him they had taken each day of life as the day impossible to die on, and treated it carefully, they too would have lived without end and would have grown to have behind them an endless past, like a full bolt of cloth unraveled in the sun and faded there, under the brilliance of unrelenting faith.

This touches momentarily on a conceit most of us have entertained, superficially plausible and immensely reassuring. Such a moment is as close as we ever get to Hook's thoughts or those of any other character; by contrast, Conner (as Updike himself notes in the introduction) comes across mainly as a thirty-year-old "goodie-goodie" who "should have been something more." (Curiously enough — and who knows how much to make of it? — the paragraph succeeding Hook's deep thoughts about life and death suddenly registers, in the meadow beyond the wall, a rabbit pausing, "a silhouette of two humps, without color." Hook's creator may already have been making plans to get the rabbit running.)

Moments of poetically rendered vision like this stand at one extreme of narrative style, the opposite of which is the prosing of banal talk, the stuff of daily conversation at the poorhouse. At the midday meal on fair day, a large one (meat loaf, boiled potato, broccoli), Mrs. Lucas, married to the man with the earache, expatiates on the difficulties of caring for a parakeet her daughter has unloaded upon her and which, let out of its cage for an airing, has escaped through the door suddenly opened by Mr. Lucas. Mrs. Lucas bitterly retails her daughter's thoughtlessness:

> "She bought it for her boy and the boy tired of it after a week, as you might expect. So, ship it off to Mom, and let her spend her pitiful little money on fancy seed of all sorts and cuttlebone. Let her clean the cage once a day. Let her worry with the bird's nails. They're more than a half-circle and still growing. It gets on its perch and tries to move off and beats its wings and wonders why it can't, poor thing. I thought I could take my sewing scissors and trim its nails myself; they're fragile looking; you can see the little thread of blood in there. But evidently you can't. They'll bleed unless you know just where to cut."

And on and on. A bit like one of Miss Bates's endless monologues in *Emma*, but also rather extraordinary when considered from the perspective of the young first novelist who, among other tasks, has set himself to imagine trivial anxieties of old age as embodied in the hazards of parakeet pedicure. This is the kind of challenge Updike courted in writing *The Poorhouse Fair*: that of vocalizing, in the most unremarkable speech rhythms, the dismal complaint of a boring old lady. And it is why the novel benefits, even more than most novels do, from rereading. Once you know how it comes out — or doesn't come out, since the ending is impressionistically inconclusive — you begin to pay attention to something other than story or idea; to the textures, the all-too-human polyphony that informs the book.

On rereading, we're likely to pay less attention to the futuristic paraphernalia which, important as it was in Updike's motive for writing the novel, is much less so in our experience of it. Setting a book twenty years in the future is a relatively modest leap (think, by contrast, of Wells's "The Time Machine") and feels even less breath-taking as we read it in 2000. In fact I think *The Poorhouse Fair* is least convincing when it presses hard the thematic content of a future America, even though there are good formulations along the way ("Heart had gone out of these people; health was the principle thing about the faces of the Americans"). An anonymous voice declares, late in the book, that with the disappearance of war — a pact has been made with the "Eurasian Soviet" —

> we were to be allowed to decay of ourselves. And the popula-
> tion soared like diffident India's, and the economy swelled,
> and iron became increasingly dilute, and houses more nig-
> gardly built, and everywhere was sufferance, good sense,
> wealth, irreligion, and peace.

This anonymous narrative, in its sweep of declaration, is less con-vincing and engaging than when similar sentiments are expressed directly through the consciousness of Hook, especially when he muses, commandingly, on the American past: "There is no good-ness, without belief. There is nothing but busy-ness. And if you have not believed, at the end of your life you shall know you have buried your talent in the ground of this world and have nothing saved, to take into the next." But the resonance this has is inde-pendent of the novel's futuristic dimension.

There is also an increasingly allegorical feel to things as the novel draws to its close. The most notable piece of action comes at the moment when, repairing the stone wall hit by the soft-drink truck, some of the inmates, though not Hook, in a parody of the stoning of the martyr Stephen, throw stones at Conner, wounding his pride and soul. Conner declares, "I know you all," and tells his sidekick Buddy that he "forgives" them, whatever that means. The poor-house itself, as the townspeople come to the fair, assumes a larger symbolic range of perspective: "In a sense the poorhouse would indeed outlast their homes. The old continue to be old-fashioned, though their youths were modern. We grow backward, aging into our father's opinions and even into those of our grandfathers." That last sentence is delivered very much in the voice of an Updike we shall become increasingly familiar with in fiction to come. Here, though eloquent, it feels just a shade disembodied, almost too wise for the occasion.

In a later comment on the book Updike said, unpacking the metaphor of his novel, that the poorhouse was our world, a poor house to live in, under the aspect of the spirit, but nevertheless all we had, and to be cherished for that fact. There is an appealing inconclusiveness to the way things are concluded in the novel: the narrative diffuses itself into myriad voices of the visitors — separate, random bits of conversation that overall, as to be expected, are aimless, casual. Hook, ending his day, and one day closer to the end of his life, thinks vaguely about how he must try to help Conner after the day's humiliation — must tell him something "as a bond between them and a testament to endure his dying in the world." But the book's final sentence is a question: "What was it?"

The Same Door

There is comparatively little of such tentativeness in the sixteen stories published in the *New Yorker* between late 1954 and the beginning of 1959 and collected in *The Same Door*. Updike's first collection of short fiction came at the end of a decade that had seen a number of impressive collections by American writers, among them Salinger's *Nine Stories* (1953), John Cheever's *The Enormous Radio* (1953), and Flannery O'Connor's *A Good Man Is Hard to Find* (1955). More than one critic has noted the air of self-conscious effort with which short-story writers try to say what it is that this genre attempts and what claims it makes on a reader. Such an effort is noted by John Bayley, in his study of the short story from Henry James to Elizabeth Bowen, when he quotes Kay Boyle, herself a prolific writer of stories who attempted to put it all into words: "At once a parable and a slice of life, at once symbolic and real, both a valid picture of some phase of experience, and a sudden illumination of one of the perennial moral and psychological paradoxes which lie at the heart of *la condition humaine*."[3] Bayley remarks wittily that this definition makes the perusal of a short story into more of a duty than a pleasure, and we may sympathize with his uneasiness. No such anxiety is shown, he points out, by writers of novels, who don't have to feel that they must justify their trade, whether the result is a tight, poetic operation like *The Poorhouse Fair* or a loose and baggy monster. Certainly Boyle's solemn claim, that stories render the human condition (in French), feels inappropriate to characterize the playful, unsolemn treatment of characters and situations in Updike's early ones.

Although the category has fallen out of use, a popular way of classifying and often dismissing or disparaging short fiction, especially in the 1950s and 1960s, was to attach the adjective *New Yorker* to it. *New Yorker* stories were supposedly deft, witty, but superficial (perhaps *therefore* superficial) treatments of eastern-seaboard suburban life as lived by well-off, middle-class families and as written about predominantly by American middle-class white males like Salinger, Cheever, and Updike. Characters in these stories were wholly under the author's thumb; the only disruptions allowed them were minor ones, to be remedied or absorbed by the story overall. The "typical" *New Yorker* product was narcissistic in its overriding concern for style, which rendered all action in neatly turned, elegant sentences and paragraphs. These stories' commitment to surface values opened them, predictably, to the charge of lacking depth — like the magazine in which they appeared. Their ironic, witty way of taking things made them inimical, or at least unresponsive to — so the charge ran — Life, which was disorderly, unmanageable, a matter not adequately dealt with ironically or stylishly. It is interesting that Nabokov, who published stories and the chapters of *Pnin* in the *New Yorker*, when asked whether his characters ever broke free from his authorial control, replied straight-facedly that no, he kept them severely under his thumb at all times — they were "galley slaves." But Nabokov, being an expatriate and the author of *Lolita*, was immune to the criticisms his younger American *New Yorker* contributors received.

Two years after *The Same Door* was published Updike reviewed in the magazine Salinger's *Franny and Zooey*, and before he turned to some fairly sharp criticisms of "the extravagant self-consciousness" of Salinger's later prose — especially in the overextended "Zooey" — he addressed himself to the writer's earlier work.[4] It had come upon Updike as "something of a revelation," particularly Salinger's conviction that "our inner lives greatly matter." Updike saw this conviction as consonant with the temper of current America in an age of "introversion," "of nuance, of ambiguous gestures and psychological jockeying on a national and private scale." Salinger's "intense attention to gesture and intonation," Updike wrote, made him "a uniquely pertinent literary artist." This is strong praise indeed, but not at all carelessly eulogistic; since the force with which Salinger struck young readers in the 1950s, especially those who themselves aspired to "write," can't be overstated. (It is a commonplace that those of us who began our teaching careers back then could assume that the one book every college freshman had read, probably more than once, was *The Catcher in the Rye*.)

Updike doesn't go on to point out that Salinger's penchant for "introversion" expressed itself in his fiction mainly in terms of anguish, nervous collapse, and suicide. Holden Caulfield speaks to us from the sanatorium where he's recuperating; the opening and closing pieces in *Nine Stories*, "A Perfect Day for Bananafish" and "Teddy," end with the protagonist's taking his own life. In between there is drunken anguish ("Uncle Wiggily in Connecticut"), a broken romance ("The Laughing Man"), and shell-shocked disorder ("For Esmé — with Love and Squalor"). If this writer's mood and themes were coincident with national ones, then America was in for difficult times, which proved to be the case as the 1960s unrolled. By contrast, nothing really serious goes wrong in any of the stories in *The Same Door*: some sort of nonviolent resolution always occurs, and there is almost no attempt on Updike's part to explore a consciousness with complicated, penetrating analysis. Not that Salinger goes very deep either; his introversion, his preoccupation with extreme states of nerve are more given and asserted than they are explored.

What Salinger and Updike most notably do share is, in the words quoted from Updike's review, "intense attention to gesture and intonation." The most impressive intonation in Salinger's art, and where his true originality may be said to lie, is in the immediate, direct, unaffected address to the reader with which the storyteller launches his tale — as in "The Laughing Man":

> In 1928, when I was nine, I belonged, with maximum *esprit de corps*, to an organization known as the Comanche Club. Every schoolday afternoon at three o'clock, twenty-five of us Comanches were picked up by our Chief outside the boys' exit of P.S. 165, on 109th Street near Amsterdam Avenue. We then pushed and punched our way into the Chief's reconverted commercial bus, and he drove us (according to his financial arrangement with our parents) over to Central Park. The rest of the afternoon, weather permitting, we played football or soccer or baseball, depending (very loosely) on the season. Rainy afternoons, the Chief invariably took us either to the Museum of Natural History or to the Metropolitan Museum of Art.

This first-person mode is untypical of Salinger's collection as it is of Updike's, but the detail, the parenthetical ease of "(very loosely)," the generally humorous perspective on things — all embodied in a confident, easy address to a reader from whom sophistication and irony are expected — make the "intonation" a classic American one. It is an intonation shared by at least one other writer of the period, John Cheever, all of the stories in whose first collection were also published in the *New Yorker*. Here is the beginning of its opening one, "Goodbye, My Brother":

> We are a family that has always been very close in spirit. Our father was drowned in a sailing accident when we were young, and our mother has always stressed the fact that our familial relationships have a kind of permanence that we will never meet with again. I don't think about the family much, but when I remember its members and the coast where they lived

and the sea salt that I think is in our blood, I am happy to
recall that I am a Pommeroy. . . .

Here the narrator says something like, "Let me, without even clear-
ing my throat, introduce myself to you in the most unassumingly
direct way — then we can get on with the tale." The "plots" of
Cheever's stories seem much less important, even trivial and random, compared with the steady reassurance provided by the narrative speaking voice, available to all readers who use their ears.

The young Updike had of course read these stories by Salinger
and Cheever published in his favorite magazine, whose ranks he had
just entered as a salaried contributor. What in their work would he
choose to steer clear of? Put another way, what resources had they
drawn upon that he lacked, and therefore must supply with different ones? Their first resource, surely, was eastern urban-suburban
life. Salinger grew up in New York City, knew his Fifth Avenue and
Central Park; Cheever lived there for some years before moving to
Ossining (Connecticut in the fiction) and taking over exurbia. By
contrast Updike was, as he would later call one of his fictional
stand-ins (in the story "Flight"), "a homely, comically ambitious
hillbilly," a country boy whose family's move to the farm in
Plowville, Pennsylvania, in 1945 made him feel more like a "hick"
than his classmates from Shillington. But this was also his major
resource: he had, as he put it later, "a Pennsylvania thing to say" and
in the mid-1950s he was saying it in the autobiographical novel
(Home) while working other material into New Yorker stories. A
good strategy, except that, as noted earlier, when he moved to
Ipswich in 1957, he decided to scrap the novel, going to work
instead on The Poorhouse Fair — another "Pennsylvania thing" but
not an autobiographical one.

"Pennsylvania" thus enters only glancingly into the stories collected in The Same Door. It is there in the earliest one, "Friends from
Philadelphia," where the boy, John Nordholm, is asked by his mother
to procure a bottle of wine to serve some Philadelphia people who
are coming for dinner. John enlists the help of Mr. Lutz, the breezy

father of one of his friends, who purchases a bottle for John, ostensibly with the two dollars the boy has given him. At the story's end John glances at the label, CHÂTEAU MOUTON-ROTHSCHILD 1937, unaware that he has been benignly tricked by Mr. Lutz. It is the purest O. Henry ending of any story in Updike's oeuvre, and for that reason looks like a youthful experiment in a mode that was not to prevail. Other loosely based Pennsylvania tales include "Ace in the Hole," about an ex–basketball star, a trying out of the character who would become Rabbit Angstrom and the first story in which the town is called Olinger; "The Kid's Whistling," set in a department store in what sounds like Reading; and a couple of school tales, one about a high-school teacher, another about a new girl in elementary school. It's not until the final and by far the best story in the book, "The Happiest I've Been," that the Olinger scene gets a fuller treatment and where we hear an intonation in the narrative voice predictive of Updike's best writing. Otherwise, except for "Dentistry and Doubt," where the protagonist visits an Oxford dentist, the scene of the stories is New York City. For the most part Updike's New York is sketched in pretty lightly, the focus being on a recently married man and his wife, sometimes with a baby daughter. They live on the upper West Side, later in a small apartment in the Village. There are a couple of Salingeresque efforts with clever titles ("Who Made Yellow Roses Yellow?" and "A Trillion Feet of Gas"), while "A Gift from the City," the collection's longest story, is a nod to the Cheever mode. (A young couple becomes involved in increasingly complicated relations with a black man to whom they've given money and who keeps returning for more.) From this group of urban tales I single out the two that seem most original, that could not have been written by Salinger, Cheever, or any writer except Updike: "Toward Evening," and "Snowing in Greenwich Village."

The first of these feels like a slight thing indeed, a "sketch" only eight pages in length but also distinctive insofar as it's difficult to name its subject precisely. A young man, Rafe, headed home from work in midtown and carrying a just-purchased mobile his wife has suggested he buy for their daughter, boards an uptown bus in front of

St. Patrick's Cathedral, then proceeds past Columbus Circle and up Broadway until he alights at Eighty-Fifth Street, where he lives. The ride consists of Rafe first assisting a fat woman in black to board the bus, then gazing at two women who rouse him to erotic thoughts. He first regards a beautiful, stylishly dressed white woman who looks as if she speaks French and — since she sports a copy of Proust's A l'ombre des jeunes filles en fleurs — probably does. Then, standing, he eyes a desirable, inaccessible "Negress" seated beneath him, and his steady look at her turns from a lustful fantasy to consideration of "the actual Negress" — "the prim, secretarial carriage of her head, the orange skin, the sarcastic Caucasian set of her lips." When he alights from the bus she has "dwindled to the thought that he had never seen gloves like that before." In between his gazings at the two women, Rafe's eye is caught by an advertisement on the bus for Jomar Instant Coffee, ingeniously constructed so as to afford two versions of a man enjoying his coffee. But Rafe is too close to the ad for its ideal desired effect to work, and instead he begins to feel bus-sick.

Upon reaching home, he plays with his daughter, producing the mobile he has carried home. It is not a success: his wife had expected something more Calder-like and his daughter is simply not interested. After his "favorite" dinner of peas, hamburger, and baked potato, Rafe smokes a cigarette and looks across the Hudson to the Palisades where he notes that the Spry sign has gone on. The sign — an actual phenomenon of the 1950s — is described in close detail, and an imaginary account of it is conjured up by Rafe to explain how such an object came into being. (Among the amusing details of the account is a directive from the head office to turn it slightly south, since "Nobody at Columbia cooks.") After the fantasy about the Spry sign's genesis is completed, this paragraph concludes the story:

> Above its winking, the small cities had disappeared. The black of the river was as wide as that of the sky. Reflections sunk in it existed dimly, minutely wrinkled, below the surface. The Spry sign occupied the night with no company beyond the also uncreated but illegible stars.

This is the first moment in the collection when, having finished the story, a reader might well ask, what of it? What is this story "about" — indeed, is *story* the right name for it? After all, nothing happens, characters aren't "developed," there is no conversation between the husband and wife (Updike excised, from the version published in the *New Yorker,* what little there was), and the wife doesn't even speak. Events over the course of eight pages are linked only in the most tenuous way as moments in the mind of an inventive, rather playful consciousness. Yet the final paragraph sounds a deeper note, feels elevated and somber, out there on the edge of something with that black river, those sunken reflections on what one might call the loneliness of the Spry sign as imagined by a watcher, himself alone. For want of a better term, it may be called a poetic moment in which the language's density is out of proportion to anything it is "saying," and where the sequence in that final four-sentence paragraph is more heard than seen, aurally resonant even while visually precise. It is quite distinct, in its way of concluding, from the kind of thing either Salinger or Cheever provides, and a *New Yorker* reader who encountered it in the issue of February 11, 1956, might well have taken such note.

The story that follows "Toward Evening" in *The Same Door,* "Snowing in Greenwich Village," is probably the best known of Updike's New York City efforts, also of interest since it inaugurates what he would later call the Maples stories, about the fortunes of a married, then divorcing, couple and their children. It's also Updike's first story to savor of the illicit — sexual temptation and the married man's close escape (or is it his failure?). The word *close* is rather flagrantly highlighted at the beginning and end of the story: Richard and Joan Maple have just moved from the West Eighties to West Thirteenth Street and decide to invite for drinks a friend living in the neighborhood, Rebecca Cune, "because now they were so close." The third-person narrative is centered on Richard; his wife has a cold; the three of them talk and drink sherry and eat cashews; at one point they rush to look out the window as six mounted police gallop down the street. It is now snowing and for

Joan at least, we are told, the snow comes as a sort of benediction on their marriage. When Rebecca, who has entertained them with a number of amusing, slightly odd stories, gets up to leave, Joan insists that Richard accompany her, "close" as she lives to them.

Earlier in the story Richard had helped Rebecca off with her coat, thinking to himself how "weightless" the coat had seemed, how gracefully he had managed this act. Generally he has been pleased with himself as host, presiding at this minor entertainment with a satisfaction not untouched by vanity. But when Rebecca invites him to come up and see her apartment, "in a voice that Richard imagined to be slightly louder than her ordinary one," he becomes nervous. Opening the door to her room, Rebecca announces that "It's hot as hell in here" but doesn't remove her coat; nor does Richard offer to help remove it, noting instead the prominent presence of a double bed. They look out the window, make further small talk, then Richard moves toward the door, deciding she has been standing "unnecessarily close" to him. Leaving, he makes a weak joke, delivered with a slight stammer, and she — seeing he has attempted a joke — laughs before he's finished it:

> As he went down the stairs she rested both hands on the banister and looked down toward the next landing. "Good night," she said.
> "Night." He looked up; she had gone into her room. Oh but they were close.

The story is artful and satisfying for the way it tempts a reader into interpretive moves while refusing to endorse any of them. When, in reviewing Salinger, Updike declared the current temper in America to be one of "nuance," of ambiguous gestures and psychological "jockeying," he used terms that fit the temper of "Snowing in Greenwich Village." Is Rebecca out to seduce Richard or just to tease him? Or is she innocent, and does she keep her coat on so as to respect his status as a married man? Or is she inviting him to help her take it off, then see what happens? Is Richard correct in deciding her moves are provocative, or is he deluding himself, as a somewhat vain,

self-important, and insecure young married man might do? With retrospective knowledge of the Maples stories to come, are we justified
in seeing this small instance of temptation as the entering wedge? If
this is a story about fidelity and temptation, of suspicion directed at
both the hero and The Woman, of desire and *anger* at desire, of self-
satisfaction at having resisted the temptation for now — how much
of these mixed feelings does Richard Maple's author share with him?
Does Updike know something Richard doesn't know? To answer
these questions unambiguously is to prevail over the story by ignor-
ing other, contrary possibilities. What the tempted but undeluded
reader responds to instead is, I think, something more like nuance,
as felt in the ring of that "Oh" in the final sentence — "Oh but they
were close." Whatever happens in "Snowing in Greenwich Village,"
no one including the narrator is about to say exactly, to name it any
more closely than does the final sentence. We're closer to the atmosphere of Chekhov than of O. Henry, or for that matter of either
Salinger or Cheever.[5]

But it is in "The Happiest I've Been," concluding and best story in
The Same Door, that Updike first taps the rich vein of nostalgic, guilty
affection that animates the "Pennsylvania thing" he had it in him to
say. It is also the only story in the book told in the first person singular. Its style is distinct from both the impressionistic montage of
"Toward Evening" or the tight, economical, rather taciturn presentation of "Snowing in Greenwich Village." It rejects the virtues of
ambiguous gestures and psychological jockeying in favor of a more
open, "sincere," even good-hearted vision of things. While it is still full
of nuance, of delicate noticings and expressively voiced reflections,
such noticings and reflections are put in the service of a perspective on
life that is appreciative, wondering, accepting. At one moment the
narrator, John Nordholm (back from "Friends from Philadelphia"),
confides to us that he had "nearly always felt at least fairly happy."
Whether his creator ever said something like that about himself, there
is surely a temperamental affinity between the nineteen-year-old
Nordholm, a sophomore at college, and the about-to-be twenty-seven-
year-old Updike, who published this story, set in late December 1951,

in the January 3, 1959, issue of the *New Yorker*. Wordsworth's declaration that "The Child is Father of the Man" seems relevant to mark the
continuity between someone about to leave his teens and a somewhat
older writer concerned to celebrate the adolescent becoming man,
which is the burden of "The Happiest I've Been."

The correspondence between the particulars of John Nordholm's
life, as laid out in the opening paragraphs of the story, with those of
his creator's suggests that Updike was anxious *not* to hide behind the
anonymous resources of fiction. Like his hero, Updike was nineteen
in late December 1951, was in his sophomore year at Harvard, had
met the "girl" (Mary Pennington) he fell in love with "in a fine
arts course" (she was a student at Radcliffe). In the story John
Nordholm is going to visit this young woman at her parents' home
in Chicago, where Mary Pennington's father was a Unitarian minister. John Nordholm lives, as did Updike, with his mother,
father, and maternal grandparents on a farm some four miles
from Olinger (Shillington), bordering on the city of Alton
(Reading), Pennsylvania. (The distance between the farm and
Olinger/Shillington later becomes ten miles.) As John and his
friend Neil Hovey, in whose car he is going to Chicago, leave the
farm — not directly for Chicago but first to a party with old Olinger
high-school pals — the hero takes a picture of the homeplace he
won't see again until spring:

> I embraced my mother and over her shoulder with the camera
> of my head tried to take a snapshot I could keep of the house,
> the woods behind it and the sunset behind them, the bench
> beneath the walnut tree where my grandfather cut apples into
> skinless bits and fed them to himself, and the ruts in the soft
> lawn the bakery truck had made that morning.

One says, seeing those bits of apple and those ruts in the lawn, that
no one is making this up: its authority comes from an "I" who was
also "really" there — who had the experience.

Updike's self-confidence in openly trusting himself to speak truly
in fiction about his younger self may be a matter of having picked

exactly the right moment to bring that younger self back to life. He once declared his conviction that the first great wave of nostalgia hits us when we're done with high school and moved away from our hometown, launched on some sort of independent life, yet close enough to what life was once (and not so long ago) that we can be both involved with and detached from the experience.[6] There is a moment during the party John and Neal attend when John, "sitting alone and ignored in a great armchair," watches his ex-classmates dance to records, still 78s ("Every three minutes with a click and a crash another dropped and the mood abruptly changed"). He notes the "female shoes" scattered about the room, and is suddenly moved to feel "a warm keen dishevelment, as if there were real tears in my eyes." The tears have to do, he thinks, with how things are superficially unaltered, how it's the same party he's been going to throughout his life, and how people have changed very little — "a haircut, an engagement ring, a franker plumpness." Yet, the implication is, everything has changed, is different, unforeseen, potentially "tragic" — a word the narrator uses about John's perception.

Among the quite ordinary events that follow, Neil Hovey proceeds to get drunk, sitting in the den and listening over and over again to Gene Krupa's "Dark Eyes" on the phonograph, while an unidentified girl keeps him company, silently reading issues of *Holiday* and *Esquire*. The girl has been brought by Margaret Lento, another acquaintance of John's, also drunk and now furiously dancing by herself, having been ditched by the host, who has taken off with another girl. Neil has promised to drive Margaret and the other girl home (they live on the far side of Alton, away from Olinger) and while John waits for him to pull things together, he amuses himself by reading in volume 2 of Thackeray's *Henry Esmond,* which he's removed from a glass bookcase. Finally Neil appears, addresses him affectionately as "Norseman," and says, "Let's go to Chicago." But first they must deliver the girls home, and the evening — now middle of the night — prolongs itself when Margaret invites them in for instant coffee. Neil and Margaret's friend retire to the couch for some necking, while Margaret and

John, discussing her ex-boyfriend's character, have a satisfyingly intimate conversation — "the quick agreements, the slow nods, the weave of different memories; it was like one of those Panama baskets shaped underwater around a worthless stone." She draws his arm around her shoulder and eventually falls asleep, wakened only by the milkman making his morning rounds. The boys leave, drop the other girl off, and in a short concluding section to the story head out, at 6 AM, for Chicago.

That concluding section, one of the best pieces of writing to be found anywhere in Updike, shows him exploiting, for the first time, the full resources of a remarkable voice. In "The Happiest I've Been" that voice builds in interest as the boys drive back through the dead stillness of Alton and Olinger, then pass close enough to John's house so that he imagines shooting out a pane of his parents' bedroom window with a .22. He thinks of his grandfather stamping around, waiting for his grandmother to make breakfast; then the turnpike entrance looms and he is "safe in a landscape where no one cared." At which point Neil asks him to take the wheel — even though previously he had never trusted John with his father's car — and promptly falls asleep. The landscape where no one cares unrolls itself:

> We crossed the Susquehanna on a long smooth bridge below Harrisburg, then began climbing toward the Alleghenies. In the mountains there was snow, a dry dusting like sand, that waved back and forth on the road surface. Further along there had been a fresh fall that night, about two inches, and the plows had not yet cleared all the lanes. I was passing a Sunoco truck on a high curve when without warning the scraped section gave out and I realized I might skid into the fence if not over the edge. The radio was singing "Carpets of clover, I'll lay right at your feet," and the speedometer said 81.

But nothing momentous happens, except in Updike's sentences, as Neil sleeps on, even providing an accompaniment of homely snoring.

The promise of those words from the song "For You," the magical, providential sense that nothing bad will occur to them — that the landscape where no one cares isn't, on the other hand, malign, and that the future really does lie ahead — these and other feelings coalesce in a wonderful moment as they navigate the tunnel country and begin the descent to Pittsburgh. Neil wakes up, scratches a match to light his cigarette; at which point John experiences an extraordinary happiness that he accounts for in the story's concluding sentences:

> We were on our way. I had seen a dawn. This far, Neil could appreciate, I had brought us safely. Ahead, a girl waited who, if I asked, would marry me, but first there was a vast trip: many hours and towns interceded between me and that encounter. There was the quality of the 10 A.M. sunlight as it existed in the air ahead of the windshield, filtered by the thin overcast, blessing irresponsibility — you felt you could slice forever through such a cool pure element — and springing, by implying how high these hills had become, a wide-spreading pride: Pennsylvania, your state — as if you had made your life. And there was knowing that twice since midnight a person had trusted me enough to fall asleep beside me.

It's those final two sentences that makes the story's ending so powerful, convincing us that, indeed, this is the happiest John Nordholm has been and that he's more than right to feel that way. The penultimate sentence is long, complex, almost going overboard as it twice punctuates itself with dashes, suspending us over the course of the first one until we see that the participles ("blessing," "springing") are in apposition. There follows the lovely appreciation of "Pennsylvania, your state" followed by the recognition of such appropriation as extravagant, though forgivably so — "as if you had made your life." Then, ushered in by the innocuous "And," comes the final revelation, directly stated, about the human circumstances that have made such happiness fitting, almost inevitable.

Updike knew what he had done here, at least so it seems when in 1985 he said about the story that "I had a sensation of breaking through, as if through a thin sheet of restraining glass, to material, to truth, previously locked up."[7] Amusing and agile as the light verse is on occasion, technically impressive and resourceful as is *The Poorhouse Fair*, this final story in *The Same Door*, especially its conclusion, is the happiest Updike had yet been as a writer.

THE NOVELIST TAKES OFF
Rabbit, Run

I n his 1995 introduction to the Everyman edition of his Rabbit tetralogy, *Rabbit Angstrom*, Updike addresses the composition of the book that would be the catalyst of a literary career:

> *Rabbit, Run* was begun, early in 1959, with no thought of a sequel. Indeed, it was not yet clear to me, though I had one short novel to my credit, that I was a novelist at all. At the age of twenty-seven I was a short-story writer by trade, a poet and light-versifier on the side, and an ex-reporter for *The New Yorker*. I had come, two years before, to New England to try my luck at freelancing. *Rabbit, Run* at first was modestly conceived as a novella, to form with another, *The Centaur*, a biune study of complementary moral types: the rabbit and the horse, the zigzagging creature of impulse and the plodding beast of stoic duty. *Rabbit* took off; as I sat at a little upright desk in a small corner room of the first house I owned, in Ipswich, Massachusetts, writing in soft pencil, the present-tense sentences accumulated and acquired momentum. It was a seventeenth-century house with a soft pine floor, and my kicking feet, during those excited months of composition, wore two bare spots in the varnish.[1]

By September 11 of that year he had finished the handwritten draft, which he then typed up and sent off to Knopf, "just as the decade ended." By the end of the next decade *Rabbit, Run* would run through numerous editions, would be translated into eleven European languages, under such piquant titles as *Hasenherz, Hare Hop,* and *Corri, Coniglio,* and would become, even more than its successors in the tetralogy, one of the most frequently taught novels in American college classrooms.

Inevitably, as successive Rabbit books followed, *Rabbit, Run* (with forty-seven printings by 1989) took its place as the opening novel in a sequence, and its characters were compared with their reincarnations later on. This process of familiarization, even as America in the late 1960s turned disaffected and violent beyond anything dreamed in *Rabbit, Run,* had somewhat the effect of domesticating a book that originally struck many readers as something new and disturbingly immediate in its portrayal — some saw it as a very hostile one — of American life. It was an aggressive book that assaulted readers: by its present tense you-are-there way of narration; also by its "hyperexpression" (Whitney Balliett's word), as if the novelist had six or seven senses; and most certainly because of the presence of events and language that had no place in the stories and short novel Updike had thus far published. Foremost among these "events" are the two sex scenes with Ruth, the sometime prostitute whom Rabbit lives with for a time, and the scene in which his wife Janice accidentally drowns their baby when, intoxicated, she tries to give Rebecca June a bath. But it would be wrong to speak of the "content" of sex and death as the sole reason why the novel unsettled people, since that unsettling was importantly a product of the way Updike wrote and of the moral perspective his writing gave — or refused to give — on the book's content.

Coming at the end of a decade, *Rabbit, Run* was a good candidate, retrospectively though not so much at the time, to be read as diagnostic novel "about" the 1950s — a decade that acquired, rather soon after its completion, the reputation as a time when young people were passive, complacency ruled the roost, and Eisenhower presided placidly over American consumerism. In fact this is not a rewarding way to read the novel, and Updike himself called *Rabbit,*

Run a product of the 1950s, rather than a postmortem on them. Paul Goodman's diagnostic *Growing Up Absurd*, published a year before *Rabbit, Run*, has a legitimate claim as a book that set out to say, in no uncertain terms, what had gone wrong with 1950s America; but diagnosis cannot be well conducted in the present tense. It's worth pointing out also that to those of us who spent our twenties in the decade, the 1950s were a very exciting time to be alive — nothing placid about them, but full of confusion and discovery and a fair share of that *angst* we were invited to characterize our souls as ridden with (and that forms the first five letters of Rabbit's surname). Encountering *Rabbit, Run* nearly forty years after it was published, it is difficult to see what the fuss was about or to imagine how this book could have provoked such strong reactions from its first readers and reviewers. It wasn't the sexual passages that disturbed them — anyone who read Joyce or Lawrence or Nabokov's *Lolita* would not have been unnerved — so much as the novel's overall view of humanity, more specifically humanity in its lower-middle- and working-class manifestations as observed in southeastern Pennsylvania. More than one reviewer found the attitude permeating Updike's novel to be an unqualified expression of dismay, indeed disgust. As perceptive a critic as John Thompson called it "literally a damnation," insisting that "what is damned is all the poor effort of humanity."[2] This antihuman aspect of the book's ungenerous morality, Thompson felt, made its verbal acrobatics revolting. Whitney Balliett, who had admired *The Poorhouse Fair*, also admired the style of *Rabbit*, but agreed with Thompson that it was at the service of a moral and aesthetic point of view that "detests" humankind.[3] The degree to which the book's protagonist, Harry Angstrom, is excepted from this overall condemnation — the degree to which we're invited to endorse his quest for something more, his "religious" spirit — was and has continued to be a matter for debate, though not I think a very fruitful one.

My guess is that Updike must have been unhappy about being saddled with such an antihumanity point of view. Certainly we should have little cause, on the basis of his previous three books, to predict the misanthropy some found central to *Rabbit, Run,* its overriding sense of disdain and rejection. On the other hand, it might be replied, could not *Rabbit, Run* be seen as an attempt to cut loose from the "tame creatures" — light verse, elegant sentences, humorous stories — that made up Updike's earliest volumes? When, as he said about the writing of it, the novel "took off," couldn't that mean a release into more extreme, less ironically and humorously controlled responses to life, especially as made through the consciousness that so dominates the book?

Consideration of these questions has to begin, and maybe to end, with the novel's third-person, present-tense mode of narration. Updike said that this way of telling was a "happy discovery" for him and that it had previously been sparingly used in English-language fiction. He quotes a character in a Dawn Powell novel who refers to the present tense as a "stevedore style," and notes that he himself encountered it only in Joyce Cary's novel *Mister Johnson* (1939), which Updike read in the mid-1950s. Cary had written that the present tense, used in a novel, can give a reader the "sudden feeling of insecurity" such as travelers feel who have lost their way; for Updike, the effect of Cary's novel was "rebellious and liberating." Of course since 1960 the practice has been much more common: one thinks offhand of contemporaries like Ann Beattie, Raymond Carver, Bobbie Ann Mason, and Sue Miller, all of whom have exploited the mode; no reader encountering it today would raise an eyebrow. Yet it is frequently said, and about *Rabbit, Run,* that present-tense narration provides and encourages a feeling of immediacy in the reader; that we are acted upon, beset by the sentences in stronger, less resistible ways than in the more common third-person past tense.

What reason is there to credit such claims that the forceful immediacy of the third person present crowds the reader into a responsive if uncertain relation to the narrative? Here is the often-quoted first paragraph of *Rabbit, Run:*

> Boys are playing basketball around a telephone pole with a
> backboard bolted to it. Legs, shouts. The scrape and snap of

Keds on loose alley pebbles seems to catapult their voice high into the moist March air blue above the wires. Rabbit Angstrom, coming up the alley in a business suit, stops and watches, though he's twenty-six and six three. So tall, he seems an unlikely rabbit, but the breadth of white face, the pallor of his blue irises, and a nervous flutter under his brief nose as he stabs a cigarette into his mouth partially explain the nickname, which was given to him when he too was a boy. He stands there thinking, the kids keep coming, they keep crowding you up.

Admittedly Rabbit is being introduced to us, so we haven't yet settled into registering, along with him, the look and feel of external things or the impressions and ideas of his psychological being. But the technique of this opening paragraph establishes what will be true throughout the novel: that there's a difference between what the protagonist can be said to take in ("Boys are playing basketball around a telephone pole with a backboard bolted to it") and what the writer provides by way of more densely filling in that protagonist. For example, there is the remark that, because of his height, "he seems an unlikely rabbit"; there is the exemplifying detail of the cigarette that with "a nervous flutter" he "stabs" into his mouth; and there is the explanation that he was given the nickname as a boy. In other words, from the first paragraph on there is a writerly presence here, making something out of Rabbit that he can't make out of himself, on his own.

It is this writerly presence, as much as the presumed immediacy of third-person present tense, that makes Updike's novel distinct from others written in the first or third person. It's really not all that far from the style of this opening paragraph to a passage that seems more extravagant and ornate. Having left his wife and moved in with Ruth, Rabbit takes a job — on the recommendation of the concerned minister, Jack Eccles — as a gardener on the estate of a widow, Mrs. Smith. The opening sentences of springlike effusions are stylistically aggressive:

> Sun and moon, sun and moon, time goes. In Mrs. Smith's acres, crocuses break the crust. Daffodils and narcissi unpack their trumpets. The reviving grass harbors violets, and the lawn is suddenly coarse with dandelions and broad-leaved weeds. Invisible rivulets running brokenly make the low land of the estate sing. The flowerbeds, bordered with bricks buried diagonally, are pierced by dull red spikes that will be peonies, and the earth itself, scumbled, stone-flecked, horny, raggedly patched with damp and dry, looks like the oldest and smells like the newest thing under Heaven.

It doesn't signify that Rabbit is nominally absent from these sentences, since he will be present in the ones to come, in which the sights, smells, and sounds of the garden are further embellished. For whether there in name or not, he is the beneficiary of the elevated, resurrected sense of nature that lives in the sentences Updike creates. Rabbit can see, perhaps identify, daffodils and narcissi, but does he see them "unpack their trumpets"? Does he intuit that the grass "harbors" violets, or that "invisible rivulets running brokenly make the low land of the estate sing"? Does he see the earth, along with its other qualities, as "scumbled" — a painterly word not to be found in small dictionaries but used more than once in Updike's writing? The point would not be worth laboring except that failure to grasp it has led too many critics of *Rabbit, Run,* and indeed of the whole tetralogy, into irrelevant arguments about whether it is "in character" for this noneducated ex–high school basketball star to see and feel so much, in such vibrant language.

In other words, once you assume that Rabbit Angstrom is a created character with some kind of existence independent of the sentences that are constantly making him up and unmaking him, you can argue about whether Updike approves or disapproves of his hero and the "quest" he's engaged in. And having stabilized Rabbit, whether in a positive or a negative light, or some mixture of lights, you can then take him to reflect an authorial point of view about life, or humanism without God, or America in the 1950s. But

Rabbit is less stabilized than that, harder to pin down and define, to know what his "mind" can or can't contain. One doesn't make this claim about any protagonist in any novel, or indeed in any third-person present novel: for example, in the precursor, Cary's *Mister Johnson*, Johnson is a clearly established, bounded figure whose perceptions and speech are always appropriate to our sense of what he would be likely to say or do or "register." Even Joyce's Leopold Bloom, from the book Updike acknowledged as massively influential on *Rabbit*, has a core of monological impressions that seems to emanate from some believable psychological center, as when he's deciding what to have for breakfast: "Ham and eggs, no. No good eggs with this drouth. Want pure fresh water. Thursday: not a good day either for a mutton kidney at Buckley's. Fried with butter, a shake of pepper. Better a pork kidney at Dlugacz's." Admittedly Bloom is later the recipient of mythological splendors and humiliations; still he's easier to stay with than Updike's hero, who is stylistically everywhere and nowhere in particular.

The other main characters in *Rabbit, Run* — Janice, Ruth, the minister Eccles and his wife, the old basketball coach Tothero, Rabbit's and Janice's parents — are all treated in a more conventional novelistic way. Either they are observed and described through conversation, as when Eccles visits the Springer and Angstrom households, then pays a call on Kruppenbach, the minister of Rabbit's church; or they are allowed interior, Molly Bloom–esque monologues, as when Ruth thinks about sex and men, or Janice provides a play-by-play account of the intoxicated, streaming thoughts that culminate in her drowning the baby. But Rabbit is always intoxicated, whether driving south in the famous abortive attempt to get to Florida, or playing golf with Eccles, or gardening, or running from the cemetery after his daughter is buried. Although he is not the sole narrative focus (he is offstage while his women perform or the minister queries others about him), his overriding presence in the novel makes it difficult, indeed impossible, for anyone else to "compete," in the sense of drawing comparable readerly sympathy and interest.

In an essay on several American male writers, the novelist Mary Gordon is angry about what she takes to be the congruence between Rabbit and his creator's attitudes toward women: for both of them, Gordon is convinced, women are impediments, mired in housework and babies, messy and "dumb" like Janice, or fat and promiscuous like Ruth, in one way or another standing in the path of the male's freedom — like the boys playing basketball in the book's first paragraph, they keep "crowding" Rabbit.[4] It's true that the present-tense accounting of Rabbit's actions and words and thoughts makes it difficult if not impossible to measure the degree of Updike's identification with or detachment from his hero. But this is exactly how the novelist designed it. To measure, as Gordon would have us do, both protagonist and author by adducing their fear of and incipient violence toward women is no measurement at all, especially since such extravagant behavior in extravagant language is allotted Rabbit. By the same token, we could identify Nabokov with Humbert Humbert and hold them equally responsible, in their manly irresponsibility, for the death of Charlotte Haze and the debauching of her daughter. The stunning success of *Lolita*, its proximity to the writing of *Rabbit, Run*, and Updike's growing admiration for Nabokov must surely have had an effect on his own ambitions as a novelist — may have incited him to try things he hadn't yet tried. And for all their differences, the suave multilanguaged European, Humbert Humbert, and the blundering American misfit, Harry Angstrom, are continuous, brothers in the realm of verbal expressiveness.

But if Nabokov gets away with depicting heartless "immoral" behavior in a protagonist whom, it seems, he is not interested in judging, Updike's task is a more difficult one. He must persuade us to suspend disapproval of Rabbit's actions, even to the point of making us complicitous with them, in a novel that (unlike *Lolita*) is not a comic one. Before his Bech stories and the Nabokovian *A Month of Sundays*, Updike was not thought of as a writer of comedy; yet there's plenty of it in the early poems and in the stories from *The Same Door*, and it occasionally surfaces in the first Rabbit book. Its particular nature, which, like Joyce's use of Bloom, presents Rabbit as both the butt of

humor and a humorous critic of others, can be seen in the finely inventive scene at the novel's beginning when, after playing basketball with
the boys, Rabbit reaches his house on Wilbur Street in Mt. Judge, a
three-story frame house built in a 1930s development, shingled, with
"scabby clapboards" in the front. He pauses in the vestibule, smells the
ever-present smell — something like cabbage cooking or just decay —
climbs the stairs to the top floor, and finds the door locked. He unlocks
it to discover Janice watching television from an armchair, an Old-
Fashioned beside her. Rabbit quizzes her on why the door was locked
("It just locked itself," she answers) and twits her for being afraid —
"Whodeya think's gonna come in that door? Errol Flynn?" He asks
her where the car is and gives her a sarcastic retort when she says
it's in front of her mother's: "That's terrific. That's just the frigging
place for it." Then he identifies and becomes interested in the show
she's watching, the famous 1950s after-school favorite *The Mickey
Mouse Club*, in which various Mouseketeers — most notably, Annette
Funicello — provide fun and games and good advice for young people.

Rabbit listens attentively as Jimmy, the "big Mouseketeer," delivers a homily about getting to "Know Thyself, a wise old Greek once
said." Each of us, Jimmy tells his audience, has a special God-given
talent that we must work to develop, for this is the only way to happiness. Rabbit, who has been working four weeks as a salesman
and demonstrator of a kitchen implement named MagiPeel, is
impressed, and the style of his response can be seen in the paragraph
that follows Jimmy the Mouseketeer's pinching his mouth together
and winking at his audience:

> That was good. Rabbit tries it, pinching the mouth together
> and then the wink, getting the audience out front with you
> against some enemy behind, Walt Disney or the MagiPeel
> Peeler Company, admitting it's all a fraud but, what the hell,
> making it likable. We're all in it together. Fraud makes the
> world go round. The base of our economy. Vitaconomy, the
> modern housewife's password, the one-word expression for
> economizing vitamins by the MagiPeel Method.

The humor here is not really at Rabbit's expense, even though he's credulous toward Jimmy's ability to deliver useful tips. The histrionic mouth-pinching, as he tries on the style; the easy ring of "what the hell, making it likable"; and the cynical acceptance, for the moment, of "Fraud makes the world go round," invite our complicity through a blend of Rabbit-thinking and Updike-invention. This blend is something heard: it moves the passage and provides a glimpse of the character available only to the reader; that is, no one within the novel can see Rabbit in this way. In succeeding volumes of the tetralogy, Rabbit's point of view, especially as he relaxes a bit from existential concerns, becomes increasingly humorous and ironic — the irony directed both at those outside him and at himself. But even in *Rabbit, Run*, there are stirrings to be felt.

The most impressive effort by a critic to give some account of the difference Updike's style makes, particularly in its employment of the continuous present, is in an essay by Philip Stevick that points to the calculated loss, in this novel, of "a sense of memory, or virtual memory, implicit in the narration. . . ."[5] Stevick contrasts it with the opening of James's *Portrait of a Lady* ("Under certain circumstances there are few hours in life more agreeable than the hour dedicated to the ceremony known as afternoon tea"), a narrative conducted with "deliberate, retrospective distance, with an illusion of recollection," and he makes the following summary statement of how an absence of such recollection informs the atmosphere of Updike's novel:

> Without a retrospective narration, without the interposition of a period of time between the events and the telling of them, without the appearance of a mediating consciousness and a strenuous memory, the events seem slightly dislocated and decontextualized, the characters more than a little fragile and vulnerable.

This seems to me just right by way of naming the slight dislocation, not an unpleasurable one, we experience in reading and that peaks, later in the first section, in the great night car trip south, as Rabbit

attempts, vainly but vigorously, to escape the "trap" of social and familial nets in which he's caught. What does he get instead?

> On the radio he hears "No Other Arms, No Other Lips," "Stagger Lee," a commercial for Rayco Clear Plastic Seat Covers, "If I Didn't Care" by Connie Francis, a commercial for Radio-Controlled Garage Door Operators, "I Ran All the Way Home Just to Say I'm Sorry," "That Old Feeling" by Mel Torme, a commercial for Big Screen Westinghouse TV Set with One-Finger Automatic Tuning . . .

and on and on, the continuous present in which these items are recorded as random, discrete, and uninterpreted as it's possible for continuity to be. Clearly Updike listened to the radio one night and took notes: the effect is more telling than one might think.

Although the novel is filled with 1950s junk — the paraphernalia, as one reviewer put it, of our "obese" American life — it's hard to see *Rabbit, Run* as a criticism of that life. Updike's adherence to his Pennsylvania places — pedestrian, cramped Mt. Judge and dismal, clotted Brewer — is so faithful, even loyal, that it seems to emanate from someone who never learned to regard his hometown with contempt. One thinks, by contrast, of a novel published the year after *Rabbit* that casts a very cold eye indeed on the local life of its protagonist. *Revolutionary Road,* the fine novelistic debut of Richard Yates, has as its province not a hometown but a suburb in Westchester or Connecticut where Frank and April Wheeler live. Their social class is higher than Rabbit's, a well-off upper-middle-class world of lawns and well-tended houses to which the hero returns from New York at the end of each day. This novel about the opulent desolation of the suburbs, as it was termed, has been hailed as a triumph of realism. But its realism has to do with things carefully observed and described, with voices in conflict full of "natural" American speech rhythms. Behind all this observation and recording, however, is a fictive narrative voice that assumes (in Philip Stevick's terms) plenty of deliberate, retrospective distance. For example, part 2 of the novel begins when the Wheelers decide (fatefully) to save their marriage and individual souls by picking up and leaving suburbia for a life in Paris: "There now began a time of such joyous derangement, of such exultant carelessness, that Frank Wheeler could never afterwards remember how long it lasted." The reader feels the opposite of "dislocated" here, is reassured rather by the authoritative, composed, wholly trustworthy taleteller in charge of things. It is exactly the absence of such qualities that makes the "realism" of *Rabbit, Run* such a different thing.

If it is an error to treat the novel, as I have done so far, as one whose originality lies wholly in its technique, a still more common error is treating it as a "crisis" fiction notable for its portrait of the struggle between humanism and religion, with Rabbit as the inarticulate quester who believes in something he can't put into words. That "something" is the subject of Rabbit's golf game with the Reverend Jack Eccles. As the two play, Eccles, representative of "humanism" and skeptical of the "it" — "this thing that wasn't there" and that, Harry tells him, has caused him to leave Janice — instructs Harry in the true faith: "Christianity isn't looking for a rainbow. . . . We're trying to *serve* God, not *be* God." Eccles teases him reproachfully about the nature of his quest for "it": "What *is* it? . . . Is it blue? Is it red? Does it have polka dots?" Whereupon Rabbit, whose golf game has been pretty ragged up to this point (he is learning), tees off and hits the first fine drive in Updike's fiction:

> his ball is hung way out, lunarly pale against the beautiful black blue of storm clouds, his grandfather's color stretched dense across the north. It recedes along a line straight as a ruler-edge. Stricken; sphere, star, speck.

After it makes a perfect fall, Rabbit, with "a grin of aggrandizement," tells Eccles, "That's *it*."

There's no need to choose up for Rabbit here at the expense of the minister, whose skepticism about "it" has something to be said for it and gets said in the exchange. But the heightened prose testifies that Updike has much invested in his hero's aspirings and that a perfect tee-off in golf isn't the worst metaphor for something precious —

"transcendent" if you will — that life can on occasions manifest. The attractive poise in the game of question and response between Rabbit and Eccles makes it a mistake, on any reader's part, to identify with a single viewpoint determined to be right and endorsed by the author. In an analogous manner, the inadequate humanist responses of Eccles and the other nonbelievers in the book (except for the fierce Lutheran, Fritz Kruppenbach, only Rabbit can be said, however vaguely, to "believe") aren't traduced or mocked: they're doing the best they can in their respective ways. Nor is the urban American landscape of Brewer and Mt. Judge, for all its ingloriousness, an object for satiric contempt. When, after their first lovemaking, Rabbit next day persuades Ruth to hike up to the top of Mt. Judge, they ascend through a city park that looks like this:

> The trash baskets and movable metal benches have not been set out yet. On the concrete-and-plank benches fluffy old men sun like greater pigeons, dressed in patches of gray multiple as feathers. The trees in small leaf dust the half-bare ground with shadow. Sticks and strings protect the newly seeded margins of the unraked gravel walk.

They pass the empty bandshell and observe a derelict stretched out, plus a few young "toughs" smoking near an equipment shed on which is painted in red, "TEX & JOSIE, RITA & JAY." Rabbit thinks:

> Where would they get red paint? He takes Ruth's hand. The ornamental pool in front of the bandshell is drained and scum-stained; they move along a path parallel to the curve of its cold lip, which echoes back the bandshell's silence. A World War II tank, made a monument, points its (empty) guns at far-off (clay) tennis courts. The nets are not up, the lines unlimed.

How many American towns and cities after the Second World War had something like that tank, displayed in some small park or other as a reminder of what no one in the town was interested in remembering any longer? When is a "park" not quite the way a park should be? The academic critic may find in the scene an ironic version of pastoral, whose landscape does not answer to the imagination's needs. But Rabbit and Ruth don't seem terribly bothered by it, even though their feet hurt as they climb the mountain. And I see no reason to claim that Updike is "bothered" by it, in the sense that he would like to take things in hand and improve them, remove the red paint and get rid of the scum on the pool.

Robert Frost once wrote to a young poet named Kimball Flaccus, who Frost decided wanted the world "to be better than it is, more poetical," telling him that "I don't want the world made safer for poetry or easier. To hell with it. That is its own lookout. Let it stew in its own materialism. No, not to Hell with it. Let it hold its position while I do it in art." Updike doesn't flaunt himself in this way, but his and Frost's artistic principles are similar, as were those of a third American writer, the poet William Carlos Williams, who in a section of *Paterson,* book 2 ("Sunday in the park"), writes of

> oaks, choke-cherry,
> dogwoods, white and green, iron-wood:
> humped roots matted into the shallow soil
> —mostly gone: rock out-croppings
> polished by the feet of the picknickers:
> sweetbarked sassafras
>
> leaning from the rancid grease:
> deformity—

Updike may or may not have read *Paterson* by 1960, but he would I think have recognized the park, held in less-than-glorious position while Williams did it in art.

There is a similar evenhandedness in *Rabbit, Run* in the writing about sex. Although writing about writing about sex seems a deadly prospect, the subject deserves comment since it marks Updike's entry into a subject he will be concerned with variously in the fiction and poetry to come; and it has a not insignificant place in the movement toward literary freedom in the treatment of sex that surfaced in the late 1950s. In discussing the changes and cuts in the erotic scene which first Knopf, then Updike's English publisher Gollancz, asked him to make (Gollancz declined to publish the cut version and Updike settled down with the firm of André Deutsch), Updike mentions certain books and writers as "models in sexual realism." For him these include Edmund Wilson (*Memoirs of Hecate County* had been successfully prosecuted in 1946), D. H. Lawrence, Erskine Caldwell (whose *God's Little Acre* was a steamy book for adolescents in the 1940s), James M. Cain, and Joyce. Henry Miller is absent from the list, and in fact Updike never thought much of him as a writer.

Joyce's presence is felt not so much in the sex scenes as, derivatively, in Ruth's Molly Bloom–esque monologue about sex and men, Rabbit in particular. The actual scenes of sexual encounter — the night when he moves in with Ruth and they make love; a later occasion when she, rather unwillingly, performs fellatio on him; and the scene when Rabbit tries to use Janice for ejaculatory purposes (*not* anal sex, as Mary Gordon mistakenly claims) — are all written in a direct, gritty style quite different from the lyrical one Updike would adopt for some of the lovemaking in, say *Couples*. Here are Rabbit and Ruth:

> his hand abandoned on the breadth of her body finds at arm's length a split pod, an open fold, shapeless and simple. They enter a lazy space. She rolls further, turning her back, cradling her bottom in his stomach and thighs. He wants the time to stretch long, to great length and thinness. Between her legs she strokes him with her fingertips. She brings back her foot and he holds her head. As they deepen together he feels impatience that through all their twists they remain separate flesh; he cannot dare enough, now that she is so much his friend in this search; everywhere they meet a wall. The body lacks voice to sing its own song. She floats through his blood as under his eyelids a salt smell, damp pressure, the sense of her smallness as her body hurries everywhere into his hands, her breathing, bedsprings' creak, accidental slaps, and the ache at the parched root of his tongue each register their colors.

This writing proceeds largely without Lawrence's mystical — and often quite confusing — directions; impressionistic, but without being fancy, it is the opposite of pornographic. At one preorgasmic point Ruth responds to Harry's rather sweetly boyish remark, "You're pretty," with the imperative, "Come on. Work." So Updike works at the writing here, suggesting that real sex is something different from a good time or reckless abandon or rich human sharing. When, after Ruth has an orgasm, Rabbit asks her what it was like, she doesn't say that the earth moved but that "it's like falling through." And when Rabbit pushes her — "Where do you fall to?" — she says, quite sensibly, "Nowhere. I can't talk about it." In itself this exchange would be a candidate for an achievement in sexual realism, as written in 1960.[6]

The scene in which Ruth provides oral sex to Rabbit ("sucking you off" as she refers to it in the later version) is left pretty much undescribed and none the less effective for that. Rabbit is attempting to punish her for her behavior with Ronnie Harrison, an old basketball teammate whom Rabbit dislikes and who was a previous client of Ruth's. They run into Harrison at a club in Brewer where Rabbit's sister Mim, whose precocious sexuality Rabbit worries about, also shows up with a man, disturbing her older brother. Getting Ruth to "do it" to him will, he thinks crudely, prove she's "his." Ruth wants to hold on to Rabbit and is willing to go along with something he promises he'll never ask her to do again. She takes off her clothes as he stands "by the dull wall," then "leans awkward and brings one hand up and hangs it on his shoulder not knowing what to do with it." But the point of view, interestingly enough, is hers, not Rabbit's:

> Sliding her last clothes off, her arms feel cold touching her sides. This last month she's felt cold all the time; her temperature being divided or something. In the growing light he shifts slightly. She closes her eyes and tells herself, they're not ugly. Not.

At which point the scene ends. The writing is deliberately the opposite of arousing, but it's wrong to adopt the other extreme and see it as ruthlessly clinical, by way of demonstrating his selfishness and her passivity. It's an unhappy coming together, rather, handled with just the right amount of cool regard, and readers of the novel in the early 1960s didn't forget it.

Near the end of "The Dogwood Tree: A Boyhood," Updike names the "three great secret things" — sex, religion, and art. The art of *Rabbit, Run* is devoted in part to an exploration of the first two of these great things, done mainly through the consciousness of a somewhat inarticulate man, though also, thanks to Updike, a keen registrar of impressions. Unlike the sexual "thing," the most direct treatment of "religion" in the novel occurs with Rabbit offstage, in the argument between the liberal Eccles and the unreformed Kruppenbach. But at the core of the novel is something that, while surely related to sex and religion, is an even greater secret Rabbit is allowed to discover and that, for the first but by no means the last time, makes its appearance in Updike's writing. This is the sense of transience, of loss, that surfaces with exceptional power and beauty at one moment and is most firmly and delicately rendered, though not, like the sexual passages or the drowning of Janice's baby, one that everyone remembers.

Before Janice and the new baby, Rebecca June, come home from the hospital, Rabbit, who has also come home, has cleaned up the apartment, and is occupied with being a useful citizen and father, takes his son Nelson on walks about the town. They watch softball together and share an orange soda, the "artificial sweetness" of which "fills Rabbit's heart." One day he and Nelson go to the playground and after pushing the boy gently in the swings and dabbling in the sandbox, Rabbit suddenly has a vision:

> Over at the pavilion the rubber thump of roof ball and the click of checkers call to his memory, and the forgotten smell of that narrow plastic ribbon you braid bracelets and whistle-chains out of and of glue and of the sweat on the handles of athletic equipment is blown down by a breeze laced with children's murmurings. He feels the truth: the thing that has left

his life has left irrevocably; no search would recover it. No
flight would reach it. It was here, beneath the town, in these
smells and these voices, forever behind him. The fullness ends
when we give Nature her ransom, when we make children for
her. Then she is through with us, and we become, first inside,
and then outside, junk. Flower stalks.

The grass withereth, the flower fadeth — that, sadly, is all ye know
on earth and all ye need to know. And Rabbit, here, knows as much
as he ever will, even in the novels to come, about this great and
painful secret. So that his final flight, when he bolts away from the
society of mourners at his daughter's grave, is doomed in advance,
feels even more futile than the abortive car trip south, which was
undertaken at least with a sense of possibility. We take leave from
him in the novel's final paragraph, the wind in his ears as "out of a
kind of sweet panic growing lighter and quicker and quieter, he
runs. Ah: runs. Runs." Although Rabbit's panic may seem to grow
lighter, any reader listening to the cadence Updike provides here
will hear more than a sigh in that perfectly executed "Ah."

THREE

THE PENNSYLVANIA THING
Pigeon Feathers • *The Centaur* • "Leaving
Church Early" • *Of the Farm*

When in 1964 Updike decided to publish a volume titled
Olinger Stories, containing the short fiction he had written
about his boyhood in Pennsylvania and his later returnings to
that place, he concluded the foreword by admitting that if he had
to pick a few stories to represent him, these would be the ones.
For many readers like me who began to discover Updike in the
early 1960s, it was these stories — even more than the first
Rabbit novel or *The Centaur* — that made the largest impact. To
some degree their popularity has worked against Updike's reputation overall, by prompting the claim that his excellence lies in
shorter rather than longer fiction. Yet there is no need to deni-
grate one genre by hoisting up another. After all, as Randall
Jarrell sagely remarked, a novel is a prose narrative of a certain
length that has something wrong with it; some of Updike's stories
have, as it were, nothing wrong with them. But as can be seen
from his most ambitious work in the 1962 collection *Pigeon
Feathers*, he was concerned to break up the boundaries of the
"well-made" story ("Snowing in Greenwich Village," for example)
in the interests of a more meditative, wandering, and associative
pattern of writing. More often than not a "story" of this sort works
through nonsequential, imaginative linkings, so that even when
the progression is straightforward enough — as in "The Happiest
I've Been" — there is a leisurely feel to things quite different, for

example, from the taut drivenness of a story by his contemporary Flannery O'Connor.

His unpublished novel, *Home*, is the mother lode from which the Pennsylvania stories and *The Centaur* are mined. In the form in which he bequeathed the manuscript to Harvard's Houghton Library, it is a work of some six hundred typed pages, heavily corrected and revised throughout, often using the reverse side of stories he was working on concurrently — such as "Friends from Philadelphia" and "Who Made Yellow Roses Yellow?" — that would appear in *The Same Door*. A quick recital of some of its parts may suggest the continuity between *Home* and the published work that followed. Its focus is on a nineteen-year-old woman, Elsie (or Lucy) Baer, who lives with her mother and father in a town much like Shillington/Olinger. She makes an unsuccessful attempt at being a seventh-grade substitute teacher in the public school, whose principal is named Tothero (Rabbit's high-school basketball coach). We follow her to her senior year at Lake College in Pennsylvania, where she meets and later marries Jorgeson (George) Hanema, that surname later to be encountered in *Couples*. There are glimpses of George and Lucy's honeymoon and its unsatisfactory commencement. After a few years a boy, David, is born, a dogwood tree planted to commemorate his birth. George Baer, like George Caldwell in *The Centaur*, teaches in the public school and is the recipient (as is Caldwell) of the principal's unfriendly reports. There are scenes of David reading to his grandfather or going to the movies. Near the end of the novel's first half there is a debate about selling the house and moving to the farm, some miles from town. This move having been accomplished, we hear in part 2 of David's fear of death, sparked by a reading of H. G. Wells's *Outline of History*. David has a dog named Copper and eventually a girlfriend about whom his mother makes hurting comments. This is perhaps enough to suggest similarities in material between the unpublished *Home* and Updike's published fiction of the early 1960s, also to see why he decided not to persist with the autobiographical novel. Surely he was aware of the risk involved in beginning a literary career with a lengthy family chronicle which included, among other things, the writer's birth and what happened afterward. To hold nothing back at the outset of things would have been to spend copiously, within a single book, what might be more variously and subtly exploited in different fictional and autobiographical forms.[1] So from 1959 to the beginning of 1962 he brought out in the *New Yorker* the major evidences of his preoccupation, stories that remain among the very best of his work.

Pigeon Feathers

Olinger Stories arranges the stories according to the age of Updike's protagonist — high-school boy, young married man visiting his parents after a year in England, older father of four returning, in fact or imagination, to the Pennsylvania farm. In *Pigeon Feathers* the "Pennsylvania" stories appear in the following nontemporal order: "The Persistence of Desire," "Flight," "A Sense of Shelter," "Home," "Pigeon Feathers," "The Blessed Man of Boston, My Grandmother's Thimble, and Fanning Island," and "Packed Dirt, Churchgoing, A Dying Cat, A Traded Car." Of these, in addition to "The Happiest I've Been," I take "Flight," "Pigeon Feathers," and the final two portmanteau efforts to be of primary interest in establishing Updike as an original artist in shorter fiction.

As usual it is he himself who best put his finger on the impulse animating the *Pigeon Feathers* stories, as well as the three novels — *Rabbit, Run, The Centaur,* and *Of the Farm* — published between 1960 and 1965. In all of them he identifies "a central image of flight or escape or loss, the way we flee from the past, a sense of guilt."[2] The sense of guilt has to do with the fact "that in time as well as space we leave people as if by volition and thereby incur guilt and thereby owe them, the dead, the forsaken, at least the homage of rendering them." This is his great theme, mainly absent in the stories from *The Same Door,* hinted at from time to time in *Rabbit, Run,* but emerging full-blown in the best stories in *Pigeon Feathers* and continuing through his career.

For literary antecedents to Updike's portraits of adolescents and young men living in small towns, bound by familial — especially maternal — bonds, and trying, with whatever mixed feelings, to get loose from them, we must go to the early 1920s, when American writers importantly began to register this struggle. There are vivid evidences of it in the letters of Hart Crane to his father and mother, as Crane attempts to move away from and beyond Cleveland, Ohio. There is Hemingway's returning soldier, Harold Krebs (in "Soldier's Home"), a grown-up adolescent painfully striving for release from his mother even as he prostrates himself before her. Most predictive of Updike is Sherwood Anderson's *Winesburg, Ohio* chronicle, which one critic has invoked as a progenitor of Updike's story "Flight" — the youthful protagonist's mother a stronger version of *Winesburg's* Elizabeth Willard, another mother with aspirations for her son to fly beyond the provinces into a wider world.[3]

There is justice in the comparison, but also immense difference between Anderson's handling of Elizabeth Willard and her son George (in the *Winesburg* story "Mother") and what Updike does with Allen Dow and his mother. The difference is to be found in the comparative subtlety and complication of Updike's treatment. As Elizabeth Willard observes her gifted son, she says things to herself: "He is groping about, trying to find himself. . . . Within him there is a secret something that is striving to grow. It is the thing I let be killed in myself." And in the story's final page, when George says he will have to go away, his mother "wanted to cry out with joy because of the words that had come from the lips of her son," although she is too embarrassed to give expression to her feelings. By contrast, Updike's "Flight" begins in the embarrassment of the seventeen-year-old son rather than his mother's, as one day she hikes with him to the top of Shale Hill where they look down on Olinger, its homes, stores, gas stations, movie theater, elementary school, and Lutheran church. The vision widens to include the entire Pennsylvania county, as suddenly the mother announces,

> "There we all are, and there we'll all be forever." She hesitated before the word "forever," and hesitated again before adding, "Except you, Allen. You're going to fly." A few birds were hung

far out over the valley, at the level of our eyes, and in her impulsive way she had just plucked the image from them, but it felt like the clue I had been waiting all my childhood for. My most secret self had been made to respond, and I was intensely embarrassed, and irritably ducked my head out from under her melodramatic hand.

The reflective, first-person narrator is still, in retrospect, both moved and embarrassed by the gesture, seeing the notion of flight as a metaphor too easily plucked from the birds, but also as the something big he has been waiting for. This resonant voice is continuous with the one in "The Happiest I've Been," and it immediately opens up possibilities in a way that Anderson's heavily omniscient third-person voice cannot. The interest and energy of Updike's writing lies not in any "points" it makes about mother or son, but in its shifts and changes of voice, its flights and perchings (to steal a metaphor from William James) that constitute Allen's stream of thought. Some decades after "Flight" was published, Updike wrote an appreciation of *Winesburg, Ohio* in which he treated it as part of a tradition in American writing:

> The Protestant villages of America, going back to Hawthorne's Salem, leave a spectral impression in literature: vague longing and monotonous, inbred satisfactions are their essence; there is something perilous and maddening in the accommodations such communities extend to human aspiration and appetite.[4]

Anderson and Sinclair Lewis had done the work of showing the repressive cruelty of American villages such as Winesburg and Gopher Prairie; Updike determined to put a fresh spin on the "accommodations" such communities did and did not offer the spirit. The determination was consonant with, in "The Dogwood Tree," riding "a thin pencil line" out of Shillington, but complicated also by the recognition of how attractive the "inbred satisfactions" of village life could be. In "A Sense of Shelter," the story in *Pigeon Feathers* that follows "Flight," William Young loves being the smart boy in school, always knowing the right answers and feeling the "snug sense of his work done, of the snow falling, of the warm minutes that walked through their shelter so slowly." His vision of his own future — in which he will become a brilliant, revered professor and die, like Tennyson, with a copy of *Cymbeline* beside him — is nothing more than an untroubled extension of the life he's already leading. William will receive his comeuppance when the beautiful girl to whom he declares his love, responds, "You never loved anybody. . . . You don't know what it is."

But not to the extent that he is wholly shocked out of his dream world, for Updike is canny enough to resist moments of conversion in these stories when suddenly the protagonist sees the error of his ways and is enlightened into harsh truth. He resists such melodramatic transformations partly by deflecting the story's curve away from steady presentation of its hero, so that in "Flight" Allen Dow isn't the sole and solemn focus of attention, even though his first-person voice is always there. Indeed the opening two sentences invite us to view him, as does his retrospective narration, with sympathetic, humorous detachment: "At the age of seventeen I was poorly dressed and funny-looking, and went around thinking about myself in the third person. 'Allen Dow strode down the street and home.' 'Allen Dow smiled a thin sardonic smile.'" The first half of the story is taken up with establishing, by way of familial and geographic detail, why the mother wants Allen to fly away from Olinger. Here, material presented at length in *Home* is compressed into succinct portraits of the mother in her younger days, her college education and her desire to move to New York City, her inability to do this, and her consequent marriage to Victor Dow. These, along with brief histories of her mother and father, coalesce into a portrait of the trap, "the inheritance of frustration and folly that had descended from my grandfather to my mother to me, and that I, with a few beats of my grown wings, was destined to reverse and redeem."[5]

The action of "Flight" is a simple one: Allen travels with three members of his debate team — all girls — to participate in a contest ("Should the Federal Republic of Germany . . ."), stays out late talking and necking with one of them, Molly Bingaman, loses the debate next morning, and comes back to Olinger with a new girl-friend. No one, least of all his mother, thinks the relationship a good idea; they break up more than once, then one night, when Allen nervously parks in front of her house but doesn't knock on the door, Molly suddenly appears and comforts him. After leaving her, he eats three hamburgers and drinks two glasses of milk at an all-night diner, then goes home to find, at 2 A.M., his mother lying on the sofa, still awake, listening to Dixieland as it emerges by way of New Orleans and Philadelphia, the family Philco with "the orange disc of its celluloid dial" her only company. His mother appalls him by asking, "How was little hotpants?" and they proceed to spar, then are suddenly interrupted:

> Upstairs, close to our heads, my grandfather, in a voice frail but still melodious, began to sing, "There is a happy land, far, far away, where saints in glory stand, bright, bright as day." We listened; and his voice broke into coughing, a terrible rending cough growing in fury, struggling to escape, and loud with fear he called my mother's name. She didn't stir. The voice grew enormous, a bully's voice, as he repeated "Lillian! Lillian!" and I saw my mother's shape quiver with the force coming down the stairs into her.

The son too feels this force, feels angry, and hates "that black mass of suffering," even as he realizes he is "too weak to withstand it." He tells his mother that she's won, but won for the last time, and she responds "with typical melodrama, 'Goodbye, Allen.'" It is a power-ful moment, in which Updike invests a great deal, as can be seen from his singling it out in an interview and confessing to its autobi-ographical truth: "This is the way it was, is. There has never been anything in my life quite as compressed, simultaneously as commu-nicative to me of my own power and worth and of the irremediable grief in just living, in just going on."[6] This I take to be the voice of a writer already tired of being praised or dispraised as a "stylist," a writer who wants, like his hero, to flee home, to get beyond his own well-shaped sentences into truth — what the family, what "home" really is like. Coleridge once wrote, "All the images rose up before me as things," and something of that sense of overpowering presence is felt in this scene.

David Kern, a slightly younger version of Allen Dow, is the hero of the book's title story, which has an episodic feel to it similar to "Flight." The opening section of "Pigeon Feathers" begins with the family's move to David's mother's farm, some miles from Olinger, and with the attendant displacement and rearrangement of objects, particularly the collection of books, acquired mostly by David's mother. They include, along with P. G. Wodehouse, Sinclair Lewis, and Will Durant's *The Story of Philosophy*, a four-volume set of H. G. Wells's popular classic, *The Outline of History*, a work that graced the shelves of somewhat bookish people in the 1930s and 1940s. Leafing through it David discovers, more or less fortuitously, Wells's naturalistic account of Jesus of Nazareth, an "obscure political agitator" who survived his own crucifixion and on whom a religion was founded. Wells's denial of the divinity of Jesus has a terrible impact on the youth: how could such a brain as Wells's, "black with the denial of Christ's divinity," have been permitted to exist, write books, win honors? If Wells spoke truth, then David's world is "a jumble of horror. The world outside the deep-silled windows — a rutted lawn, a whitewashed barn, a walnut tree frothy with fresh green — seemed a haven from which he was forever sealed off. Hot washrags seemed pressed against his cheeks." As strong a presentation of personal crisis as is to be found in Updike's work, this experience seems unlikely to have been something merely thought up by a writer, rather than suffered by an actual boy. As with the closing moment in "Flight," Updike might have said about it, with reference to his younger self, "This is the way it was, is."

The crisis extends and intensifies when, while using the outhouse, David has a vision of his death and burial, the "impending oblivion" that reading Wells has caused him to imagine. Returning to the farmhouse, he finds his parents arguing about whether the land has a "soul," with his father taking the "scientific" ("nothing but chemicals") perspective and his mother a more poetic one. David looks up the word *soul* in *Webster's* and is slightly comforted to find that it is "separate in nature from the body and usually held to be separable in existence." He looks for confirmation of this from his Lutheran minister the Reverend Dobson (whom his father thinks an intelligent man) at the catechetical class in the Firetown church. At question time David asks the minister where the soul resides in the period between our death and the Day of Judgment. Dobson is uneasy, suggests that we can think of our souls as asleep, and of Heaven as existing the way Abraham Lincoln's goodness lives on after his death. David is inwardly scornful of this way out and, like the boy in Philip Roth's story "The Conversion of the Jews," takes things into his own hands — though, not, as Roth's hero does, by climbing out on the roof and threatening to jump.

Instead he searches the Bible and questions his mother about God, but is dismayed when she tells him both that God has given us everything and that man has made God. He can't accept this: God has to be different, and neither his mother, who gives him Plato's allegory of the cave to read, nor his father, who says death is a wonderful thing ("Get the garbage out of the way"), can help. He loses his appetite for reading, feels distracted only by such temporary respites as the comforts of school — especially the pinball machine at the Olinger luncheonette — or calming his dog, Copper, when he recoils from the noise made by David's gun, a Remington .22 his parents give him for his fifteenth birthday. Still, the four volumes of Wells's *Outline* remain "adamant," like "four thin bricks" he can't dislodge from his consciousness.

The story then takes a surprising and unobvious turn toward "action" when David's mother urges him, at the request of his grandmother, to shoot some of the overabundant pigeons cluttering up the barn. The motive behind the request is partly to give the boy something to do, sunk as he is in dark speculation. David at first demurs, not wanting to kill anything, then agrees to do it, at which point a "pleasant crisp taste entered his mouth with the decision."

The story's closing pages describe, with precise and complicated verbal energy, the contents and physical layout of the barn, especially the small round holes through which the pigeons enter and exit. Their attempt to exit, after David begins to shoot, is presented with disturbing force:

> Now others shook loose from the rafters, and whirled in the dim air with a great blurred hurtle of feathers and noise. They would go for the hole; he fixed his sight on the little moon of blue, and when a pigeon came to it, shot him as he was walking the ten inches of stone that would have carried him into the open air.

Dabs of gray pop in and out, the pigeons' cooing becomes shriller, and David, "fully master now," begins to feel like "a beautiful avenger": "A tiny peek, probe, dab of life, when he hit it, blossomed into a dead enemy, falling with good, final weight." Eventually he climbs the ladder and trains his sights on a particularly stubborn foe that, caught in the hole, refuses to fall one way or the other, even as David pumps a clip of bullets into the bird's shadow. Meanwhile the remaining pigeons escape, and he grows tired of the whole business. With his mother's aid he buries the dead pigeons, studying them as he does so and finding how wonderful their feathers are, with their designs of color. The closing sentence has often been quoted: "As he fitted the last two, still pliant, on the top, and stood up, crusty coverings were lifted from him, and with a feminine, slipping sensation along his nerves that seemed to give the air hands, he was robed in this certainty: that the God who had lavished such craft upon these worthless birds would not destroy His whole Creation by refusing to let David live forever."

Updike likes to finish his stories with a flourish, and because of the religious theme, carefully developed earlier in this one, there is a temptation to rush in for the kill, to pick out and hold high the plum of wisdom gained. So the writer of a study of pastoral patterns in Updike's fiction finds that David has undergone an initiation here, is now complicit with sin and death, having killed the pigeons, but also enabled by the experience: "Having created death through the act of shooting, the boy achieves transcendental insight through contemplation of his kill."[7] The trouble with such a formulation, apart from its not being very interesting (literature, after all, is filled with characters achieving transcendental insights), is that it's deaf to the play of tone that is Updike's, not David's. The return to faith ("That the God who had lavished such craft . . .") is hedged round by a sympathetic but ironic voice in its account of how "David" would surely live forever. Just as Updike refrains from condescending to or moralizing about David's shooting the birds, portraying it rather for what it was, a thrilling and unsettling rite, so the story's end doesn't oblige us to see the boy as either triumphant or merely duped. The motive behind that sadly humorous twist in the final sentence about God, the pigeons, and David Kern is surely a mixed one.

In an essay written the year after *Pigeon Feathers* was published, Saul Bellow recognized Updike's "virtuosity" but made the following, rather chilly, comment about the ending and overall quality of the title story:

> Nevertheless, there is nothing to see here but the writer's reliance on beautiful work, on an aesthetic discipline and order. And sensibility, in such forms, incurs the dislike of many because it is perceptive inwardly, and otherwise blind. We suspect it of a stony heart because it functions so smoothly in its isolation. The writer of sensibility assumes that only private explorations and inner development are possible and accepts the opposition of public and private as fixed and indissoluble.[8]

Coming from the novelist who, seven years previous, had given us *Seize the Day* — a virtuoso performance of its hero, Tommy Wilhelm's, suffering sensibility — Bellow's reservations seem less than convincing. Perhaps the fact that he was about to publish *Herzog*, his most ambitious attempt to connect public and private realms, makes the demur about Updike more understandable. But to exercise, in Bellow's terms, "aesthetic discipline and order" so as to produce not only "beautiful work" but work that is about a large, "public" enough subject (a crisis in religious faith) seems to me not at all to exhibit stony-heartedness or writerly isolation, but nothing more nor less than the satisfaction of art.

In Updike's stories from *The Same Door*, religious matters of inti-mate and ultimate concern were largely absent, or present in rela-tively superficial ways. (In "Dentistry and Doubt" a graduate student at Oxford, writing a thesis on the sixteenth-century divine Richard Hooker, goes to have his teeth repaired and has thoughts about his earlier morning attack of skepticism.) With *Pigeon Feathers* the reli-gious concern surfaces noticeably, and not only in the title story. In "Lifeguard," for example, the voice speaking is that of a divinity student who spends nine months of the year poring over theolog-ical texts — in particular, "the terrifying attempts of Kierkegaard, Berdyaev, and Barth to scourge God into being" — then spends the summer months "attentively perched" on his chair overlooking the sea's immensity and the lust-provoking "texts of the flesh." This short story might be called Updike's first exercise in the sermonic mode, one which with *A Month of Sundays* will be developed into a literary technique. In an even shorter piece, "The Astronomer," a young man similar to Rafe in "Toward Evening," living with his wife in a West Side apartment overlooking the Hudson, is visited by an old Hungarian classmate now teaching astronomy at Columbia and possessing "an air of seeing beyond me, of seeing into the interstel-lar structure of things." The "I" narrator finds this upsetting; he fears the astronomer's visit, he tells us, because "I was twenty-four, and the religious revival within myself was at its height." There follows a good description of his recent discovery of Kierkegaard in the handsome books published by Princeton University Press. In true 1950s intellectual style, Updike was reading his Kierkegaard, but even more important to him was the presence of Karl Barth, to whom he paid tribute in a 1962 review of one of Barth's books. In *Rabbit, Run* we meet a Barth-like figure in the Reverend Kruppenbach who, when visited by Eccles for the purpose of enlist-ing his concern for Rabbit's marital difficulties, fiercely rebukes the liberal clergyman for his concern with marital and social adjustment rather than with preaching the word of God. In his foreword to *Assorted Prose* (1965), Updike's first collection of nonfiction pieces, he says unequivocally that his debt to Barth's theology was immense, for "at one point in my life [it] seemed alone to be supporting it." And in "Faith in Search of Understanding" from that same volume, he quotes with approval Barth's scornful words about the "liberal churches" dedicated to the cause of human righteousness. For Barth, Updike writes, "The real God, the God men do not invent, is *totaliter aliter* — Wholly Other. We cannot reach Him; only He can reach us." We may surmise that Updike found in Barth the answer to David Kern's worries in "Pigeon Feathers" about who made God, as well as to David's dissatisfaction when his mother tells him that man made God.

However that may be, the heart of these stories does not lie in the loss or recovery of faith, but rather in the familial and provincial affirmations enacted through conflict and tenuous resolution, first by the Pennsylvania youths of "Flight" and "Pigeon Feathers," then, even more intimately, by the older Massachusetts surrogate for Updike who narrates the two closing stories with their long, pieced-together titles. To emphasize the superior weight and subtlety of these Pennsylvania stories isn't to deny virtue to others in *Pigeon Feathers,* like "Should Wizard Hit Mommy?", "Wife-Wooing," "A Crow in the Woods," or "Home"; but the more lasting writing is found in the four longer, less storylike efforts. On one occasion Updike recognized this; when asked to contribute something of his published work to a *This Is My Best* anthology in 1970, he selected the final story in *Pigeon Feathers,* not quite the longest one but the one with the longest title: "Packed Dirt, Churchgoing, A Dying Cat, A Traded Car." He said that it was his "best" because it contained the most truth for him, and that it came — as did the preceding "triptych," "The Blessed Man of Boston, My Grandmother's Thimble, and Fanning Island" — from a time in the spring of 1961 when "my wits seemed sunk in a bog of anxiety and my customary doubts that I could write another word appeared unusually well justified."[9] The two "farraginous" narratives, particularly the second one, contained, he felt, "a bigger, better kind of music." He warns us that there's plenty of "conscious art" in the narrative and "more fiction than meets the eye." Still, one feels in both stories, but especially the second, in which the protagonist identifies his occupation as that of a writer, that the line between fiction and autobiography is most tantalizingly thin, and that Updike is able to get imaginative mileage out of that fact.

It may be more important to assert that these portmanteau, glued-together efforts were therapeutic in pulling him out of a slump than to argue about whether they "succeed" in ways superior to more conventional stories. He used them for the occasion and didn't continue in the mode, although he would continue to practice sudden turns in narrative focus. In the triptych story it is the middle, longest section about the grandmother's death that centrally absorbs us; in the "quadriptych" story the final "A Traded Car" pages, describing a drive from Massachusetts to Pennsylvania and back on a visit to his sick father, are not only superb but also connect with the earlier sections in satisfying ways. The pretext, stated explicitly in "My Grandmother's Thimble," is that the different parts constitute "unwritten stories," a paradoxical claim inasmuch as the writing is as dense, as passionately *written*, as anything Updike had yet done. The strong autobiographical hook is underlined to the extent that, at one point in the "Grandmother" section, the narrator recalls spending summer afternoons in his grandmother's bedroom, reading and writing in a rocking chair at the foot of the bed where she lies crippled by Parkinson's disease, her powers of speech all but gone. One day the grandson is writing "a piece of light verse about what I imagined the sea voyage I was soon to take would be like" (he is headed for a fellowship year in England):

> That line is the horizon line.
> The blue above it is divine.
> The blue below it is marine.
> Sometimes the blue below is green.

These lines had already been published in Updike's poem "Shipbored," so they invite us to erase the line between fiction and autobiography.

The "Grandmother" part of the triptych begins when the narrator's memory is triggered by stumbling across his wife's sewing basket and discovering an old thimble of his grandmother's: this stimulates him to "tell how once there had been a woman who now was no more, how she had been born and lived in a world that had ceased to exist." He moves into the past, remembers arriving at the farm for a visit when he and his wife find his grandfather has unexpectedly died; years later his mother calls to tell him of his grandmother's death. He resolves to go to a Lutheran church the next morning in memory of her, but then neglects to go. The italicized *I did not go* further precipitates more intimate memories of his grandmother when as a teenager preparing to go out on a date, he would clown with the old woman: "Delirious, humming, I would swoop and lift her, lift her like a child, crooking one arm under her knees, and cupping the other behind her back," lifting and twirling her tiny body as his parents look on nervously. "Giving my past a dance," he calls it, and the dance of words now brings the grandmother to life:

> She never to my knowledge went outside the boundaries of Pennsylvania. She never saw a movie; I never saw her read. She lived in our nation as a fish lives in the deep sea. One night, when she thought — wrongly — that she was dying, I heard her ask, "Will I be a little debil?" I had never before heard her curiosity range so far.

Those who like to simplify Updike into a writer with only one style — ornate, extravagant, verbally lush — should ponder the above as an example of direct and unaffected, absolutely telling sentences. Or the following one that summarizes the woman in relation to her grandson: "She was projected onto my own days by her willed survival; I lived with her and she loved me and I did not understand her, I did not care to."

"Details are the giant's fingers," he writes in the triptych's closing paragraph, and it is in "Packed Dirt, Churchgoing, A Dying Cat, A Traded Car" that the details are most memorably revealing. Schematically its four sections begin with the reflections about "human erosion" and the way "We in America have from the beginning been cleaving and baring the earth." The way our feet make paths, pack down the dirt, is our testimony to a "human legacy" — a legacy that leads into memories of churchgoing, especially David Kern's with his father, ushering at Lenten Wednesday-night services in the country church. On rare occasions Updike strikes a wrong note by making the narrative voice too portentous, the association too forced, as when a transition sentence between the first and second parts declares, "One thinks of John Dewey's definition of God as the union of the actual and the ideal" — where a reader wants to say that perhaps one doesn't. And sometimes the thematic nugget of a particular section is almost too visible, as when in section 3, "A Dying Cat," a slight incident is recorded in which David, in Oxford, his wife in hospital about to give birth to their first child, comes across on a night prowl a dying cat to which he ministers, but whose dying (or perhaps dead) body finally admonishes him to *"Run on home."* It feels a shade rigged.

But in the longest and most impressive of the sections, "A Traded Car," the art is powerful and wholly convincing. David learns that his father is in the hospital after a heart attack; he drives from New England to the Pennsylvania farm in an old car that is about to be traded, sees his mother, talks to his father, drives back to Massachusetts the next night. Yet within that "story" is another story in which, previous to getting the news about his father, David and his wife have been to a party where something like a mutual pass is made between him and the woman with whom he is dancing. He and his wife return home, make love, but there follows "the wrinkled, azoic territory of insomnia," in which we see that David's youthful crisis of faith, in "Pigeon Feathers," hasn't resolved itself. He thinks about Jesus' saying that lusting after a woman in thought is the same as committing adultery; if so, it follows that "The universe that so easily permitted me to commit adultery became, by logical steps each one of which went more steeply down than the one above it, a universe that would easily permit me to die." Next day, on his birthday, his mother telephones with news of his father; David is instantly relieved, restored to health by deciding that his father "had engaged the enemy and it would be defeated." Next day, after going to church, he decides to drive to Pennsylvania in an about-to-be-traded old car, giving it one final fling. *Run on home*, he thinks to himself as he leaves his family and heads south.

The confluence of illicit sexual desire, terror at human life without God, and thoughts of death will be explored in *Couples*, six years hence. But this moment in "A Traded Car" is an important one in Updike's career, since it's the first fusion of concerns — the child, the adult, the believer, the lover — that will remain central; the call to *Run on home* David hears is not solely a moral call to be with his sick father but a way of escaping, momentarily, the married man's adult terrors and temptations. Nor is it surprising that the preferred vehicle of escape should be an automobile. In "The Happiest I've Been," John Nordholm's life as a man begins when his friend Neil tells him to take the wheel on the Pennsylvania Turnpike and falls asleep beside him. Harry Angstrom's first attempted escape from wife and family is made in his Ford headed for the "white sun of the south" he's destined not to reach. Perhaps the best sequence in *The Centaur* involves the boy and his father's efforts to get their old car started in the morning, then vainly trying to get it back home through the snowstorm. And in the story "Home," from *Pigeon Feathers*, the Updike-son figure (there called "Robert"), home from a year abroad, is greeted by his father at the boat. The father looks incredibly old, but while driving to the farm has a confrontation with another Pennsylvania motorist and wins glory in his son's eyes. "We in America make love in our cars," declares the narrator of "A Traded Car," and is unsurprised that the American landscape is sacrificed "to these dreaming vehicles of our ideal and onrushing manhood." These associations of the automobile with masculine testings and rites of passage are part of the larger imaginative design of Updike's fiction — just as *"Run on home"* cleverly alludes to the novel that preceded it, *Rabbit, Run*, as well as the unpublished *Home*. If one is tempted, as I am, to identify the first-person narrator of "A Traded Car" with the biographical Updike, one should be reminded that for all David Kern's authoritative, even slightly stagy, remarks about American cars and the American landscape, he is, as he was at the end of "Pigeon Feathers," a boy and man who acts and suffers, a dramatic character, explored and to some necessary extent ironized by his creator — just as the speaker of a Shakespeare sonnet, however much he sounds like "Shakespeare," is in fact less than, different in kind from, Shakespeare the poet. But both Shakespeare and Updike are strong enough artists to make us, at moments, forget this truth.

On Route 128 in Massachusetts, David picks up a hitchhiking sailor who rides with him as far as New York, even drives the car for a couple of hours in Connecticut — a reversal of "The Happiest I've Been," since it's now the narrator who tells us he trusts the sailor ("guileless, competent, mildly earnest") at the wheel. The sailor is identified as an "American" product and at one point asks David if he's a teacher. David, impressed by the question since his grandfather and father were teachers and it was assumed he would be one too, answers no, that he's a writer:

> He seemed less offended than puzzled. "What do you write?"
>
> "Oh — whatever comes into my head."
>
> "What's the point?"
>
> "I don't know," I told him. "I wish I did."

The response is partly disingenuous, partly humorous modesty in not wanting to claim too much for the literary trade, but also possibly reflexive if we presume Updike to have been less certain about the "story" he was welding together in four parts than about more contained efforts in *Pigeon Feathers* like "The Persistence of Desire" or "A Sense of Shelter." There's an improvisatory, slightly reckless quality to the whole proceeding, beginning of course with the improvised, homemade, patched-together title, absurdly long as it is.

David drops the sailor at the entrance to the New Jersey Turnpike in the rain, glimpses, as the windshield wipers beat, "the wonderland lights of the Newark refineries," and waits to stop for food until he crosses into Pennsylvania soil, where the very Howard Johnsons are "less crowded, more homelike in their furnishings." The Pennsylvania aura deepens as home gets closer: the music improves — he hears a Benny Goodman quintet record he loved in high school — and the car itself runs effortlessly, its speedometer attaining seventy with ease. There is magic to this night journey, even down to the moment when, after arriving home and greeting his mother, he goes to bed, is wakeful, then covers himself with an old overcoat of his father's and is magically "tipped into sleep." His mother had greeted him with the announcement that "Daddy says he's lost all his faith," an ironic echo to the son's own crisis — although, his mother adds, his father was never a great one for faith, but "strictly a works man." The next day we see some of those works. David's father, barefoot but untypically in pajamas, puts the son at ease, commiserating with him over his work ("I couldn't do what you're doing if you paid me a million dollars a day"), joking with him, relieving him of the burden of embarrassment. He praises the hospital and all the "wonderful gentlemen" it contains, then tries to put at her ease a girl from the Lutheran Home Missions who visits him as a member of the parish. He accepts the pamphlet she gives him to read, tells her he knows how sincere she is in wishing him a speedy recovery, and — when she asks to be excused to make other calls — dismisses her with a jovial "Of course. You go right ahead, sick Lutherans are a dime a dozen. You're a wonderful woman to be doing what you're doing."

But he has not yet done with good works. When David offers to stay another night so he can visit him again, his father says No, and the son who has run on home says he will drive "home," back to his family in Massachusetts. There occurs what David later perceives as a blank in his father's face, "swallowing the realization that he was no longer the center of even his son's universe," but it is only for a moment:

Having swallowed, he told me how good I had been to come
all this way to see him. He told me I was a good son and a good
father; he clasped my hand. I felt I would ascend straight north
from his touch.

Henry James decided at one point that he possessed "the imagination
of disaster"; nowhere in Updike's writing is the imagination of virtue
more present than at this moment in "A Traded Car." Something like
the swallow David's father takes may take place as well in a responsive reader, looking at and listening to words he almost wonders
whether he should be privy to. One thinks of other American stories
about fathers and sons, like Hemingway's with that very title, in
which Nick Adams and his boy are driving through country, the son
asleep as Nick thinks about *his* father: "His father was with him, suddenly, in deserted orchards and in new-plowed fields, in thickets, on
small hills, or when going through dead grass, whenever splitting
wood or hauling water, by grist mills, cider mills and dams and always
with open fires." Hemingway pulls out all the lyric stops and we end
up thinking more about the writer — the stylist — than the father. I
don't think this is the case with Updike's passage.

In the story's final pages, as David drives home, the ascension
straight north is not quite as uniformly smooth as he had imagined
when his father touched him. On a tide of lyric writing that keeps
us continuously in touch with real roads, real places, David drives as
the sun sets, through the "enchanted" Pennsylvania countryside,
then negotiates New Jersey, with Manhattan making its "gossamer
splash at its favorite hour, eight o'clock." From there the trip runs
"more steeply uphill," up the "meaninglessly coquettish" Merritt
Parkway and the "maddeningly obstinate" light-controlled stretch
below Hartford (famous to drivers in the 1950s as the Berlin
Turnpike and still extant). Then the car, as when it crossed into
Pennsylvania, seems to take things over on its own, assumes an
independent being even as "its soul the driver had died." He reaches
his backyard, notes the stars "frozen in place," and in a final paragraph gives a valediction to the car, soon to be traded in:

My father traded in many cars. It happens so cleanly, before you expect it. He would drive off in the old car up the dirt road exactly as usual and when he returned the car would be new, and the old was gone, gone, utterly dissolved back into the mineral world from which it was conjured, dismissed without a blessing, a kiss, a testament, or any ceremony of farewell. We in America need ceremonies, is I suppose, sailor, the point of what I have written.

The last sentence, like others in Updike's short fiction, has been objected to as unnecessary flourish, too much of an attempt to clinch things memorably. But I wouldn't want to lose it, especially for the graceful way it picks up the sailor's earlier question about what the point of writing was. In its ceremonious close, this final story in *Pigeon Feathers* is Updike's most pointed and fully articulated testimony to the value of writing as the only way to come to terms with — to find terms for — the passing of the past. In the closing lines of Frost's "Carpe Diem,"

But bid life seize the present?
It lives less in the present
Than in the future always,
And less in both together
Than in the past. The present
Is too much for the senses,
Too crowding, too confusing —
Too present to imagine.

The Centaur

In his "This Is My Best" explanation of why he chose, as his best, the final story in *Pigeon Feathers* ("Packed Dirt . . ."), Updike said that in David Kern's "plunge into terror" after an erotic moment with a woman not his wife, the sexual themes of his later work were first stated. But the main action in what was planned to be the last of his Pennsylvania stories lay somewhere else: "the heart of the story, toward which all tends, is of course the father, his generous and comical manner of dying. As might as well be said of the subsequent novel, *The Centaur:* it is a good story because it has a good man in it." On another occasion he expressed his preference for *The Centaur* over his other novels, calling it "my gayest and truest book."[10] By way of justifying the adjective *gayest,* he recalled himself rereading and laughing at passages in which one of the characters reveals his or her mythological dimension; as if in writing *The Centaur* a comic wit became available to him in a way it hadn't been before. One may take mild issue with these otherwise justifiable remarks on the author's part: *The Centaur* is not a "good story" just because it has a good man in it — stories can't be made good that artlessly; and for all the play, which delighted Updike, between real life and mythological resonance, the overall elegiac note of *The Centaur* isn't caught by calling it the "gayest" anything. But it is quite possibly Updike's "truest" book. It sparked his career by winning him the National Book Award in 1964; it was reviewed widely, sometimes trenchantly — especially by Renata Adler in the *New Yorker* — though not always favorably. Decades after the fact, *The Centaur* grows in the mind upon rereading, making my own early objections to the excessive cleverness and pedantry of its mythological scheme bulk increasingly less large. The book's generosity, its willingness to tolerate, and with affection, different kinds of human behavior — some of it maddening — and the spirited energy of its narrative throughout make it an extraordinary achievement. In 1997 Updike's *Toward the End of Time* would offer another mythological tale, but with exhaustion, depression, and depletion its keynote themes. By contrast, *The Centaur* is vibrantly alive and hopeful, the product of a thirty-one-year-old writer operating with ambition and audacity at the height of his powers.

From the outset, discussion of the novel was understandably occupied with the relation between its realistic narrative of three days in Pennsylvania, January 1947, and the mythological story of Chiron the centaur's wounding and eventual sacrifice to release Prometheus from imprisonment. Did this mythical dimension enhance and enrich the realistic account of George Caldwell, the Olinger school-teacher weighed down with psychic and physical ailments, and his son Peter, an Updike-like brilliant student and aspiring painter who is afflicted with a deeply embarrassing — though also exciting — case of psoriasis? Was the alternation between myth and realism, the invitation to identify mythic analogues in "ordinary" characters (and vice versa), a brilliant fictional achievement in post-*Ulysses* creation, or an annoyingly strained effort by an author who was try-ing too hard to be major? The early reviews show there was much to be said on each side of the debate. Most critics of *The Centaur*, how-ever, did find unhelpful the mythological index Updike, at the sug-gestion of his wife (he said), placed at the novel's end. In it, num-bers of pages are listed on which, say, Philyra or Pholos or Poseidon appear — no matter that the reader may well have no previous acquaintance with Philyra or Pholos (though he may be familiar with Poseidon). In his introductory note to the index, Updike tells us that "Chiron and Prometheus, being ubiquitous, are omitted," and that the referents to many characters are unstable, as with a member of the Olinger High swimming team who at one time or another is "now a centaur, now a merman, and sometimes even Hercules." One hears more than a hint of mischief in such a prof-fered aid to the bewildered reader. At any rate, the index has been of no use to me, nor am I tempted to consult it as I read the novel — though doubtless Updike had a good time compiling it as an appendage to his "gayest" book.

One possible response to the mythological dimension of *The Centaur* is something like what Hazlitt recommended to the reader puzzled about how to deal with Spenser's allegory in *The Faerie Queene* — that if you don't bother the allegory it won' t bother you. So at the novel's opening section — "Caldwell turned and as he turned his ankle received an arrow" — after acknowledging the nod to Chiron's wound we can follow the narrative in a readerly manner similar to that we will give Caldwell's son Peter's account of waking up to go to school at the beginning of section 2. We observe George Caldwell's painful progress through the building ("The feathered end of the arrow scraped on the floor with every step") to Hummel's Garage, adjacent to the school, where the mechanic painfully extracts the arrow. We may note that Hummel "is" also Hephaestus, his garage an underworld-supernatural repair shop (remember that word *vulcanized*), but we attend rather to the fantastic action by which the arrow is extracted. It is little different from following the "romance" narrative in a Hawthorne story, or tracking the progress of one of Spenser's knights as he falls and is magically restored. "Maintaining a more or less continuous parallel between contemporary events and history," as Eliot said Joyce's *Ulysses* had done, surely provided Updike a challenging writerly task, that of artfully manipulating the narrative materials out of which he constructs his book. But the narrative that results has its eyes on the reader's feelings and responses; it is rhetorical rather than hermetically sealed, and we aren't asked merely to "figure out" what it really means.

As distinguished from the Pennsylvania stories Updike had published, and from his earlier novels as well, *The Centaur* has a number of distinct rhetorical modes. Its central one, in terms of the pages in which it prevails, is Peter Caldwell's first-person account of the three days that elapse between getting up for school Monday morning, driving into Olinger with his father, then because of (first) car failure, and (second) a snowstorm, having to spend one night in an Alton hotel, then a second one at Vera Hummel's house in Olinger. Father and son arrive back at the farm late Wednesday afternoon, and Thursday morning Peter, sick in bed with a cold, looks out his window to see his father once more headed for work in what, on the mythological level, is Chiron's "sacrifice" for Prometheus; on the naturalistic one, it is Caldwell's acceptance of mortality and his return to another day in the classroom for the sake of his son. But there are also sections in which Caldwell, in a blend of naturalistic and mythological presentation, is at the third-person center of things. There is as well the occasional mock-heroic presentation of life in a high school; there is a short section in which we see Chiron instructing his pupils, and a slightly longer one in which Peter/Prometheus lies stretched out on the rock of his psoriasis and is visited and inspected by the community. There is also a small-town newspaper obituary for "the late George Caldwell," Olinger's good citizen, and a final epilogue in which Zeus sets Chiron in the Zodiac as the constellation Sagittarius.

These shifting narrative and rhetorical perspectives have made for anxiety on the part of critics, who feel the need to reassure us that the whole thing is a dream, an imaginative fantasy emanating from the mind of the mature Peter Caldwell. As a boy his hero was Vermeer; as an adult he is, he tells us, a second-rate abstract expressionist painter, living in Manhattan with a woman he refers to as his "Negro" mistress. The writing in which Peter addresses her about his childhood ("Hey. Listen. Listen to me, lady. I love you, I want to be a Negro for you . . .") is the least convincing of any in the book. (An essay could be written about the appearance of black men and women, usually as a species of exotica, in Updike's early fiction, and the fiction of this mistress-listener seems contrived and unnecessary.) But in fact there's no need to centralize Peter in the effort to give the novel a presiding consciousness — the way Eliot in his note to *The Waste Land* tried to convince us that Tiresias was somehow the ever-present, unifying figure in the poem. It is better to think of all the perspectives as Updike's, made interesting by their surprising changes and juxtaposings, and by the way they complicate his rhetorical address to the reader.

In *The Centaur's* brilliant opening section Caldwell heads back from Hummel's garage, dragging his wounded leg behind him, to teach his class in General Science, the lesson for that day having to do with the age of our earth. He finds that his antagonist — the school's principal, Zimmerman — has appeared in class and means to stay and observe Caldwell while he teaches. As in Joyce's "Cyclops" or "Circe" episodes in *Ulysses*, the technique of Updike's first section is transformation, of a comic and grotesque sort. Caldwell hands the "cold, sleek arrow shaft" to Zimmerman, who remains unsurprised and unmoved by the teacher's concern over the assault. The principal takes a seat in back "behind the cup ears and blazing acne of Mark Youngerman" (students are of course seated alphabetically), but soon, Caldwell notes, moves over to peek down the blouse of the plump beauty, Iris Osgood. Distracted, Caldwell launches gamely into his explanation of temporal aeons, writing numbers with endless zero-digits on the blackboard in the attempt to help the class imagine what five billion years is like. Then in an inspired shifting of terms, he invites them rather to assume the universe is three days old, the big bang having occurred on Monday last. (The Thursday on which this lecture occurs is prior to the novel's realistic time frame, which begins on a subsequent Monday.) He struggles on, giving the equivalent of a quite impressive popular science lecture, and is undeterred as a piece of chalk turns to a warm white larva in his hand, or a paper airplane unleashed by a student becomes an "open-faced white flower" that yowls like a baby. As Zimmerman fondles Iris, and Diefendorf — a thuggish member of the swimming team Caldwell coaches — caresses another girl's throat, the general current of noise steadily increases. Caldwell introduces an organism called the volvox by whose ministrations cells will not go on to live forever, "potentially immortal," but take on specialized functions and thus incur death: "It dies sacrificially, for the good of the whole." In the humorous, harassed idiom that typically characterizes his speech, Caldwell takes his hat off to the cells, "the first altruists who got tired of sitting around forever in a blue-green scum and said, 'Let's get together and make a volvox.'" At this point, and with death introduced into the universe as a prefiguration of his own at the end of the novel, Caldwell/Chiron doffs his cap in pantomime and "the class screamed." There occurs the equivalent of a big bang in the schoolroom; as with Joycean transformations in the Cyclops or Circe sections of *Ulysses*, anything is liable to happen:

> Mark Youngerman jumped up and his acne leaped to the wall; the paint began to burn, blistering in slowly spreading blotches above the side blackboard. Fists, claws, cocked elbows blurred in patch-colored panic above the scarred and varnished desktops; in the whole mad mass the only still bodies were those of Zimmerman and Iris Osgood.

Caldwell is not finished, but his words now have magical effects; for example, mention of the word *trilobite* causes one boy to empty a paper bag of living trilobites on the floor: "As they scuttered along the scrolling iron desk-legs," looking like "partially unrolled condoms," "their brainless heads and swishing glabellae brushed the ankles of girls who squealed and kicked up their feet so high that white thighs and gray underpants flashed." Boys drop their books on the creatures, and one girl, transformed into a "huge purple parrot feathered with mud," crunches and chews one of them in her beak.

Kenneth Burke once defined the literary mode of "grotesque" as "the cult of incongruity without the laughter," and Updike's classroom is perhaps closer to inspiring fear and disgust than humorous pleasure. In fact the classroom has never been a subject many novels dared or deigned to look at for very long (there are exceptions in Dickens, D. H. Lawrence, Joyce) and never in such a radically violent light. But the sentences registering these grotesque happenings manage to keep the lid on by behaving in grammatically and imperturbably correct fashion, while they convey a madcap version of high-school dailiness. As a boy who spent, so he tells us, many happy hours in Shillington classes — usually, like Peter Caldwell, equipped with the right answers should teacher ask — Updike's imagination is energized by a classroom in which things go wrong, get out of control. Near the beginning of the unpublished novel *Home*, Elsie Baer's disturbing inability to control the class in which she serves as a substitute teacher is imagined with real and painful sympathy. The chance, in the first section of *The Centaur*, to blow the whole place up was irresistible, and an indication of how much active fun Updike took in its writing, even as he keeps (with his own father in mind) a steady, sympathetic gaze on Caldwell's daily humiliations.

But of course the mythic derangement of teacher-student relations is only one way of presenting pedagogy in the novel. As Renata Adler pointed out in her review of the book, *The Centaur* contains a number of variations on the theme of pedagogy, as Caldwell takes his students through matters of evolution, creation, mathematics, geology (he tries to help out a slow student by asking her the questions that will be on tomorrow's quiz), and translating Virgil. In Adler's apt words, "Each rings so fresh and true that the reader wears a continual smile of assent and revived memory."[11] The rhetoric provided Caldwell, in his comments on the profession in which he finds himself, is a fine mixture of sarcasm, self-pity, and cynical good sense, as when he harangues the dull student Diefendorf about the state of things educational:

> "The Founding Fathers," he explained, "in their wisdom decided that children were an unnatural strain on parents. So they provided jails called schools, equipped with tortures called an education. School is where you go between when your parents can't take you and industry can't take you. I am a paid keeper of Society's unusables — the lame, the halt, the insane, and the ignorant. The only incentive I can give you, kid, to behave yourself is this: if you don't buckle down and learn something, you'll be as dumb as I am, and you'll have to teach school to earn a living."

And so it happens when Peter reveals that years later he met Diefendorf and finds that he has indeed become a teacher.

Caldwell's character, the vividly humorous, self-displaying idiom he employs so that his wife accuses him justly of putting on performances, has been rightly admired, even by readers who find the book's mythological scheme pretentious. But an achievement almost equal, only just a shade less difficult to bring off than imagining this father-teacher, is Updike's presentation of his son, Peter. We have met the young high-school boy previously in some of the *Pigeon Feathers* stories, but never with quite the immediacy given him in *The Centaur*. Allen Dow, the protagonist of "Flight," speaks in the first person, but very much retrospectively, from the distance of mature years. "Pigeon Feathers," in its third-person narrative of David Kern's religious crisis, puts some distance between writer and character — we remember the gentle irony in the story's final sentence about God not destroying "His whole creation by refusing to let David live forever." The portmanteau stories at the volume's end also have vivid moments of life on the farm, but filtered through the married man's memory. In the second chapter of *The Centaur*, however, it seems that nothing stands between us and the immediate circumstances of Peter's waking up on a cold Monday morning in January and preparing to join his father in their trip to Olinger High.

A single instance must do by way of illustrating the rich particular fidelity and immediacy with which Peter's experience is given to us. The farm has electricity but as yet, in 1947, no indoor plumbing; so Peter goes outside to urinate and brush his teeth. His dog, Lady, greets him excitedly from her pen, responding especially when Peter asks her, "Sleep well? Dream of rabbits? *Rabbits!*" Then these two paragraphs:

> As I squatted, the cold came up behind me and squeezed my back. When I stood, the squares of wire my hands had touched were black, my skin having melted the patina of frost. Lady leaped like a spring released. She came down with a foot on her pan and flipped it over and I expected to see water spill. But the water was ice solid with the pan. For the instant before my brain caught up with my eyes, it seemed a miracle.
>
> Now the air, unflawed by any motion of wind, began to cake around me, and I moved quickly. My toothbrush, glazed rigid, was of a piece with the aluminum holder screwed to the porch post. I snapped it free. The pump dragged dry for four heaves of the handle. The water, on the fifth stroke rising from deep in the stricken earth, smoked faintly as it splashed the grooved brown glacier that had built up in the pump trough. The rusty water purged the brush of its stiff jacket, but when I put it in my mouth it was like a flavorless square lollipop. My molars stung along the edges of their fillings. The toothpaste secreted in the bristles melted into a mint taste. All the time, Lady watched my performance with a wild delight that swelled and twitched her body, and when I spat, she barked in applause, each bark a puff of frost. I replaced the brush and

> bowed, and had the satisfaction of hearing the applause con-
> tinue as I retired behind the double curtain, the storm door
> and the main door.

This is the quintessence of realism, some sort of last word in how to
catch things on the fly, as they occur, and to find the absolutely
right words to fix and dignify their givenness. Like the water frozen
solid with the pan, it seems a miracle, at least a performance of dazzling skill, a major version of the minor one Peter gives Lady as he
spits, eliciting her barks in applause. Randall Jarrell's charming
poem "Well Water" is about gulping what he calls "the dailiness of
life," and there is nothing in Peter's ablutions that does not take
place, more or less, every day. That doesn't make them any less
extraordinary when rendered in sentences like the ones quoted. The
two paragraphs don't "mean" anything; they just *are*, are there for
themselves, as if that were enough significance. And so it is, as Peter
moves back into the house, trying to gulp down an inadequate
breakfast before it's time to depart.

As a character, Peter gets much help from his creator, who can
enter into the boy's fifth stroke of the pump when water arises from
the "stricken earth," or melt the toothpaste from its lodging in bris-
tles to a taste in the mouth. Like Rabbit Angstrom, Peter is, even at
the realistic level, more than a figure with discernible bounds and
dimensions, thus he eludes judgments about his moral composition:
we're not invited to see him as good or not so good, but rather as an
important means of vision in the novel. His father, on the other
hand, is indeed — as Updike called him — a good man, but more
to the point an impossible one, at least for his son to get a fix on and
deal with as a rational being. On that cold Monday morning when
they head out in the car for school, and after a well-rendered
description of the touch-and-go business of getting the old Buick
started, Peter notices his father isn't wearing the leather gloves he
had bought him, at some financial effort, for Christmas. He wants
his father to "care about his clothes and his comfort, like the fathers
of my friends." But after wearing the gloves for a day, Caldwell

leaves them on the front seat, then the back, and Peter asks, "Why don't you ever wear them?"

"They're too good," he said. "They're wonderful gloves, Peter. I know good leather. You must have paid a fortune for 'em."

"Not that much, but aren't your hands cold?"

"Yeah. Boy, this is a bitter day. We're in Old Man Winter's belly."

"Well don't you want to put the gloves on?"

Caldwell's answer, which is and isn't an answer, avoids the question by transposing it into another of his performances: "When I was a kid, if anybody had given me gloves like that, I would have cried real tears." The diversionary tactics, the willingness of Caldwell to put himself on stage by turning the gloves into what he never had as a child (therefore they belong in the backseat, unworn) is comic and touching, and — for those in his family who deal with it daily — infuriating. It's unsurprising that by the end of section 2 the gloves have disappeared, confiscated by a deplorable hitchhiker the father picks up on the way to school. Caldwell's response, typical of him, is "Well . . . he needs 'em more than I did. That poor devil never knew what hit him."

After the impressive first two sections of *The Centaur*, in which Peter and his father have been fully established as realistic characters (even while Caldwell also doubles as Chiron), the third, very short, section is more problematic, since it exists wholly on the mythological plane. In it Chiron is seen instructing his students — "Jason, Achilles, Asclepios, his daughter Ocyrhoe, and the dozen other princely children of Olympus abandoned to his care." After he and his students sing a hymn to Zeus, Chiron begins to discourse on the Love that "set the Universe in motion" and on the original, Arcadian pastoral landscape in which death was not to be feared, no more than sleep. The section closes with "Then her scepter passed to Uranus . . ." after which, presumably, something less than Arcadian came into effect. The trouble with this section is that, after the first two, it seems empty of content and rather monotonous, an occasion for Updike to sport his ingenuity by providing Chiron with his "anciently acquired druggist's knowledge" of plants and roots and of which drugs have the most virtue. It has the effect, mainly, of making us eager to resume the realistic narrative that picks up again in section 4 ("After school, I went up to my father's room, Room 204. Two students were in there with him"), an eventful seventy-page sequence that is the novel's heart and that contains, among other things, Caldwell's visit to the doctor, Peter's meeting with his girlfriend Penny at Minor Kretz's luncheonette, the breakdown of the Caldwells' car, and their lodgment overnight in a rather seedy Alton hotel.

After the whiff of Arcady in the previous section, we are now placed in modern, urban reality, in a thinly disguised Reading (Alton) Pennsylvania, another of the "small ugly cities of the East ... Trenton, Bridgeport, Binghamton, Johnstown, Elmira, Altoona," where Peter's father worked as a cable splicer before the depression. Ugly or not, Caldwell loves it: "its asphalt and streetlights and tangent façades spoke to him of the great Middle-Atlantic civilization, bounded by New Haven in the north and Hagerstown in the south and Wheeling in the west, which was his home in eternal space. To walk beside my father down Sixth Street was to hear the asphalt sing." So, right under our eyes, mythology reasserts itself, and if we had never before thought of the Middle-Atlantic civilization as great, or even a civilization, it is given embodied credibility here in the likes of cities such as Hagerstown and Wheeling. Caldwell's love for the city is contagious; at least by the time he and Peter are established for the night in their hotel room overlooking "the radiant tangle of Weiser Square" ("For two blocks Weiser was the broadest street in the East"), Peter is moved to the following dense appreciation of it:

> Now here headlights swam as if in the waters of a purple lake
> whose surface came to my sill. The shopfronts and bar signs
> made green and red grass along the banks. The windows of

Foy's, Alton's great department store, were square stars set in six rows; or like crackers made of two grains, the lower half of light yellow wheat and the upper half, where the tan shade was drawn, of barley or rye. Across the way, highest of all, the great neon owl by means of electric machinery winked and unwinked as a wing regularly brought to its beak, in a motion of three successive flashes, an incandescent pretzel. Beneath its feet, polychrome letters alternately proclaimed:

OWL PRETZELS
"None Better"
OWL PRETZELS
"None Better"

It is a moment of merging, and for Peter predictive of the future which, in a single sentence, is named: "City." Peter is a would-be artist (a Vermeer perhaps), a small-town aspirant who yearns to breathe more deeply, to experience something other than provincial constriction and sameness. Yet looked back on, recalled through the dream or fantasy of the now mature Peter, second-rate expressionist painter in his New York loft, the richness is all in the past, all back there in the "radiant tangle of Weiser Square."

Next morning he and his father take the trolley from Alton to Olinger High, getting off at Hummel's Garage adjacent to the school. As they walk toward their destination "a little whirlwind sprang up before us and led us along." Through dead leaves, a candy wrapper, chaff from the gutter, Peter sees his father continue to strive in a kind of Dante-Virgil mini-inferno that disappears as quickly as it appeared. But when they part, using different entrances to the school, Peter watches him walk away down the long hall, growing smaller and smaller, and the son is seized by terror. It is appropriate then that this long central section is followed by a very short one consisting of an obituary for George Caldwell, dead at fifty. The obituary's pious, rather plummy tone, not out of character for such a small-town appreciation, turns the centaur's daily grind of teaching into a sacred calling: "To sit under Mr. Caldwell was to lift up one's head in aspiration. Though there was sometimes — so strenuous and unpatterned was his involvement with his class — confusion, there was never any confusion that indeed 'Here was a man.'" Various other good works are duly noted as making up the life of this good man. But his son stays alive to suffer: after Caldwell's presumed death in the obituary's "objective" account, we see Peter, in section 6, stretched out, like Prometheus on the rock, exhibiting his psoriasis for the assembled — especially various girls who have come in a bus to gaze upon his disgrace. At the section's end he somehow catches up with his father, tells him that fifty is too early an age at which to die, assures him that he has "hope," a quality he owed to the father. The stage is then set for the two final sections, mainly realistic in presentation, that take father and son through the day, into the impassable snowstorm, and back to Olinger for a second night away — this time at the Hummels'. Eventually, they come home to the farm.

Joyce Carol Oates once observed that Updike's genius "is best excited by the lyric possibilities of tragic events that, failing to justify themselves as tragedy, turn unaccountably into comedies."[12] I'm not sure why Oates says "unaccountably," since the turn is very much accounted for by Updike's refusal to inflate his homely materials to tragic dimensions. For example, there is Olinger High with its overworked, underpaid teachers; there is the malfunctioning 1936 Buick, defeated by internal and external circumstances; there are Caldwell's worries about the pain in his gut, a nagging tooth to be extracted, an unexplained missing bloc of tickets to the night's basketball game — tickets for which he's responsible. These, like the daily domestic trials at the Caldwell farm, are not the stuff of tragedy but a proof of how hard it is to write — as Frost once put it — "the Russian novel in America." Caldwell is convinced he has cancer, but the X rays show nothing, and Dr. Appleton's Latin diagnosis, revealed to Caldwell only when he and Peter finally reach home and get the word, is *Mucinous colitis,* something that can be lived with.

Nor do Peter's agonies about his psoriasis live up to Prometheus on the rock, for when, at halftime in the basketball game, he reveals his secret to Penny by literally showing her his wounds, she takes it very much in stride — and indeed, as Peter turns up his sleeves to show her the underside of his arms, he finds there are fewer spots than he expected. Godlike figures such as the principal Zimmerman (Zeus) and Vera (Venus) Hummel show themselves as all-too-human, imperfect vessels of mythological power: like Caldwell, they're just doing the best they can. The narrator's address to his readers at the beginning of section 8 opens with a *tour de force* memory of the art museum in Alton he and his mother used to visit, which memory ends with a fountain where a naked lady is eternally unable to drink the water that splashes an inch from her mouth. The narrator imagines this endless stream of water ceasing with the coming of night, and announces that "my story is coming to its close." In other words, we are assured by the storyteller that his hands are capable ones, that we will not be abandoned to misery, will not — as Shelley's poet claims he does in the West Wind ode — "fall upon the thorns of life" and "bleed." Like the "staunched" flow of water in the museum's statue, the tale will resolve itself, and not in horror.

Still, Oates's comedy-rather-than-tragedy claim for the book is too exclusive and unsubtle to fit *The Centaur*. Much of the novel is devoted — like Updike's other early fictions — to settling on things in their actuality and rendering them so that their look and feel are indelibly etched on our consciousnesses. Something like this passion for realism (an inadequate word, granted) is felt by Peter when he wakes up the morning after they reach home and, sick with one of his frequent colds, looks through his bedroom window at his father headed out to the black Buick with the ruined grille that, after he digs it out of the snowdrift, will carry him yet once more to Olinger High for another day in the life. Peter in his fever "burns" to paint it and suddenly realizes that "I must go to Nature disarmed of perspective and stretch myself like a large transparent canvas upon her in the hope that, my submission being perfect, the imprint of a beautiful and useful truth would be taken." This is the realist's dream and its boyhood lineaments are rather different from the large canvases that sprawl about the adult Peter's Manhattan loft. But that dream bears a closer relationship to Updike-the-artist's sense of what matters most.

It is worth specifying a little more fully the literary quality of the "imprint" of Updike's canvas, and here a single example will have to do, from the paragraph near the book's end in which Peter reflects on the artist he hopes to become. Looking out the window he sees his father,

> an erect figure dark against the snow. His posture made no concession to the pull underfoot; upright he waded out through our yard and past the mailbox and up the hill until he was lost to my sight behind the trees of our orchard. The trees took white on their sun side. The two telephone wires diagonally cut the blank blue of the sky. The stone bare wall was a scumble of umber; my father's footsteps thumbs of white in white.

Peter knows that this is "a patch of Pennsylvania in 1947" but is also in his "softly fevered state mindlessly soaked in a rectangle of colored light." He may not know, as William Blake knew, that all knowledge exists in minute particulars, but Updike's sentences confirm that they do and that the truth they hope to tell, through words, is "beautiful and useful." A further word that comes to mind is *poignant,* as in the opening lines of Richard Wilbur's "Clearness": "There is a poignancy in all things clear, / In the stare of the deer, in the ring of a hammer in the morning." This poignancy, whose clarity is perhaps its chief attribute, suffuses *The Centaur,* making it something more mixed than terms such as *tragic* or *comic* can encompass.

Oates called it "the most psychologically satisfying" of Updike's books for the way it expresses "its author's considerable idealism in the guise of adolescent love, for Woman and for Father." What in *Rabbit, Run* was a choked, baffled, intermittently brilliant sense of the world's body, always expressed through the pressing present tense, becomes in *The Centaur,* in Peter's retrospective creation, a more ample, leisured, contemplative, and indeed humorous thing

— psychologically satisfying, if you will, insofar as it speaks to more human impulses than Updike had hitherto spoken to. The challenge it presented him was to write about a high-school boy without falling into sentimentality and self-pity — without claiming too much for his subject. In *Practical Criticism* I. A. Richards deftly treated the issue of sentimentality in poetry and why, or how, it was to be avoided. Defending a poem, D. H. Lawrence's "Piano," against students who found it mawkish and sentimental, Richards strongly disagreed, finding that Lawrence had built into the poem an understanding of the human impulse toward sentimentality, rather than a wallowing in it: "The glamour / Of childish days is upon me, my manhood is cast / Down in the flood of remembrance, I weep like a child for the past." "Piano" shows more than a weeping "I," since there is a perspective and a purchase taken on the act of abandoning one's adulthood, and Richards then generalized about sentimentality, and its avoidance, in these words: "The only safe cure for a mawkish attachment to an illusory childhood heaven . . . is to take the distorted sentiment and work it into close and living relation with some scene concretely and truthfully realized."[13] It is a task impressively performed in *The Centaur*, especially the close and living relation established among Peter, his father, and the high-school scene in which they enact their roles. In that sense it justifies itself as Updike's "truest" book.

"Leaving Church Early"

Working possibly exaggerated sentiments about "an illusory childhood heaven" into "close and living relation with some scene concretely and truthfully realized" is what Updike also achieved triumphantly in a poem that appeared in 1975, more than a decade after *The Centaur*. "Leaving Church Early" was written not long after his mother had turned seventy (Linda Hoyer was born in 1904) and its "Envoi" is addressed directly to her — she, along with her son, the only survivors of the old family group of five. It is a poem of 149 lines, divided into seven leisurely blank-verse paragraphs and the concluding envoi. The verse paragraphs are of varied length, the lines themselves are Frostian loose iambics, some of them accommodating up to thirteen and fourteen syllables. The poem's manner is that of expansive, reflective speech, as the remembering adult calls up a summer Sunday afternoon in 1940s Pennsylvania when time seemed endless — in fact, maddeningly so. "Leaving Church Early" begins with four people (grandfather, father, mother, child) departing church "as the last anthem was commencing" and moving "*bump* and whisper, down / the side aisle" to head back to the farm in their black 1936 Buick (George Caldwell's chariot in *The Centaur*). "What, I wonder, were we hurrying to," the poem begins and goes on to provide, not exactly an explanation for their impulse to leave, but an account of what they had left church early to resume:

> What had we hurried back to? There could be
> no work: a mock-Genesiac rest reigned
> in the bewitched farmland. Our strawberries
> rotted in their rows unrummaged-for;
> no snorting, distant tractor underlined
> the rasp of my father's pencil as he marked,
> with his disappointed grimace, math exams.
> The dogs smelled boredom, and collapsed their bones.
> The colors of the Sunday comics jangled,
> printed off-key, and my grandfather's feet,
> settling in for a soliloquy, kicked up fuzz.
> My father stood to promenade his wounds.
> I lay down, feeling weak, and pulled a book
> across my eyes the way a Bedouin
> in waiting out a sandstorm drapes his sheet.

Mother and grandmother "clucked and quarrelled" in the kitchen as they cooked dinner and "A foody fog / arose." Each figure is doing its usual thing, keeping "the axis of its own theatric chore" to give performances that have by now become wholly expected by all the actors, especially by the boy, book draped over his face like a Bedouin's sheet, who waits for . . . for what?

"Jesus," my father cried, "I hate the world!"
"Mother," my mother called, "you're in the way!"
"Be grateful for your blessings," Grandpa advised,
shifting his feet and showing a hairless shin.
"Ach," Grandma brought out in self-defense,
the syllable a gem of German indignation,
its guttural edge unchipped, while I,
still in the Sabbath shirt and necktie, bent
my hopes into the latest Nero Wolfe, imagining
myself orchidaceous in Manhattan and
mentally constructing, not Whodunit,
but How to Get Out of Here: my dastardly plot.

The poem resists two ways of sentimentalizing — either by inflating
nostalgic recall of Sundays at home, or by glorifying the adolescent,
chafing under the awful boredom of it all — through the poise of its
lively wit. Nero Wolfe, Rex Stout's detective hero in 1940s mys-
teries, is perfect here, as is the absurdity of "orchidaceous" by way of
setting up the glamorous unreality of such imaginings on the boy's
part, or, picking up the Nero Wolfe metaphor, brandishing the "dastardly plot" (itself a worn cliché) of "How to Get Out of Here." The
family's immobile, separate existence is contrasted to the modern
family, grouped around the television, watching. Nobody is coming
to the farmhouse this afternoon:

Outside, a lone car passed; the mailbox held
no hope of visitation — no peacock magazine,
wrapped in brown paper, rife with ads, would come
to unremind us of what we were, poor souls
who had left church early to be about
the business of soaking ourselves in Time,
dunking doughnuts let fall into the cup.

They are all there, enclosed in "Hot Pennsylvania, hazy," a group of
cells "diseased, unneighborly, five times alone, and quick." That
peacock magazine, the *New Yorker*, surely won't be coming this day.

As the poem continues to accumulate details, whether comically, ruefully, or regretfully observed, its surface, bristling with implication, becomes ever more solid; the way things *were* in their mere fact feels increasingly more potent than any wish or possibility that they might have been otherwise. The heavy, unchanging recalcitrance of family theatrics is as immutable as the Pennsylvania haze surrounding it all, and once more the adult speaker asks a question of the scene, then answers it in a passage of quietly growing raptness, as the place and group within it take on the enchantments of myth:

> What was our hurry? Sunday afternoon
> beckoned with radioed ball games, soft ice cream,
> furtive trips in the creaking auto, naps
> for the elderly, daydreams for the young,
> while blind growth steamed to the horizon of hills,
> the Lord ignoring His own injunction to rest.
> My book grew faint. My grandfather lifted his head,
> attentive to what he alone divined;
> his glasses caught the light, his nose
> reclaimed an ancient handsomeness.
> His wife, wordless, came and sat beside.
> My father swished his hips within his bath of humor
> and called his latest recognition to the other
> co-captain of dissatisfaction; my mother
> came to the living room doorway, and told us off.

She is their prison, they her captive who "shake our chains, amused." The question of why they left church early is finally answered:

> here to this house, this mythy *then*, we hurried,
> dodging the benediction to bestow,
> ourselves upon ourselves, the final word.

But the final word has now been bestowed, and the "Envoi," spoken directly to the mother, is lamely apologetic and uneasily anxious in the summary attempt at a moral formulation: "we had no time, of course, we *have* no time / to do all the forgiving that we must do."

Extended quotation from this poem is perhaps the only way to suggest its warmth and depth, the rounded sincerity it brings to the presentation of a family. Its felicity of language, its wit, are conveyed through rhythms that, as in other Updike poems, sometimes seem rough and imperfect — although in this case they work to guard against a too-smooth flow of reflection. Yet "Leaving Church Early" is a piece of art so dependent upon its content — someone having been there in "that mythy *then*" and remembering what it was like — that some of Updike's prose reflections by contrast sound artificial and overstudied. If he had written no other poems but this one, his contribution to the genre would still be a matter of record.

Of the Farm

Two years after the award-winning *Centaur*, Updike published a short novel, *Of the Farm*, "in part" — as he put it in an interview three years later — "a look at the world of *The Centaur* after the centaur had indeed died."[14] The "indeed" was his way of emphasizing that at the end of the earlier novel it is Chiron who dies, while George Caldwell lives on, enacting his daily sacrifice for others, especially his son Peter. In *Of the Farm* the son, now named Joey Robinson, is visiting his mother at the farm the year after his father's death. Joey brings back with him his second wife, Peggy (he has divorced his first one, Joan), and her eleven-year-old son Richard. They arrive on Friday and stay till Sunday afternoon, in the course of which visit Joey encounters his past, listens to and does or doesn't mediate between the awkward conversations of Peggy and Mrs. Robinson, who are having their first extended meeting. The three of them, along with the questioning, precocious, good-humored Richard, provide a note that Updike later described as of "chamber music, containing only four voices."[15] The novel's resolution doesn't quite resolve; its conclusion is inconclusive, yet something has undeniably happened to the participants.

Two things in particular struck me about *Of the Farm* when I read and admired it thirty-five years ago. The first, less important observation was that Updike, then a married man with four children living — it was well known — in Ipswich, chose for his now familiar figure of the son returning to his homeplace (as did David Kern in "Packed Dirt . . .") a divorced man, recently remarried. Admittedly there is no reason to expect a sharing of marital or other traits between author and protagonist: after all, in *The Centaur*, Peter Caldwell lives in New York City with his black mistress. But it was not an obvious thing to do, to make the representative Updike figure into a divorced, remarried man, a condition the author himself would enter into only in the middle 1970s. It may well be that, as in T. S. Eliot's formulation, "The test of a true poet is that he writes of experiences before they have happened to him." So much for the first distinctive feature; the second, much more significant, one was that this brief novel stood virtually alone in its probing examination of a husband caught between and pulled in different directions by his mother and his wife. The great precursor of such a situation is of course Lawrence's *Sons and Lovers*, except that Paul Morel is not married to Miriam and the combat between the women for his soul is hardly fought on even ground — Miriam being no match for Gertrude Morel. Also, the dynamics between mother and wife in *Of the Farm* are complicated further by Mrs. Robinson's invoking Joey's previous wife, who is compared — usually to Peggy's disadvantage — with his present one.

With such a thematic concern wholly evident in the novel's pages, it is puzzling that some reviewers of it took the Podhoretz line about Updike having nothing to say. This implied demand that a novel "say" something important seems crude enough, and seems as well an irritated response to the writer's precocity and early success. Like the novels and stories that precede it, *Of the Farm* has its quota of elaborate "poetic" writing (especially Joey's comparison of his wife to the field he's about to mow) that struck the unimpressed as eloquence in need of having its neck wrung. But by far the canniest response to something different in the writing of the new book was that of Charles Thomas Samuels, a young critic who later interviewed Updike for the *Paris Review* and wrote a useful monograph

on him. Although Samuels admired the earlier novels, he also felt
in them a straining toward significance, what he called "the devices
of a fervent will toward meaning," that marred both *Rabbit, Run* and
The Centaur but were also the visible embodiments of a writer having too much, rather than too little, to say.[16] What one feels in the
opening sentences from *Of the Farm* is, as Samuels pointed out, the
speed and lightness with which things are managed:

> We turned off the Turnpike onto a macadam highway, then off
> the macadam onto a pink dirt road. We went up a sharp little
> rise and there, on the level crest where Schoelkopf's weathered
> mailbox stood knee-deep in honeysuckle and poison ivy, its
> flopped lid like a hat being tipped, my wife first saw the farm.

In the amusing conversation that ensues, Peggy and Richard question Joey about the farm's size (eighty acres) and what it contains:
no livestock, no chickens, "Just some dogs and a barn full of swal-
lows," answers Joey, to which Richard poses the question that introduces and is at least partially answered by the novel to follow:
"What's the point . . . of a farm nobody farms?" From the outset
Updike is adept at employing something like the plain style rather
than the grand one — though note the caginess with which "my
wife first saw the farm" is delayed so that the mailbox may be fanci-
fully and with visual accuracy compared to a tipped hat. And in
Richard's pointed question about the point of such a farm may be
heard the humor and vernacular bite that inform the quartet of
voices in the novel. This sprightly and taut compression of characters in action is in part what makes *Of the Farm* impressive; but the
comparison Samuels and other reviewers of the novel make of
Updike to Henry James is less convincing. Granted that Updike
shares with James a tendency toward preciosity in language, at least
shares a reverence for "style" as the real right thing that (in James's
words) "*makes* life, makes interest, makes importance." Yet it is only
by a feat of abstraction that we can connect James's intense and —
in his later works — oblique conversations between his characters,
where "substance thins gaseously beyond the edges of the moral

issue" (Yvor Winters), with the thrust and parry, often deliberately crude and misjudged in execution, that make exchanges among the characters in *Of the Farm* so telling.

The ostensible purpose in visiting the farm is twofold: Joey, using his mother's old tractor, will mow the "shaggy fields" that the Commonwealth of Pennsylvania has now decreed must be mowed; while his mother will "deepen her acquaintance with my wife, to learn, if possible, to love her." But Peggy falls asleep during the first night's after-dinner conversation, soon after she and Mrs. Robinson have had their first confrontation. In response to the mother's statement that the two main things she wanted in life were the farm and a son, and that her husband George gave her both, Peggy asks, challengingly, what she gave him in return — what, in effect, Joey's father got out of the deal. His mother answers, "expansively spreading her hands," that she gave her husband "his freedom." At which point Joey as narrator makes the first in a sequence of disloyal moves toward his second wife by terming the mother's answer "this daring vindication of her marriage" in which "all her old wit sprang to life." It dismays him to see that "Peggy was puzzled," although she responds with a rather forceful and relevant question, "Can you give a person freedom?" Joey perceives she is angered, not for the last time on the visit.

The question of how to think about freedom is raised in the novel's epigraph, another of Updike's heavy-hitting ones (earlier epigraphs were from Bergson, T. S. Eliot, Kafka, Pascal, and Barth), this time from Sartre who writes that once we recognize man as a free being who "can want only his freedom," we then "want only the freedom of others." It's another example of the "fervent will toward meaning" Charles Samuels mentions, and it hints, with a flourish, at a level of depth and significance — of allegorical overmeaning — that is a good deal less interesting than the page-by-page drama as it unfolds in the novel. In that unfolding drama people's wants are less nobly inevitable than claimed by Sartre's formulation, as their individual voices struggle with each other for dominance and control. Mrs. Robinson is especially artful and ruthless in her bid to control her son's responses and persuade him to accede to her view of things. After Peggy retires and Joey feeds the dogs in their pen, he returns to the house to find his mother lying in the dark on the sofa feeling, as she puts it, "queerly." Though his wife awaits him upstairs, he sits down momentarily in his grandfather's rocking chair for the following exchange:

> "The boy," my mother said, "seems bright."
> "Yes, I think he is."
> "It's interesting," she continued, "because the mother doesn't seem so."
> This blow was delivered in the darkness like a pillow of warmth against my face. I felt myself at the point at which, years ago, in this same room, I had failed Joan. Yet I respected — was captive within — my mother's sense of truth. My response was weak. "Not?"

Pressing her advantage, Mrs. Robinson goes on to express her surprise that Joey needs a "stupid woman" to give him confidence and says that he has turned into a man his dead father wouldn't recognize. This is strong stuff, too much, and Joey strikes back, asserting himself and defending his wife. But the blow has been received and is not removed by his mother's assuring him that she's "just a crazy old woman." The whole encounter is a replay of Allen Dow's late-night confrontation (in "Flight") with his mother, in which she insults the rival girlfriend. Joey Robinson is thirty-five, however, and on his second wife, yet the mother-son battle is still to be fought, unresolved by the son's flight. It's not that easy to escape the farm.

A powerful scene like this one incites embarrassment on our parts, embarrassment that is an important ingredient of the novel's psychological drama. But some qualification about the nature of that drama and its psychology must be made, not just in reference to this scene but throughout the work. In arguing that the third-person present tense of *Rabbit, Run* gave its hero an advantage by constantly making us privy to his thoughts and feelings, however subtle or crude they were, I was distinguishing Rabbit from other characters in the novel who are treated more conventionally. In *Of the Farm* Joey Robinson similarly has an advantage, since his first-person recital of the weekend's events reveals himself to us much more fully than his wife and son are revealed, or even his mother — we are given his perspective on her actions and comments, but hers on his only through quoted speech. In other words, and as with *Rabbit, Run,* Joey's character is infused with authorial energy and imaginative verve; he is the beneficiary of Updike's sentences in a way that the other actors can't be. In his interesting review of the novel Anthony Burgess, after complaining about certain Updikean prose excesses, said that "on the whole the thing works. It is the sort of thing that brings poetry back to the novel — not the poetry of action or casual close description but the poetry of digression, the only kind really admissible."[7] While I don't fully understand Burgess's distinction here, "the poetry of digression" seems an excellent way to describe what's effective and powerful about Joey's narrative.

The cowriters of an early book on Updike analyzed Joey as follows: "[he] remains an imaginative man. The poetic impulse has not died in him. Yet the powers of the imagination that might have enlarged his life have not been disciplined or directed into true creativity. Since he met Peggy, his mind has turned mostly to romantic-erotic images. . . ."[18] But the use of past tense ("Since he met Peggy") is a tip-off that something is wrong with their analysis, which assumes that Joey is a real person with a mind whose history can be charted. Rather, and like Rabbit Angstrom, he can become anything Updike wants to make of him at the moment, for the occasion. The most notorious of such occasions occurs when Joey mounts the tractor and mows the field he's come to mow. At the beginning of this sequence he confides to us that "My wife is wide, wide-hipped and long-waisted, and, surveyed from above, gives an impression of terrain. . . ." Its final paragraph, about Joey's mowing, is as follows:

> Black-eyed susans, daisy fleabane, toadflax, goldenrod, butter-
> and-eggs each flower of which was like a tiny dancer leaping,

legs together, scudded past the tractor wheels. Stretched scat-
terings of flowers moved in a piece, like the heavens, constellated by my wheels' revolution, on my right; and lay as drying
fodder on my left. Midges existed in stationary clouds that,
though agitated by my interruption, did not follow me, but
resumed their self-encircling conversation. Crickets sprang
crackling away from the wheels; butterflies loped through their
tumbling universe and bobbed above the flattened grass as the
hands of a mute concubine would examine, flutteringly, the
corpse of her giant lover. The sun grew higher. The metal
hood acquired a nimbus of heat waves that visually warped
each stalk. The tractor body was flecked with foam and I,
rocked back and forth on the iron seat shaped like a woman's
hips, alone in nature, as hidden under the glaring sky as at
midnight, excited by destruction, weightless, discovered in
myself a swelling which I idly permitted to stand, thinking of
Peggy. My wife is a field.

This is lyrical but also witty writing, characterized — as usual in a
passage of Updike observation — by an easy intimacy with the
names and appearances of things. An extraordinary tractor driven,
we might think, by a mower who notes "a scattering of flowers . . .
constellated by my wheels' revolution" on one hand, drying fodder
on the other. Or who registers butterflies loping above the universe
like a concubine examining "the corpse of her giant lover," then
caps it all off with himself achieving what the English call a "stand"!
If this passage were misread as simply a solemn hosanna to the rich
fertility of nature and by analogy the female principle ("My wife is
a field"), then surely Updike could be accused of overreaching,
obliterating his character in a gush of fine writing. That it must be
understood otherwise is a consequence of the style's playful consciousness of its own extravagance. It is like the difference between
a straightforwardly heroic mode of presentation and one closer to
mock heroic. It doesn't lose sight of the blunt fact that this is a thirty-
five-year-old fellow who still lusts after his wife (maybe even more

so with his mother around) and for whom a good rocking tractor "flecked with foam" is just the thing to make things swell up down there. Joey, as it were, becomes king for a day, or at least for a timeless moment, there at the top of things; he will soon come down to earth, revealing himself as rather less than a god.

Saturday afternoon, after he mows most of the field, a storm gathers, eventually breaking into steady rain. The psychological storm that has been gathering from the moment of their arrival also breaks, especially when the farm becomes a subject of discussion. What is it for? What's the point of, in Richard's terms, a farm nobody farms? Mrs. Robinson suggests it be thought of as "a *people* sanctuary" where the old come to compose themselves before they yield to death. Not too tactfully, Peggy intervenes by questioning the metaphor: "a funny sanctuary . . . Like a concentration camp" — at which point Joey's mother takes offense, abruptly leaving the lunch table and slamming the front door. Things continue, by turns accommodating, then erupting into further unpleasant exchanges between the women: Peggy asks Mrs. Robinson whether she thinks Richard should be a farmer and receives in reply, "I think it would take more imagination than you'll permit him to have," a clear insult however "sincerely" meant. Joey tries to defend his wife, not very successfully; his mother tells her she shouldn't be jealous of Joey or of Richard. Peggy responds in disbelief ("You're fantastic"), defending herself by claiming she is the first woman who has ever let Joey be "a man." As it continues to rain steadily, Joey perceives that "The air of the house had taken a wound"; then suddenly his mother, with no attempt to pretend it is an accident, breaks one, then another plate in the kitchen. This is too much for Peggy, who says she's leaving, but is cajoled by Richard into staying. Joey tries to clown his way out of the mess, saying to Peggy, "God, no; don't leave me woman!" in a comic tone, to which she responds, after smiling rather significantly, "The cute thing about you, Joey, is you're really sort of a bastard."

That remark is sometimes quoted as if it were, more or less, the "point" of the book — that Joey's vacillation between wife and

mother, and his pusillanimous behavior in letting the mother bully
him into derogating Peggy, can be accounted for as a character flaw.
One of Updike's best critics, Donald Grenier, speaks of Joey as passive, weak, and manipulable, to his discredit as a human being.[19]
The trouble is that Joey isn't a human being but a character in a
novel; moreover a character endowed with special privileges of perspective and commentary. This sometimes makes for strange effects,
as when following close on the heels of Peggy's observation that he's
"sort of a bastard," Joey — instead of woundedly taking her words to
heart — notices the quality of her skin: "My wife's skin blanches
when she is angry, grows very smooth in making love, and takes a
tan briefly, as if the atoms composing it dance with especial rapidity."
There is more of such observation, guaranteed to disconcert and
annoy readers who want clear and sensible responses from the hero
to the words of another character. Such directness is sacrificed or
replaced by the poetry of digression Anthony Burgess speaks of, per-
vasive in a novel narrated by one of its main characters.

That Saturday evening Joey's wife and mother talk to one another
for an hour and a half, while Joey, ostensibly reading Wodehouse,
formulates the conflict thus: that Peggy thinks Mrs. Robinson
destroyed Joey's father by undervaluing him, by bringing him to the
farm he didn't want; and that Mrs. Robinson thinks that Joey "the
center, the only child, the obscurely chosen, the poet" has been
taken away from his first wife by Peggy and forced into "the shide-
poke [Pennsylvanian for *infra dig*] sin of adultery and the eternal
damnation of my children's fatherlessness." He decides that perhaps
they are both right; yet of the two "darknesses" manifested by these
women in collision, that of his mother is the more nurturing and
alive one. In point of fact, Peggy really has little chance against the
cumulative weight of the past — "of the farm" he shares with his
mother. Thus what truly shocks us, when Peggy goes to bed and Joey
sits talking with Mrs. Robinson — the fullness of his capitulation to
the mother and betrayal of the wife — is also inevitable, to be
expected. Joey admits to her that he was "wrong" in leaving his first
wife, that he left his three children out of account, put his life out

of joint, and that — knowing it was a mistake even while he made it — he nevertheless persisted. Moving in for something like the kill, his mother proposes that "You've taken a vulgar woman to be your wife," a charge that receives not denial, but a three-word comment: "It was true." And, eagerly capitulating, Joey goes on to overegg the custard by insisting, "She *is* stupid. . . . Remarkably stupid." The word echoes Rabbit's characterization of his wife, Janice, as well as Peter Caldwell's calling his sweetheart Penny "My poor little dumb girl," and in both earlier cases some dramatic justification is provided for the judgment, at least by way of demonstrating the male's nervous attempt at dominance. But Peggy is another matter: as Elizabeth Tallent observed, in her sharp monograph on Updike, Peggy "seems rather quick on her feet for a stupid woman."[20] I think any reader of the novel must agree with Tallent, which leaves us the choice of supposing either that Joey's condescension and assumed superiority are repeatedly endorsed, consciously or not, by Updike; or that Joey knows more about Peggy than we do (but such presumed knowledge doesn't get dramatized in the novel); or that in attempting to underline Joey's capitulation to his mother, Updike has sold out Peggy, and also Joey, in the process. It's surely not enough to spoil the book, but it momentarily disturbs its poise, its balanced play between alternatives. It may be that the betrayal of Peggy is not perpetrated simply by Joey.

A way of countering this objection, indeed obviating it, would be to claim that Updike's purpose, achieved in *Of the Farm*, was to present an uncommitted, morally dubious man, protecting himself by registering only superficially the winds that blow him one way and another. For it's not just Mrs. Robinson who steamrollers him: after Joey and his mother attend church on Sunday morning, where an artful sermon is preached about the proper relations between man and woman and about man's ethical ties to the earth (the farm), Mrs. Robinson has an attack, in the car on the way home, of heart-related breathing problems. She takes to her bed, Joey calls the doctor, and he and Peggy have an exchange with reference to his first wife, Joan. Peggy speaks with firmness and power, quite the opposite of the "stupidity" with which she has been saddled by mother and son:

> "One thing I want very clear with you, Joey. Don't throw Joan in my face like that again. You made your choice. I had no power over you and tried to be honest with you and you made your choice. If you have anything constructive to say to me say it, but don't tease me like you did that dog. Don't keep showing me the hole. If I have to make any sacrifices so your mother gets proper care of course I'll make them, but I'm not Joan and we all knew it at the time and I'm not going to be sorry."

(The canine reference is to Joey as a boy teasing his dog by showing him the pipehole in which the dog had once gotten stuck.) Joey's reply to her is casual and evasive — "Don't be dumb. You're great" — but he feels that she has "come between me and my momentary vision of the farm"; that "my failure to be able to see both her and the farm at once seemed somehow a failure of hers, a rigidity that I lived with resentfully, in virtual silence, until at two-thirty promptly the doctor came, smelling of antiseptic soap and sauerkraut."

Here again we have the problem — the novel's problem — of how to come to terms with its protagonist-narrator. For there are really three Joeys here: the apologetic nice guy who reassures his wife because he's been jolted by her attacking him; the deeper "thematic" thinker who over the book's course has made the farm mean something rich, significant, and imperiled; and the humorous writer who gives us a way out with Doc Graff's arrival, all antiseptic soap and sauerkraut, in good Pennsylvania Dutch medical fashion. How can a reader, tempted to make a moral judgment to Joey's disadvantage, get around the charm and reassurance provided by soap and sauerkraut? Writing of this sort, multileveled and slippery in its movement from one style of address to another, makes it impossible for us to feel that the novel is in any coherent way a working out of its Sartrean epigraph about "freedom." But that fact makes the book more rather than less interesting: for all the patent experimentality of *The Centaur* and its mythological lode, *Of the Farm* may be more truly adventurous, insofar as it explores its subject without presuming to come out anywhere definitively. In doing (or not doing) that, it shares something with the way our lives and our relations with others also may not "come out" anywhere, at least an anywhere that we can formulate.

Indeed the final chapter, directly following on the exchange between Peggy and Joey, is brief, uneventful, and reconciling, as the three visitors prepare to head back to New York City, urged along by Mrs. Robinson who assures them, quite handsomely, that she'll be all right: "You've done your duty, all three of you, and you've made this old woman very happy, and it's not your fault her arteries couldn't take so much happiness." Mother and wife agree that Joey is "a good boy," Peggy grinning at him as she repeats the phrase, and Mrs. Robinson invites her, should Peggy come back to visit again, to have their picture taken together. It feels as if it's time for the novel to conclude itself and that the characters know this, so step back from the various traps and verbal pitfalls into which they fell over the just-passed weekend. Mrs. Robinson's last request to Joey is that when, after her death, he sells "my farm," he should manage to get a "good price" for it:

> We were striking terms, and circumspection was needed. I must answer in our old language, our only language, allusive and teasing, that with conspiratorial tact declared nothing and left the past apparently unrevised.
> "*Your* farm?" I said. "I've always thought of it as our farm."

Circumspection, conspiratorial tact, allusive and teasing language, the striking of terms, and the significant use of *apparently* in reference to leaving the past unrevised — it is a paragraph that performs, in a single sentence of some complexity, its stated subject. The note of just-managed equilibrium achieved by the players is, we're made to feel, something to have been achieved.

When someone unacquainted with Updike's works asks me which one I would suggest as place to begin, I usually recommend *Of the Farm*, since it has a subject — marital and domestic accord and disharmony — that is perhaps Updike's central one, here "worked up" into a beautiful and satisfying (despite my earlier qualification) work of art. It seems to me, along with Saul Bellow's *Seize the Day* (1956), a novella of approximately the same length, a distinct liter-ary triumph that stands out from anything produced by American fictional contemporaries, midcentury and after. You might even say that neither Updike nor Bellow did anything more finished, more verbally and imaginatively pleasing page by page, than these two books from early in their careers — despite the larger efforts they both would go on to undertake, often with impressive results. Looking back at his early work, *Tale of a Tub*, Swift is supposed to have exclaimed on what genius he had back then. A similar response from Updike or Bellow, decades after they produced these two short novels, wouldn't be out of line.

FOUR

ADULTERY AND
ITS CONSEQUENCES
The Music School • *Marry Me* • *Couples*

In the spring of 1963, concurrent with publication of *The Centaur*, Updike wrote a story titled "Couples" and submitted it, as was his wont, to the *New Yorker*, which rather uncharacteristically rejected it. Then, in the two-year interim between *The Centaur* and *Of the Farm*, in addition to publishing his usual spate of stories, poems, and reviews, he wrote a draft of a novel that was eventually published as *Marry Me* in 1976. In his note to a limited edition of "Couples: A Short Story," also published in 1976, he refers to the "bedeviled manuscript" of *Marry Me*, into which details from "Couples" found their way, and he notes also that the story and the novel were "among my first attempts to write about suburban adultery."[1] The two works emanated from a troubled period in Updike's life when, in the wake of a passionate love affair, he strongly contemplated the possibility of divorce and then retreated from it. In his memoirs, *Self-Consciousness*, he speaks of the "grayness" of a period in 1962, when he was trying to "piece together those last fragmentary stories in *Pigeon Feathers*," and when "I tried to break out of my marriage on behalf of another, and failed, and began to have trouble breathing." With respect to this period in Updike's life, Yeats's painful question near the end of the second part of "The Tower" comes to mind:

> Does the imagination dwell the most
> Upon a woman won or woman lost?

> If on the lost, admit you turned aside
> From a great labyrinth out of pride,
> Cowardice, some silly over-subtle thought
> Or anything called conscience once;
> And that if memory recur, the sun's
> Under eclipse and the day blotted out.

It is the woman lost and the circumstances of loss that stir up much of the energy in Updike's writing from these years.

The writings dealing with adultery and its consequences include a story, "Leaves," and the poem "My Children at the Dump" (originally "My Children at the Dump at Ipswich"), written in the fall of 1962; there is as well the story "Couples" and the *Marry Me* project; also an essay on Denis de Rougement that follows "Couples" closely in time, as does a poem, "Report of Health." A number of densely meditative stories that treat in one way or another the theme of eros and its effects on the lover were published in 1964 and 1965 — "The Morning," "The Dark," "The Music School," "The Stare," and "Harv Is Plowing Now" — and would be collected in *The Music School* (1966). At the distant end of this period, the novel *Couples* appeared in early 1968, propelling its author into a *cause célèbre* and bestsellerdom. In some ways these writings make up the part of Updike's oeuvre that is now the least read, certainly as compared to the early stories and novels, or to the later Rabbit novels, or to the Maples stories, most of which were written after 1965, and the best of them — "Separating" and "Here Come the Maples" — in the 1970s. The stories from *The Music School* listed above are familiar only to the Updike expert, and as "stories" they provide little of the traditional satisfactions associated with the genre — brooding, darkly introspective, and curiously static as they are.

The Music School; "Couples"

Asked, in 1974, to contribute to another of those "my favorite" anthologies, similar to the one for which he had previously chosen "Packed Dirt . . . ," Updike selected "Leaves": "A shy child," he commented, written in "a mode of mine, the abstract-personal, not a favorite with my critics."[2] It is true that when *The Music School* was reviewed in 1966 there were even more than the usual number of complaints about how Updike's "exquisitely artful" writing (the words were Robert Martin Adams's in the *New York Times Book Review*) failed to find subjects commensurate with its pretensions.[3] In response to a reviewer who expressed impatience with such "lace-making," Updike noted quietly that if "Leaves" were lace, "it is taut and symmetrical lace, with scarce a loose thread." Yet what he characterizes as his unpopular mode, the abstract-personal one, becomes within the less-than-five pages "Leaves" occupies, very personal indeed. The story begins and ends with a first-person meditation on what a man sees outside his window: the curious beauty of grape leaves as emblematic of nature — that which exists outside of us but includes our bodies, "our shoes, their laces, the little plastic tips of the laces" — in contradistinction to the inner man, the spirit, the subject capable of feeling guilt. It is a wholly Emersonian division, as Emerson expressed it in *Nature*, between nature and the soul, between the "Not Me" and the "Me," but with an immediate emphasis — in the opening paragraph of Updike's story — on the soul's propensities for suffering. The man recognizes that the grape leaves are beautiful, and this feeling is strange to him "after the long darkness of self-absorption and fear and shame in which I have been living." Strong assertions like this one are unlikely to occur in a story that is mere lace-making, and the assertion is reiterated as the man rejects the palliative of a possible return to nature, an untroubled entry into "Time's haven of mortality" in which our spirits "sink composedly among the mulching leaves." Rather, his situation, as in the Barthian epigraph to *The Centaur* (man as "the creature on the boundary between heaven and earth"), is irreconcilable with any such merging: "we stand at the intersection of two kingdoms, and there is no advance and no retreat, only a sharpening of the edge where we stand."

These abstract-personal meditations in the short-story form devote themselves to sharpening that edge by giving poignancy and

self-punishing force to it. In "The Stare" a man visits New York City
and spends his day looking for, expecting, and not quite meeting the
woman with whom he'd had an affair and had eventually broken it
off: when she had asked him whether he didn't love her, he had
replied "Not enough." Back in New York "he discovered himself so
healed that his wound ached to be reopened." Part of the motive
behind these short pieces is to reopen the erotic wound, now healed
or healing. About halfway through its short transit, "Leaves" moves
from the abstract to the personal mode when the man remembers
"the black of my wife's dress as she left our house to get her divorce."
He then, "divorced," drives through a landscape of turning leaves
and meets the other woman, his "wife-to-be" — only to feel, to his
horror, "the inner darkness burst my skin and engulf us both and
drown our love." He tells us then that "By telephone I plucked my
wife back," a happening perhaps in imagination only, since he next
tells us that "The pain does not stop coming." We are left with him
alone, thinking, reading a few pages from Whitman's *Leaves of Grass*
and bequeathing us the leaves of pages we have just read. The story,
for all its formal and formed art, feels like it is negotiating a
tightrope, the leaves he has produced making up, in Robert Frost's
words about poetry, a "momentary stay against confusion" that is
extremely tenuous.

The verb *plucked*, in "I plucked my wife back," occurs twice in
"Leaves": earlier in the story, even while the man is "upheld in a
serene and burning universe of leaves," something "plucks" him
back into inner darkness and guilt. The poem "My Children at the
Dump," written concurrently, opens with an imminent divorce:
"The day before divorce, I take my children / on this excursion."
Surrounded by waste, wonderful in its lavishness — "Sheer hills of
television tubes, pale lakes / of excelsior . . . sparkplugs like nuggets,"
the man finds that these objects "pluck" at his "instinct to con-
serve." But although his children want to revive some of the waste,
perhaps a bent tractor that could be brought to life, he knows better, knows that he has come "to add / my fragments to this universe
of loss, / purging my house, ridding a life / no longer shared of rem-

nants." The stay against confusion in this sad poem, which has scarcely enough rhythm line by line to hold it taut, is so little evident that we feel guilty at being onlookers of his guilt. By contrast to the poem, the unhappy stories from these years show Updike at his most Hawthornesque, at moments making us think as well of Poe, a writer to whom he seems otherwise alien. The penultimate paragraph to "The Stare" finds the man, in the evening, near Rockefeller Center, staring at many faces, no one of which is his lost beloved's:

> The moon gratuitously added its stolen glow to the harsh illumination around the iceless skating rink. As if sensing his search, faces turned as he passed. Each successive instant shocked him by being empty of her; he knew so fully how this meeting would go. . . . What was that element that had been there from the beginning and that, in the end, despite every strenuous motion of his heart, he had intensified, like some wild vague prophecy given a tyrannical authority in its fulfillment? What was the thing he had never named, perhaps because his vanity refused to believe that it could both attach to him and exist before him?

At such a moment Updike's writing is as close to attempting the inexpressible, the unsayable, as it ever will be. I take this effort to be an indication of how much feeling there is churning behind the handsome sentences, and how much an error it is to see the effort as nothing more than figure skating or lace-making, the production of one arabesque after another. The right way to read these stories is to be unsettled by them — as we feel, for all their art, the writer of them is unsettled. For perhaps the first time in his work, the author of "The Happiest I've Been" sounds unhappy, both high spirits and irony drained away together.

At moments in the abstract-personal stories and in "Couples," the voice tries to move beyond its solipsistic pain, its encasement in guilt and unhappiness, into some formulation that would universalize the plight and to that extent mitigate it. In "The Music School,"

a father waits for his eight-year-old daughter to finish the piano lesson to which he has driven her. Held in the basement of a Baptist
church filled with the sounds of many instruments, and with children and mothers arriving and leaving, the "school" is presented as
something the man loves and on which he lavishes affectionate
powers of description and evocation. It is only when he drives his
daughter home, confiding to us how much he loves this driving her
to and from the lesson, that he finally explains why he is doing it: it
is because his wife is visiting her psychiatrist and that "She visits a
psychiatrist because I am unfaithful to her." He claims not to understand the connection between these facts, but assumes there is
one. A couple of pages later, after associating the music school's
satisfactions with those of his remembered days attending a country
church — and after having confessed that he is also currently seeing
a psychiatrist — he rises to generalization:

> My friends are like me. We are all pilgrims, faltering toward
> divorce. Some get no further than mutual confession, which
> becomes an addiction, and exhausts them. Some move on,
> into violent quarrels and physical blows; and succumb to sex-
> ual excitement. A few make it to the psychiatrists. A very few
> get as far as the lawyers.

The germ of *Couples* is to be found in these sentences, which sound
authoritatively diagnostic and hopelessly unable to do anything
about the situation diagnosed. Their imaginative power in this particular story is less perhaps than their truth as index to American
middle-class marital discontents — particularized within the affluent, eastern-seaboard milieu — that broke out of hiding and went
on to flourish in the 1960s.

The motive behind these stories (made explicit in "The Stare") is
to nurse a wound that has healed enough that it aches to be
reopened. The motive is also evident in one of his poems, written
in mid-1963 but not published until six years later, perhaps because
it is so nakedly the statement of someone in pain. "Report of
Health" has three parts, of irregular lines and groups of line units

that are nothing like stanzas. Addressed to the woman to whom the man has done "wrong," it reports on that man's condition:

> I
>
> I am alone tonight.
> The wrong I have done you
> sits like a sore beneath my thumb,
> burns like a boil on my heart's left side.
> I am unwell.
>
> My viscera, long clenched in love of you,
> have undergone a detested relaxation.
>
> There is, within, a ghostly maze
> of phantom tubes and nodules where
> those citizens, our passions, flit; and here,
> like sunlight passing from a pattern of streets,
> I feel your bright love leaving.

Little needs to be said about this valentine of unhappy similes; certainly the lines lack rhythmic pressure to the point of slackness, as if they would attest to their sincerity by refusing to be formally inventive, to make the lace taut. In the poem's second section the man reveals to her that he has heard, through another, that she is "happy and well" and that no news could hurt him more than such lack of "disarray" in either her hair or her moral composure. Part 3 concludes:

> I may not write again. My voice
> goes nowhere. Dear friend,
> don't let me heal. Don't
> worry, I am well.
> I am happy
> to dwell in a world whose Hell I will:
>
> the doorway hints at your ghost
> and a tiger pounces on my heart;
> the lilac bush is a devil
> inviting me into your lair.

Did he keep the poem around for six years, before publishing it, out of a regard for privacy, or out of a sense that it was weak composition — or out of some combination of these motives? Whatever the motive, "Report of Health" violates the pleasure principle that Wordsworth insisted must be paid homage to by any true poem. The only reason for laboring this point is that refusal of some sort of satisfying "closure," however minimal, is quite untypical of Updike's artistic performance. In the conclusion to his review of *The Music School*, Robert Adams wrote that "It will be a good day for American fiction when [Updike] loses some of his prudence"; yet I doubt that Adams would have embraced an imprudent poem like "Report of Health" as the desirable alternative, even as it shows the writer in the grip of an experience whose painfulness he doesn't know how to master in words.

There is much more mastery shown in the rejected "Couples," and Updike's foreword to the 1976 limited-edition publication of it is exceptionally rich in its compressed statement of why, though imperfect, it contained something worth cherishing. He admits to having had qualms, which reconciled him to its nonpublication in 1963, about the story's faults of sentimentality and vagueness. He notes that this early attempt to write about "suburban adultery" failed to "earn the clangor of its last two paragraphs"; yet he found something worth writing about in the "sad magic" of these extramarital relations. In its imperfections, he said, "Couples" yet contained "tendernesses and exactitudes" he did not succeed in duplicating later, in further stories or in the novel of the same title. Updike's fondness for his rejected child is evident as he recalls the "innocent excitement of presentation" that characterized the story. So while he's willing to call it "clumsy" compared to others of his stories, he finds that the "possibly unkind sociological tone" of the novel *Couples* is in the story qualified by or fused with notes of personal emotion.

As with other fictions of Updike's, "Couples" is extremely unconcealing in its willingness to display biographical similarities between its first-person narrator and the author. The man and his wife, Ann, married in college and moved north to Tarbox from New York City "six years ago." (Updike moved with his wife and children to Ipswich in 1957, six years before the imagined time of the story.) Like most of the other couples they are in the latter half of their twenties, have children, and take eagerly to the "kind of playground for adults" offered by the Tarbox society: "We were playing at being adults, at being fathers and mothers and housewives," says the man from his later point of vantage in which — now living alone (as does the man in "Leaves"), separate but not wholly apart from either wife or mistress — he surveys the scene. The social activity of the couples, as in the novel to come, includes parties, dancing, games of touch football, and the like. At some unspecified date after he and Ann move to Tarbox, at the time of their third child's birth, he falls in love with Peggy Williams, first kisses her privately a year later, and begins making love with her six months after entering into "delicious sensations of freedom and elemental acceptance and new knowledge."

After he confesses the affair to Ann, she tells him that over the last couple of years, when he's been out of town, she has been visited and made love to by the husband of another of the couples. So the "rich ground of shared secrets" among the group is beginning to grow perhaps too rich, at least for the narrator's blood. He and his wife agree to hold off any decision about separation until the end of summer; at the end of August he breaks things off with Peggy, then, deciding that "we need a sacrifice" (the "we" being the group of couples), goes to Peggy's house and asks her husband for his wife. At the end of the story the man, now sounding very much like a writer, gives us two paragraphs containing the unearned "clangor" Updike spoke of later, but some of whose sentences are as fierce as anything he had written. The man describes himself as "torn from my home and robbed of my enemy," then asks,

> Who is the enemy? Who is it against whose threatened
> invasions we lit our fires and erected our barricades of chil-
> dren, whose subversion we subverted with alcohol, whose

propaganda broadcasts we jammed with parties, whose intrigues and fanaticism we counteracted with the intrigues
and fanaticism of love; who is the enemy I was delegated to
engage alone?

He answers that this enemy is "my friend," and that "I move with
ease among his camps, the underfurnished camps of solitude." He is
in no hurry to resume his life in "the doomed axis of couples,"
although he knows that this will happen; that he and Peggy will
move away, but eventually into some other "set." The story concludes in a way reminiscent of *The Great Gatsby* as it attempts a
final mythologizing of the "couples" motif:

> I am a parenthesis — a boat adrift between two continents. At
> times I remember and foresee the world of couples eagerly, as
> a garden from which I have been banished but to which I am
> certain to return. In trying to imagine my domestic life with
> Peggy, in fondly admiring her tireless touch with furnishings, I
> have slighted the coast that is not yet christened America.
> And time, time that knits and unravels all blessings, will pass
> before this paradise becomes a bewitched armaments factory
> whose workers, in their frenzy to forge armor for themselves,
> hammer, burn, and lacerate one another.

That final trio of verbs — *hammer, burn*, and *lacerate* — invites us
to take this voice as not just that of man adrift but one who has
seen something like hell. Updike was doubtless right in saying that
he needed a wider compass, a more extensive space than this story
in which to develop his vision of adulterous marital pleasures and
sufferings; in this connection we may note, by contrast, the length
of *Couples* (458 pages) and the deadpan declarative tone of its conclusion. So the intensities of "Couples" were displaced into a cooler
and more leisured treatment that gained in control what it lost in
the "innocent excitement of presentation" Updike speaks of with
fondness.

Marry Me

Marry Me is continuous with the stories and poems written or published in the period 1962–65 and can be claimed as Updike's principal imaginative preoccupation during those years. (This isn't to
say that he was Johnny one-note: his story about Harvard, "The
Christian Roommates," the longest and perhaps most finished one
in The Music School, reveals a more familiar and more traditionally
objective way of presentation, in its anthropological exploration of
a group of Harvard freshmen thrown together: there is nothing here
of the dark musings of "Leaves" or the passionate cry at the end of
"Couples.") In writing Of the Farm, he thought he was saying the
last of what he had to say about the "Pennsylvania thing"; meanwhile his imagination had been energized by "the muffled heart of
Couples, the theme of friendship — of friendships and their
inevitable, never-quite-complete betrayal by, if by nothing else,
time." This is from the foreword to "Couples," and the story itself
generalizes about how

> Relationships between couples are squares of which two sides
> are the marriages and the other two whatever comradely and
> respectful feelings the persons of the same sex share. It is not
> enough that affection make connections along all four sides.
> The square is hollow unless dotted diagonal lines of attraction
> exist between the opposite corners; it is these illicit lines that
> hold the square taut.

Here is the germ not only of the later novel but, more simply and
schematically, of the interaction between the two couples — Jerry
and Ruth Conant, Sally and Richard Mathias — that constitutes
the burden of Marry Me.

In Marry Me the diagonal "illicit" lines exist most strongly
between Jerry and Sally, who have an affair, are found out, and also
fall in love; less strongly between Ruth and Richard, who conducted
an earlier, rather businesslike affair, kept it secret, and broke it off
when they agreed things had gone too far. The novel's clever, "W,"
five-chapter organization is framed, at beginning and end, by Jerry's

narrative ("Warm Wine" and "Wyoming"), the first of which is followed by Sally's "The Wait," that wait being the airport chaos in which she and Jerry try to get back home after their tryst in Washington. Then the focus is Ruth's ("The Reacting of Ruth") and, though much less intensely, Richard's ("The Reacting of Richard"). In his note to the novel, Updike compared its "recalcitrance" to a just-built bookcase that reveals "constructional defect," but also the "symmetrically alliterative" form that gives him pleasure.[4] The novel's center, "The Reacting of Ruth," which he says was much reduced in length, is also its most "inward" section, and certainly Ruth's psychology is more interesting, since more created and explored, than that of the other three principals.

Updike's feelings on completing the first draft somewhere between 1963 and 1965 were doubtless mixed. One of the sources of his uneasiness might have been the closeness between the time when the book was written and the time in which it is set (1962). Although he had negotiated a similar closeness between writing time and novel time in *Rabbit, Run,* the third-person present tense may have felt easier to work in — everything is happening *now* — than the relatively detached, storylike mode he used for his tale of the lovers. There is also the matter of the subtitle of *Marry Me* — *"A Romance."* Added somewhere between the book's first draft and its eventual publication, it could have signified, in 1976, the remoteness of these fifteen-year-old events occurring in a time previous to assassinations, war, and presidential impeachment. In a 1978 interview Updike suggested that his unease at the lack of "sociology" in the novel led him to add the subtitle as a way of cutting it off from his other novels; also that the characters behaved "romantically" in a way that had gone out of fashion.[5] But more to the romantic point are the words Jerry speaks to Sally as they try to catch a plane back from Washington in time so that their mates will not suspect anything untoward. By way of distinguishing his and Sally's relationship from marriage, he says, "I see it so clearly. What we have, sweet Sally, is an ideal love. It's ideal because it can't be realized. As far as the world goes, we don't exist. We've never made love, we haven't been in Washington together; we're nothing. And any attempt to start existing, to move out of this pain, will kill us."

The words may be put next to Updike's 1963 review of a collection of Denis de Rougemont's essays (in *Assorted Prose*), where he formulated the main idea informing de Rougemont's *Love and the Western World* as follows: "Love as we experience it *is* love for the Unattainable Lady, the Iseult who is 'ever a stranger,'" and who "'rouses in the heart of a man who has fallen a prey to the myth an avidity for possession so much more delightful than possession itself.'" For de Rougemont, in Updike's view, "Eros is allied with Thanatos rather than Agape; love becomes not a way of accepting and entering the world but a way of defying and escaping it." This sort of passion is of course incompatible with marriage, but also, as Jerry Conant puts it in the novel, isn't to be satisfactorily found in adultery — at least not American adultery. Jerry tells Sally he doesn't want her as a "mistress" (she has used the word) since "our lives just aren't built for it. Mistresses are for European novels. Here, there's no institution except marriage. Marriage and the Friday night basketball game." Although, he goes on, they have "love," that love must also have a "blessing," which blessing can't come from themselves: "For some reason it must come from above." For all the difference between the theorist de Rougemont's sophistications and Jerry the TV commercialist's fumbling attempts to rationalize what he and Sally are doing, they share, as mediated by Updike the reviewer and novelist, a certain rough agreement about the incompatibility of marriage and passion — about the absolute gulf between the woman won and the woman lost. Later on the same page, in a summary remark of Jerry's made after the "blessing" passage, and sounding more like a novelist "explaining" the situation than an independent character, Jerry proposes that "Maybe our trouble is that we live in the twilight of the old morality, and there's just enough to torment us, and not enough to hold us in." (Significantly, the sentence is quoted on the book jacket to *Marry Me*.) It sounds, at any rate, like the voice of a man committed to playing a losing game, which is the game that the novel will show us. Of course, decades after Jerry's worry about the old morality and the new whatever-it-is that's replacing it, such binds may no longer seem troubling.

Later Updike would write, in *Self-Consciousness*, about the difficulties of successfully combining sex and marriage in the same package:

> My notions of heterosexual love had been derived from Hollywood movies and pornographic comic books and then such modernist benchmarks of sexual realism as *Lady Chatterley's Lover*, the last chapter of *Ulysses*, Henry Miller's *Tropics* books, *The Story of O*, and the memoirs of Frank Harris; perhaps I was disappointed when an overworked mother of four failed to follow these scripts.

This is candid; but his inclination (if such it were) to write, in 1963, a novel that would be not a novel but a "romance" may well have had as much to do with aesthetic as personal motives. That is, the human reference felt in some of the anguished stories and poems he was writing at that time is only part of the impulse that issued in *Marry Me*. With the appearance of *The Centaur* in 1963, he had published three novels, all of them elaborate in different ways, each of them dense and full of the "digressive poetry" Anthony Burgess found in *Of the Farm* and that is the major constituent of meditative stories like "Leaves" and "The Stare." In *Marry Me* the symmetry of the two couples, the dividing up of narrative focus on each person, the relatively high proportion of conversation to narrative exposition that speeds up the novel's pace — these may have been appealing possibilities for a fresh fictional effort on his part, a style he hadn't yet tried.

In fact when the novel was published it met with a less enthusiastic response than any of his previous books. Objections were made to his too-gentle treatment of the affluent Connecticut shore community of which the two couples are citizens, as well as to the couples themselves. Some reviewers felt that Richard Mathias, all cynicism and leering self-pity, was too simply conceived; others objected to the vacuity of the romantic lovers, Jerry and Sally, and especially to Jerry himself, his "existential" discontents and his willingness to make vasty pronouncements about the need for a "blessing" or the twilight of the old morality. Such philosophizing seemed to fit ill with an animator of TV commercials, a failed cartoonist who, like Peter Caldwell or Joey Robinson, settled for abstraction (painting, business) instead of particularity (Vermeer, poetry). The lovers' talk, especially in their opening tryst at the beech ("Warm Wine"), contains a fair share of "Hey"s and "Hi"s, as well as Jerry asking Sally, "Want me inside you?" In fact this short, opening idyll in which such words and sentiments get exchanged may bulk too large in one's memory of the novel, which in fact settles down to a more convincing realism in succeeding chapters. But Jerry Conant remains a bit lightweight for the concerns he's made to embody, even as he manages — either through Updike's kindness or a refusal to take Jerry seriously enough — to avoid moral criticism and judgment at the hands of his creator.

An English reviewer of the book perceptively raised an issue worth thinking about, especially in relation to *Marry Me*, where the novelist seems most detached from his creations, but by extension to Updike's fiction generally. The reviewer, Brian Way, quoted Updike from a television interview done when he was living in England in 1970, in which he said that he didn't want to stand "like a hanging judge over my characters; everyone has a case."[6] Such reticence, Way pointed out, helped avoid foreclosure by allowing characters a certain amount of freedom from authorial judgment and punishment. (We may be reminded of D. H. Lawrence's inveighing against the novelist, like Tolstoy in *Anna Karenina*, who put his thumb on the scales instead of allowing for "the full play of all things.") But the other side of this admirable reluctance to applaud or condemn a character may seem like uninvolvement, an inability to make us care much one way or the other about the fates, in *Marry Me*, of Jerry or Sally or Ruth or Richard. Updike has more than once rejected the notion that he is a satirist, saying that he has no interest in showing up his people that way; "You can't be satirical at the expense of fictional characters," he once said in interview with Jane Howard, "because they're your creatures. You must only love them."[7] But kindliness, an unwillingness to distinguish the admirable motive and action from the not-so-admirable one, can issue in a blurred sense of characters insufficiently distinguished from one another. Updike has said that as a novelist he is more interested in "conflict" than in "resolution," which again may be taken as a warning against the too-glib resolvings and concludings of simpleminded fictions. But with reference to *Marry Me*, it may also be an unsuccessful rationalization of his failure to end the novel in a convincing way. Never trust the artist, trust the tale — another directive from D. H. Lawrence whose burden is not easy to spell out. Updike attempts to obey the directive by holding back and refusing to pronounce judgment on Jerry, concentrating rather on the conflict in a man for whom the word *conflicted* is a massive understatement. He is the sort of hero who is a setup for abuse: reviewing the book savagely, Brigid Brophy quotes the following sentence: "[Jerry] looked up, a tall child with wet cheeks, a cut knee, a hopeful smile," and claimed that in the face of his repellent "boyishness" she began to hope "that the two women who inexplicably love him would turn out to be elderly homosexual men in drag."[8] Such florid abuse from a reviewer might be understood as a response to Updike's willingness to show the worst about his lead player, yet stop short of satirical denigration — not an easy balancing act to bring off. In fact Jerry Conant is a particularly egregious example of what another critic of the novel trenchantly referred to as the "passivity and histrionic narcissism" of Updike's protagonists generally.[9] The line may be traced from Rabbit Angstrom's troubles all the way up to the plaints and complaints, thirty-seven years later, of the protagonist in *Toward the End of Time*. When asked in an interview with Charlie Rose about what he thought of this character, the not-so-nice Ben Turnbull, Updike grinned and said that he rather liked him, which I take to be a comment directed less at the character's moral and human makeup than at the novelistic energies that went into thinking him up, making him reveal himself on the page.

What's good about *Marry Me* are its scenes of conflict and chaos. Undoubtedly the book's best piece of action is the extended scene at Washington's National Airport where Jerry and Sally get caught up in airline chaos, canceled flights, the abortive attempt to rent a car, and an eventual — though late — flight home. The narrative mastery over this bit of commercial confusion is especially welcome in a novel where so much of the "action" is up-close talk within the little world of the four principals. But chaos can happen there too as when, in "The Reacting of Ruth," Jerry, needing to confess his adultery to her, suddenly loses control at the dining table and slaps his youngest child as she tries to join in the grace he's saying. There ensues a family free-for-all, at the end of which — things having quieted down — he finally tells his wife about Sally. Conflict or chaos is also strongly present in the excruciating conversation between the two couples when (in "The Reacting of Richard") after Sally tells her husband about the affair, the Conants are invited to the Mathiases' to talk things out in a session presided over by the slightly demonic Richard, master of these sad revels. At a crucial moment late in the novel, after the adulterous secret is out and the marriage of Jerry to Sally seemingly set in motion, Jerry visits her at her house and asks whether she doesn't feel as if "We're two children caught with our hands in the cookie jar." He is then moved into a less cozily acceptable set of feelings:

> He sat in her bright kitchen, the glitter of its knives and counter edges and pâté molds at intervals dulled as clouds swallowed the sun, and talked of Richard and Ruth; they found it difficult to talk of themselves. Their love, their affair, had become a great awkward shape, jagged, fallen between them. Jerry was ashamed of his desire not to touch her; he wanted to explain that it was not a change in her, but a change in the world. Richard's knowing had swept through things and left them bare; the trees were stripped, the house was polished and sterile like a shopwindow, the hills dangled as skeletons of stones, so that lying embraced even in the earth Jerry and Sally could be seen.

This state of exposure, depletion, and shame could have been a fitting place for *Marry Me* to have ended, in which case the subtitle "*A Romance*" would have been an ironic one indeed. But Updike didn't leave it there and wrote a final section, with alternate possibilities for what finally happened to Jerry and Sally. Granted that the novelist should be in charge of how he ends his book; yet *Marry Me* seems at its close giddier and more unsubstantially fanciful than it does in the paragraph above about Jerry's desolation in his lover's bright kitchen. Whether or not the alternate endings were part of the original draft, they surely bear relation to the married life of John and Mary Updike in 1962: "I tried to break out of my marriage on behalf of another, and failed, and began to have trouble breathing." At any rate he put the novel on the back burner and saved its publication for the year, 1976, in which his divorce became final.

Couples

The April 26, 1968, cover of *Time Magazine* featured a full-scale presentation of "Author John Updike," complete with green turtleneck and set against a backdrop of what looks like marsh grass, perhaps of the Ipswich variety. Draped diagonally across the top of the page is the caption, "The Adulterous Society." Inside, in the book section, there is a lengthy six-page account of *Couples* and its author's career leading up to it; there are also photos of Updike, his family, his parents, and even a map — drawn by a *Time* artist — of the mythical town and environs of Tarbox, in Plymouth County, Massachusetts. If readers were so inclined, they could trace out the different residences of the couples (conveniently featured in red ink), along with locating the Tarbox parking lot, post office, and Congregational church. The account of the novel itself speaks excitedly of "desperate tribal rites" in which the couples engage, and *Time*'s anonymous critic moves from a cleverly sketched account of the book's story to a consideration of its author's habits. We learn, for example, that Mr. Updike writes in a room above a restaurant on the Ipswich green, "romps" with his four children at home, plays in a recorder group with his wife, and may be seen on a winter morning heaving a snowball against the corner stop sign or, in summer, doing a little lettuce cultivating, Rabbit-like, in his garden. Alternatively, he can be seen driving his dented 1963 Corvair down to Crane's Beach for a walk and sometimes, at low tide, to swat a few golf balls. As for the novel's place in his literary career, it contains the "explosive expression of his theme" that his earlier, highly crafted but limited stylistic enterprise lacked. The charge of "irrelevance," made by the critic Leslie Fiedler, no longer applies. Updike, it seems, has broken through to something.

Couples made the best-seller lists for a while and made Updike a lot of money (a million dollars, he said in an interview). It has also suffered the fate likely to afflict a book published to a lot of notoriety and hoopla — that of being, years later, written off or at least discounted as an overcelebrated production by a writer who had produced and would produce better, less celebrated things. Its length and the relative slowness of its reading pace may have told against it as well; certainly it is, as a novel, capaciously unselective in what it chooses to include. Updike himself was willing to admit, in later comments, that at 458 pages *Couples* was perhaps too long, and he used the pertinent adjective *upholstered* by way of characterizing the novel's manner and weight. That upholstery may be felt when the protagonist, Piet Hanema, attending a Tarbox town meeting with his wife Angela, looks about him and intuits a hovering "miasma of alcohol, of amber whiskey, of martinis hurriedly swallowed between train and dinner, with the babysitter imminent." Piet intuits also that the town is changing:

> Each year there were more commuters, more young families with VW buses and Cézanne prints moving into developments miles distant from the heart of historical Tarbox. Each year, in town meeting, more self-assured young men rose to speak, and silent were the voices dominant when Piet and Angela moved to town — droning Yankee druggists, paranoid clammers, potbellied selectmen ponderously fending off antagonisms their fathers had incurred, a nearsighted hound-faced moderator

who recognized only his friends and ruled all but deafening dissents into unanimity.

This is expert observation, animated with an insider's sense of place, and it could go on and on (indeed it does) with no more justification needed than that of providing further evidence of a real place, in real time, described with real fullness. The passage, however, doesn't come early in the book, as one of the establishing pegs in its structure, but rather in its final, fifth section, on page 386, in the middle of a page-and-a-half paragraph devoted to the town meeting. In other words, Updike has interests that are broader, less intensely focused on the development of his main theme: the attractions and disengagements between couples in what one of the wives calls "the post-pill paradise."

All of Updike's earlier books contained epigraphs; some of the books were dedicated, some not. As if to signal the expansive ambitiousness and seriousness of this long novel, Updike dedicated *Couples* "To Mary" and provided a double epigraph for it. The first was from Paul Tillich, comparing today's "average citizen" to the Roman subjects who felt powerless about "decisions relating to the life of the society," a state, Tillich claimed, "favorable for the resurgence of religion but unfavorable for the preservation of a living democracy." The other epigraph is four lines from Alexander Blok's "The Scythians," beginning "We love the flesh: its taste, its tones, / Its charnel odor, breathed through Death's jaws." Epigraphs are chosen to be provocative, to give the book or poem to come some sense of stability, however delusory; and to suggest the concerns about to be represented and explored: to my mind the juxtaposed Tillich and Blok epigraphs raise matters of ultimate concern — sex, death, religion, the state and its citizens — in a manner both grand and teasing. And the novel to which they adhere, in its overall "feel" or atmosphere, is equally suggestive and elusive.

By this I mean to indicate how hard it is to say with confidence what *Couples* is doing, since it's doing various things and in different ways, many of which are extremely satisfying, full of the usual

Updike observation, charm, and wit. There is nothing frivolous or insufficiently thoughtful about this novel: to dismiss it as a cynical literary exploitation of the sexually permissive society is in itself a merely cynical response. If anything, *Couples* is all too earnest in pursuing its theme, to the extent perhaps of overreaching itself and exhausting its material. Whatever one thinks about the novel, moreover, it must be acknowledged that Updike, by setting it in the years 1963–64, was most attentively registering something important. Recall the opening stanza of Philip Larkin's "Annus Mirabilis," in which the year of miracles is celebrated with mordant wit:

> Sexual intercourse began
> In nineteen sixty-three
> (Which was rather late for me) —
> Between the end of the *Chatterley* ban
> And the Beatles' first LP

Three stanzas later we are invited to affirm, in conclusion, that "life was never better than / In nineteen sixty-three," when the postpill paradise became available to all. But Larkin's *jeu d'esprit* requires little more from us than a wry smile of wisdom at the vanity of imagining there is any sort of panacea that will make life "better." Updike writes a long novel to demonstrate, so the thematic burden of *Couples* seems to have it, that, like the story "Couples," the world of adultery is a hell in which, it will transpire, the inhabitants "hammer, burn, and lacerate one another." It's not Marry or Burn, but Marry and Burn.

In no other of his books had he so hammered in a theme through the words and feelings of his hero Hanema, the good carpenter, adulterer, and eventual lover of Foxy Whitman, married to another. The theme can be expressed comically and smartly, as when Piet tells his wife that his virility is the result of a "stiffening sense of sin." Insomniac after the party for the new Whitman couple, he thinks about his dead father and mother, his wife and his lovers, and prays "God help me, help me, get me out of this." Three hundred pages later, with Foxy pregnant by him, Piet vouchsafes to her that

"We know God is not mocked." A hundred pages after that, after Foxy's abortion and as Piet's marriage unravels, he attempts to shore things up by promising that his adulterous days are over, and he thinks that "there was, behind the screen of couples and houses and days, a Calvinist God Who lifts us up and casts us down in utter freedom, without recourse to our prayers or consultation with our wills." Yet a little later — Foxy having left her husband and gone to visit in Florida, while Piet, separated from Angela, lives alone — he finds that he misses not so much friends, but something else: "a nostalgia for adultery itself — its adventure, the acrobatics its deceptions demand, the tension of its hidden strings, the new landscapes it makes us master."

This formulation, like others of Piet's in the novel, is dazzlingly well put, and indeed Piet is a man of many parts. He is verbally and physically playful, good at doing stunts (as Updike was said to be) such as standing on his head; he is a thoughtful and proficient builder; he is a relatively dutiful father (there are nice touches between him and his two daughters), and even an uxorious husband — if that can go along with a penchant for other female liaisons. (Updike once said that the precursor of *Couples* was *Liaisons Dangereuses*.) Piet also attends church and, except for Foxy, is the only one in the set of couples who does. Like Rabbit Angstrom, he is singled out as a "believer." He has a sense of sin, stiffening or not, and seems to be in touch with the Calvinist God evoked in his speech to Foxy. Although we never catch him reading anything, and though he never graduated from college, he comes across as literate, sophisticated, very much at ease with language as well as with parties. Ranges of feeling are allowed him that are allowed to no one else, with the possible exception of Foxy, who is at least the nominal subject of a lovely passage of reflection early in the novel. It is time for the couples to break up and go home after their Sunday-afternoon touch-football game (the men play, the women watch — it is 1963), and Angela asks Foxy to stay for a drink. Foxy, "truly sad," says "we must get back" and we are told that

> She was to experience this sadness many times, this chronic
> sadness of late Sunday afternoon, when the couples had
> exhausted their game . . . and saw an evening weighing upon
> them, an evening without a game, an evening spent among
> flickering lamps and cranky children and leftover food and the
> nagging half-read newspaper with its weary portents and atroc-
> ities, an evening when marriages closed in upon themselves
> like flowers from which the sun is withdrawn, an evening
> giving like a smeared window on Monday and the long week
> when they must perform again their impersonations of working
> men, of stockbrokers and dentists and engineers, of mothers
> and housekeepers, of adults who are not the world's guests but
> its hosts.

The repetitions in the lengthening sentence as it imitates the long
evening to come, the sympathetic and horrified vision of marriages
closing in on themselves, the romantic sense of loss, as with nostalgia, permeating the passage — it is hard to believe that Foxy is
capable of entertaining all this, though her creator surely is.

In both *Rabbit, Run* and *Of the Farm* the male protagonist is the
privileged beneficiary of qualities, often discordant, that the more
"ordinary" characters in the book simply don't show. Since the central focus of these books is, respectively, on running Rabbit or on the
first-person presence of Joey Robinson, the privileging seems appropriate, or at least only incidentally damaging to overall credibility.
But *Couples* is a more conventionally structured novel, both in length
and in its successful creation of the Tarbox young married society. (It
could be argued that the novel's long second section, "Applesmiths,"
is unconventional insofar as it serves as background for the Piet-Foxy
love story.) Yet even as we're invited to take as not just credible but
definitive Piet's large, theological pronouncements — which "work
out" in the novel, right down to the burning of the Congregational
church — we must ask just how it all goes together. On one hand here
is a book full of the most expert observation of manners; of the inte-
riors and exteriors of houses; of the landscape of the Tarbox/Ipswich

marshes; of games — physical and verbal — the couples play with one another; of the wisecracks, allusive chatter, insults, and confidence-boosters they trade among themselves. On the other hand there are, intermittently, Piet's deeply gloomy and prophetic thoughts that point out the book's large thematic ambition.

When *Couples* was published, eyebrows were raised at how many people in the set were sleeping, at one time or another, with how many others of that same set. I remember wondering about the extent to which Updike's picture was a true and believable one of the erotic life in an eastern-seaboard town in 1963; at any rate the one I was living in (admittedly not on the sea) didn't quite measure up, in colorful variety of entanglements, to Tarbox. Was Updike's scene exaggerated by novelistic license or the attempt to show that nearly all the members in his group were sexually of interest? Was the novel a kind of erotic tall tale with the "marvelous" mode exploited with an eye more toward the fantastic happenings of romance than the sober, plausible accountings of the realistic novel? I was puzzled as well by the lack of a clear moral position in the book: were these adulterous couplings to be accepted as the way we lived now (then), or were they to be deplored, or looked upon as welcome liberations from marital tyrannies? Was this lifestyle appropriate for some people though not for others? Was "it" given its comeuppance in the dramatic resolution of the novel? To these questions Updike would answer, probably, that his job as novelist wasn't to judge his characters and their affairs but rather to render them. Fair enough, yet the questions persist in rereading the book.

What more than anything else animates *Couples*, as it does *Liaisons Dangereuses*, is the excitement and dangerous pleasure of talking about, planning, and executing illicit love. When Foxy says to Piet, late in the game, "Adultery. It's so much *trouble*," his reply, "reluctant to agree," is "It's a way of giving yourself adventures. Of getting out in the world and seeking knowledge." The novel never denies this truth nor acts as if there is a superior alternative that, if Piet had only thought harder about things, might have proposed itself. Nor do Updike's retrospective comments about the book suggest there is anything self-deceiving or "wrong" about Piet's answer. The only answer, to him and for him, is a theological or melodramatic one depending on how convincing one finds it — that of the Calvinist God he believes in. Updike rationalized the denouement as follows:

> At any rate, when the church is burned, Piet is relieved of morality and can choose Foxy — or can accept the choice made for him by Foxy and Angela operating in unison — can move out of the paralysis of guilt into what after all is a kind of freedom. He divorces the supernatural to marry the natural. I wanted the loss of Angela to be felt as a real loss — Angela is nicer than Foxy — nevertheless it is Foxy that he most deeply wants. . . . So the book does have a happy ending.[10]

We can't reprove the novelist for saying perhaps too much in retrospect about his own novel, but Updike works awfully hard here in the service of inviting us to extract meanings from the book. It's as if he wants us to understand something about Piet that Piet can't understand about himself ("He divorces the supernatural to marry the natural"). Of course the novelist always "knows" more about his protagonist than the protagonist can know about himself (that's how novels work), yet in certain fictions the hero attains, at the end of the book, a wisdom clearly endorsed and underlined by his creator. Think of *Crime and Punishment,* in whose last pages Raskolnikov in prison thinks about Sonya: "He remembered how ceaselessly he had tormented her and harrowed her heart; he remembered her pale thin little face; but these memories now hardly troubled him: he knew with what infinite love he would now expiate all her sufferings." And Dostoyevsky continues with the confident self-analysis, having finally provided Raskolnikov with the novelist's unquestionable truth. *Couples* has its crime and punishment, sort of, but also "a happy ending" insofar as the hero gets what he most deeply wants. Why can't one have his cake and eat it too?

Piet's wife Angela, in some ways the most attractive character in the novel, is also quite mysterious and not really there on the page.

When she finally asks Piet to leave, and he prepares to move out, the two of them put their children to bed, pack (jointly) a suitcase for Piet, share a last brandy in the kitchen, then Piet backs his pickup truck down the driveway only to hear a noise from Angela he thinks is to call him back:

> He braked and she rushed to the side of his cab with a little silver sloshing bottle, a pint of gin. "In case you get insomnia," she explained, and put the bottle dewy in his palm, and put a cool kiss on his cheek, with a faint silver edge that must be her tears. He offered to open the door, but she held the handle from the other side. "Darling Piet, be brave," she said, and raced, with one step loud on the gravel, back into the house, and doused the golden hallway light.

On the basis of this act (greater love hath no wife than she will offer up a pint of gin to the husband she's asked to leave the roost), I too along with Updike agree that Angela is "nicer" than Foxy. But I don't see that the novel clarifies her any further than that, nor do I see that Piet knows what to make of her or what to do with this "cool kiss . . . with a faint silver edge that must be her tears." The writing, as writing, is more engaging, indeed sparkling, than any meaning it cumulatively possesses as an index of Angela's character or of Piet's response to it. One feels Updike wants to be kind to all his people, wants to say what he can say, positively, for each of them; it is an impulse very far away in spirit from a satiric treatment of character, though these characters are sometimes treated comically. But even the self-appointed evil one, the Satanic dentist Freddie Thorne, is allowed tremendous life in his tasteless jokes, quick repartee, and felicitous way with names (he regularly addresses Piet Hanema, whom he dislikes and for good reason, as Handlebar or Handyman). The surface life of the novel, so lively and done with such relish, works against our attempts to take seriously, to care enough about its main actors in the Piet-Angela-Foxy triangle in the ways we care about Raskolnikov, or Dorothea Brooke, or Leopold Bloom, or even Rabbit Angstrom.

In his note to "Couples" Updike addressed somewhat wearily the distance he had traveled from the story's moments of remembered immediacy to the "lofty, sociological tone" of the novel. When writing *Couples* he found those earlier moments to have gotten "overlaid with too many incidents," and found himself becoming "an author-god lifted above his personae." Certainly the big, carefully worked-over event of the Tarbox church burning is a prime example of that author-god taking out his vengeance on the scene he's been witnessing below. (On the other hand, the Congregational church in Ipswich really did burn down.) Yet I can imagine how that scene might also be taken as a parody of a cataclysmic event, cataclysm being much too grand to visit the imperfect lives that watch the church burn. And after the fire the central actors pretty much disappear or become shadow versions of their earlier selves. We hear from Foxy, who with her baby is spending time in the Virgin Islands; there is space devoted to showing, briefly, the other couples sealing themselves off from Piet; he himself watches crane operators rescue the golden weathercock from the ruined church, and "Affected by this scene of joy, seeing that his life in a sense had ended, Piet turned and realized he was standing where he had first glimpsed Foxy. . . ." The novel's final paragraph, in a time shift almost as drastic as the one Keats effects at the end of "The Eve of St. Agnes," tells us that now, some years later, the town scarcely remembers Piet; that Angela, divorced, still lives there, is teaching school in Braintree; that Piet and Foxy married and that he works as a construction inspector in the Boston-Worcester area. In a final sentence, "The Hanemas live in Lexington, where, gradually, among people like themselves, they have been accepted, as another couple."

We may hear in that ending an echo, perhaps conscious, of Fitzgerald's final disposition of Dick Diver in *Tender Is the Night*: "his latest note was post-marked from Hornell, New York, which is some distance from Geneva and a very small town; in any case he is almost certainly in that section of the country, in one town or another." Like Fitzgerald, Updike signals the close of his novel by permitting the hero to fade away, in one small town or another, from the scenes and characters in which he's figured. Yet in some ways Piet has never quite been on the scene, but always detached, somehow unaffected by the turmoil of which he's been a part, indeed significantly contributed to. This may be saying no more than that Piet's psychology doesn't go very deep, not deep enough; he doesn't get wholly free — as he would have to do for the novel fully to weigh as a dramatic one — from the sociological tone informing the book. When Updike does let him get free, momentarily, it's done through a poetic mode which, though handsomely managed, doesn't quite emanate from our heroic carpenter. For example, at the end of the novel's third (of five) sections, "Thin Ice," Piet — having woken up full of the desire to confess his adultery to Angela — creeps downstairs and outdoors:

> The stars had wheeled out of all recognition. They were as if seen from another earth, beyond the Milky Way, rich in silence and strangeness. Treading lightly upon the rime-whitened grass, ice to his bare soles, he finally located, southward above the barn ridge with its twin scrolled lightning rods, a constellation gigantic and familiar: Orion. The giant of winter, surprised in his bed. So the future is in the sky after all.

And he returns to his house, satisfied that a crisis in his love for Foxy had passed, "that henceforth he would love her less." The power of this as writing is incommensurate with the sealed-in "social" world of the book, but is another example of why *Couples*, with whatever reservations one has about it as a wholly successful novel, yet remains in the mind as a bold, sometimes unforgettable piece of writing.

FIVE

IMPERSONATIONS
OF MEN IN TROUBLE (I)
Midpoint • *Bech: A Book* • *Rabbit Redux*

> Deepest in the thicket, thorns spell a word.
> Born laughing, I've believed in the Absurd,
> Which brought me this far; henceforth, if I can,
> I must impersonate a serious man.

These four lines conclude Updike's five-part poem "Midpoint," written after *Couples* appeared in early 1968. He was then thirty-six years old, flush with money and publicity, ripe for stepping back from a prolific ten years of production — five novels, two volumes of poetry, three collections of stories, a book of prose — to take stock. "Midpoint," which is also the title of the book of verse he would publish the following year, is forty-one pages, a "long, philosophical poem" he called it later, whose five parts differ strikingly from one another. The introduction, written in freewheeling terza rima, recapitulates family memories from Shillington and considers "dear Chonny's" (his childhood name) present condition as a married man with four children setting out on the downward slope of "the Hill of Life," a drawing Updike made when young. In that drawing the five Updike/Hoyers, each of them situated, according to age, in appropriate position on the Hill of Life, are either climbing or descending that hill. Now, in 1968, he contemplates his "reward": "fame with its bucket of unanswerable letters, / wealth with its worrisome market reports, / rancid advice from my critical betters" and himself transformed into public unrecognizability —

> From *Time*'s grim cover, my fretful face peers out.
> Ten thousand soggy mornings have warped my lids
> and minced a crafty pulp of this my mouth.

Still, he discerns at the end of the introduction a "hopeful burning" in himself and vows to keep going, his talisman an "untoward faith in the eye / I pun." Accordingly, the second section ("The Photographs") consists of three pages of pointillist reproductions of family snapshots taking him from infant to newly married father.

In ten years, the young man who brought out *The Carpentered Hen* (1958) has solidified into a respected literary figure. The poems he had published, after his second collection, *Telephone Poles*, appeared in 1963, were predominantly of the "serious" rather than "light" variety, though few readers thought of him as a poet of significance. Yet that Updike should choose, in "Midpoint," to inspect this figure — whether in verse or prose — is less surprising if we think of Frost, whose first book of poems, *A Boy's Will*, published by a small English press in 1913, marked his literary debut; ten years later his fourth book of poems, *New Hampshire*, won him the Pulitzer prize. In the title poem from that volume Frost went on stage as the public figure whose bardlike career an audience was presumed interested enough in to hear about:

> I may as well confess myself the author
> Of several books against the world in general.
> To take them as against a special state
> Or even nation's to restrict my meaning.
> I'm what is called a sensibilitist,
> Or otherwise an environmentalist.
> I refuse to adapt myself a mite
> To any change from hot to cold, from wet
> To dry, from poor to rich, or back again.

In other words, I am a public literary icon, available for display, insofar as I can conduct the display myself; the public Updike, whom we encounter for the first time in "Midpoint," is operating out of similar assumptions.

The overall shape of this long poem may suggest how this public man went about putting on an engaging performance for his readers. The photographs, made up so as to emphasize "the coarse dots, calligraphic and abstract" (Updike's words from the second section's opening "Argument"), are a teasing way of pretending that a picture is worth a thousand words, then stopping the slide show by way of making us wonder whether the maxim is true. *Midpoint's* jacket blurb alludes to "the photographic techniques of concrete poetry" as one of the means employed in constructing "a joke on the antique genre of the long poem." This joke continues in the poem's next two sections, with part 3 — "The Dance of the Solids" — being nothing less than eleven Spenserian stanzas in which much scientific playfulness is expended on solids like ceramic, glass, and polymers. Here as elsewhere, we are invited to be dazzled by Updike's determined ability to use the materials of science in, of all places, an autobiographical poem. Recall Wordsworth's pledge in his preface to *Lyrical Ballads* that "the remotest discoveries of the Chemist, the Botanist, or Mineralogist will be as proper objects of the Poet's art as any upon which it can be employed, if the time should ever come to us when these things shall be familiar to us." It is unlikely that Wordsworth's pious hope could have imagined the jaunty manner in which Updike dances through the solids:

> The *Polymers*, those giant Molecules,
>   Like Starch and Polyoxymethylene,
>   Flesh out, as protein serfs and plastic fools,
>   This Kingdom with Life's Stuff. Our time has seen
>   The synthesis of Polyisoprene
>   And many cross-linked Helixes unknown
>   To *Robert Hooke*; but each primordial Bean
>   Knew Cellulose by heart. *Nature* alone
> Of Collagen and Apatite compounded Bone.

It is the sort of performance guaranteed to reduce the reader to speechlessness, seasoned with wonder that such a thing could be done at all, also wondering whether it's worth doing. Section 4, "The Play of Memory" (the longest section of the poem), contains further verbal and typographical stunts, as the previously observed photographs and other concretions take their place in a discontinuous, dizzying series of autobiographical evocations, mainly erotic, which the herald of "The Adulterous Society" (*Time*'s headline) might be expected to highlight. It's not clear how or whether the reader is expected to put it all together coherently.

That coherence, however, is what the final section ("Conclusion") in its long march of heroic couplets seems to promise, even though near its end the poem claims that "The time is gone, when *Pope* could ladle Wit / In couplet droplets, and decanter it." Nevertheless Updike devotes his conclusion to praising old heroes of his — Barth, Kierkegaard, Vermeer, and Henry Green — while acknowledging that the world of the late 1960s is a violent one: "The world boils over; Ho and Mao and Che / Blood-red inaugurate a brighter day. / Apocalpyse is in; mad Eros drives / The continents upon a shoal of lives." Updike's response to all this turmoil is mild, sensible, private, even complacent: seize the moment, appreciate the created world in its richness and individuality, "Cherish your work," "Applaud your neighbor," and "Don't covet Mrs. X; or if you do, / Make sure, before you leap, she covets you." Although the section began with a ringing declaration — "An easy Humanism plagues the land; / I choose to take an otherwordly stand" — the stand he ends up taking is a rather worldly one, appropriate, he seems convinced, to a man on the downward slope of the Hill of Life. There was an earlier time when things were different:

> The playground dust was richer, once, than loam,
> And green, green as Eden, the slow path home;
> No snows have been as deep as those my sled
> Caressed to ice before I went to bed.

But the forward-looking couplet to follow is not reassuring: "Perhaps Senility will give me back / The primitive rapport I lately lack." The poet concludes with an homage to Chilmark Pond (the spot on Martha's Vineyard where Updike completed "Midpoint") and a new resolution: "I must impersonate a serious man."

One of the ways not to become a serious man is, of course, to impersonate one, and "Midpoint" is full of impersonations, the major one that of a poet undertaking the formidable task of writing a long poem, after it has been done by predecessors like Spenser, Milton, and Wordsworth. Decades previously Virginia Woolf, in her essay "Mr. Bennett and Mrs. Brown," had declared portentously that "we must reconcile ourselves to a season of failures and fragments." Updike's comically fragmented send-up of the long poem, with its intermittent hints of necessary failure (" — all wrong, all wrong"), was also a serious attempt to speak largely and autobiographically about himself as a performing self in late-1960s America. In a book by that title (*The Performing Self*, 1971) Richard Poirier has a second chapter consisting of an essay he published two years earlier, when *Midpoint* appeared. Titled "The Politics of Self-Parody," it argues that contemporary self-parody, which Poirier finds rampant in novelists such as Pynchon, John Barth, Mailer, and Borges, could be distinguished from earlier forms of parody in that the contemporary form "makes fun of itself *as it goes along*": such self-parody is importantly directed at any effort to verify "standards," even to verify them through the activity of its own writing.[1] (This would, presumably, distinguish Barth and Pynchon from Alexander Pope, although Byron's verse in *Don Juan* makes fun of itself, along with other things.) Although Poirier didn't include Updike in his list, "Midpoint" can be seen as an illustration of such literature, insofar as it makes its own aspirations and uncertainties the subject of narrative unravelings and discontinuities, even while it speaks out in favor of some old-fashioned humanistic values. For Updike, as for some of his contemporaries, the way we lived in the late 1960s could be credibly expressed only by a literary style that called into question the standards or sanctities of its own representation.

Bech: A Book

A year after *Midpoint* appeared Updike brought out *Bech: A Book*, in which he impersonates a Jewish novelist whose literary career is in the doldrums. Henry Bech, a sufferer from writer's block, finds himself touring Eastern Europe (the Soviet Union, Bulgaria, Rumania), regions Updike had visited in 1964 as a representative of the State Department. The bright yellow dust jacket of *Bech* features a caricature of the novelist, bestriding international urban architecture like a colossus, his curly gray-white hair filled with the faces of seemingly willing maidens (a dream, doubtless). In a foreword Bech writes a "Dear John" letter, congratulating Updike, more or less, for publishing this "short yet still not unlongish collection" that brings to mind various contemporary Jewish writers. He mentions productive ones like Mailer, Bellow, Philip Roth, Singer, Malamud, and a further triad — Henry Roth, Daniel Fuchs, and Salinger — whose "noble renunciations" are heroic versions of Bech's ignoble failure to produce enough books. Along with echoes of these Jews, Bech claims to hear, in the seven stories, "something Waspish, theological, scared, and insulatingly ironical," a quality he surmises derives from the non-Jew, Updike. After a number of instances in which Bech demonstrates how "America reduces her writers to imbecility and cozenage," he concludes with declaring that, though no maker of puns himself, he doesn't suppose "your publishing this little *jeu* of a book will do either of us drastic harm."

Bech: A Book not only did Updike no harm, it provided the occasion for reviewers who had mixed feelings about the earlier books, especially *Couples*, to praise the comic lightness and *brio* of these relatively undemanding, good-humored tales. One can understand why this happened; after all, *Bech* is a book where the issues, the motives out of which he had made his books — theology, metaphysical guilt and despair, family entanglements, adultery, Pennsylvania — are largely absent, though Bech does have a bout of *angst* while visiting a southern women' s college. The prose is crisp, witty, fully articulated throughout, as in this single example from "Bech Panics" in which the novelist attempts an illicit evening out with his mistress, Bea (he has recently broken things off with her sister, Norma). By separating her from her children he hopes to spend quality sexual time with her alone, although he must return her home by midnight so the baby-sitter can leave:

But the overfilling meal at a boorish roadside restaurant, and
their furtive decelerated glide through the crackling gravel
courtyard of the motel (where a Kiwanis banquet was in
progress, and had hogged all the parking spaces), and his
fumbly rush to open the tricky aluminoid lock-knob of his door
and to stuff his illicit guest out of sight, and the macabre interior of oak-imitating wallboard and framed big-eyed pastels that
embowered them proved in sum withering to Bech's potency.

The piling on of detail (that aluminoid doorknob, that crackling
gravel, those merry Kiwanians) is what any reader assumes Updike
will provide, but the tone and manner of treatment are not of the
sort commanded by Rabbit or Joey Robinson or Piet Hanema. For
example, the adjective *boorish*, to describe the roadside restaurant
where the portions were too large, rings with a contemptuous superiority reminiscent of Nabokov's Humbert; and indeed Updike's
impersonation of Nabokov is evident in *Bech: A Book*, in its introductory and concluding frames, in the introductory letter from Bech
to Updike, and in a concluding appendix (the second of two) in
which a bibliography of Bech's work is provided, along with a
selected list of critical articles concerning him ("Prescott, Orville,
'More Dirt.' *New York Times*, 12 October 1955"). This is good fun
and the appendix gave Updike the opportunity to index detractors
of his own work such as "Podhoretz, Norman," "Aldridge, John,"
and "Fiedler, Leslie." (There are also some lovely free-floating creations like "Minnie, Moody, 'Myth and Ritual in Bech's Evocations
of Lust and Nostalgia,' *Wisconsin Studies in Contemporary Literature*,
v.2, [Winter-Spring 1964] 1267–1279.")
    Like any humor, Updike's is infused with various degrees of ani-
mus that — under the cover of the aging Jewish writer Henry Bech
— he feels free to indulge in. So when in "Bech Swings?" the novelist visits London and is interviewed at length by a fatuous young
journalist named Tuttle (who will later publish a denigrating piece
on him in the *Observer* — "Bech's Best Not Good Enough"), he
responds to Tuttle's question about whether Bech has an affinity

with Ronald Firbank by declaring, "Only the affinity . . . I feel with all Roman Catholic homosexuals." This is an excellent one-liner, of the kind that filled Roth's *Portnoy's Complaint*, published the previous year. One can imagine Updike himself making it, if ever in an interview he allowed himself to be more disgruntled, sarcastic, and disruptive than in fact he did. As Bech's interviewer proceeds, the novelist's mind becomes more playful, anarchic, and daring, qualities encouraged by his talking into a tape recorder:

> He was an Aristotelian and not a Platonist. Write him down, if he must write him down as something, as a disbeliever; he disbelieved in the Pope, in the Kremlin, in the Vietcong, in the American eagle, in astrology, Arthur Schlesinger, Eldridge Cleaver, Senator Eastland and Eastman Kodak. Nor did he believe overmuch in his disbelief. He thought intelligence a function of the individual and that groups of persons were intelligent in inverse proportion to their size. Nations had the brains of an amoeba whereas a committee approached the condition of a trainable moron. He believed, if this tape recorder must know, in the goodness of something vs. nothing, in the dignity of the inanimate, the intricacy of the animate, the beauty of the average woman, and the common sense of the average man.

Soon after this the delighted interviewer leaves and Bech falls asleep. But in fact there is less here of Bech, the blocked Jewish writer, than of a series of declarations to which Updike, as a canny individualist, a nonsubscriber to and nonjoiner of groups, can subscribe, if without overmuch enthusiasm.

In other words, it turns out that Updike's "impersonation" of a writer ostensibly distinct from his own prolific, Protestant, married-with-children self is less convincing as an impersonation of otherness than as an opportunity for aggressive self-definition. Compared to such definition, Bech's sexual and writerly confusions seem adopted for the occasion, not to be explored or even taken seriously: it is the satiric observations that emanate, most strongly and believably, from

Bech's creator. An example: the "docile tourist and interviewee" Bech has supposedly become in his visit to London is exemplified by a list of meaningless activities, like appearing on the BBC's Third Programme or at a cocktail party at the American Embassy. But although it may be extremely meaningless to participate in a television discussion program on the "Collapse of the American," Bech's brief characterization of the other panelists is sharp and a shade nasty, not powerless at all: "an edgy homosexual historian whose toupee kept slipping; a mug-shaped small man who thirty years ago had invented a donnish verse form resembling the limerick; a preposterously rude young radical with puffed-out lips and a dominating stammer; and, chairing their discussion, a tall BBC girl whose elongated thighs kept arresting Bech in mid-sentence." These observations were, for various reasons, impossible for Updike's earlier fictional protagonists to make; with Bech, he can let himself go and engage in mockery of late-1960s manners and morals.

Clearly the nine months Updike spent with his family in London provided material for the most richly observed of these stories, "Bech Swings?" "Minority Report," a poem Updike wrote and published in England during his stay there, is a sort of love letter to the land he had temporarily left, as he sits in his flat overlooking Regent's Park and his new Citroen, "exiled by success of sorts." It is America's "dear barbarities" he recalls with relish, and, addressing his country, he tells it not to worry:

> They say over here you are choking
>   to death on your cities and slaves,
>   but they have never smelled dry turf,
>   smoked Kools in a drugstore,
>   or pronounced a flat "a," an honest "r."

"Don't read your reviews," he tells America, "you are the only land." Years later in the controversial chapter from *Self-Consciousness*, "On Not Being a Dove," Updike filled in the feeling behind "Minority Report" by describing his stubborn unwillingness to line up with condemners of his country's involvement in the Vietnam War.

"Minority Report" feels like a willful, even petulant response to those in another country who claim to know the real truth about the United States, a situation familiar to anyone visiting or residing abroad for long.

When Bech arrives in London (the occasion being his publisher's decision to bring out an anthology, *The Best of Bech*), he strolls about the city with awakened senses, engaged with the English poetic tradition in a way Updike must have been and that his prose buoyantly celebrates:

> He arrived with the daffodils. The Viscount banked over Hampton Court, and the tinge of their yellow was visible from the air. In Hyde Park beside the Serpentine, along Birdcage Walk in St. James's, in Grosvenor Square beneath the statue of Roosevelt and in Russell Square beneath the statue of Gandhi, in all the fenced squares from Fitzroy to Pembroke, the daffodils made a million gold curtseys to those tourists who, like our hero, wandered dazed by jetlag and lonely as a cloud. *A poet could not but be gay*, Bech recalled, *In such a jocund company.*

Meanwhile the denizens of swinging London from Oxford Street to Trafalgar Square "formed another golden host, beautiful in the antique cold-faced way of Blake's pastel throngs, pale Dionysiacs, bare thighs and gaudy cloth, lank hair and bell-bottoms, *Continuous as the stars that shine / And twinkle on the milky way.*" This wholly delightful and witty coupling of Wordsworth, wandering lonely as a cloud, with urban London 1969, is a further instance of what makes *Bech: A Book* satisfying in its freewheeling invention, even as it keeps in touch with the registered places and persons of Abroad.

It may not be an exaggeration to claim, as Cynthia Ozick did in writing about the book, that Updike loves his protagonist best when Bech "is most openly, most shrewdly, most strategically, most lyrically Updike."[2] Compared to this, Ozick found the Jewish furniture provided for Bech not very convincing, and also noted that, interested as Updike has always been in "how divinity works through

Gentiles," he shows no such curiosity as regards his Jewish hero. What novelistic need, then, did *Bech* serve? Noting the dominance of Jewish writers in the 1960s, Ozick recalls that some have suggested it was the example of Norman Mailer that "taunted" Updike into the "sexual adventurism" of *Couples*, and she wonders whether some analogous, "external" prompting may have helped generate *Bech*. Surely it's implausible to credit Mailer with provoking *Couples*, since small-town adultery had been central in Updike's work for some years. The question of what Bech himself calls the Jewish writer's "domination of the literary world" is equally impossible to establish as having stimulated him to write the Bech stories. There is no argument, to be sure, that a decade which, among other productions early on, saw Salinger's *Franny and Zooey*, Heller's *Catch-22*, Malamud's stories in *The Magic Barrel*, Bellow's *Herzog*, then closed itself with *Portnoy's Complaint* and *Mr. Sammler's Planet*, and that was seasoned throughout with Mailer's fictional and journalistic reports, might have inspired on Updike's part a can-you-top-this set of mind: let me, a Protestant, churchgoing exception to the literary rule, get into the act. Beyond that lies no profound explanation, other than that Updike, always looking to bring off something new and unexpected, managed to produce something not at all to be predicted on the strength of *Couples*. Nor is the Jewish motive the only one behind *Bech*; its formal high jinks — its mock foreword and appendices — remind us that Nabokov's *Lolita* and *Pale Fire*, as well as the metafictional playfulness of John Barth in his work from the 1960s, are also in the background. That the possibilities of free-floating, "authorial" commentary — the expression of strong opinions under the protective guise of a fictional character superficially unlike John Updike — proved attractive is shown by his returning to Bech later in his career, for two further collections. As he remarked in a 1975 interview, the Bech stories "did open, somehow, a door in me that hadn't opened before."[3] Another way to put it would be to say that Bech was as useful an alter ego to his creator as Rabbit had been and would be; both characters exist at greater distance from the writer than do the protagonists of *Marry Me* and *Couples*.

Rabbit Redux

It's arguable that the years 1968–73 were the most turbulent ones America had experienced since the Civil War, and these fireworks were visible in the arena of fiction, where the most significant reputations produced, if not their best work, work whose power to shock and entertain was undeniable. The novel (and nonfiction versions of it like Mailer's *Armies of the Night*) was the place to get America's news, the news William Carlos Williams once wrote that we were dying every day for lack of. Consider the following titles by some of our established fiction writers: Barth's *Lost in the Funhouse* (1968); *Portnoy's Complaint* (1969); Mr. *Sammler's Planet* (1970); Malamud's *The Tenants* (1971); E. L. Doctorow's *The Book of Daniel* (1971); Pynchon's *Gravity's Rainbow* (1973); add to them Mailer's reports on the 1968 political convention *(Miami and the Siege of Chicago)*, the space adventure *(Of a Fire on the Moon)*, and women's liberation *(The Prisoner of Sex)*. Robert Lowell's *Notebook* published in 1969 and in enlarged, revised form the succeeding year, was a further powerful attempt by the poetic imagination to take, among other things, contemporary American society and politics as a subject for unrhymed sonnets. At a lesser level of farce and travesty there was Roth's *Our Gang* (1971). Excess was the keynote, sometimes the excess of minimalist titles of forgotten novels from the period like *Superworm* or *Up* or *Saw* or *Quake*. On *Rowan and Martin's Laugh-In*, a popular television send-up of current events, there was a female character given to enthusiastic bursts of approval, such as "Wild" and "Far Out!" If inclined toward reading fiction, she would have so responded to many novels of the period.

Rabbit Redux stands in the middle of these years. Updike's account of its genesis is, as always, full and smoothly persuasive, if we accept that his decision to write a sequel to *Rabbit, Run* was a sudden rather than a long-considered one. With his projected novel about James Buchanan failing to declare itself, Updike said that he returned to the States from England and found himself, at the beginning of 1970, without a likely prospect for the novel he and his publisher had mutually agreed would alternate with his other (less profitable) books of poems, short stories, and criticism. So he proceeded to write the second Rabbit book, producing a finished typescript by April 1971 in time for Knopf to bring out the book later in the year. The cover jacket of *Rabbit Redux* was designed for catchy appeal: a flaglike full-page pattern of red, blue, and white (more like gray) stripes; a smallish moon in the upper-right-hand corner; a centered circle, cutting into the stripes, with book title and author's name in black and white; inside the jacket, a short blurb, surely written by Updike, with a dictionary definition of *redux*, then a paragraph gloss on the novel — "1969's lurid confusion of technology, fantasy, and emergency. Rabbit is abandoned and mocked, his home is invaded, the world of his childhood decays into a mere sublunar void; still he clings to semblances of patriotism and paternity." The note is aggressively protective of our hero, virtually turning him into a scapegoat who suffers but hangs on to things as best he can. Updike is frank, in the introduction to *Rabbit Angstrom*, in admitting that the protagonist served "as a receptacle for my disquiet and resentments, which would sit more becomingly on him than on me." More becomingly, of course, because literary people, sensitive and "liberal" ones certainly, were not supposed to harbor "low" motives and impulses such as unexamined patriotism, support of one's president in prosecution of an unjust war, or nervous feelings about racial minorities.

Updike called *Rabbit, Run* a "product" of the 1950s rather than being "about" them. With *Redux*, the emphasis moves toward "about" in that the diagnostic commentary — however crude we may feel the diagnosis to be at any specific moment — is largely directed at observable social facts in America, 1969. Perhaps the most significant of these facts was the emergence of black people from invisibility, and Rabbit registers their presence as he rides the bus home from his job at the linotype plant in Brewer to the suburban Penn Villas where he and Janice have a small house in a development:

> The bus has too many Negroes. Rabbit notices them more and
> more. They've been here all along, as a tiny kid he remembers

streets in Brewer you held your breath walking through, though they never hurt you, just looked; but now they're noisier. Instead of bald-looking heads they're bushy. That's O.K., it's more Nature, Nature is what we're running out of. . . . Read somewhere some anthropologist thinks Negroes instead of being more primitive are the latest thing to evolve, the newest men. In some ways tougher, in some ways more delicate. Certainly dumber but then being smart hasn't amounted to so much, the atom bomb and the one-piece aluminum beer can. And you can't say Bill Cosby's stupid.

It's Rabbit's attempt at fair-mindedness, his clumsy attempt at sympathy, that makes these reflections more than just crude. When in *Rabbit, Run* he caught the bus to Mt. Judge, having learned that his infant daughter had drowned, his thoughts were, understandably, more inward — he saw only his own mind. In *Redux* Updike allows him to be more relaxed, less existential, and thus more humorous, able to express his irritation at the "Negroes" in ways it would be unobservant simply to dismiss as racist:

> But against these educated tolerant thoughts leans a certain fear: he doesn't see why they have to be so noisy. The four seated right under him, jabbing and letting their noise come out in big silvery hoops; they know damn well they're bugging the fat Dutchy wives pulling their shopping bags home. Well that's kids of any color: but strange. They are a strange race.

It's Rabbit's somewhat detached observation of the annoyed "fat Dutchy wives" that saves this from racist cliché, even makes for a mind lively enough to inhabit. What will that mind think of next?

> It's as if, all these Afro hair bushes and gold earrings and hoopy noise on buses, seeds of some tropical plant sneaked in by the birds were taking over the garden. His garden. Rabbit knows it's his garden and that's why he's put a flag decal on the back window of the Falcon even though Janice says it's corny and fascist.

There follows a long paragraph in which, more objectively and with Updike's passion for naming and classifying visibly at work, the urban decay of West Brewer is surveyed, from Jimbo's Friendly Lounge to the West Brewer Dry Cleaners, to a toy store named Hobby Heaven, to a Rialto movie house featuring, on its "stubby marquee," "2001: SPACE OD'SEY". The survey continues on into mock-Tudor ranch house villages of Penn Park and eventually to Vista Crescent, Rabbit's street in Penn Villas.

Perhaps the most authentic and striking note of observation in *Rabbit Redux*, as the country makes its leap into space in quest of other worlds, concerns the urban world of cities like Brewer — stagnant, dying, still trying to breathe. In the novel's opening paragraph, Updike's handsome prose bids to assist that breath:

> but now in summer the granite curbs starred with mica and the row houses differentiated by speckled bastard sidings and the hopeful small porches with their jigsaw brackets and gray milk-bottle boxes and the sooty ginkgo trees and the baking curbside cars wince beneath a brilliance like a frozen explosion. The city, attempting to revive its dying downtown, has torn away blocks of buildings to create parking lots, so that a desolate openness, weedy and rubbled, spills through the once-packed streets, exposing church facades never seen from a distance and generating new perspectives of rear entryways and half-alleys, and intensifying the cruel breadth of the light.

The elegiac sense of things is sharpened by the way it directs us to something most of us, revisiting in the 1960s the "revived" cities of our youth, have experienced — something not seen before, shockingly revealed from a new perspective. *Rabbit Redux* is at its strongest, inevitably, when the poetry of urban blight and the pathos of attempted renewal are in the foreground; this gritty motif makes the hoopla of moon-venturing seem flashy and opportunistic by comparison, something other than human.

The note of stagnancy, decline, and diminishment in the landscape of Brewer is not merely particularized but extended to

American experience generally, through Harry's nostalgic take on things. In *Rabbit, Run*, the most eloquent of such moments occurs when Rabbit takes Nelson to the playground and "feels the truth: the thing that has left his life has left irrevocably; no search would recover it . . . it was here, beneath the town, in these smells and these voices, forever behind him." This moment of lyric poignancy, replayed in *Redux*, itself feels diminished, the feeling gone a bit sour. When Harry and his father-in-law take Nelson to a baseball game to see the Brewer Blasts, they are waved into a parking lot by "a little colored boy." Harry thinks "about America, it's still the only place," but the next paragraph begins with *but*:

> But something has gone wrong. The ball game is boring. The spaced dance of the men in white fails to enchant, the code beneath the staccato spurts of distant motion refuses to yield its meaning.

Although Harry's game was of course basketball, baseball is America's game, "a game whose very taste, of spit and dust and grass and sweat and leather and sun, was America." Yet "America" somehow isn't there this Saturday afternoon:

> Sitting behind first base between his son and his father-in-law, the sun resting on his thighs, the rolled-up program in his hand, Rabbit waits for this beauty to rise in him, through the cheers and the rhythm of innings, the traditional national magic, tasting of his youth; but something is wrong. The crowd is sparse, thinning out from a cluster behind the infield to fistfuls of boys sprawling on the grass seats sloped up from the outfield. Sparse, loud, hard: only the drunks, the bookies, the cripples, the senile, and the delinquents come out to the ball park on a Saturday afternoon.

After hearing someone catcall about a player, "Kill the black bastard!" Rabbit "yearns to protect the game from the crowd; the poetry of space and inaction is too fine, too slowly spun for them."

Updike not only protects Rabbit here, he allows him a sympathy and delicacy in his feelings that it would be hard for any mere individual baseball game, on a Saturday afternoon in 1969 or whenever, to live up to. It is all back there someplace, available only in memory: "The eight-team leagues of his boyhood have vanished with the forty-eight-star flag. The shortstops never chew tobacco any more." A harbinger of baseball as it has turned out decades later, this game goes on for too long, "with a tedious flurry of strategy." Although Nelson assures his grandfather that the game was "neat," Harry can read the boy's mind, knows that "the screen of reality is too big for the child," knows that he misses "television's running commentary, the audacious commercials." The sudden, painful realization of childhood's loss in *Rabbit, Run* has now become almost programmatic, to be expected. How could Nelson possibly be enthusiastic enough in his reponses to satisfy Harry? After all, he never heard of Rabbit Maranville and all those other tobacco-chewing shortstops.

As with *Rabbit, Run*, no other character really has a chance to compete with Harry's strong memory, guardian of his own past as well as Brewer's and Mt. Judge's, even — as with the baseball game — of America's. This is why the futuristic space adventure holds so little appeal for him; it can't be made to play a role in the great drama of what once *was*. But Updike, in the effort to avoid solipsism, works at developing, at least to some extent, other characters, especially Janice. Housebound and "dumb" in the first Rabbit book, she not only is allowed to run off and have an affair with Charlie Stavros, her coworker at Springer Motors, but is also given some private sexual feelings (she masturbates while Harry sleeps) and more lively, intelligent responses than she gets in *Rabbit, Run*. She has become, more or less, self-sufficient. Still, the central focus of energy is the mind of Harry Angstrom, a mind that Updike here and throughout the tetralogy devotes his full energies to impersonating. Eight years after *Redux* was published, Philip Roth's *The Ghost Writer* appeared, initiating Roth's Zuckerman sequence of novels. When asked by his *Paris Review* interviewer, Hermione Lee, what happened when he, Roth, turned into Zuckerman, the novelist replied:

> Nathan Zuckerman is an act. It's all the art of impersonation,
> isn't it? That's the fundamental novelistic gift. . . . Making fake
> biography, false history, concocting a half-imaginary existence
> out of the actual drama of my life *is* my life. There has to be
> some pleasure in this job, and that's it. To go around in dis-
> guise. To act a character. To pass oneself off as what one is not.
> To *pretend.*[4]

Admittedly the parallels between Roth and his fictional hero are
closer, since Zuckerman is a novelist who wrote a sensational best-
seller that sounds much like *Portnoy's Complaint*. But there is no
essential difference between Roth's relation to his character and
Updike's to Rabbit. The art of impersonation governs each.

What was controversial about *Rabbit Redux* when it appeared, and
I suspect is still a source of troubled dissatisfaction for some readers,
including this one, is the working out of story in which (in the
words from the jacket cover) "Rabbit is abandoned and mocked, his
home is invaded. . . ." The invaders are two: a young woman, Jill,
daughter of an affluent Wasp family, a runaway caught up in the
drug scene whom Rabbit takes into his house; and Skeeter, the
black, self-styled prophet who soon joins them and Nelson at Vista
Crescent — Janice having moved in with Stavros. The novel's second and third sections are titled respectively "Jill" and "Skeeter,"
and they trace an increasingly hectic atmosphere in which Skeeter
runs evening "teach-ins" on black history from slavery to Vietnam.
This highly verbal, teacherly activity is complemented by drug use
(Rabbit mildly participating), sex between Jill and Skeeter (more or
less forced by Skeeter, watched by Rabbit), and the eventual burning of the house, presumably by disapproving vigilante-type neighbors, on an evening when Rabbit and Nelson are elsewhere. In the
fire Jill dies; Skeeter, aided by Rabbit, flees town. A grim list of
events, which is not erased in the final section of the book when
Janice and Rabbit are reconciled.

If, as I suspect is the case, *Rabbit Redux* is the most problematic
novel in the tetralogy, it may have to do with Rabbit's strange wel-

coming passivity in the face of this invasion by aliens and his inability to do anything about forestalling or preventing the violence it provokes. Why should puzzlement at or disapproval of a fictional protagonist's behavior in any way be a ground for adverse judgment on the novel in which it occurs? Why, despite admiration for the virtuosity and range of *Redux*, does one have reservations about the overall product? The reasons are two, the first of which has already been broached in relation to *Couples* and to Updike's previous treatment of his male heroes. It has to do with the novelist's principled avoidance of appearing to "correct" or censure his characters, especially the central one. With *Couples* the difficulty of keeping Piet Hanema in focus had to do with his reckless, but also feckless, sexual adventuring, combined with his punitive theological explanation and condemnation of it ("We know God is not mocked," he tells Foxy). Rabbit Angstrom has access to no such religious vocabulary, but he is endowed, from moment to moment — as at the baseball game — with reflections that invite us to take him seriously as a human being. After all, how can you not sympathize with someone whose relation to putting up combination storm windows is presented as follows:

> You slide up the aluminum screen, putting the summer behind
> you, and squirt the inside window with the blue spray, give it
> those big square swipes to spread it thin, and apply the tighter
> rubbing to remove the film and with it the dirt; it squeaks, like
> birdsong. Then slide the winter window down from the slot
> where it has been waiting since April and repeat the process;
> and go inside and repeat the process, twice: so that at last four
> flawless transparencies permit outdoors to come indoors, other
> houses to enter yours.

(Updike is especially eloquent about old-fashioned, wooden-framed storm windows. "The Melancholy of Storm Windows" concludes by contrasting our human predicament with that of the windows — "Ambiguous, we have no place / where we, once screwed, can say, *That's* it.") Such a moment can either be understood as the author taking over — and admired or deplored as intrusive — or can be taken as yet one more aspect of the hero's responsiveness to things. If you do the latter, then Rabbit's acute *presence* in dealing with storm windows makes his *absence*, when dealing with Jill and especially with Skeeter, troubling, something we yearn to do something about — to shake him, wake him up, if not for his own sake then for that of his thirteen-year-old son. And in fact Rabbit's putting up of the windows occurs when things at Vista Crescent are about to burst into flames — when the house-burning is imminent.

In his negative review of *Redux* in the *New York Review of Books*, cleverly titled "Flopsy Bunny," Christopher Ricks unequivocally stated the case against Updike's treatment of his characters: "as a writer Updike is all mercy and no justice, his benignity so remorseless as to leave cruelties and oppressions, both personal and public, merely mentioned."[5] If this is too triumphantly said, on Ricks's part, it points to a real question about the novel: namely, whether its measure of its hero has been sufficiently taken. Updike does give Harry a moment of remorse in which, waking from a dream of Jill, he realizes her absence and "grief rises in him out of a parched stomach, a sore throat, singed eyes" — and he weeps. But that is it, as far as second thoughts go; indeed, one can barely call them thoughts. Rabbit's memory, so vividly poignant when directed at natural transience and decline, as in the yearly ritual of window-preparation, doesn't seem to involve what Eliot in "Little Gidding" called "the rending pain of re-enactment / Of all that you have done, and been . . . the awareness / Of things ill done and done to others' harm." A voice might counter, why should Updike compete with Eliot in the guilt sweepstakes? Yet Rabbit's awareness of others seems, to say the least, deficient, and Updike lets him off pretty easily, Nelson's recriminations to his father notwithstanding.

Critical opinion of the novel was most divided about the third, "Skeeter," section, which consists of a number of performing monologues by the black prophet as he instructs, and, in more than one sense, "turns on" his rapt listeners — Rabbit, Nelson, and Jill. What did Updike know about black revolutionary rhetoric of the sort

Skeeter spouts? Isn't this improbable character, made up out of newspaper accounts of African-American rhetoric in the late 1960s, a parodic simplification of any "real" black militant? Don't the chunks of American history, served up by an impassioned revision-ist, feel undigested and go on for too long? Yet Updike has brought much together here, made the attempt to write about what was hap-pening under our eyes and ears as we watched the Vietnam War on TV, or shook our heads over riots in the cities and the universities. Skeeter is a voice, and Updike's ventriloquizing it, his impersonat-ing of it, is never less than resourceful. One instance may suffice, as Skeeter answers Rabbit's earnest question, "Is our being in Vietnam wrong?" with the following:

> Wrong? Man, how can it be wrong when that's the way it is? These poor Benighted States just being themselves, right? Can't stop bein' yourself, somebody has to do it for you, right? Nobody that big around. Uncle Sam wakes up one morning, looks down at his belly, sees he's some cockroach, what can he do? Just keep bein' his cockroach self, is all. Till he gets stepped on. No such shoe right now, right? Just keep doing his cock-roach thing. I'm not one of those white lib-er-als like that cracker Fulldull or that Charlie McCarthy a while back gave all the college queers a hard-on, think Vietnam some sort of mis-take, we can fix it up once we get the cave men out of office, it is *no* mistake, right, any President comes along falls in love with it, it is lib-er-al-ism's very wang and ding-dong pussy.

There may be a trace in this of Mailer's black disc jockey who gave us the news in *Why Are We in Vietnam?* (1967), and Skeeter is espe-cially inventive in his renaming of white "lib-er-als" such as "John Kennel Badbreath and Leonard Birdbrain." Much of what animates the Updike/Skeeter show is the novelist's own dissatisfaction with white liberal anti-Vietnam feeling, while the fatalism with which Skeeter responds to Rabbit's question about the morality of Vietnam has its analogue in Updike's sympathy with the embattled Lyndon Johnson and his stubborn sense that once committed there was no way out of Vietnam except to push ahead. (One remembers the comedian Tom Smothers risking trouble with his producers by singing, on his television show, "We're waist-deep in the Big Muddy, / The big fool says to push on.") In a similar way, there is no stopping Skeeter, and when Nelson cries to his father, witnessing Skeeter's treatment of Jill, "He'll *kill* her Dad," Harry responds, inadequately, with "No he won't. He's just high. She's all right." When Skeeter calls himself "The Christ of the new Dark Age" and asks Rabbit, "Do you believe?", the latter, dragging on a joint, replies, "I do believe." (Waist-deep in the Big Muddy, the big fool says to push on.) Whatever *belief* means here is impossible to say; but to be ruthlessly literary about it, the reason Rabbit doesn't stop Skeeter and lets him proceed to the final disaster and death is that the novelist wants to squeeze everything he can get out of his Skeeter impersonation. Issues of morality, fictional "justice," any attempt to draw the line and say thus far and no farther are as nothing compared to the manic invention that fuels things for the configuration. In that sense, *Rabbit Redux* is a ruthless book.

In fact, squeezing everything that can be gotten out of his material is especially characteristic of Updike's performance in the novel, where everything is seen in terms of everything else. Christopher Ricks pointed out what was well known already, that Updike is "exceptionally observant," though Ricks thinks that the novel "shows the severe limits which are set to a work of art that commits itself so unremittingly to being observant." But it's not that the problem is too much observation; rather, what makes for uneasiness, more than once in the book, is a too-ready propensity to reach for multisignificance by fusing disparate, "contemporary" orders of event. So when Janice and Rabbit make desperate love after she confesses her affair with Stavros (and before she departs to live with him), it's not just lovemaking that goes on in their bedroom:

> To help them see when darkness comes, Janice turns on the
> television set without sound, and by the bluish flicker of mod-
> ule models pantomiming flight, of riot troops standing before

smashed supermarkets, of a rowboat landing in Florida having
crossed the Atlantic, of situation comedies and western melo-
dramas, of great gray momentary faces unstable as quicksilver,
they make love again, her body a stretch of powdery sand, her
mouth a loose black hole, her eyes holes with sparks in them,
his own body a barren landscape lit by bombardment, silently
exploding images no gentler than Janice's playful expert
touches, that pass through him and do him no harm.

The imperial ambition to synthesize — by the novelist's own playful, expert touches — love, war, and extraterrestrial exploration
results in prose that somehow passes through the reader without
effecting the kinds of emotional resonances it aspires to. "The barren landscape lit by bombardment" (Mailer's *Of a Fire on the Moon*
had appeared the previous year) threatens to swallow up the merely
human characters. The novelist may have wanted it that way, but
the novel sometimes feels like more of a three-ring circus than is
good for its representation of a human drama. As usual, Updike
anticipated and went about incorporating or defusing such criticism
by marking, in the preface to *Rabbit Angstrom,* the 1960s as a decade
most "violent and bizarre": thus "the possibly inordinate emphasis
on sexual congress — and enthusiastic mixture of instruction man-
ual and de Sadeian ballet — also partakes of the times."

In that preface he also claimed that Rabbit's crossing of the "color
line," in his interaction with Skeeter, constitutes a "tortured form of
progress." But, always wary of making explicit claims for what the
hero has "learned," the novelist hedges round that progress with
hesitations and qualifications. In the book's concluding section,
Harry's sister Mim — a professional courtesan, American syle —
comes home for a visit and asks her big brother about the meaning
of what he's been through recently. Harry tells her, "I learned some
things," and when Mim asks, "Anything worth knowing," he
replies, "I learned I'd rather fuck than be blown" — to which Mim
says that it sounds "healthy," "rather unAmerican though." Then,
trying to become serious, he tells her that as a result of the reading

sessions and discussions with Skeeter, he has learned that his country wasn't and isn't perfect. But immediately there follows: "Even as he says this he realizes he doesn't believe it, any more than he believes at heart that he will die." This is surely the verbal equivalent of Rabbit running, yet once more, away from any claim for maturing wisdom, for accepting decline and imperfection in either his country or himself. When, in the novel's final paragraph, Rabbit and Janice, reconciled more or less, rent a motel room for a little reacquaintance (they fail to have sex), he confesses to her that he feels guilty "about everything." Janice tells him to relax, that not everything is his fault, to which he replies, "I can't accept that." But that's as far as he goes in the moral redirection game, as Updike the writer takes over, framing the now landed couple in the space theater of the book: "He lets her breasts go, lets them float away, radiant debris. The space they are in, the motel room long and secret as a burrow, becomes all interior space." Nestling against Janice, "He finds this inward curve and slips along it, sleeps. He, She. Sleeps. O.K.?" This mischievous ending, in the monosyllabic way each novel in the tetralogy ends, is especially teasing here because it is directed at the reader rather than the couple. How does one take in, let alone speak back to, the voice (is it even, now, a voice?) of a narrator who ends his novel with "O.K.?" It reads like an ending that's not an ending but rather a short sleep of ten or so years when Rabbit will wake up again.

SIX

**IMPERSONATIONS
OF MEN IN TROUBLE (II)**

A *Month of Sundays* • Short Fiction 1967–79

Updike's father, Wesley, died in 1972; two years later his son and Mary separated, with Updike taking an apartment in Boston. In 1976 they were divorced and he moved to Georgetown, Massachusetts; the following year he and Martha Bernhard would be married. Near the end of the story "Separating," published in 1975, the protagonist, Richard Maple, tells his son Dickie that he and Joan are about to separate. In a guilty agony he assures the boy, "I hate this. *Hate* it. My father would have died before doing it to me." It seems likely that the death of Wesley Updike may have made at least marginally easier his son's decision to separate and divorce. At any rate Updike's writings from this period are heavy with the whiff of promises betrayed, an old thing coming to its end, a new thing trying to bloom in its aftermath. *Marry Me*, finally published in the year of his divorce, had imagined, when written more than a decade earlier, its possibility; the Maples stories, some of which appeared in the 1960s, five more in the final section of *Museums and Women* (1972), had brought a couple's marriage to its breaking point. Their divorce became final in "Here Come the Maples" (1976) — along with "Separating," the richest and deepest of the Maples stories. These two were collected with earlier Maples ones in *Too Far to Go* (1979); related postseparation and postdivorce stories, published in the later 1970s, appeared in *Problems* (also 1979), a further collection of short fiction.

A Month of Sundays

In the middle of these years A Month of Sundays (1975) provided a most intemperate and mischievous account of a minister undone from marriage and society by his adulteries, even as he celebrates them aggressively and outrageously in a flamboyant literary style. The novel received decidedly mixed responses from its reviewers; in fact, of the books Updike published between 1969 and 1976, only *Bech: A Book* and *Rabbit Redux* were really well received. The poems from *Midpoint* generated little attention; the stories in *Museums and Women* were treated as effective, yet familiar, treatments of old themes; the play *Buchanan Dying* received a percipient review from the historian Arthur Schlesinger Jr., but was largely ignored; and *Marry Me* was judged as failing to measure up to earlier work. A *Month of Sundays* brought out especially strong distaste from one female reviewer, who called upon this "enormously charming" writer to "take himself more seriously and forgo the tricks of his trade — titillation, verbal pyrotechnics, philosophical chicanery, and factitious mushy theologizing."[1] She urged readers to say "No, No" to its repetitive sexual encounters and obsessively named anatomical parts.

Unlike *Marry Me*, whose mode was lyrical and comic, A *Month of Sundays* is polemical and provocative, indeed is meant to provoke, and its comedy is harsher than any previously encountered in Updike. One instance by way of illustration: when the disgraced minister, Tom Marshfield, retraces for us the steps by which he came to sleep with and eventually marry the daughter of Dr. Chillingworth, his divinity-school professor of ethics, we learn that

> Jane was slow to say she loved me. Of her virginity (a mere wet inch away) she said she should "save herself." For some other? As the logical positivists thought to end human confusion by careful reference to the dictionary (see C. L. Stevenson, *Ethics and Language*, 1944, and the final text Chillingworth assigned), I introduced the word "marriage." Jane nodded, silently. I saw her as "wife"* and went blind with pride.

The asterisk in the last sentence directs us to the bottom of the page where we find, "The word, by the way, is just the Anglo-Saxon *wif*, for 'woman.' My wife, *ma femme*, this cunt indentured to me. Sad to say, lib-lubbers." Here is coattailing of a most aggressive kind, flaunting the early rhetoric of women's liberation ("I want to be treated as a person, not a sexual object") by converting wife to indentured body part in a thumbing-the-nose footnote.

Does Updike invite or expect us to be critical of, detached from, his "I" narrator? Does he hold his protagonist, Tom Marshfield, in some sort of ironic perspective? The question could be raised about any passage in the book, and with equal uselessness. Updike's impersonation of a rogue minister, sent away into a wilderness "retreat" somewhere in the Southwest and instructed to write himself into some sort of stocktaking, *is* what the book is about. There is no way a reader, caught up in the verbal surface fireworks, can separate the nasty-clever, fast-talking wordman who turns out these diary pages from the creator who authorizes them. That is, except for our own moral sense (admittedly an important "except"), there is no available "depth" of corrective second thought to act as an ironic check on the excesses and indecorums of the sentences as they flash past. An epigraph from Paul Tillich, "This principle of soul, universally and individually, is the principle of ambiguity," provides the principle out of which this novel is written. The other epigraph from Psalm 45 — "my tongue is the pen of a ready writer" — proves itself on every page of the "sheaf of blank sheets" with which Marshfield is provided, his only task being to "sully" them.

It is the essence of this ready writer to give his tongue, his pen, the typewriter provided him by his "keepers," the freest rein, indeed to flog these instruments into nonstop verbal play:

> The month is to be one of recuperation — as I think of it, "retraction," my condition being officially diagnosed as one of "distraction." Perhaps the opposite of "dis" is not "re" but the absence of any prefix, by which construal I am spiritual brother to those broken-boned athletes who must spend a

> blank month, amid white dunes and midnight dosages, in "traction." I doubt (verily, my name is Thomas) it will work. In my diagnosis I suffer from nothing less virulent than the human condition, and so would preach it.

Such reflexive energies make even Nabokov (in *Lolita* and *Pale Fire*) pale by comparison, and make also for a patent unreality of "realistic" character about the Reverend Marshfield. This is not a mark against the novel, necessarily, although insofar as *A Month of Sundays* aspires to say something about "the human condition," it risks obfuscating any such saying by its overbearing, twitching, linguistic antennae. At any rate, Marshfield's incorrigibility is built fully into every sentence of his narrative; readers who can't stand the verbal heat had better not even enter the kitchen.

His supervisor at the desert retreat — and the female presence to whom, along with the reader, his pages are addressed — is a Ms. Prynne; his wife's maiden name was Chillingworth. The allusions to Hawthorne, which will be extended in two later novels of the "trilogy" (*Roger's Version* and *S*), are strongly foregrounded. Given Updike's admiration for Hawthorne as a writer and man of letters (his essay "Hawthorne's Creed" was first delivered as a lecture in 1979), the connection invites attention, which it has received from more than one critic.[2] Certainly it is possible to stress filiations between the writers by thinking of the adulterous minister's tale as representing Dimmesdale's version of things, to be juxtaposed with Chillingworth's and Hester's in the novels to come. And since Updike has spoken of Hawthorne as the most important (almost the only) nineteenth-century American novelist of heterosexual relations, there are historical and cultural continuities. Yet for this reader only a feat of abstraction makes it possible to think about *The Scarlet Letter* while reading *A Month of Sundays*, since there is no relation — except that of forcible reaction in a quite different mode — between Hawthorne's measured, even plodding way of moving through his narrative and Updike's mercurial, wised-up performance. Although parallels have been noted — Dimmesdale at his looking glass, Marshfield at his mirror — the stylistic disparity between the novels is so great that comparison seems willful. In a similar vein, it does not seem useful to suppose that one of Marshfield's women — his wife Jane; the organist, Alicia Crooke, with whom he first betrays Jane; Frankie Harlow, a member of the congregation with whom he is impotent; or the mythical Ms. Prynne to whom he addresses his desert epistles — "is," or at some moment is like, Hawthorne's Hester Prynne.

Each Sunday in this month of Sundays, Marshfield, deprived of his parish pulpit, works all the harder to preach in his pages a dazzling sermon, the first of which takes as its text a moment in John's gospel when Jesus says to the woman taken in adultery, "Neither do I condemn thee." He also tells her, "Go and sin no more," words not quoted by Marshfield. The omission is significant, since the whole sermon is an example of what Samuel Johnson called talking for victory. In a novel whose principle is ambiguity, the sermon is quite unambiguous in its spirited, ingenious, and deliberately perverse defense of adultery as the vehicle by which American men and women recover their sense of worth. The tone of Marshfield's delivery assumes that there are no ifs, ands, or buts about the matter — that his argument is delivered "verily":

> Verily, the sacrament of marriage, as instituted in its adamant impossibility by our Saviour, exists but as a precondition for the sacrament of adultery. To the one we bring token reverence, and wooden vows; to the other a vivid reverence bred upon the carnal presence of the forbidden, and vows that rend our hearts as we stammer them. The sheets of the marriage bed are interwoven with the leaden threads of eternity; the cloth of the adulterous couch with the glowing, living filaments of transience, of time itself, our element, our only element. . . .

This brilliant writing is employed in the service of a simple message: "We *are* an adulterous generation; let us rejoice."

Marshfield should know, since he is no garden-variety adulterer but came to it robed in ecclesiastical garments. Later in the book he admits that, yes, he did sleep with a few of his female parishioners "by way of being helpful." An empty church was an especially commodious place to conduct such activity, and Updike's own fondness for the physical insides of churches has been celebrated elsewhere (see especially "The Deacon" in *Museums and Women*). Marshfield feelingly evokes the church as "a hushed, capacious treasure of accommodating nooks: the robing room, smelling of clean linen and old paper; the nap mats in the Sunday-school nursery; the ladies' parlor with its Oriental rug and lockable door; my office with its rather sticky and sneeze-inducing horsehair sofa." He admits to never having tried, with a partner, "the nave and its pews," but is impressed by "how unfussily these seducing women sought out the scrotal concealed in the sacerdotal, how intuitively religious was their view of sex." To top it all off, he invites us to contemplate the grandeur he has experienced when, presiding at the communion rail, he has placed a wafer "between the parted lips of a mouth that, earlier in the very week of which this was the Sabbath day, had received one's throbbingly ejaculated seed."

This is writing designed to make all but the most accepting (or blasé) readers wonder if it's not over the line, whether it doesn't exceed the bounds of, violate the canons of taste. But what can the principle of taste (good taste?) have to say about that throbbingly ejaculated seed taken in by parted lips? For the moment, Marshfield is indulging himself in an imitation of porn dressed up in oh-so-literary garments. Nabokov's Humbert admonishes us never to trust a murderer with a fancy prose style; Updike's sinister minister is likewise a fetcher from far of tropes that all too perfectly answer, on every page, to the fetcher's pursuit of *le mot juste*. The self-enclosedness of the whole operation, brilliant as it is, can be off-putting as well, although as usual Updike has anticipated such a complaint by telling an interviewer that he wanted to make the book "kind of offensive and abrasive."[3] This remark, applied to any of his earlier books, would make absolutely no sense; it is forward-looking in that it will apply to more than one of the novels to come — especially to *Roger's Version* and *Toward the End of Time*.

Rather than its offensive and abrasive atmosphere and tone, what really prevents A *Month of Sundays* from being something more than a virtuoso display of manic — sometimes mean — high spirits directed at various targets is Updike's inability to live up to his own best motives. For in the same sentence from the interview in which he brings out the style's capacity to give offense, he said also that his aim was "to show a life in a human being whose profession demands that he stand up at least on Sunday and try to give other people reason to keep on living." This motive sounds conventional enough, also sympathetic, inviting us to find in the novel something admirably positive, even heroic, in its portrayed life of a clergyman. But unless I have seriously missed it, that life can't be found in the actual book Updike wrote, whose hero seems to conceive of other people, whether or not he's sleeping with them, in wholly two-dimensional terms: they are described and analyzed only as they do or don't serve Tom Marshfield's purposes at any moment. There is no disinterestedness in him, nothing of the "witness" a serious minister might be expected to bear. Marshfield, in fact, is less a clergyman than a lively and resourceful novelist, in as satiric a novel as Updike would ever write.

I should say that the "positive" and three-dimensional aspects of a minister who tries "to give other people reason to keep on living" simply can't fit into a novel as ironic and self-corrective, as verbally active in its behavior as A *Month of Sundays*. The only "third dimension" — and a very large one, admittedly — is the dimension of language so central to its every page. In line with these motives, the novel becomes in its conclusion even more self-reflexive than it was earlier on, when Marshfield, preparing to pack up and leave his desert retreat, speculates on the events that brought him there and the pages he has produced as penitential atonement for those events. He asks Ms. Prynne, his ideal reader, to forgive him for "preaching out of season," and tells her that he is "not only a sinner but a somewhat cheerful one" — a "clown," but one who has been cruel to his wife. And he entertains the question that, surely, Updike in 1975 had given more than a month's thought to: "When is it right for a man to leave his wife?" Marshfield answers it thus: "When the sum of his denied life overtops the calculated loss of the children, the grandparents if surviving, the dog, and the dogged *ux.*, known as Fido, residual in himself." What begins as a large, eloquently presented question about marital separation, considered and answered in as good a way as any to answer it, concludes with the witty verbal move from dog to "dogged *ux.*, known as Fido, residual in himself." In other words, the clown's language is such that it encourages, nay provokes, irrepressible cheer to break in on the uncheerful reflection.

As the book prepares to end, Marshfield frames his foregoing pages in a summary manner that suggests the archetypical or universal aspect of its theme:

> Not, you say, a very edifying or conclusive narrative. A man publicly pledged to goodness and fidelity scorns his wife, betrays one mistress, is ompotent* with another, exploits the trust and unhappiness of some who come to him for guidance, regards his father and his sons as menacing foreign objects, and through it all evinces no distinct guilt but rather a sort of scrabbling restiveness, a sense of events as a field of rubble in which he is empowered to search for some mysterious treasure.

The telling detail here is that the minister has experienced, out of the whole process, "no distinct guilt" — "scrabbling restiveness" rather, of the sort suggested by the asterisk after "ompotent," taking us to the bottom of the page where the verbal "slip" leads to play with omnipotence and potency and an allusion to Meister Eckhardt's reflections on the subject. The "mysterious treasure" for which this unguilty-feeling man is in search is to be discovered, time and again, in the treasure of words he exploits. Against this consuming activity, the claims of wife, mistress, father, and sons are decidedly subordinate.

So it is unsurprising that Ms. Prynne, his "keeper" at the resort — whom he has been wooing by leaving his written pages where she can read and, he hopes, improve them — knocks on his doors and proceeds to give herself to him. Or is that what happens? (Updike has noted that "Ms. Prynne" is very close to "misprint.") She is experienced at "lightly drawing my penis up into its ideal shape," but was the outcome similarly ideal? "Was I worthy? You have brought me to an edge, a slippery edge. And nothing left for me to do, dear Ideal Reader, but slip and topple off, gratefully." The book ends with an address to each of us as potentially Ideal Reader, an address that is grandly and vaguely universal: "What is it, this human contact, this blank-browed thing we do for one another?" A question not to be answered, any more than is the "O.K.?" that ended *Rabbit Redux*. But the writing becomes extremely lyrical:

> There was a moment, when I entered you, and was big, and you were already wet, when you could not have seen yourself, when your eyes were all for another, looking up into mine, with an expression without a name, of entry and alarm, and of saluta-tion. I pray my own face, a stranger to me, saluted in turn.

That odd usage — "I pray my own face" — and the uncertain status of "saluted" in the final sentence bid to take the Reverend Marshfield, if he hasn't been taken out of it already, away from any possibly adverse judgment in human and moral terms. Perhaps it is a sentence that only an Ideal Reader can understand; at any rate, an imperfect "real" reader like this one feels both uplifted and baffled. But we remember our Tillich from the epigraph: "This principle of soul, universally and individually, is the principle of ambiguity," noting also that we are dealing with an other, a presence, a speaker whose "tongue is the pen of a ready writer."

Short Fiction: 1967–1979

Midpoint; Bech: A Book; Rabbit Redux; A Month of Sundays — each of these works has its individually distinct form through which Updike's impersonations of men, in trouble of one sort of another, find embodiment. But the consummate art he produced at this mid-point period in his life — from roughly age thirty-five to forty-five — is to be found in his short fiction, specifically those stories whose protagonist is a man coming to the end of his marriage, separating from wife and children, living alone while visiting both wife and lover, eventually divorcing and remarrying. These stories include the final five from *Museums and Women,* grouped under a rubric "The Maples," and ten to fifteen others, published during the 1970s, that found book form in *Problems* and in *Too Far to Go* (subtitled *"The Maples Stories"*). In dedicating *Problems* to his four children, Updike speaks of "the curve of sad time it subtends"; yet the fictional art of these tales, however weighted toward the comic or the more grave, shows the writer at his most inventively alive, bristling with implication, complication, and, indeed, love.

"Snowing in Greenwich Village," first of the Maples stories, published in 1959, ended with Richard's almost-sexual encounter with Rebecca Cune, a friend of the Maples whom he has walked home after they've entertained her: "Oh but they were close" — Richard's concluding reflection — is, when looked back on from the vantage point of the stories to come, the beginning of the end of a marriage. But closeness is in many ways the essential fact of all these stories. The Maples stay close to home, and except for a visit abroad ("Twin Beds in Rome") their limit of awayness is Boston, reached in an hour or less by car or train. Richard and Joan go there occasionally (for him, reluctantly) to give blood ("Giving Blood") or to march in a civil rights demonstration ("Marching through Boston"). We know that he works in Boston because (in "Eros Rampant") he takes his secretary, Penelope Vogel, to lunch and a possible affair that doesn't materialize. Richard — unlike Joey Robinson *(Of the Farm)* or Jerry Conant *(Marry Me),* both of whom have barely specified jobs in the business and commercial world — is identified and characterized by no nameable work. He's always around the house, either on a weekend, or on a weekday when he has a cold ("Your Lover Just Called"). The Maples' closeness is centrally that of a couple, of a family; typically they spend their time talking to each other, after the party guests have gone home ("The Red-Herring Theory"), about those guests and their possible sexual affiliations. They go to lots of parties but, unlike in *Couples,* these parties aren't described — it's the verbal aftermath that counts. Most interestingly, perhaps surprisingly for the author of Couples, there is, aside from the occasional embrace (between Richard and Eleanor Dennis in "The Taste of Metal" or Joan and Mack Dennis in "Eros Rampant") no physical lovemaking to be observed. It seems to be going on, and quite a bit of it, but not in the Maples' bedroom, nor outside it as far as represented in these pages.

Though not officially one of the Maples stories (the separated couple in it have different names from Richard and Joan), "Domestic Life in America" can serve as an appropriate title for the whole group: assuming, that is, a reader who accepts that domestic life in 1970s America is a life of separation and divorce, in which a man shuttles between wife, mistress, and two sets of children. This man repairs a lock, buries the household dog, or helps his teenage son with geometry. At crucial moments in the stories he is presented alone with his "separated" thoughts, which on occasion make a bid for visionary status. At the end of "Domestic Life in America" Fraser, the first of Updike's divorcing protagonists whose last name begins with F, returns to Boston on the train after a weekend spent with his wife and two of their children, his wife-to-be and three of hers. It is bitter cold as he walks home across Boston Common to his small apartment on Beacon Hill:

> In his life alone, he welcomed discomfort, as somehow justifying him. The trees in the Common had been festooned with their Christmas strands, but they were unlit. There seemed no life afoot but his, no spark of life but the image cupped in his head of his apartment, his room-and-a-half, its askew rug and unmade bed, its dirty windows and beckoning warmth. Proceeding toward this domestic vision numbly, he crossed the lagoon bridge in the Public Garden, dividing a lunar perfection down the middle. On either side of him, his walking rolled smears of light across the icy whiteness. Above Beacon Hill, in the general direction of his lawyer's, an electric sign announced in alternation, remarkably, 10:01

and 10°. Fraser regretted there was no one with him to help witness this miracle.

The moment is saved from self-pity by its humor, at once sly and grim (what kind of "miracle" is this, anyway?), as well as by the always fully specified particularities of the man's bachelor life, leaving his bed unmade as visible sign of discomfort and guilt.

It is doubtful that the Maples stories and their related successors in *Problems* can affect readers at this century's close with the force they did in the 1970s, even though they remain, I'm convinced, no less powerful as art. Back then they struck us as important news, to be found, for example, in the second paragraph of "Separating": "Years ago the Maples had observed how often, among their friends, divorce followed a dramatic home improvement, as if the marriage were making one last effort to live; their own worst crisis had come amid the plaster dust and exposed plumbing of a kitchen renovation." This truth may have true before 1970, but registered as such to me only then and in immediate years afterward as I observed friends and acquaintances, usually though not always male, moving out from the spousal nest into one or another underfurnished place, sometimes indeed after a quite ambitious "dramatic home improvement" had been made or attempted. Returning from England in the summer of 1969 with three children to an undersized house, my wife and I decided to effect such a home improvement by way of enlarging things. Unlike the Maples, we survived our own worst crises, but the scene around us looked like a different one from what we were used to. These and related disruptions, it was said, were products of "the sexual revolution," the freedom provided by the pill, and the women's movement that seemed inevitably to follow upon it. When had gossip, the revelations of who had left whom and for whom, ever been so interesting? This is the domestic life in America Updike writes about, and it was surely the product of something larger than one writer's self-absorbed fantasies.

It would be wrong, however, to presume that, because Updike refers to "the curve of sad time" in which these stories are located and which they render in words, the fictional upshot is mainly grave, sober, "sad." Rather than sentimentalizing Richard Maple, Updike presents him as often an unpleasant, even nasty fellow, vain, self-regarding, and unfeeling as, miserable with a cold and having marched through Boston, he lies in bed mocking out loud the rhetoric of King and Abernathy by crudely and cruelly imitating the voice of the enslaved ("Ah kin heeah de singin' an' de banjos an' de cotton balls a-bustin'"). Above all else, Richard is a tease, especially of his less playful spouse, and the brittle comedy in the earlier Maples stories, such as "Your Lover Just Called" or "Eros Rampant," has his demanding selfishness at their center. Yet like Updike's other male protagonists, Richard is granted the power of shaping a moment into something artful, indeed artistic. In "Your Lover Just Called," after Richard and Joan spar with one another about what or whose possible lover it might have been on the phone, Richard ventures out to purchase cigarettes and bitter lemon, preparatory to having drinks with the recently separated Mack Dennis (in whose wife's arms Richard had ended up, having crashed his car, in "The Taste of Metal"). Returning, he looks in the kitchen windows and sees Mack and Joan, drinks having already been poured, in an embrace, kissing. But Richard sees a lot more than improper conduct:

> Behind them an open cabinet door revealed a paralyzed row of erect paper boxes whose lettering Richard could not read but whose coloring advertised their contents — Cheerios, Wheat Honeys, Onion Thins. Joan backed off and ran her index finger down the length of Mack's necktie (a summer tartan), ending with a jab in the vicinity of his navel that might have expressed a rebuke or a regret. . . . The scene had the fascinating slow motion of action underwater, mixed with the insane silent suddenness of a television montage glimpsed from the street.

He keeps on looking, sees his eldest daughter come to the upstairs window, unaware that he is watching, scratching her armpit while she studies a moth beating on her window screen. These happenings "gave Richard a momentous sense, crowding his heart, of having been brought by the mute act of witnessing — like a child sitting alone at the movies — perilously close to the hidden machinations of things." Obviously, one might say, he has X-ray vision, the poet's gift (or curse) of reading an armpit, a moth, some Cheerios and related foods in "erect paper boxes" that are also "paralyzed." In *Middlemarch* George Eliot reminds us that it is our good fortune to walk around with ears "well-wadded with stupidity"; otherwise we should hear the squirrel's heartbeat and the grass growing, sensations that would cause us to die from the "roar on the other side of silence." There is a similar motive at work here in Richard's intense perception of "the hidden machinations of things."

In his foreword Updike speaks of the couples' relation to one another as a "musical pattern" that as their separation approaches is "ever more harshly transposed." But in the climactic "Separating" harshness itself is transposed into something sadder and more impersonal; the overall tone and atmosphere of things has a fullness congruent with Updike's sense of marriage as a mixed blessing. The story's opening three sentences, handsomely directed and varied in length, introduce us to the long-awaited, long-postponed day of reckoning:

> The day was fair. Brilliant. All that June the weather had mocked the Maples' internal misery with solid sunlight — golden shafts and cascades of green in which their conversations had wormed unseeing, their sad murmuring selves the only stain in Nature.

The plan has been to defer news of Richard's leaving until the four children are assembled and can be told in turn, more or less from eldest to youngest. Richard, occupied with "battening down the house against his absence," attends to various repairs while Updike's prose establishes another sense of "separating" — removing the barrier Richard and his wife have held against their children's knowing: "Each moment was a partition, with the past on one side and the future on the other, a future containing this unthinkable now." He feels his new future waiting there for him, someplace "beyond four knifelike walls," and — in language it's impossible to imagine Richard using about himself or even "thinking" — we're told that "His skull cupped a secret, a white face, a face both frightened and soothing, both strange and known, that he wanted to shield from tears." So the battening down of things, the "purposeful desolation" with which he performs his tasks of repair, even as he prepares to break things apart, is given a metaphorical, poetic force that can't easily be translated into nameable meanings.

Things break apart at the supper table when Richard finds himself in tears that pour out uncontrollably. But this potentially sentimental scene in which the floodgates are unlocked is cagily preceded by a wonderful paragraph devoted to his efforts, eventually successful, to replace the lock to a door on the screened porch, "deliberately rendered obsolete by manufacturers":

> Another hole had to be gouged, with bits too small and saws too big, and the old hole fitted with a block of wood — the chisels dull, the saw rusty, his fingers thick with lack of sleep. The sun poured down, beyond the porch, on a world of neglect. The bushes already needed pruning, the windward side of the house was shedding flakes of paint, rain would get in when he was gone, insects, rot, death. His family, all those he would lose, filtered through the edges of his awareness as he struggled with screw holes, splinters, opaque instructions, minutiae of metal.

(Updike later wrote a sonnet, "Enemies of a House," which names those enemies, beginning with dry rot and concluding with "voracious ivy; frost heaves; splintering; / carpenter ants; adultery; drink; death.") So when at the table Richard's tears suddenly come, they have as antecedent the strenuous particularity of repair that was supposed to hold against such collapses of partition:

> The tears would not stop leaking through; they came not through a hole that could be plugged but through a permeable spot in a membrane, steadily, purely, endlessly, fruitfully. They became, his tears, a shield for himself against these others. . . .

> Tears dropped from his nose as he broke the lobster's back; salt
> flavored his champagne as he sipped it; the raw clench at the
> back of his throat was delicious. He could not help himself.

Everything has come unlocked, but the writing does something
other than invite us to wallow in Richard's tears; after all, he admits
that the "raw clench" (fine word, *clench*) is "delicious," champagne
mixed with tears in a way that makes grief not only grief but also satisfying in its taste. "He could not help himself": the cliché is here
re-created, made strong and poised in its active affirmation of passion, of passivity.

The scene turns into a parody of itself when fourteen-year-old
John interrupts his parents' mollifying attempt to explain their
actions and immediate future plans by crying, "We're just little
things you *had*," then responds to his father's denial by breaking a
cigarette in half and stuffing it in his mouth. Richard leads the boy
outside, and they walk hand in hand past the recently built tennis
court, a dramatic home improvement. John confesses his unhappiness at school and Richard holds out the possibility of transfer:
"They had said what they could, but did not want the moment to
heal, and talked on. . . ." Eventually they return to the house to find
the three females amiably drinking white wine, getting along all
right, it seems, without Father. But as Joan reminds Richard, his task
is not yet completed; he must tell their older son the news after
Dickie returns from a rock concert in Boston. This Richard proceeds to do, his heart heavy as he meets the 1:14 A.M. train. Dickie
seems to take what his father calls the "sad news" pretty equably,
asks Richard about how the other children took it, laughs when he
hears of John's antics. Then, in his longest burst of speech, Richard
tells the boy how much he hates doing this, how the last hour has
been the worst of his life, how (in the assertion quoted earlier) *his*
father would never have done this to him. But as with the supper-
table tears, that admission is placed in wider perspective by three
brief sentences that follow: "He felt immensely lighter, saying this.
He had dumped the mountain on the boy. They were home."

Yet it is not to be so smoothly effected, this news of separation. When Dickie goes to his room, his father listens for the sounds of a "tantrum"; but no, "The door closed normally, gently. The sound was sickening." Richard wakes up Joan to tell her he's told their son; she goes in to say good night to him, then is joined by Richard, who exchanges some final words with the boy, pleading that "No matter how this works out, I'll always be with you. Really." In conclusion:

> Richard bent to kiss an averted face but his son, sinewy, turned and with wet cheeks embraced him and gave him a kiss, on the lips, passionate as a woman's. In his father's ear he moaned one word, the crucial, intelligent word: *"Why?"*
>
> *Why.* It was a whistle of wind in a crack, a knife thrust, a window thrown open on emptiness. The white face was gone, the darkness was featureless. Richard had forgotten why.

The white face that, earlier, Richard had hoped to save from tears is now no longer salvageable, disappeared out the window into darkness, featurelessness: it has no referent. But the moment remains, perhaps the most poignant one of any in Updike's fiction, long or short, as our mixed feelings are directed not at father or son or at any character, rather at the situation, the play of voices and forces — the play of art. "Separating" is not a tragic story; no one is destroyed, things will heal, Richard will doubtless remember "why," absence will be replaced by something substantial, present. Still, the sense of never again — of the end of something, since all things under heaven must end — is persistent and strong.

"Separating" may be said to mark the peak of something like a "tragic" awareness in these Maples stories. "Here Come the Maples," which concludes the volume and which appeared the year after "Separating" (the year that Updike's divorce became final), provides a note of human resolution in the comic spirit and gives a kind of answer to Dickie Maple's question "Why?" The witty title sets the tone of things with a riff on the courtroom's legal "Now come . . ." language of the divorce hearing, while it sturdily suggests the couple's strong union at their final moment of togetherness before legal disuniting. The story, as usual narrated through Richard's consciousness, shuttles between Cambridge City Hall ("the rounded Richardsonian castle, red sandstone and pink granite"), unchanged since the day more than twenty years before when Richard and Joan had procured their marriage license. Now in quest of his "unlicense," he travels to Central Square on the T from Boston while reading a popular science article about the behavior of "quarks" (weak forces in the gravitational field) and as memories of his and Joan's wedding and honeymoon mingle with the present. Waiting for his affidavit to be notarized, he remembers "the white creature trembling beside him at the altar" whom, in his excitement, he had forgotten to kiss by way of sealing their vows.

It was his fault then, but now, early in the morning of their "no-fault" divorce hearing as he drives Joan to City Hall, he realizes how, throughout their marriage, "he had blamed her for everything." But such blame is at an end: "No longer: he had set her adrift from omnipotence. He had set her free, free from fault." A moment like this one, so much the product of Updike's writerly sensibility, so fertile in its verbal connections (the no-fault/fault play being only the most obvious), fends off critical commentary that would fix it into stable significance. So when one critic says, about Richard's setting Joan "free from fault" — "This new innocence, however, occurs too late, and only as a function of their divorce. No indicators of the path back exist; it is indeed 'too far to go'"[4] — we feel that while the formulation isn't exactly wrong, it is not right enough to catch the moment's literary tone. Instead it moralizes by knowing better ("occurs too late") and forcing things into a larger pattern ("It is indeed 'too far to go'") in a way that throws them off-key. Mainly it misses Updike's persistently humorous way with perception, with language, the incorrigible mark of an art that converts the imperfect endings of life, like a divorce, into something enduring.

This conversion at its most impressive and irresistible is achieved in the perfect conclusion to "Here Come the Maples." The couple confer with their respective lawyers, who are uncertain about what this new "no-fault" ruling involves: what will Richard say if the judge should ask him for a specific cause of the "irretrievable break-down" their marriage has suffered?

> They entered the courtroom two by two. The chamber was
> chaste and empty; the carved trim was painted forest green.
> The windows gave on an ancient river blackened by industry.
> Dead judges gazed down from high on the walls. The two
> lawyers conferred, leaving Richard and Joan to stand awk-
> wardly apart. He made his "What now?" face at her. She made
> her "Beats me" face back.[5]

Mythological dimensions — the chaste, empty chamber, the ani-mals entering the ark, the forest into which Hansel and Gretel wan-dered, the Styx-like Charles River outside, judgment day with all those dead judges gazing down — make the couple's playful face-making in the face of it all attractively humanized. Finally Joan decides, drawing on her expertise as a fine arts major, that "It's a Daumier." The tableau is broken as the judge summons them up in turn, Richard first, to swear that their marriage has suffered an irre-trievable breakdown. Richard allows that it has, but — when his wife similarly swears — "knew" that she doesn't believe it. He's not about to give up, even at this moment of consummation, the fiction that he knows what Joan really does or doesn't believe. Whatever his own ironic distance from the legalese of "irretrievable break-down," he refuses to allow her a similar distance from her words — in parody of the marriage ceremony — "I do."

Everything has worked out perfectly, there are no questions from the judge to complicate matters, the case has been settled amicably and finally. But the final paragraph gives a fully composed picture of the resolution whose concluding gesture is not required by law:

> The judge smiled and wished them both good luck. The
> lawyers sagged with relief, and a torrent of merry legal chitchat
> — speculations about the future of no-fault, reminiscences of
> the old days of Alabama quickies — excluded Joan and
> Richard. Obsolete at their own ceremony, the Maples stepped

back from the bench in unison and stood side by side, uncertain of how to turn, until he at last remembered what to do; he
kissed her.

Commentary isn't needed to bring out the humorous delicacy and
sadness of this wholly original way to present an American moment
that, in 1976, had become expected and was nobody's fault. Of
course the charming gesture here is Richard's, the male's, bidding to
make venial in comparison his past infidelities and betrayals. "All
mercy and no justice": Christopher Ricks's words about *Rabbit Redux*
might in fairness be applied by a reader who knows what fairness is
and wants fiction to observe something like ideal balance. But, as
reiterated, Updike's fiction transforms, turns this moment of divorce
into a moment that never was on sea or land, even down to the
lawyerly chitchat marvelously telescoped in two words, "Alabama
quickies." At the end of the final story in *Pigeon Feathers*, "Packed
Dirt . . . ," the narrator addresses the now absent hitchhiking sailor
who asked him what was the point of writing: "We in America need
ceremonies, is I suppose, sailor, the point of what I have written."
One such needed point is provided us by the ending of "Here Come
the Maples."

Nine months after this concluding Maples story was published,
and the year Updike remarried, he published "The Egg Race," a
story about a recently divorced and remarried man investigating his
past. With "Domestic Life in America," published at the end of
1976, Updike declared an end to the trials of Richard and Joan
Maples by naming his separated, not-yet-divorced man "Fraser."
Fraser has other incarnations in other short stories from these
months; he is Sapers in "The Man Who Loved Extinct Mammals,"
and Tod in "Love Song, for a Moog Synthesizer." In "The Egg Race"
he has become Ferguson, an archeologist who lives with his second
wife and her son in Maine. But the fictional disguise is a thin one
indeed, as in the story's second paragraph Ferguson has a dream in
which he and his father, dead five years, are traveling together. As
with the earlier, Olinger stories, Updike is ready, even eager, to

underline the congruence between his own and Ferguson's life; for not only had Wesley Updike died five years previously — Ferguson remembers how, at the funeral in "Hayesville," there was an outpouring of testimony to their beloved teacher by his former high-school students — but Ferguson even reiterates the words spoken by Richard Maple to his son about the impending separation: "He had long contemplated this last," thinks Ferguson about leaving his first wife, "but would never have done it had his father been alive."

The egg race itself is out of Ferguson's past ("or was it called the spoon race?" he asks in the opening paragraph), a playground event where he held an egg in front of him on a spoon and tried not to drop it in the course of beating competitors to the finish line. Like most of us, Ferguson never won the race, "but lately he was visited, as if grown permeable in middle age, by recollections and premonitions." It makes sense to call this story Updike's recognition and acceptance of his own middle age, as felt in Ferguson's archaeological interest in his past as it filters through a "permeable" consciousness (the word also used about Richard Maple's tears in "Separating"). Ferguson does a number of things in the story: goes to the Smithsonian Institution on business, visits a senior colleague dying of lung cancer, and — most significantly — returns to his hometown for a high-school reunion. But over everything he does there is an air of detachment, bemusement, a sense of the oddness of things, which a spectator of life rather than a participant in it is privileged to register. In fact, one way to distinguish Ferguson from his predecessor, Richard Maple, is to note that Ferguson is no longer caught up in the comi-tragic world of relationships, marital strife, and extramarital excitements. There is a been-there, done-that quality to his view of experience.

Ferguson's "recollections and premonitions" involve a fair component of guilt, and indeed the story following "The Egg Race" in *Problems* — hardly a story at all, a poetic meditation, rather — is titled "Guilt-Gems," in which several such gems are displayed. "A guilt-gem is a piece of the world that has volunteered for compression," observes the story's protagonist, Ferris, another divorced man grown skillful at calling up his past. He remembers, for example, a softball game between his and a neighbor's children in which, pitching for both sides, he was powerless to prevent the neighbor's children from feasting off his underhand offerings; they pounded the ball vigorously, while Ferris's own children, despite his best efforts to give them fat pitches to hit, produced only pop-ups or feeble grounders. On one of these dribbles to the mound, Ferris has no choice but to tag his daughter as she tries to get from first to second base:

> The child didn't have a chance; his legs were longer. He could think of no way not to make the play. In the moment before the tag, she looked at him with a smile, a smile preserved as in amber by a childish wild plea on her face. She was out.

A particular gem of a guilt-gem, this seems. In "The Egg Race" Ferguson's guilt toward his children is not so compressed, but diffused into a sense of belatedness, as if the time of growing up had conspired against him by *not* being the time of his own childhood. So when, in the dream, Ferguson and his father travel in some benign adventure, he reflects, waking, on his failure to show his own children the great wide world out there. Not only did he lack his father's "authentic late-Christian flair — stoic yet quixotic, despairing yet protective" — there was also lacking the "threadbare" environment in which those qualities stood out as heroic ones:

> It was no longer the Depression, trolley cars no longer swayed through the center of cities, people no longer boarded railroad trains in their Sunday best, coal no longer sparkled in the weedy rights-of-way, the next town was no longer another planet. Ferguson's children graduated from ten-speed bikes to driver's licenses, and toward the end scarcely needed him to take them places. He had left them, he felt, only a little before they would have left him.

This nostalgia for the lean, as it might be called, is a way of making personal guilt the inevitable result of mobility upward, from threadbare to affluent (those ten-speed bikes). The implied question is, how, possibly, can your childrens' childhood live up to your own, in its remembered sweet deprivations and gritty realities?

Ferguson's attitude toward the past, toward his own past, is stubborn, contradictory, willful, poetic; he is both beyond it (on the other side of it), relieved that it is over, but at the same time contemporaneous with it, still living it. Two vignettes bring out this imaginative doubleness: on a trip to the Smithsonian the archaeologist visits an exhibit of Americana in which there is an "antique classroom," a blackboard chalked with examples of Palmer-method penmanship, a portrait of George Washington, a sepia map of spice trade routes on the wall, an asphalt playground outside the windows: "Ferguson stood baffled. What was historical about this exhibit? He had studied in such a classroom. If it were not for the glass, he could walk in — a shabby little overachiever, often the first to arrive — and take his seat." At another moment, after visiting his dying colleague in the hospital, he looks at life from the greatest distance with a version of Shakespeare's seven-stages-of-man speech: from infancy, to boyhood, to married man with children ("The motions of changing a diaper still lived in Ferguson's hands, and the feel of a small child's gritty grasp on a single finger during the bedtime song"), up through the "divorcing man, haggard yet lightened." He knows what the future holds, but is relieved that "These roles, thoroughly performed, need not be performed again" — relieved "that he would never be asked to be young again."

What saves the archaeologist from terminal detachment, the loss of "affect," is the high-school reunion he decides to attend. Glazed by bourbon, saturated with song hits from the 1940s — "Near You," "Tangerine," "Rag Mop," and "Across the Alley from the Alamo" — he "perceived that amid these old children, these accents, and these melodies he had experienced Paradise." Even so, he wishes he were back in Maine. He admires the still-admirable breasts of Linda Weed, now Gottfinger, and observes Nasty Kegerise, the class pest, flip back one of the leaves of her bodice so as to reveal a breast "as perfect as an egg." Finally, as the band finishes off with, appropriately, "So Tired" (Updike correctly notes "the soul-chilling wah-wah of the

muted trumpets" in Russ Morgan's otherwise undistinguished recording), the class athlete informs him how much more of a man than
Ferguson was Ferguson's father, to which the son can only agree.

Next day he prowls his lost town, the boarded-up high school, the
candy store where he can still buy "the old candies," the playground
suggesting to the anthropologist "a Hopi village on a mesa, a skele-
tal village of swing sets and jungle gyms," the site on which Ferguson
never won the egg race. He decides that perhaps that race, "meant
to be festive" had struck him instead as "tragic," and wonders
whether that premonition of the tragic has not dogged his life.
Almost without our registering the metaphor, and without the writer
making it explicit, life turns out to be an egg race, and not just back
in its earlier years. Returned home, finding that his colleague has
died, he watches his wife take up a tray upstairs for her child sick in
bed. Ferguson is propelled into thoughts of his own childhood ill-
nesses, of staying home from school and having breakfast off the
lovely tray his mother prepared. In one of Updike's longest sentences
(quoted here in part) the sickbed is lovingly exfoliated —

> the fever-swollen mountains and valleys of the blankets where
> books and crayons and snub-nosed scissors kept losing them-
> selves, the day outside the windows making its irresistible arc
> from morning to evening, the people of the town travelling to
> their duties and back, running to the trolley and walking
> wearily back, his father out suffering among them, yet with no
> duty laid upon the child but to live, to stay safe and get well,
> to do that huge something called nothing.

It is one of the fine moments in Updike's fiction in which everything comes together, the particularities of one child's sickbed
unobtrusively comprehending all our childhoods. With a final rise
into apostrophe, the child becomes — as he was already — truly
father to the man, and something like a blessing is pronounced:

> The house in all its reaches attended to him, settling, ticking,
> clucking in its stillness, an intricately worked setting for the

jewel of his healing; all was nestled like a spoon beneath his
life, his only life, his incredibly own, that he must not let drop.

I can think of no better words to characterize this passionate, brilliantly articulate awareness of self than those the jazz critic Otis
Ferguson once employed about the tone, the music, of Bix
Beiderbecke's cornet playing — "as fresh and glittering as creation
itself."

I have spent some time in laying out parts of the story and pointing to their interrelations and coherences in order to suggest what
impressive plastic powers of shaping — both spatially and temporally
— Updike employs in constructing this not-well-known story. In
rehearsing its "plot," circumstances, episodes, small actions, and in
quoting liberally its sentences by way of addressing how style, tone,
voice perform "meanings," I am aware of a central problem in dealing with such a various and prolific writer. For how many readers —
general ones, or even devoted ones of the writer in question — can
be expected to recall "The Egg Race" in any specificity and fullness,
from among the two-hundred-odd stories Updike has written? Yet as
suggested earlier, this story is a watershed moment in a literary
career, insofar as it translates its protagonist to a different, slightly
remote and detached plane, from which not just his past but his
present and future experiences are regarded. At forty-five, no great
age for anyone these days, Updike's representative man has become
old, sadder, wiser — a state he seems to have attained almost
overnight.

There is a touching recognition of that state in the final story
from *Problems*, an allegorical fiction titled "Atlantis." Atlantis is the
mythical kingdom in which Farnham and his second wife — not
then married to one another — used to live, where parties and pic-
nics on the beach of the Atlantic occurred, along with love affairs
and marital breakups. No longer: he and his wife now live "inland,
in a state people confused with Ohio," where there is indeed corn as
high as an elephant's eye. "Inland" is of course a very unusual spot
for the Updike man to live, but Farnham, we are told, who spent all

his life "in one city or suburb or another, within a few miles of the sea," got out of the scene just in time:

> Atlantis was now sunk beneath the sea. It had been sandy, marshy, permeated by glistening water like something very rotten, and doomed. Odd moments of his life there, as detailed and difficult of explanation as religious visions or archeological finds, returned to him. . . .

Sitting with his wife in the land of corn, he recalls one of those moments, a tryst with a woman at her house near a tidal river, and the second Mrs. Farnham accuses him of thinking about old girlfriends, saying that she can tell "By the light in your eyes. They get green." She is right in perceiving this, in catching him gripped by an "archaeological find," a moment when "the alien corn outside his window dimmed, became husky, negligible, permeated by the memory of Atlantis, its curving waterways, its towering cities, its endless parties." The prose itself glows with reflected light.

At the end of this short tale, driving with her husband along the Connecticut coast to the wedding of his daughter in Westerly, Mrs. Farnham is moved, seeing a water tower in the vicinity of New London, to think of a man she knew after she left her first husband. The man was a "frogman" whose job consisted in making sure submarine trainees got out of their subs without panicking, were blowing the requisite amount of bubbles. His curiosity piqued, Farnham asks her how well she knew the man, and receives a one-word answer, "Pretty." He observes that her eyes are green, and the story concludes: "Farnham, headed toward his daughter's wedding along the mazy coast, prayed: O rise, frogman, smoothly and without panic, up from the depths, trailing your train of air; bring us news of sunk Atlantis, our fabled pasts. Keep us in touch." But the prayer has already been answered in that past's retrieval and renewal through the art of fiction.

SEVEN

EXTRAVAGANT FICTIONS
The Coup • *The Witches of Eastwick* •
Roger's Version • *S*

The Maples stories, and the related ones from *Problems* — a number of them written during the years of marital separation and remarriage — testify to Updike's powers as a realist, an observer and recorder of domestic life in America the way it was lived at a certain moment in our culture. Yet even as he was writing them, we can imagine him plotting how to break out of his encapsulation as the small-town chronicler of, first, Pennsylvania boyhood, then New England adult life. *A Month of Sundays*, with its flagrantly provocative tone and texture, was the first step in that direction. In 1978, the year after his marriage to Martha Bernhard, Updike produced, to the surprise of more than one of his readers, a novel that in its pace and characters seemed as far as one could get from Middle-Atlantic reality. In its fabulous account of an African dictator, his American past, and his present decline into private citizenship, *The Coup* showed a different Updike from a writer who after twenty years of fiction might have been content to rest on realist laurels. Instead he came across as dazzler and showman, as Nabokovian illusionist, in a more radical way than he had hitherto demonstrated. Predictably, and as was the case with the "extravagant" novels that followed it in the 1980s, *The Coup* was ambiguously received and — as with those novels to come — consensus is lacking about its artistic place and value in Updike's work.

The most severe and heavily weighted criticism of his fiction from this period — coming as it did from an American critic of distinction — was Frederick Crews's essay in the *New York Review of Books*, on the publication of *Roger's Version*.[1] Crews's argument, simplified, was that anxiety about religion was at the core of Updike's work, and that the earlier "affirming" celebrations of the world's body — as in the Pennsylvania stories and novels — increasingly ceased to serve him in the 1970s and beyond. Crews notes, correctly, that after the 1960s Updike begins "experimenting with a cooler, more sardonic artistic strategy," often embodied in a Nabokovian manner devoted to keeping the reader off-balance. This strategy was a way of dealing with what Crews saw as the novelist's growing crankiness and "class-based misanthropy," directed at various social classes and ethnic groups, "liberated" women, and other disruptions of political, social, and cultural order. By more and more frequently casting the protagonists of his novels as notably over the line, like an adulterous, defrocked minister, a black African dictator, a witch, or a bilious, obsessed professor of religion, Updike both cast doubt upon the veracity of his narrator and at the same time, in Crews's words, he "could let fly with all the dour and spiteful reflections that had found no outlet, or perhaps no need for it, in his early works." When, in a follow-up letter to the *New York Review of Books*, I charged Crews with eviscerating Updike for the illiberal views his dramatic persons sometimes revealed, Crews replied that, no, he was trying rather "to account for the morally ambiguous, self-undermining character of certain novels and for Updike's eventual adoption of a sardonic, cat-and-mouse manner," a character and manner that he, Crews, found "uncongenial."[2]

Such attacks on Updike's fiction, as they periodically occur, invite us to consider his literary career in broader terms than merely stylistic ones. Or rather, they suggest that stylistic verve and density, admirable as they occur in sentences and paragraphs, may be put to moral and human uses that are not so admirable. Implicit in the attack is an assumption that the later, displeasing, Updike is to be contrasted with an earlier, agreeable one. "He no longer feels at home in the here and now," wrote Crews, by way of contrasting the later, "negative" attitudes with earlier ones. But even if for the moment we grant the presence of strongly negative, satiric, or dissatisfiedly alienated sentiments in the four novels from *The Coup* to *S*, isn't there something wrong with identifying and reducing the essential Updike to these sentiments? Recall that in the ten-year span he also produced, in addition to the four novels in question, a number of other books. *Rabbit Is Rich* (1981), compared to its two predecessors in the Angstrom saga, shows its hero settling down and his creator's narrative tone relaxing, accommodating more comedy and an ironic acceptance of human life. In the continuation of the Bech stories (*Bech Is Back*, 1982) there is a finely poised, seventy-five page comedy, "Bech Wed," that shows Updike's genial powers at their peak, as they bring back to life his newly married but still uncomfortable hero. *Hugging the Shore* (1983), his largest collection of critical prose thus far, provided further instances of his balance and sanity as a critic. And a volume of poems, *Facing Nature* (1985), showed him still at the practice — though it drew little attention — of producing determinedly "un-major" but agreeable efforts like this one, "The Code," completed in 1983:

> Were there no rain there would be little noise,
> no rustle on the roof that we confuse
> with our own bloodbeat on the inner ear,
> no braided gurgle in the gutter, no breathing
> within the tree whose shelved and supple bulk
> sifts the rain to a mist of small descents.
>
> A visitor come from a cloudless planet
> would stand amazed by the tumults of our water
> and feel bereaved. Without the rain
> the taxi wheels would pass like wind on sand
> and all the splashing that excites our lovers
> fresh from drinks would be a chastening calm;

the sky would be devoid of those enormous
witnesses who hang invisible
until our wish to see brings forth in focus
their sliding incandescent shapes.
Without the rain the very links of life
would drift still uncemented, a dream of dust.

Were there no rain the windowpanes
would never tick as if a spy outside,
who once conspired with us to ferret out
the secret code, the terms of full concord
with all that is and will be, were signalling
with a fingernail, *I'm back. I've got the goods.*

Like many of his poems, some of the lines seem too casually struck
off, not quite scannable, certainly lacking tautness; yet "The Code"
is nevertheless a poem one is pleased to have and to read.

My point is partly defensive: that Updike's desire not to be easily
typecast, not to be characterized "essentially" as the Rabbit-man, or
the chronicler of suburban adulteries, or the exquisite appreciator of
natural process, sights, and sounds — to say nothing of the responsible critic producing interestingly varied reports on all manner of
subjects — may have stimulated him into writing novels in which
the protagonist's "take" on the world has a strong component of dissatisfaction with various forms of life in our century's late decades.
One remembers the critic F. R. Leavis shaking his moral finger at
Flaubert for that novelist's impulse to "do dirt on life." Without
examining the question of how or whether "doing dirt" is a likely
way to assess Flaubert's morality as a novelist, it may at least be
entertained as a possibility that one of the validly human ways of
responding to life is to do some dirt on it. But the extent to which
such a charge fits the particular novels about to be taken up should
also be qualified by our knowledge that there were — concurrently
with their composition — other impulses, other responses to "life"
in the books Updike was turning out.

The Coup

The Coup came as a real departure for those readers who took Updike to be a portrayer, merely, of suburban manners and morals — especially since its immediate predecessor, *Marry Me,* was a distinctly "Updikean" novel of marriage, affairs, and separation. To have stepped out of that familiar role and into the shoes of an African politico in a remote land seemed nothing short of refreshingly bold, even dangerous, as an imaginative venture. In 1973 Updike had spent three weeks traveling and lecturing in Africa for the State Department (Nigeria, Kenya, and Ethiopia mainly), but three weeks of observation, even for such a remarkable observer, is incommensurate with the wealth of specification on every page of *The Coup.* The acknowledgments — the first deemed necessary for any of his books — name a multitude of sources for his African history and other information. And in his comments about the novel Updike sounds both enthusiastic about it and eager to share sources and analogies for it:

> Behind *The Coup* you can find, jumbled together, Nabokov, impressions of Ethiopia, readings on the Sahel, African novels (I'm mad about African literature — it's a different world, where magic really works), but particularly, to begin with, the works of Joyce Cary, who lived in Nigeria in the 1920s: *The American Witch* and *Mister Johnson.*[3]

He also said that it took him a year and a half to write, that it was an attempt to get away from the "domestic subject," that it "was based on the country's rejection of Nixon" (there was a sort of global parallel in the fall of his dictator, Elleloû), and that the "Nabokovian unreality," the "made-up country" resulted in a book, he hoped, that among other things had "layers as in *The Centaur,* in a way, bubbling up and merging."

The made-up-ness of the country Updike calls Kush was, not surprisingly, a problem for some readers in a way that, say, Saul Bellow's wholly imaginary and largely unspecified Africa in *Henderson the Rain King,* or Paul Theroux's comparatively realistic portrayals of

Malawi and Uganda in *Jungle Lovers*, was not. On the one hand, and selecting the novel's opening chapter for example, the narrator, Hakim Félix Elleloû, now a retired citizen living in the south of France within sight of the sea, provides us with many statistics on matters like the natural resources, life expectancy, per-capita gross national product, form of government, and many other features of the Kush over which he once presided. Yet at the same time as he provides this information he confesses that "I am copying these facts from an old *Statesman's Year Book* . . . so some of them may be obsolete." It is a high-handed Nabokovian disclaimer, worthy of Humbert Humbert, and it indulges slightly in the postmodernist gesture of reminding the reader that "facts" are words copied and perhaps obsolete, mere writing rather than truth.

Of course "writing" is to the fore of any Updike novel, and *The Coup* is densely written. But its peculiar kind of density signals its affiliation with *A Month of Sundays* rather than with Updike's more realistic works. This may be seen from one example, a longish paragraph in which Elleloû, having introduced himself to us, addresses the question of narrative — of whether to speak of himself in first or third person (Updike will vary such presentation throughout the novel):

> Yet a soldier's disciplined self-effacement, my Cartesian schooling, and the African's traditional abjuration of ego all constrain this account to keep to the third person. There are two selves: the one who acts, and the "I" who experiences. This latter is passive even in a whirlwind of the former's making, passive and guiltless and astonished. The historical performer bearing the name of Elleloû was no less mysterious to me than to the American press wherein he was never presented save snidely and wherein his fall was celebrated with a veritable minstrelsy of anti-Negro, anti-Arab cartoons; in the same spirit the beer-crazed mob of American boobs cheers on any autumnal Saturday or Sunday the crunched leg of the unhome-team left tackle as he is stretchered off the field. Elleloû's body and career carried me here, there, and I never knew why, but submitted.

This virtuoso paragraph suggests why Elleloû, even more than earlier Updike characters such as Rabbit Angstrom or Joey Robinson or, surely, Tom Marshfield, is in no conventional novelistic sense a "character" — someone whose intellectual, emotional, and spiritual boundaries can be more or less charted. Indeed, at one moment in the paragraph the narrative voice and declaration sound like nothing so much as Thoreau's in *Walden*: "I only know myself as a human entity; the scene, so to speak, of thought and affections; and am sensible of a certain doubleness by which I can stand as remote from myself as from another. However intense my experience, I am conscious of the presence and criticism of a part of me, which, as it were, is not a part of me, but a spectator, sharing no experience, but taking note of it; and that is no more I than it is you." Thus one part of Elleloû is that of reflexive commentary — in a most highly sophisticated mode — on narrative method. Then later in the paragraph we are moved, in one of his many anti-American diatribes, invariably conducted with high energy, to consideration of the way his fall was celebrated by the American press, a way comparable to that practiced by American boobs. This is the Nabokovian/Humbertian voice, reveling in its diction, its clever nonce creations such as "the unhome-team," and its highly compressed verbal adjectives like *crunched* and *stretchered*. How, we might ask, would one get to know or "understand" a narrative voice so lordly in its expression, so unlikely ever to be at a loss for words, indeed for none but the most glittering words?

"The border of Kush in the northwest is nine-tenths imaginary," Elleloû tells us early in the novel as he is about to confront the American State Department representative in charge of distributing a mountain of breakfast cereal, cream soups, and sundry useless items that his government has had flown in to drought-plagued Kush. But it's not merely the northwest border of Kush that is nine-tenths imaginary, since the whole book itself is so, even as it appears to specify with relentless detail the country's lineaments, or makes use of impossible-to-work-out time schemes, or traces the mysterious routes Elleloû takes on his various trips from the capital into the interior. As suggested by the paragraph from Elleloû's narrative quoted above, it's he himself who is the most "imaginary" of all the creations in the novel, to an extent that puts him well beyond our capacities for sympathetic identification. Evelyn Waugh's *Black Mischief*, with which *The Coup* has been compared, is in part about the rise and fall of a character named Seth who comes back from an Oxford education to become (but not for long) Emperor of Azania. (Elleloû received his formal education at an imaginary campus called McCarthy College in Franchise, Wisconsin, and some of the book's best comedy recalls that experience.) Seth's progressive aspirations and his inexperience make him a clear candidate for exploitation and disaster, and Waugh's narrative, for all the made-up trappings of his imaginary kingdom, is basically operating in a realistic mode with nothing "magic" or even difficult in the sequence of his sentences. By contrast, *The Coup* was and remains one of the least straightforward of Updike's novels, and one that presents plenty of resistance to a reader; it cannot be read swiftly, and it doesn't become much easier on rereading. This is due to what may be called, if inadequately, the prose's density: the countless things it invites us to notice, register, and assimilate sentence by sentence.

A single instance will illustrate how much resistance the writing presents to a "fast" reading. In the first section Elleloû recalls his journey north, accompanied by his two bodyguards — in a Mercedes, complete with refrigeration and weapons — to visit a Soviet rocket installation. (Elleloû's and Kush's affiliations are with Russia politically, Islam religiously.) When the party reaches the installation the Russians are drunk, and swamp the president and his men "with hairy embraces, Cyrillic barks, and splashing offers of vodka." Elleloû reminds them that his religion forbids strong drink; eventually his protestations

> won for myself and my small party the right to respond in chalky Balkan mineral water (fetched from the sub-cellar) to their interminable toasts and to observe with sobriety this foreign enclave. The Russians had been here since the secret

SAND (Soviet-Allied Nuclear Deterrants) talks of 1971 and in
the two years since had amply furnished the bunker in the
stuffy tsarist style of Soviet supercomfort, from the lamps with
fringed shades and soapstone bases carved in the shape of tussling bears resting on runners of Ukranian lace to the obliga-
tory oil paintings of Lenin exhorting workers against a slanted
sunset and Brezhnev charming with the luxuriance of his eyebrows a flowery crowd of Eurasiatic children. The linguist
among them, a frail steel-bespectacled second lieutenant
whose Arabic was smeared with Iraqi accent and whose
French sloshed in the galoshes of Russian *zhushes*, fell dead
drunk in the midst of the banquet; we carried on with minimal
toasts to the heroes of our respective races.

Later in the same paragraph we are introduced to the leader of the
Russian group, Colonel Sirin, thus making explicit the Nabokovian
homage (Nabokov once assumed "Sirin" as his pen name). It's not
writing that invites "interpretation"; to read it well demands nothing more or less than responsive antennae and a determination *not*
to complain of overload — a determination not shared by all readers. Among a plethora of things to be noticed are the unnecessary
but welcome adjective *chalky* to characterize the Balkan mineral
water; or the comments on the interior decoration of the bunker,
those lamp shades and bases with tussling bears and Ukrainian lace.
As if it were insufficient merely to be given pictures of Lenin and
Brezhnev, we must be directed to the "luxuriance" of the latter's eyebrows (did we ever think about Brezhnev's eyebrows before? certainly we registered them) charming the children. And then there
is the fate of that frail linguist "whose French sloshed in the galoshes
of Russian *zhushes*." This riotous feast of abundance, like the
"Soviet supercomfort" it celebrates and parodies, moves the focus
far away and beyond any character named Elleloû with whose fate
and personality we are seriously concerned.

With her usual critical acuity about Updike, Joyce Carol Oates
put her finger on the essential literary fact about *The Coup* when she

contrasted it with Garcia Marquez's novel about a dictator, *The Autumn of the Patriarch*. She points out that whereas Marquez's patriarch was "seen from without, filtered through the voices of a number of close observers," Updike's procedure is utterly different. Elleloû, she notes, has sent many people to their deaths and is personally responsible for decapitating the king, Edumu, who has been like a father to him: "but the reader hasn't the sense, any more than Elleloû does, that he *is* a murderer; his elaborate syntax convinces us otherwise."[4] Or, let us say, it convinced Oates, who admires the novel, as do I. But one will admire it a good deal less if it registers as a crippling defect that the all-pervasive voice of the novel is so overbearingly Updike's as to persuade us there is really no dictator there, no Elleloû with his wives and lover, no "Africa." If it's all, or nine-tenths of all, "imaginary," the argument might run, then the presiding imagination is beyond morality, beyond the sympathetic commitment to other minds, impossible to care about, inhuman. At the end of the passage from *Walden* in which Thoreau delineated the distinction quoted previously between the "me" who experiences, often intensely, and the "I" who is detached, critical, imaginative, he adds almost as an afterthought, "This doubleness may easily make us poor neighbors and friends sometimes" — as if he were almost loath to confess it. Something like that charge might be brought against *The Coup*, as lacking in human "reference." Yet the book has so much life that such an objection is less than compelling.

In focusing, perhaps owlishly, upon the critical problem presented by *The Coup*, I have neglected its complicatedly inventive plot and range of characters. Especially attractive are Elleloû's intermittent reminiscences of his college days at McCarthy in the 1950s, of annual football games between McCarthy and Pusey Baptist ("an even more northerly academic village of virgins and bruisers"), of cheerleading, of drugstores on "Commerce Street," and much else. Elleloû puts it this way: "Everything in America, through that middle bulge of the Fifties, seemed to this interloper fat, abundant, and bubblelike, from the fenders of the cars to the cranium of the President." Nowhere is the presence of Nabokov's *Lolita* more strongly felt, and not it seems to me to Updike's disadvantage: his own creation is equally contemptuous, genial, disbelieving, admiring. Comparing the novels, however, brings out a problem of "voice." The narrative voice of *Lolita* is surely Nabokov talking, but also believably that of the urbane, cynical, sophisticated, neurotic, and European Humbert Humbert. Updike's version of a similar voice, emanating from an African dictator, is harder to accept, needs more of a suspension of disbelief to make it work. The attempt nevertheless was a bold one: in "Through a Continent, Darkly," a prose piece from the "Africa" section of *Picked-Up Pieces*, Updike placed himself in a long line of predecessors who have taken Africa as "an invitation to the imagination." One of the ways he makes his contribution to the list is by imagining America through the focus of the angry and bemused, but also enchanted, Elleloû.

The Witches of Eastwick

In an interview, Updike made a connection between *The Coup* and *The Witches of Eastwick* as books he'd written "in which I tried to animate conceptions" — thus underlining the difference between such novels and the realism of the Rabbit tetralogy. At least one critic of *Witches*, Harold Bloom, found its animation of conceptions not only brilliant but the only instance in Updike's work where this "minor novelist with a major style" became something more.[5] What Bloom liked about the novel was the way Updike's usual "religious polemic," which Bloom found distasteful, came into productive conflict with "the natural otherness of particular human lives," as embodied in the three women who dominate the book. Bloom found the novel moved beyond satire and touched on true horror, and although he declared, sniffily and pontifically, that "the American Sublime will never touch [Updike's] pages," he almost made an exception for *Witches*. Other admirers of the book found it a healthy development in Updike's portrayal of the sexes, claiming that it showed "a promising new direction in the author's engagement . . . with sexual and religious questions at the core of human life," and that in it the sexes were reaching out to each other in ways previously uncharacteristic of the author's work.[6]

Updike himself has been more cautious in his remarks, confirming what any reader of the book would already have perceived, that witchcraft is the "venture" of "women into the realm of power." In fact the book's opening pages tell us that "this air of Eastwick empowered women," and such empowering, consonant upon the previous demise, indeed dissolution, of each woman's husband, is the "given" of the novel. We view the lives and mutual friendship of Alexandra Spofford, a sculptress (she makes womanly clay figures called "bubbies"), Jane Smart, a serious cellist, and Sukie Rougemont, a gossip columnist on the local paper. All three have children to whom they pay as little attention as possible (the children are barely there in the novel); they also have lovers — various married men of Eastwick — and every so often they cause extraordinary things to happen, as when, in a relatively benign manifestation of power, Alexandra raises a sudden storm to clear the beach, on which she's walking her dog, of human beings. Into Eastwick comes Darryl Van Horne — the devil, we are meant to understand — who installs himself along with his pop art collection in an old mansion, newly decorated with what must be diabolic inventiveness. Each of the women is fascinated by Van Horne; he flatters each, plays with them, and invites them to communal frolickings on his tennis court and in his pool. The witches' solidarity is compromised by Van Horne's erotic and magical presence, but he forsakes them all and marries Jennifer Gabriel, the daughter of Sukie's dead lover, then eventually absconds with Jennifer's brother to New York City. In the meantime the witches' tricks have turned nastier, more malevolent, the most vicious instance of which is the hexing of Jennifer and her subsequent death from cancer. In the end the women lose their power, are supplanted by other female members of the community inimical to them, and, in a coda, each remarries and settles down happily more or less ever after.

This simplified, schematic account of the novel's "story" may suggest how, like *The Coup*, the narrative of *Witches* is a fabulous one that has affinities with romance and fairy tale. (Its nod at magic realism, as perpetrated by Garcia Marquez in the 1970s to much acclaim, is also palpable.) *Witches* is set in an unspecified year — Vietnam is happening, Nixon is president — but Updike's imagining of "empowered" women could only have come, I think, some years after the women's movement of the early 1970s had registered itself. Less time-bound is the novel's visual, geographical setting, one of its strongest and truest, if overlooked, delights. Whatever disagreement there might be about the weight or seriousness of the novel, its evocation of little Rhode Island is undeniably vivid:

> Rhode Island, though famously the smallest of the fifty states, yet contains odd American vastnesses, tracts scarcely explored amid industrial sprawl, abandoned homesteads and forsaken mansions, vacant hinterlands hastily traversed by straight black road, heathlike marshes and desolate shores on either side of the Bay, that great wedge of water driven like a stake clean to the state's heart, its trustfully named capital.

This narrator knows everything, although he is himself unspecified, at times speaking as the voice of the community, a "we," but more tellingly as the traditional Updike narrator — from *Rabbit, Run* through *Couples* and *The Coup* — who is gifted with at least six senses. These he employs on the texture of Rhode Island, after giving some religious and historical dimensions to the state:

> There is a kind of metallic green stain, bitten deep into Depression-era shingles, that exists nowhere else. Once you cross the state line, whether at Pawtucket or Westerly, a subtle change occurs, a cheerful dishevelment, a contempt for appearances, a chimerical uncaring. Beyond the clapboard slums yawn lunar stretches where only an abandoned roadside stand offering the ghost of last summer's CUKES betrays the yearning, disruptive presence of man.

Could that metallic green stain really be there? Does this cheerful dishevelment truly appear as one crosses the state line either from

Massachusetts or Connecticut? Realism is magical when a reader can't just say that the writer is "making it up" but is stimulated rather to exercise his own senses and cross the state line (I usually cross it at Woonsocket) to see whether such a "subtle change" occurs. At any rate, this is prose with immense authority and perfect auditory ease: it could reasonably be maintained that Updike has never written better.

But the surprise of this novel lies less in the writing's assurance (what else would we expect by now, in Updike's career?) than in the sympathetic inwardness with which he treats two of his three witches, Alexandra and Sukie. Especially Alexandra, whom Bloom is persuaded Updike loves "better even than he loves Rabbit Angstrom." Without choosing up, we can agree that, certainly, he speaks comfortably from within Alexandra, the witch most concerned with her body — she runs toward overweight, fears she will develop cancer — and the most human, most prone of the three to guilt, especially in her painful second thoughts about the lethal trick the three women have played on Jenny Gabriel. The ease with which Updike inhabits her can be felt in the scene where she takes her dog Coal for a walk on a Narragansett beach, passes an "over-muscled male trio" of longhaired Frisbee players, and thinks she hears the word *hag* or *bag* directed at her:

> Alexandra felt irritated and vengeful. Her insides felt bruised; she resented the overheard insult "hag" and the general vast insult of all this heedless youth prohibiting her from letting her dog, her friend and familiar, from running free. She decided to clear the beach for herself and Coal by willing a thunderstorm. One's inner weather always bore a relation to the outer; it was simply a question of reversing the current, which occurred rather easily once power had been assigned to the primary pole, oneself as a woman.

A virtuoso passage follows in which the "forbidden names" are invoked and, "A blast of cold air hit from the north, the approach of a front that whipped the desultory pennants on the distant bath-house straight out from their staffs," at which point the offending Frisbee players and others are packed off the scene. At one level typical magic, but the "empowering" of the heroine asserts itself in the prose's effortful activity — we are very much in favor of this witch having her way. At other moments besides this bravura one, such as the witches' meetings with one another, conducted mainly through gossip, telephone conversations, and weekly gathering for drinks, we hear conversations skillfully orchestrated, sometimes amusing. The women are very much *there* at the level of the social, the thrust and parry of daily exchange.

The trouble comes when Van Horne and the witches do their thing at the mansion in Darryl's marvelous pool that opens, upon the press of a button, to the night sky. How you render a "credible" devil is a problem, one that Updike was quite aware of when he told his interviewer he really didn't know much about devils but that Van Horne gives the women "a theater in which they can explore their mutual fondness and, I guess you could even say, their latent lesbianism."[7] (This last subject is more latent — if that's the word — than patent in the novel.) Van Horne is thus a "facilitator," but it's hard to know whether one should take the devil's "theater" with any degree of seriousness; and if not with seriousness then with what? Just how good is the entertainment it provides, not for the witches but for the reader? Consider a moment in the revels when, after Janis Joplin and Tiny Tim do their songs over the great sound system, "Sukie and Alexandra swayed in each other's arms without their feet moving, their fallen hair stringy and tangled with tears, their breasts touching, nuzzling, fumbling in pale pillow fight lubricated by drops of sweat worn on their chests like the broad bead necklaces of ancient Egypt." Our anonymous narrator may be working too hard here, and in this portrait of Van Horne: "his empurpled penis rendered hideously erect by a service Jane had performed for him on her knees, pantomimed with his uncanny hands — encased it seemed in white rubber gloves with wigs of hair and wide at the tips like the digits of a tree toad or lemur. . . ." One is put in mind, and without pleasure, of Jack Nicholson's over-the-top performance in the film version of the novel. Of course there is doubtless sly humor in Updike's exploitation of the "devilish attributes": "On the black velour mattresses Van Horne had provided, the three women played with him together, using the parts of his body as a vocabulary with which to speak to one another; he showed supernatural control, and when he did come his semen, all agreed later, was marvelously cold." Who are we to gainsay it? Yet such cavortings go a good way toward making the women's lives something we may not want to invest much of our sympathies in. In other words, the book's realism sits uneasily with its farcical, fantastic qualities — at least when the devil is onstage directing things.

Violence, death, and extreme suffering are facts of life that from the beginning Updike largely avoided treating in his fiction. The deaths in the first two Rabbit books are an exception; usually the death of a pet, as in the affecting poem "Dog's Death," is about as far as he went. It wasn't until *The Coup* that murder raised its head in Elleloû's dispatching of the king and incinerating of the American foreign service hand on a pyre of breakfast cereals and cream of celery soups. In a novel of political turmoil and intrigue, death is appropriate and to be expected. *The Witches of Eastwick*, on the other hand, might be expected by virtue of its affinities with fantasy and tall-tale extravagance to transpose what violence might occur into a slightly remote key, leaving us relatively unaffected by it. But in fact the suicide of the newspaper editor Clyde Gabriel, following hard upon his murder, with a poker, of his intolerable wife Felicia, is a painful episode indeed, presented by Updike with gravity and attentive care. (Clyde's doing away with himself by hanging may remind one of Julian English's suicide in a novel Updike admired, John O'Hara's *Appointment in Samara*.) Later, offstage, we hear graphic and unpleasant news, circulated among the witches, of the lingering death of Clyde's daughter Jenny, for which they are, so it seems, also responsible. On a less ultimate but memorably disgusting level there is the witches' tormenting of Felicia and of Brenda Parsley, wife of the fatuous curate who leaves her and joins a revolutionary cult (he is blown up by a mismanaged bomb).

Strange objects issue forth from the mouths of these hectoring, highly verbal women, such as straw, feathers, saliva-coated pennies, thumbtacks, or "a small straight pin and what looked like part of an art-gum eraser." Even after more than one reading of the novel, these inventions and transformations strike with some horror.

At the end of the second section of *Witches* ("Malefica"), the narrator steps back from the action to survey, in a long paragraph, not only his heroines' activities but the deeper meaning they offer, in human terms, to all of "us":

> We all dream, and we all stand aghast at the mouth of the caves of our deaths; and this is our way in. Into the nether world. Before plumbing, in the old outhouses, in winter, the accreted shit of the family would mount up in a spiky frozen stalagmite, and such phenomena help us to believe that there is more to life than the airbrushed ads at the front of magazines, the Platonic forms of perfume bottles and nylon nightgowns and Rolls-Royce fenders. Perhaps in the passageways of our dreams we meet, more than we know: one white lamplit face astonished by another.

Here is detectable a thematic push toward depth by way of assigning a moral function to witchery: it reminds us, or scares us into admitting, that the "more" to life is not the upward impulse toward transcendence but a downward one into the accreted, often unlovely matter of our lives, the nature whose material underside we share. One is reminded of Kenneth Burke's remark about Swift's satire, that it devotes itself to showing how every ideal fulfillment has its gross and revolting natural or material parody. To that extent Updike wants to rub our noses in it.

But he also wants to do so in an entertaining way, the way novels should be entertaining. When Kathleen Verduin noted what she termed a "suspiciously puckish" quality to Updike's tone in *Witches*, she was surely right, although we might ask, why "suspiciously"?[8] For this is Updike's most mischievous novel, in the spirit of his heroines; like them, he is devoted to unsettling all things, and his more unlucky characters have to pay the price for such unsettling. So if, as it seems to me reasonable to claim, this is the cruelest book he has produced, its impulse may be accounted for. Accounted for, yet it's hard to be totally at ease with it, accepting of it, unless — like Harold Bloom — you're wholly pleased with the way the religious, "transcendent" impulses that had informed his art are here defeated — at least severely shaken up. Let us call the novel a wicked entertainment, leaving those two ambiguous words hedged round with the reservations one doesn't have about, say, *The Centaur:* another novel in which Updike set out to "animate conceptions."

Roger's Version

Wicked entertainment: the phrase could be used, without raising eyebrows, about the next novel Updike published, yet *Roger's Version* is a richer book than *The Witches of Eastwick,* as well as a daunting one, inasmuch as it demands of readers an engagement with various languages that put us sorely, if exhilaratingly, to the test. At one point Roger Lambert, the divinity-school professor whose "version" of things the novel relates, concludes a paragraph in which matters of "creationist" thought and scientific, mathematical information meet unresolvedly: "Follow, you who can," Roger instructs us, to which the hard-pressed reader might well reply, "I'm not sure that I can, quite." This situation occurs more than once in the book, Updike's most difficult and knotty composition, to which, in his note to the Franklin Mint edition, he said he had "done more adjusting and fine-tuning" than in any previous novel.

Much of the critical writing about *Roger's Version* has dealt with its Hawthorne aspect, as the second in what is called Updike's *Scarlet Letter* trilogy.[9] While not denying that many interesting connections can be made in terms of Updike's revisions or playful overturnings of his predecessor, and while recognizing the full force of his claim that Hawthorne in *The Scarlet Letter* wrote "the one classic from the lusty youth of American literature that deals with society in its actual heterosexual weave,"[10] I am concerned here — as with *A Month of Sundays* — to describe a few of the actual appeals and difficulties of the novel, for a reader experiencing rather than interpreting it. In those terms, the place to begin, it seems to me, is by acknowledging part of the charge Frederick Crews brings against this book and others from Updike's 1980s "post-realist" period. There is admittedly a sardonic, fastidious, not-nice, even actively unpleasant air emanating from Roger Lambert's first-person narrative. But — moving beyond Crews by way of correcting him — that narrative, rather than simply revealing Updike's increasingly crusty pessimism and bad-spiritedness about things American, makes up a novel that is appealingly comic, however sardonic. It is also an original take on themes that are characteristically his.

The crustiness and self-absorbed superiority that inform Roger's opening confidences to us are too blatant for even the most credulous and trusting listener to miss. He is visited, in his divinity-school office, by a young research assistant in a computer lab who claims mutual acquaintance with Roger's niece Verna and her illegitimate child, who are also living in the city — not named, but clearly Cambridge/Boston. Dale Kohler, the young man, has what he considers to be a groundbreaking theory about proof of God's existence, and in this role he will be cast as Roger's antagonist. As the interview proceeds we learn a number of things about Roger's preferences and temperament: that Dale is "the type of young man I like least"; that he, Roger, is "a depressive" and that it is important for his mental well-being to keep away from "areas of contemplation that might entangle me and pull me down"; that although he smokes a pipe as a helpful defensive strategy in dealing with others, he finds the mannerisms of other pipe-smokers "stagy, prissy, preening, and offensive." Cleveland, where Roger grew up, is "that most dismal and forsaken of rust-belt metropolises, to which nothing but funerals has induced me, for thirty years, to return." In the old days, he remembers most vividly about his half-sister Edna, Verna's mother, that when she began to menstruate "the days of her 'period' flooded the house with her sticky, triumphantly wounded animal aroma, even to the corners of my room with its boyish stink of athletic socks and airplane glue." Although, of course, Roger is aware of his "dark side" — "a sullen temper, an uprising of bile that clouds my vision and turns my tongue heavy and ugly" — he manages nevertheless to keep putting that dark side into words. These asides to the reader suggest that Roger will be, shall we say, not easy to satisfy, but never anything less than stimulating and demanding in the moves he asks language to make and invites us to follow. A less giddy Tom Marshfield, Roger has left the clergy many years earlier, divorced his first wife, and married a woman named Esther; at the divinity school he is a specialist in early Christian heresies and heretics.

The vein of self-parody evident in Roger's utterances allows us to take them with less than full seriousness. A particularly egregious example, which may suggest the attraction and appeal of this "unattractive" character, occurs when he invites Dale, along with Verna and her child, to Thanksgiving dinner at the Lambert house. When Dale arrives Roger offers him a drink, suggesting white wine or a Bloody Mary; Dale opts for cranberry juice. As he discovers some in the refrigerator, Roger is moved to the following characterization of, in his view, "this dreary liquid": "Cranberry juice depresses me, reminding me of bogs, of health food, of children with stained upper lips, and old ladies gathering in dusty parlors to pool the titillations of their dwindling days. It looks dyed." In terms of the novel's thematics, this would count as yet another item in the catalog of things that depress Roger Lambert; but the bogs, the lip-stained children, the dwindling old ladies, combine into an abusive treatment of the famous liquid that is both unjust and delightful: surely these are the first really bad words ever uttered against cranberry juice. And it feels utterly natural and expected for Roger, a few pages later, to move from the depressions induced by the juice to jaundiced reflections about "youth." He notes that Verna, who has arrived and is about to have a Bloody Mary, is "muttering" with Dale in a language Roger doesn't know:

> Youth: the mountain range that isolates it in a valley far from
> our own grows steeper, I think, as capitalism ever more fero-
> ciously exploits it as a separate market, beaming at it whole

new worlds of potential expenditure — home video games and rear-entry ski boots and a million bits of quasi-musical whining cut by laser into compact discs. Ever more informational technique, ever more inane information.

In fact the information being provided by Dale here, with the help of the boxes and lines he's sketching on the back of an envelope, has to do with circuits and binary codes and other computer things that Roger couldn't follow anyway. The point is that such animadversions on modern life, as Roger's version has it, make for much of the book's comic life but tend to be overlooked when one is asked to focus instead on parallels with and divergences from Hawthorne, or indeed any thematic aspect.

The most available peg on which to hang the narrative is of course the debate between Roger and his "inquisitor," the young man Dale who wants a grant from the divinity school so he can advance his project of proving that God exists; that he is — in Dale's excited terms to Roger — *"breaking through."* This is exactly the kind of breakthrough that Roger not only doesn't want, but finds repellent: the notion that a "complete physical description of the basic universe," with all the evidence put together and run through a computer, could establish God's reality. Roger tells Dale he finds the whole idea "aesthetically and ethically repulsive," and goes on to explain: "Aesthetically because it describes a God Who lets Himself be intellectually trapped, and ethically because it eliminates faith from religion, it takes away our freedom to believe or doubt. A God you could prove makes the whole thing immensely, oh, un*i*nteresting. Pat. Whatever else God may be, He shouldn't be pat." A Barthian, Roger remembers his youthful discovery of the great sentence in his hero, "The god who stood at the end of some human way — even of this way — would not be God." It would compromise and play false Roger's conviction were he to assume or hope that Dale's belief in the human continuity between science and a demonstrated Divinity might be entertained. So the defeat of Dale has personal stakes involved.

Early in the novel there is an odd moment of narrative in which the special character of Roger Lambert's "version" (or vision) is established. After his interview with Dale they part without shaking hands, an occasion for a minor Roger-diatribe on how there's too much handshaking in American life, along with too much wishing others a good day. He then thinks about his upcoming lecture on the heretic Marcion in which he foresees that the students will titter at his mention of Karl Barth, "my own, I must confess, rascally pet." Suddenly Roger is disconcerted by his foreseeing of Dale's future as well: "In one of those small, undesired miracles that infest life, like the numb sensation of hugeness that afflicts us when we stand after long sitting or the nonsensical, technicolor short subjects the mind runs preliminary to falling into sleep, my disembodied mind empathetically followed Dale Kohler down the hall" — which progress is then described in full detail through the long paragraph. Our narrator, in other words, is endowed with a rather extraordinary X-ray vision, with regard to his antagonist, and that keeps him in focus when he is far out of sight. So Roger's later vision, in the most pedantic and lurid detail, of his wife Esther and Dale in sexual congress (fellatio, to be specific) merely follows what has already been demonstrated — that the novel delights in playing around with "realistic" boundaries, and that Roger Lambert is a master projectionist. The movie he runs of Esther and Dale occurs in the wake of his reading and translating Tertullian from the Latin, a passage in which the heretic argues that the soul enjoys nature and the worldly elements only through the agency of the flesh (*quem elementorum saporem non per carnem anima depascitur?*). As he finds "ridiculous and sickening" Tertullian's "blessing of everlastingness upon our poor shuffling flesh," Roger closes his eyes and pictures Esther fellating Dale:

> a white shaft: tense, pure, with dim blue broad veins and darker thinner purple ones and a pink-mauve head like the head of a mushroom set by the Creator upon a swollen stem nearly as thick as itself, just the merest little lip or rounded

eaves, the *corona glandis*, overhanging the bluish stretched semi-epiderm where pagan foreskin once was, and a drop of transparent nectar in the little wide-awake slit of an eye at its velvety suffused tip.

You could call this pornographic, and it has been pointed out that Roger takes pleasure in both heresy and pornography: thus his "scripting" of Dale's relation with Esther is both a consummation of homoerotic desire and part of "a larger scheme to come out on top in their theological debate."[11] I wouldn't claim that the novel rejects such interpretive moves, but as pornography a passage like the above would stimulate, I should think, only a determinedly unironic reader, unable to catch the parodic aspects of Roger's version here, while concerned to make the passage mean something exciting.

And indeed *Roger's Version* is an eminently interpretable novel, even though no particular interpretation, however ingenious, can convince a reader who is disaffected by the whole proceedings that it is any worthier a piece of writing than he at first thought. This is by way of taking up Frederick Crews's previously mentioned charge that, in this as well as other novels from the later Updike, the "range of sympathies has contracted." What Crews intuits to be Updike's growing uncertainty about God, about the Christian "answer" to things, has resulted in the growth, in his art, of "a belligerent, almost hysterical callousness" about human beings, especially those "outsiders" who will not — as Crews adds snidely — be "golfing with Updike in the great country club in the sky." The pages I've quoted thus far would be good candidates for Crews's findings of "contracted sympathies" and "callousness," if — but it's a large *if* — one were willing to proceed directly from hearing them in Roger's voice to ascribing them as sentiments his creator endorses. But let us focus on a single extended passage, half or more of a long paragraph in which, gathered at the Lamberts' house for Thanksgiving, Dale blesses the food they are about to eat. Here is Roger's response:

A few of Dale's words bored into my brain, some kind of remembrance, before we stuffed our faces, of all the starving and homeless in the world, particularly East Africa and Central America, and my mind skidded off into wondering whether the UNICEF God Who would respectfully receive such prayers were not a frightful anticlimax to those immense proofs via megastar and mammoth tusk, and skidded further into thinking of meals and betrayals — the salt spilled by Judas, the chronic diet of Cronus, dinners whipped up by Clytemnestra and Lady Macbeth, the circle of betrayal established wherever more than two or three gather or a family sits down as one. Verna's hand was in my right hand and she had a rapid pulse. Richie's was in my left and there was heat here, too, the Oedipal animus, and on my side paternal coolness, the tigerish tendency to view the cub, once born, as a competitor as pleasant to extinguish as any other. A competitor born, furthermore, into the heart of one's own turf, which he fills with his electronic static and smelly socks and ravenous ill-educated appetite for what our cretinous popular culture assures him are the world's good things. Emerson was right, we all have cold hearts.

It goes on, the "skidding," into Jews and Christians and Greeks before subsiding into the turkey to be carved, which Roger loses no time in taking to task just for being a turkey: "Oh, those diabolically elusive, bloody, and tenacious second joints! And the golden-glazed skin that proves tougher than strapping tape!" Here is a plethora of "belligerence" about a variety of subjects, all of them sharing one attribute, that of being unsatisfactory to Roger Lambert.

Without taxing Crews unfairly over a passage he doesn't quote in his review, I would imagine he could mine it for further instances of Updike's callousness, toward the starving and homeless, toward not only the younger generation but one's very own son, and — historically and mythologically — toward the "circle of betrayal" that is "really" behind family togetherness. In order to do this, however, he would need — as he has done with other passages from the novel — effectively to suppress any trace of pleasurable sensation, of wit, that he might receive from reading it. So that even while pointing to the "sardonic fictional strategy" informing *Roger*, and its relatives *A Month of Sundays*, *The Coup*, and *The Witches of Eastwick*, Crews shows no evidence that he has responded to the book's comic dimension, evidenced here in the lively "skidding" Roger's mind undergoes from one to another deplorable instance of human folly. Yet this comedy seems to me absolutely central to the compositional principle of *Roger's Version*, and it can't be separated from the way the sentences, as in the above example, make up a prose rhythm of distinct verve and musical delight. They are more than fun to read aloud, those sentences.

In his note to the novel, Updike wrote that after bringing out *The Witches of Eastwick*, one more fiction about a small town, it was time for him to attempt "a city novel." Thus although the city is unnamed ("nameless and cavalierly distorted but perhaps not unrecognizable," he says in the note), it had preparatorily to be visited and viewed "from above." Certainly the Cambridge/Boston scene is not only "not unrecognizable," it is palpably present in its gritty end-of-the-century self. When Roger visits Verna in her shabby apartment, some distance from where, in the cozy precincts of the divinity school, his own ample three-story house stands, he passes through a very different cityscape from the one of large wooden dwellings and ancient trees that make up his residence in Malvin Lane (the Hawthorne allusion to "Roger Malvin's Burial" is there for those who want it). To stab at identifying the area more precisely, it is the industrial decayed Cambridge of Central or Inman Square, rather than the academic purlieus of Harvard Square. When Roger leaves Verna's apartment to search out the lumberyard where Dale works part-time, he passes semiabandoned houses and looks for a street near the railroad tracks:

> And there *was* a street here, devoid of houses, that led into an
> industrial limbo, surviving perhaps from an era when this sec-
> tion lay on the edge of the city, a nest of mills later engulfed

and isolated, a wilderness of rusting sheds and cinder-block warehouses, of factories whose painted names had left ghosts of letters on the brick, in the ornate style of the last century — vast shelters long since fallen away from their original purpose of manufacture, rented and resold and reused in fractions of floor space, and dropping ever lower on the rotting rungs of capitalism.

We are led on, past a coalyard, through crumbling asphalt, eventually to the fenced acres of the lumberyard. This intently observed terrain is described without the facetiousness or chilly annoyance we have grown used to from Roger, and it has less to do with Hawthorne than with the novel published just one hundred years before *Roger's Version*, Henry James's *The Bostonians*. Here is part of the view from Olive Chancellor's Boston drawing room, as seen through the eyes of Verena Tarrant, but really of James:

the long, low bridge that crawled, on its staggering posts, across the Charles; the casual patches of ice and snow; the desolate suburban horizons, peeled and made bald by the rigor of the season; the general hard, cold void of the prospect; the extrusion, at Charlestown, at Cambridge, of a few chimneys and steeples, straight, sordid tubes of factories and engine-shops. . . . There was something inexorable in the poverty of the scene, shameful in the meanness of its details, which gave a collective impression of boards and tin and frozen earth, sheds and rotting piles, railway-lines striding flat across a thoroughfare of puddles . . . loose fences, vacant lots, mounds of refuse, yards bestrewn with iron pipes, telegraph poles, and bare wooden backs of places.

Viewing the scene, Verena (a name close to Updike's Verna) thinks it "lovely"; but in James's picture things are rather more interestingly complicated and expressive. Although, compared to Updike's, James's view of things is more fully named and located, both writers are concerned to convey, with authority, the spirit of industrial place.

By car or on foot, Roger visits the crumbling city neighborhood where Verna and her child live in a ghettolike housing project, and describes in precise detail the housing project that gives an impression of "random human energy too fierce to contain in any structure." The playgrounds, for example,

> originally equipped with relatively fragile seesaws and round-abouts, had evolved into wastelands of the indestructible, their chief features now old rubber truck tires and concrete drain pipes assembled into a semblance of jungle gyms. A glittering sheet of broken glass fringed the asphalt curbs, the cement foundations, SE PROHIBE ESTACIONAR.

Its inhabitants are even more directly presented:

> The people on the street, caught between the darkening time of year and the unseasonably tepid weather, appeared bewildered about how to dress, and showed everything from parkas to jogging shorts. Two young black women in long Medusa braids and Day-Glo miniskirts flitted along like negatived Alices who had passed through a besmirched looking-glass, their jaunty and girlish innocence a sign, somehow, of its very opposite. Poverty and flash jostled along the avenue, and I was tempted to sing, heading out of my accustomed neighborhood into one where possibilities were in squalor reborn.

It is, one notes, the Christmas season. On the basis of these and other passages, Crews moves with ease from the literary character to his creator and convicts Updike of a "petty, fearful exclusivism," especially against "the black menace" or "the threat of criminal black incursion." But even without questioning the conflation of Roger and Updike, we can question the wisdom of putting the critic's attention on the presumed attitude *behind* certain observations, rather than on the observations themselves. In other words, what I take to be an impressive realism in the presentation of housing project, playground, the feel of a run-down city street and the appearance of its inhabitants is not made any less impressive by "placing" it as emanating from illiberal social, even racial, attitudes. In venturing into new territory with this "city" novel, Updike became a more inclusive, rather than a "fearfully exclusive" writer. We have come a long way from Olinger and the farm, even from Rabbit's decomposing city of Brewer.

Also new territory in this novel is the peculiar blend of feelings its hero shows in relation to his niece: fastidious distaste, lust, curiosity, then a growing interest in, even affection for, the young mother who addresses Roger regularly as "Nunc" and who, after a couple of false starts, persuades him (just for that once) into bed. There is an especially odd and poignant scene in which Roger, having urged Verna to take the equivalency exams for the highschool degree, leads her through a series of questions about William Cullen Bryant's anthology warrior "Thanatopsis," a poem, he tells Verna, Bryant wrote when he was younger than she. As Verna reads it aloud and Roger quizzes her on this or that word, or on the phenomenon of assonance ("'You think I'll have to know junk like that for the equivalency test?' 'It never hurts to know something,' I said, struck as I said it by how untrue it was"), the teacher finds himself more and more appalled at Bryant's youthful evasion of the terrible fact of death he presents in the poem. "The pattern here is the absolute pattern of every high-school valedictory address: big questions melting into fatuous, wishful answers," states irritated Roger, after which Verna touchingly puts in a qualified word in Bryant's favor. The scene ends with her saying to him, "So what's next? . . . 'The Luck of Roaring Camp' [also in the anthology], or are we going to fuck?" They don't, but the question so phrased is priceless. And there is, penultimate to Verna's departure back to the Midwest (Roger and Esther are to take care of the child, Paula), a lovely moment at the end of a dinner Roger gives her in a skytop Boston restaurant. They revolve, viewing the city from all angles — "from above," as Updike said in his note. At the end of which meal "In spontaneous mercy" Verna kisses him on the cheek: "it felt like a drop of rain in the desert," claims our untypically gratified hero.

This is to do no more than suggest how the tone of *Roger's Version* is a good deal more complicated and more interesting than it turns out to be in what we may call Crews's version. His article ends by claiming to have discovered an Updike different from the conventional celebrator of the visible universe; instead, Crews makes out a figure "morbid and curmudgeonly, starved for a missing grace, playing an unfunny hide-and-seek game with his readers"; thus the "sunny outskirts" of Updike's mind should not deceive us about "a certain bleakness at the center." But "bleakness" is not an adequate word for the much more enlivening, playful, and quite daring enterprise that is *Roger's Version*. I can't successfully follow some of the learning displayed in the disquisition on religious heretics, and the *tour de force* scene in which Dale, attempting to have God's existence reveal itself to him in the computer lab, comes to grief and defeat, resulted in something close to defeat for me. But still, I had already been warned by Roger ("Follow, you who can"). Overall it is not only the strangest but the most ambitious book Updike had written, indeed would go on to write, and as an achievement — the Rabbit books aside — it strikes me as his best novel since *The Centaur*.

S

Just before *S* was published, Updike granted the *New York Times* an interview in which he talked, freely as usual, about what he had attempted to do in the new book. Here, he said, was a novel written from the woman's viewpoint, in the form of letters and tapes sent by the exiled Sarah Worth to assorted family, friends, and acquaintances. Updike explained that he had been upset to hear that some women objected to his portrayal, in his fiction, of their sex as too exclusively domestic and sexual companions. There were no career women, no women with jobs, and though, as he said, he had no interest in writing about *male* businessmen either, that didn't quite take him off the hook. In *The Witches of Eastwick*, he noted, he had written about career women of a sort, but *S* was his first "woman's novel by a man." He also admitted that there was a lot of comedy in the book, and suggested that the larger amount of "funny" stuff in his later work had to do with becoming more "hard-hearted" and "crabbier." With *Roger's Version* just at his back, the claim seemed reasonable.

Yet in that same interview Updike couldn't resist, in his roguish manner, annoying those very readers he was claiming to serve. For featured at the beginning of things is the information, in support of having written a woman's novel, that "the binding of the book is pink. It's really sort of rose . . . but it looks pretty pink to me — a feminine, hopeful, fresh pink."[12] Such testimony was unlikely to disarm, say, Gloria Steinem, and it looks to be a deliberate cutting of the ground out from under the rendered valentine or apology. In fact S is, like the bit about pink from the interview as well as Updike's recent novels (especially the *Scarlet Letter* ones), incorrigibly mischievous and programmatically provocative. The more freedom Updike gives his female protagonist to unburden herself on all sorts of subjects, the more offense the novel and its author provided readers unsusceptible to such amusements.

One such reader was the *Times* book critic, Michiko Kakutani, who in a "Notebook" response, after S was published, to the earlier *Times* interview, assured readers that Updike's attempt to write from the woman's viewpoint was unattractive.[13] His heroine was a "careless woman," satirically portrayed, stuffed with outmoded language from the women's movement, selfish, unthinking, and just not at all the sort of "sympathetic heroine" he might or should have been attempting to create. Kakutani saw that the book was comic, but objected to the tone of its comedy, calling it "sour and brittle." (She would also object to such qualities in subsequent Updike novels, notably *Toward the End of Time*.) In fact the novelistic predecessors of S — *Roger's Version, The Witches of Eastwick,* even *The Coup* — may also be classified, for whatever good it does, as comedies. Compared to them, certainly compared to its immediate predecessor (*Roger*), S is, for all its cleverness, a relatively straightforward, even "easy" book — especially if, like me, you read quickly over the Eastern yoga ritual passages and don't spend time looking up, in the thirteen-page glossary Updike obligingly provides, the difference between "Prakriti" (matter) and "Prapatti" (passive surrender). Compared to Tom Marshfield's narrative in *A Month of Sundays*, Sarah Worth's is unlaced with ambiguity; there are not even very many second thoughts on her part, nor are there ironic ones directed at her since she is, after all, the only voice we hear. *S* is also a novel unlikely to convince readers that at long last Updike had sympathetically portrayed a postliberated American woman, since Sarah's experience is not subject to narrative placing, analysis, or the kind of "understanding" that a three-dimensional novel would provide. It is not, that is, to be confused with, or even compared to, *Anna Karenina, Madame Bovary,* or *To the Lighthouse,* to name three absorbing studies that provide rich perspectives on their heroines. *S* is two-dimensional rather, very much of the surface. It is indeed "brittle," but comedy has a place for such brittleness and can make us engaged with and amused by a heroine whom we aren't asked to take seriously as a human being the way we must take Anna or Emma or Mrs. Ramsay.

Even less than with *A Month of Sundays* and *Roger's Version* does concentration on the Hawthorne aspect contribute to increased pleasure in or understanding of the narrative. To be sure, Sarah's daughter is named Pearl, and there are letters to a Mrs. Blithedale, and the ashram has its affinities with the ill-fated utopian community in *The Blithedale Romance;* while the book's handsome dust jacket, designed by Updike himself, shows a very large red-orange letter *S* imposed upon a background of deep green (the Knopf borzoi dog is also red-orange). But I don't see that these allusions go any deeper than ones in which Sarah writes an annoyed letter to her significantly named dentist back east, Dr. Podhoretz, reproving him for the bad work he did on her teeth while overcharging her. The book lives wholly and only in the vigorous, unstoppable voice of its heroine, whether admonishing her daughter — who plans to marry a young man from Holland, bringing out much anti-Dutch feeling in the mother — or her mother in Florida who is involved with an admiral, or her friend back home, Midge, giving full accounts of goings-on at the ashram. The second letter to her husband, who has accused her of misappropriating his funds, berates him for the life she led with him:

> You speak of our bank accounts and stocks. You even write the slanderous word "theft." Were not these assets joint? Did I not labor for you twenty-two years without wages, serving as concubine, party doll, housekeeper, cook, bedwarmer, masseuse, sympathetic adviser, and walking advertisement — in my clothes and accessories and demeanor and accent and even in my body type and muscle tone — of your status and prosperity?

A few paragraphs later she has charmingly forgotten her annoyance enough to worry that, without her around, he'll become careless about keeping up the property:

> I do hope you aren't letting the lawn boys scalp that lumpy section out by the roses with that extra-wide Bunton. They should be spraying for aphids now. The peonies should be staked — the wire support hoops are in the garden shed, behind and above the rakes, on nails, in the same tangle that last year's boys left them in.

Like Sarah's other communications, all the energy is on the surface, even when she tries, occasionally, to go deep and have thoughts about Life. But that surface is, typically, solid, full of physical and social detail, and invariably energetic. To complain, as with the above diatribe to her husband about her derived status, that she is spouting clichés from the early days of the women's movement is to mistake the overall tone of the novel — a "brittle" tone, if you will, not conducive to help us comprehend, in richly sympathetic ways, the woman's plight. Yet Sarah gets off a number of good hits here at her husband's expense, enough to make for the spirited piece of writing that S for the most part is.

But it's a mistake to stay very long at the level of a character named Sarah Worth, and it was also, if not a mistake on Updike's part in the interview, a kind of red herring he threw out when he allowed that S was written from the woman's viewpoint. For that "viewpoint" is always shaped and put to narratively humorous uses by the novelist behind Sarah; her woman's viewpoint is not at all the last word. This can be demonstrated, tellingly I think, by any number of moments but in particular by the letter to her mother in which she reveals her deception by the Arhat (Shri Arhat Mindadali, M.A., PH.D., Supreme Mediator, Ashram Arhat), which deception will cause her almost immediately to leave the ashram and locate herself, at the end of the novel, on a tropical isle. What Sarah discovers is that her peerless leader is not only not a bona fide Indian sage, but an ordinary American Jewish boy from a background not of the classiest: "He's not even Jewish, technically, since his mother was Armenian — you know there's that big Armenian community in Watertown, just as you cross the Cambridge line along Mount Auburn Street, past the Cemetery — and that might give him that Asiatic quality I was so sure he had." The local specification is both accurate and amusing, but Sarah soon returns to it in manner that shows how the Watertown venue is rankling: "Maybe thanks to you and Daddy I'm such an incorrigible snob it's simply the idea that he's from Watertown — if it were Newton or Belmont or even Arlington I might not mind half so much. But I can't believe I haven't burned away even that much petty prejudice in these seven months." One critic found distasteful Updike's saddling his heroine with such base and conventional prejudices, as if it were illegitimate to draw a line, however thin, between the almost-okay Arlington and its not-so-okay neighbor in the Greater Boston area.[14] Such an objection is in line with Kakutani's complaint about how we don't get a "sympathetic heroine," and it is really wishing that — instead of giving us this comedy, absolutely linked to socioeconomic fact (there *is* a large Armenian community in Watertown, and Arlington *may* rank slightly higher in real estate values) — we should have been presented with a woman who would not stoop to admitting that she's still a snob. At any rate it is a way of distinguishing the dissatisfied reader of *S* from one like myself who, if forced to rank it among Updike's other novels, would give it minority status, while insisting that it can be read and reread with pleasure.

EIGHT

THE CRITIC AND REVIEWER

Updike's relentless productivity as a critic of other writers' productions as well as his own is acknowledged by everyone including himself. In an interview he confessed with perhaps the least hint of a boast that "I would write ads for deodorants or labels for catsup bottles if I had to."[1] By way of apologizing for such fecundity or promiscuity, he allowed himself in a foreword to his second collection, *Picked-Up Pieces* (1975), to hope "for the sakes of artistic purity and paper conservation, that ten years from now the pieces to be picked up will make a smaller heap." It was not to be, since that collection when it came (*Hugging the Shore*, 1983) had almost doubled in size, amounting to 919 pages. Its successor, *Odd Jobs* (1991), also, miraculously, came in at exactly 919 pages, and a fifth, equally large collection, *More Matter*, has recently appeared. As with comparably prolific writers — Joyce Carol Oates, Anthony Burgess, A. N. Wilson — such facility inspires skepticism and distrust in the reader who would believe that, somehow, things should come harder than they do for Updike. "Has the son of a bitch ever had one unpublished thought?" asks the annoyed, anonymous voice quoted by David Foster Wallace in that previously mentioned putdown of his elder.

How did all this offense against artistic purity and the conservation of paper come about? Temperament and inclination must be acknowledged, of course, and when Martin Amis wittily reviewed

Odd Jobs, he decided that Updike's true opposite in this respect was Samuel Beckett, whom Amis imagined staring at the wall for eighteen hours a day, at the end of which he has called up a few words — "NEVER or END or NOTHING or NO WAY."[2] By contrast, Amis wrote, Updike is a "psychotic Santa of volubility," willing and eager to turn out something pithy for a science magazine on thermodynamics, or, for a fashion magazine, ten thousand words on his favorite color, then going upstairs to blurt out a novel. By way of accounting for such volubility — along with temperament and inclination, perhaps even antecedent to them — there has been Updike's association for four decades with the *New Yorker*. It must have been a temptation to the artist's purity as well, since even for such a fast worker novels take time to write. A collection of stories must accrete over a number of years, but a review due in a fortnight or a lecture to be given next month on Melville or Howells provide the short-term obligations that can be heartening. Reviewing and lecturing are ways of keeping in trim, of getting regular exercise, the sort of exercise Updike has needed no encouragement to engage in: "Evidently I can read anything in English and muster up an opinion about it. I am not sure, however, the stunt is good for me," he said in the foreword to *Picked-Up Pieces*. The uncertainty, probably more politely turned than deeply felt, appears in successive decades to have resolved itself.

Like V. S. Pritchett, Updike's rival as an indefatigable reviewer (Pritchett only ceased to review in his nineties), who could read anything in English and write about it, Updike's critical temperament has always inclined toward generosity rather than stringency. In this he is the opposite of other prolific reviewers from recent decades — Marvin Mudrick and John Simon come to mind — whose creative juices really begin to flow when they have something awful in front of them to offend their sensibilities. On the one occasion when Updike was moved to state his principles of "rules" as a reviewer (again, in the foreword to *Picked-Up Pieces*), he set himself against any notion of "correcting" the author and invited potential reviewers to "Try to understand what the author wished to do," and to "Submit to whatever spell, weak or strong, is being cast. Better to praise and share than blame and ban," was the maxim most directly reflective of his continual practice. More interesting than this benign directive, however, is his conviction that the reviewer should engage in direct quotation, both piecemeal and with reference to at least one extended passage from the book under consideration. This caveat, which Updike has consistently adhered to, means that he doesn't write the kind of imperial review that uses the book in question as a springboard merely for launching a display of the reviewer's ingenuity. Under Updike's procedure the book's author may, whatever the verdict, be heartened to find that his words have been at least taken seriously enough to be quoted.

In one of the pieces from *Odd Jobs*, a short tribute to Edmund Wilson, Updike notes that in a period when literature became increasingly a subject of academic study, Wilson was a nonacademic, his brief stints in the classroom notwithstanding. (The titans of English book reviewing in our century's latter half — Cyril Connolly, Pritchett, Geoffrey Grigson, Julian Symons — were similarly unaffiliated with the classroom.) Updike doesn't suggest a causal relation between Wilson's unacademic career and his omnivorous capacity for books, but pays tribute to that capacity in terms he would not, assuredly, mind having used about himself: "Wilson was a great reader who communicated on almost every one of his thousands of pages of criticism the invigorating pleasure — the brisk winds and salubrious exercise — to be had in the landscape of literature." It is a fair description of Updike's own contribution to criticism, right down to the confirming reference to salubrious exercise. Such identification shouldn't obscure important differences between the two men. Wilson's criticism was essayistic: he wrote plenty of reviews, but his most enduring and challenging performances are, along with his three "subject" books — *Axel's Castle*, *To the Finland Station*, and *Patriotic Gore* — the leisurely treatments of older writers like Dickens, Flaubert, Swinburne, Bernard Shaw, John Jay Chapman, Housman, Henry James. By contrast Updike's engagement with older writers has been pretty much confined to

Americans, and his essays on Hawthorne, Emerson, Melville, Whitman, and Howells all originated as lectures to one or another specific audience. There doesn't seem to be in his case — at least compared to Wilson's — a driving motive to read up on some great or insufficiently known writer (like Chapman, say), with the aim of introducing the reader to new territories. This is not to forget that a *New Yorker* reader who followed and kept track of and read some of the books considered in Updike's reviewing of contemporary African, eastern European, and American novelists (to stop at just three of numerous categories) would have extended and enlarged his tastes and horizons. Updike is also relatively without Wilson's Taine-like aspirations to explore the interdependence of biography and history with the individual talent, though he writes about Sherwood Anderson and John O'Hara with a sharp interest in the American places from which they came and whose qualities they dourly celebrated. A further resemblance: although both Updike and Wilson wrote poetry, in Updike's case a lot of it, they mainly keep away from discussing poets or poems in their criticism. Wilson's provocative "Is Verse a Dying Technique" is a rare, theoretical excursion into the historical and modern relation between verse and prose. Updike, having written his undergraduate thesis on the poet Herrick, occasionally addresses a modern poet; but his brief accounts of Wallace Stevens, Auden, and L. E. Sissman are not undertaken in any spirit of reevaluating their work. That Stevens was born in Reading, Pennsylvania, and that Sissman was a friend provides most of Updike's motive in addressing them.

Nor in temperament and critical style do Wilson and Updike invite linkage. The deliberative, precise, relatively unadorned prose Wilson used so effectively to frame and develop his judgments feels impersonal compared to Updike's strongly metaphorical and unabashedly personal testimonies of delight or disappointment. Though he has praise for Wilson's novel *Memoirs of Hecate County*, he also detects, in Wilson's fiction generally, "something leaden and saturnine," qualities wholly foreign to anything written by Updike. The latter's inclination in the direction of praise, his avoidance whenever possible of saying the worst about a book, distinguishes him — perhaps not to his advantage — from the Wilson who assaulted with deadly effect the then high reputation of a forgotten novelist named Louis Bromfield, or who found, with detective stories, that the emperor had no clothes ("Who Cares Who Killed Roger Ackroyd"), or who judged unsustaining and overrated much of T. S. Eliot's later work.

Updike's criticism is also, in its unwillingness to claim much for itself, and in its professedly casual air, to be distinguished from Wilson's or from that of the academic critic who takes his professional role with high seriousness. The foreword to *Hugging the Shore*, a collection with a jacket cover on which the author is lounging in a rowboat in shallow water close to land, opens with this metaphorical comparison:

> Writing criticism is to writing fiction and poetry as hugging the shore is to sailing in the open sea. At sea, we have that beautiful blankness all around, a cold bright wind, and the occasional thrill of a gleaming dolphin-back or the synchronized leap of silverfish; hugging the shore, one can always come about and draw even closer to the land with another nine-point quotation.

From someone who believes in quoting from the books he reviews and who quotes aptly and illuminatingly, the activity is here seen as also protective and tame, necessarily forgoing the thrill of original composition. But it can also be taken as a salutary admission of subordination, if we remember Randall Jarrell's annoyed question in "The Age of Criticism": "Criticism *does* exist, doesn't it, for the sake of the plays and stories and poems it criticizes?" Jarrell thought that all too often criticism behaved as if it heeded no such counsel of deference to the "creative" art it served. Yet any possibly noble motive for reviewing books is complicated, indeed undercut, when Updike's foreword ends with a reference (the year is 1983) to his recent divorce: "in this land of fragmentation held together by legalities, the payment for a monthly review roughly balanced a monthly alimony payment that was mine to make." So this less-than-heroic reason for hugging the shore so consistently — even while he continued to make his usual ventures out into the deep water of fiction and poetry — is acknowledged by highlighting the economic motive, something I think that the four-times-married Edmund Wilson would have avoided (and did avoid) mentioning.

The contemporary American critic and reviewer who most challenges comparison with Updike is unquestionably Gore Vidal, who began his career as a novelist more than a decade before Updike and whose output, both critical and creative, has kept pace with the younger writer's. I say "unquestionably" Vidal, though at first thought Norman Mailer, whose career like Vidal's began in the late 1940s, might also seem — in Mailer's preferred pugilistic vocabulary — a contender. To be sure, Mailer's writerly excursions into politics, political conventions, sociological and psychological analysis, fashion and the lives of women, boxing, and Lee Harvey Oswald make for a larger, more comprehensive and daring performance as man of letters than does Updike's, confined on the whole to what we may call literature. Mailer provided, in the 1950s and 1960s, some still extremely readable literary reports on a few of his novelistic brothers and sisters in America — James Jones, Styron, Capote, Kerouac, Bellow, Algren, Salinger, Ellison, Baldwin, and others (including Updike and Vidal). He wrote a devastating review of Mary McCarthy's *The Group* (McCarthy felt it was devastating) and a brilliant excursion into the fortunes of the American novel from Dreiser to Terry Southern. But after roughly 1965, Mailer turned his attentions in any direction *but* the reviewing and criticism of American fiction.

Vidal on the other hand stuck to it, and the result is his mammoth compendium of forty years' worth of essays (*United States*, 1993). In that collection he refers condescendingly to Updike as "our literature's perennial apostle to the middlebrows"[3] even though, like that apostle, Vidal admires the work of William Dean Howells. Vidal's comments on his fictionist contemporaries usually have a sociological, culture-watching motive; he once wrote a hilarious piece characterizing each of the top ten fiction best-sellers, as according to the *New York Times* in January 1973; and, in "American Plastic," he lit into the academic "art" novel as produced by Barth and Gass, Barthelme and Pynchon. There are also a number of just appreciations of American and English writers from preceding decades. But the powerful attractions of Vidal's other interests — in the movies and television, in politics and political gossip, in sex, journalism, and the structure of American society — have prohibited his amassing the catalog of detailed reports on literature Updike has given us over decades. So that, although Vidal has been called, by at least one publication, our foremost man of letters, he is so suspicious and contemptuous of what he calls "bookchat" — especially the type indulged in by "scholar squirrels" — and so attracted by and inclined to the put-down, that he seems, for all his liveliness, a rather tendentious critic of literature.

"What can one say, critically, about a critic without seeming hypercritical," Updike once asked about Cyril Connolly.[4] The question may be rephrased: what can be said, critically, about a novelist and poet whose criticism is directed mainly at his contemporaries — sometimes acquaintances, sometimes friends, sometimes rivals in the vineyard — beyond agreeing or disagreeing with his judgments of them? If I'm convinced that Updike seriously underestimates, on the basis of *Jake's Thing*, the novelist Kingsley Amis, why should anyone be interested in my opinion? Amis himself failed to admire *Lolita* or *Portnoy's Complaint* (I admire both) and to my knowledge never bothered to express an opinion about Updike. And considering the vast numbers of novelists, distributed over countries and continents, on whom Updike has passed judgment, usually in the instance of a particular novel, to attempt a survey of his opinions and take issue with this or that one seems a useless not to say impossible task. My commentary instead will be directed at him as a writer about other American writers: first, his nineteenth-century predecessors — Hawthorne, Whitman, Melville, Emerson, and Howells; second, his novelistic contemporaries, with emphasis on his treatment of two formidable rivals, Saul Bellow and Philip Roth.

. . .

The essays on nineteenth-century writers began as lectures, each of them undertaken, in his prefatory words to the first three, "to educate the speaker as much as the audience."[5] There is no reason to doubt the sincerity of this claim if we imagine Updike challenging himself to say something fresh and adequate about the achievements of five major American prose forebears (Twain and Henry James he has as yet left uncriticized). With reference to the triad of Hawthorne, Melville, and Whitman, he notes that "The theme of religious belief that connects them emerged like a gravestone rubbing." That theme also emerges in the Emerson essay, though not in the one on Howells. In dealing with these writers and that theme, Updike surely took considerable thought for whatever possible application their examples might have to his own case as a writer for whom the "religious" aspect is seldom far from the surface of things. At any rate, each of the essays shows his presence as an aspiring reader, anxious to make clear to himself and others something important about the art of our classic writers.

The Hawthorne essay, surprisingly a brief seven pages, is a complicated answer to the question posed at its beginning: "What did Hawthorne believe?"[6] Noting the writer's conspicuous lack of churchgoing and formal religious affiliations, Updike quotes Hawthorne's son Julian's statement that his father never discussed religion in either his talk or his writings, but that his faith was expressed "in caverns submarine and unsounded, yet somehow apparent." Updike sees Hawthorne's sensibility as dualistic, its "sensation of inner delicacy" associated with providence and projected onto the world, where it is threatened with "human monomania" — with the crushing of flesh and blood and disruption generally. It is "the world versus the self," the latter of which struggles against its submergence. Updike concludes that "A very vivid ghost of Christianity stares out at us from [Hawthorne's] prose, alarming and odd in not being evenly dead, but alive in some limbs and amputate in others, blurred in some aspects and otherwise basilisk-keen." The metaphorical energy of this vivid formulation is by way of attempting to sound, without being exclusive or reductive, the "caverns" of Hawthorne's soul. In no sense does Updike discuss or evaluate the novels; rather he throws out, in brief, suggestive, and speculative fashion, the claim that their overlapping between the incompatible realms of flesh and spirit produces a "stain" — "some vast substance chemically betraying itself," the poisons of which are implicated in symbols that perform in the Gothic tradition "of which Hawthorne's tales are lovely late blooms." Updike sees the struggle between spirit and world played out in Hawthorne's own career, as "the fantasizing young hermit of the dozen Salem years" eventually becomes publicly employed, married, a successful writer who dies in an America that is attempting to expunge "the stain of slavery." This approach to Hawthorne is a plausible, if uncontroversial, one that students and scholars of the writer have also intimated and formulated. But its expression in these succinct pages of compact, figured prose is remarkable.

The Melville essay is more substantial, focused on the problem of Melville's writing after *Moby-Dick*, its failure with his readership and the resultant decline of its author into obscurity and silence. "Melville's Withdrawal," as Updike titles his piece, first delivered as a lecture at the public library in Rochester, New York, was "an excuse for repairing a gap in my own reading," that gap being post-*Moby-Dick* Melville. The admission, at the outset, that there was such a gap marks Updike's procedure as something other than the impersonal, professional one affected by critics and reviewers who speak as if they are and have been masters of their subject for decades. Instead he comes fresh to his reading of *Pierre*, Melville's attempt to follow *Moby-Dick* with a more popular treatment of American life — in Melville's words "a regular romance, with a mysterious plot to it, & stirring passions at work." *Pierre*, as is well known, was a resounding failure, "grindingly, ludicrously bad," reports Updike: "The action is hysterical, the style is frenzied and volatile, the characters are jerked to and fro by some unexplained rage of the author's." The attempt that has been made in recent years by academics anxious to rehabilitate *Pierre* — claiming that its closensss to parody is a virtue rather than a disaster — doesn't convince Updike, and here he speaks truly for the common reader, unimpressed by such recuperative moves on the part of ingenious professorial critics.

Some of the essay's pages concern the bread-and-butter aspects of Melville's publishing career, just how well paid a writer he was in his early "sea" fiction (he was well paid), and what happened to put him so seriously in debt by the time *Moby-Dick* was published. Updike argues that America at that time had an insufficiently large reading public to sustain a "free-lance" writer like Melville; but the economic motive preyed on his mind and led to exasperation: "Dollars damn me. . . . What I feel most moved to write, that is banned — it will not pay. Yet, altogether, write the *other* way I cannot," Melville is quoted from a letter to Hawthorne. As himself an economic unit concerned to make a monthly alimony payment, Updike is willing to get down to the dollars-and-cents aspect of Melville's career; the result is useful and probably more pertinent, by way of establishing Melville's situation, than any purely literary analysis could be. It is of a piece with Updike's concern, in other places, with the physical appearance — handsome or depressing — of the book he's holding in his hand for review. (His condescension to the lowly look of a small publisher's printing of some Nabokov stories inspired Nicholson Baker to pity for the poor press.)

The Melville essay also strongly exemplifies a persistent quality in all Updike's criticism, namely its ability to characterize and judge, with authority and economy, the individual works as they present themselves. In Edmund Wilson's essay "The Historical Interpretation of Literature" there is a moment when, after making a case for such interpretation and for biographical criticism, Wilson adds that of course the critic's task must still be to evaluate: "to estimate . . . the relative degree of success attained by the products of the various periods and the various personalities. We must be able to tell good from bad, the first-rate from the second-rate." This insistence, so foreign to much that passes for criticism today, is what Updike honors when in the essay he comes to Melville's late

work *The Confidence-Man*. Calling it "crabbed and inert," Updike
notes that, like *Pierre*, it "yields many evidences of ingenuity to
academic analysis," and that it anticipates later, apocalyptic writers
like Nathanael West and more recent black humorists. But he qualifies the claim:

> Black the book is and humorous its intent; but appreciation
> should begin with the acknowledgment that it is suffocat-
> ingly difficult to read. . . . Where *Pierre* is at least a bad novel,
> *The Confidence-Man* is no novel at all; it is a series of farfetched
> but rather joyless conversations upon the theme of trust, or
> confidence.

Overall *The Confidence-Man* gives the "sensation of wheels whirling
to no purpose." By contrast, there is the style of *Piazza Tales*,
Melville's collection of stories:

> though a triumphant recovery from the hectic tropes of *Pierre*,
> [it] is not quite the assured, playful, precociously fluent, and
> eagerly pitched voice of the sea-novels. It is a slightly *chastened*
> style, with something a bit abrasive and latently aggressive
> about it. However admirable, these tales are not exactly com-
> fortable; their surfaces are not seductive and limpid, like those
> of Hawthorne's tales.

As for Melville's poems, Updike notes that we have more "tolerance
for the awkwardness and obliquity" that reviewers of that time
found unappealing; still, "even the most sympathetic reader now
cannot but be struck by a feeling of deliberate and stubborn effort in
the poems, an effect of *muttering* quite unlike the full-throated ease
of the prose." In sum, Melville's poems strike "a resolute music of
iron and wood." This is impressionistic criticism of a high order,
aimed at speaking to and for the intelligent reader, not a specialist,
but one whose eyes and ears are curious about Melville's, or any
writer's, effects. The conclusion to the essay is unstartling: that after
Moby-Dick, Melville had indeed used up his one true subject, the
sea; that he was "right to withdraw" and that "turning to public

silence and private poetry" was a dignified act of preservation. If this puts a more benign cast on Melville's later years than is usually done, it also avoids blaming either him or the society in which he wrote. And it accords perhaps with Melville's own sense of privacy and his refusal to keep on playing at compromise.

Updike's essay on Whitman is the slightest one in this group on nineteenth-century writers, perhaps because the only way to make a case for Whitman's poetry is through extended quotation, commentary, and questioning of one's commentary. There is no such time and space available in a twelve-page "general" portrait of the good gray poet. The liveliest single essay written about Whitman — aside from D. H. Lawrence's profound one in *Studies in Classic American Literature* — is Randall Jarrell's "Some Lines from Whitman." That title suggests what Jarrell did so effectively, namely to pick out wonderful bits, lines and short sequences, from Whitman, quote them, then say — in a number of reiterated ways — how could anyone *not* recognize that this is great poetry? The problem in reading Whitman comes, though, not with individual lines but with experiencing them as parts of longer sequences, where much less marvelous lines than the ones Jarrell quotes tend to crop up. At moments Updike casts a cold eye on what his title calls "Whitman's Egotheism" — besides "his sometimes cloying vanity the relative unconvincingness and melodrama of the human tableaux and visitations in *Leaves of Grass*" — and he quotes with approval Lawrence's mockery of Whitman's all-too-easy identification with otherness, his sense of "One identity." (In Lawrence's example, if the identity in question were that of an Eskimo in his kayak, "there was Walt being little and yellow and greasy, sitting in a kayak.") But too quickly Updike declares that vanity and melodrama is no problem after all, quotes some lines as evidence of Whitman's "magnanimity" and simplicity, then exits by way of claiming that his "metaphysics" are those of our "distinctive 'American realism.'" The case needs more making.

With Emerson the case seems to be — and it feels like a problem in the somewhat grudging treatment Updike gives him — that

Emerson no longer bulks as large as he once did in "literary courses," except from a historical angle. Updike himself can't remember when he last read one of the "celebrated essays" which merge in his head so that he can't really tell one from another; thus his overall impression of the sage is cloudy and indistinct. The only way to make that impression less cloudy would be to confront particular sentences and paragraphs from Emerson's essays and attempt to describe the extraordinary difficulties and challenges they present a reader — difficulties inseparable from Emerson's greatness as a writer. Updike chooses instead to concentrate, as he did with Hawthorne, on Emerson's philosophy. His essay is titled "Emersonianism," and it points to habits of mind and belief rather than the habits of sentences in Emerson's prose. He is interested, for example, in comparing Emerson's charge to the students at Harvard Divinity School with the one presented by the crisis theology of Updike's favorite thinkers, Kierkegaard and Barth. In the lively pages that conclude the essay, describing a walk from his house to the train to Boston, a visit to his doctor at the hospital, and other mundane events, he demonstrates how, having been thinking about Emerson, things keep turning emblematic of one or another proverb and bit of wisdom offered by the master. But this activity of noting "Emersonianism" is rather different from the activity of reading him.

Updike's determination — as he expressed it in "The Dogwood Tree: A Boyhood" — "To transcribe middleness with all its grits, bumps, and anonymities, in its fullness of satisfaction and mystery," may have prevented or protected him from fully reaching out to embrace the creative exaggerations that inform the styles of both Emerson and Whitman. Or it may be that as above all else a writer of fiction, his sympathies most truly extend to novelists. (Although *Moby-Dick* is surely the greatest example of creative exaggeration in our literature.) At any rate, in reading his appreciation of Howells as what he calls an "anti-novelist," one feels that here is a writer whose theory and practice most truly speak to the books Updike had been writing over the past decades (the Howells essay was first delivered as a lecture at Harvard in 1987). Sentences he quotes from Howells's lecture "Novel-Writing and Novel-Reading" could serve as a fair description of Updike's own creative practice. Howells says that his ideal novelist will not rest until he has made his story "as like life as he can,"

> with the same mixed motives, the same voluntary and involuntary actions, the same unaccountable advances and perplexing pauses, the same moments of rapture, the same days and weeks of horrible dullness, the same conflict of the higher and lower purposes, the same vices and virtues, inspirations and propensities.

And in Howells's first novel, *Their Wedding Journey*, the narrator-novelist speaks of how he is able to move into the life of another and "inhabit there" — "to think his shallow and feeble thoughts, to be moved by his dumb, stupid desires, to be dimly illumined by his stinted inspirations, to share his foolish prejudices, to practice his obtuse selfishness." It is as though Updike's "inhabiting" of Rabbit Angstrom were prophesied.

His main strategy in the essay is to claim for Howells's fiction an unsettling character — unsettling to our expectations as readers — which he terms "avant-garde." Doubtless there is humorous exaggeration in presenting such a claim for a novelist who, if readers remember him at all, is associated with the production of comfortable, solid fictional products. But Updike sees Howells as interestingly unsolid insofar as he plays with readerly expectations by writing novels that are a little off-center, in the interests of a stronger realism. For example, Howells creates what Updike terms the "Not Quite Likable Hero," about whom over the course of a novel we develop decidedly mixed feelings. The culminating, most successful example of such a creation, found in perhaps Howells's best novel, is Bartley Hubbard of *A Modern Instance*, although Theodore Colville (*Indian Summer*) and Silas Lapham are also less-than-ideal "heroic" protagonists. Updike notes as well — and this is a crucial point to make about Howells's art — that his novels have a "tendency to defuse themselves, to avert or mute their own crises." Howells's plots are not memorable: just how *do* things work out in the latter chapters of *Indian Summer* or *The Rise of Silas Lapham* — not to mention lesser but wholly readable works like *April Hopes* or *The Quality of Mercy*? If my own experience of these books is typical, their outcomes are elusive, inconclusive. They have no strong curtain.

Such fidelity to the way things happen in life means that Howells (unlike, say, Dickens or Hardy) must be skeptical of "plot" as an animating and resolving principle of composition. "Life does not fall into plots," as Updike points out, and Howells's novels try to honor this truth. He does this by giving the impression of not being "wholeheartedly behind them" (his plots), by leaving "an impression of outlines not filled in, of developments not permitted." Even when, as in *A Modern Instance*, he punishes his hero (Bartley Hubbard is shot and killed in Arizona), his heart doesn't seem to be in it, as evidenced by the novel so transparently and casually putting the blame on Arizonian outlaws. As for Howells's stopping short of sexual realism — he couldn't appreciate *Sister Carrie*, for example, and was if anything too solid a citizen as regards social proprieties — he is still, Updike claims with a flourish, a "moral anarch in his art." This is surely the way Updike would prefer himself to be taken: as the sexual realist Howells failed to be; as a not-too-solid citizen, even as in public he observes, punctiliously and smilingly, the social proprieties involved with being a man of letters; as a moral anarch in his art.

The Howells essay concludes with a comparison to James, acknowledged by Updike as the first American modernist but whom he sees as more of an idol for academics to study and assign to the young than a living force emulated by practicing American novelists. Somewhat surprisingly Updike names Peter Taylor and Cynthia Ozick (and in their early work only) as the only true Jamesian "imitators" while Howells's heirs and descendants, he finds, are legion — Hamlin Garland and Booth Tarkington, Sinclair Lewis and John O'Hara and Raymond Carver, the last of whom exemplifies postmodernist exhaustion and the appeal of minimalist fiction. He concludes by quoting Howells's assertion, in response to James's likening of Howells's style to a man holding a diamond and not knowing what to do with it: "I am not sorry for having wrought in common, crude material so much; that is the right American stuff." The lecture on Howells, delivered close to the time when, in *Rabbit at Rest*, Updike would provide his most impressive rendering of such "right American stuff," seems at least in part to justify, in its concentration on the local, the regional, the domestic, and sexual, the "crude material" out of which his own art is made.

The central fact to be noted about Updike's criticism of his contemporaries in the fiction arena is that he has actively sought out opportunities to review them. This distinguishes him from significant American novelists of his generation — like Bellow, Roth, Pynchon — though not, as previously noted, from Mailer in his younger days and from Vidal throughout his career. Given the space the *New Yorker* has so obligingly provided him, his treatments of novels and novelists are leisurely, even expansive in the way they present — through quotation, plot summary, character description, and general evaluation — the book in question. Confining myself to what he has had to say about Bellow and Roth is an attempt to control, slightly, what has been an uncontrollable impulse on his part to seek out novels and novelists from Europe, Africa, Asia, and South America. If one looks for a country, indeed a continent, whose fiction he seems to have neglected, Australia might be mentioned; otherwise, give or take the lack of reference to writers from Lapland and Outer Mongolia, he has pretty much covered the globe. This is of course an amazing feat, as well as depressing to the spirits of anyone who, seriously bitten by the fiction bug, feels the necessity to "keep up" and regularly fails to do so. Although I can't demonstrate it here, my sense is, reading through Updike's reviews, that he works harder to be interested in and accepting of fiction the farther away it is from what's being produced in his own country. As far back as 1965, writing admiringly of the Argentinean Jorge Luis Borges, he took the occasion to deliver a smack, by its contrast with that writer's work, to "the dead-end narcissism and downright trashiness of present

American fiction." Whether thirty-five years later he would revise upward his estimate of that fiction is debatable.

If it is conceivable, and perhaps admirable, that Updike has cultivated openness toward fiction written outside the Anglo-American orbit, it seems to me also the case that he extends more tolerance and generosity to women (in contrast to male) novelists than, from a more objective point of vantage, they either ask for or deserve. While over the years he has paid very little attention to British male novelists since World War II — Henry Green is a notable exception, and Updike has praised William Trevor — he has been hospitable on more than one occasion to Iris Murdoch, to Muriel Spark (especially), to Margaret Drabble (with reservations), to Penelope Mortimer, to Anita Brookner (who "writes thrillingly"), and to the Canadian Margaret Atwood. Here of course one's reading prejudices assert themselves, but I find it telling that he has had no time, at least in print, for Evelyn Waugh, for Anthony Powell, for Anthony Burgess or A. N. Wilson or Ian McEwan or other English writers whose fictional art is in the main satiric and whose "take" on human beings might be accused of being diminishing or reductive. His remarks about Kingsley Amis are especially acerbic and dismissive. *Lucky Jim* is "unabashedly sophomoric"; Amis's "ambition and reputation alike remain in thrall to the weary concept of the 'comic novel,'" and he bears responsibility for the state of the "winsomely trivial" postwar English fictional product. The review of *Jake's Thing*, from which the previous judgments are taken, says the novel suffers from "contrived jokiness and unsteady perspective" although as a "portrait of a man" it is "satisfyingly ambiguous, relentless, and full." But that rather abruptly arrived-at positive judgment doesn't stop us from feeling that Amis is not at all Updike's cup of tea.

The claim that he is more generous, even more courtly, toward female than toward male novelists should be made only with an admission that it can't be proven, and that if it were true no great harm is done. I have perhaps been unduly influenced by an early but egregious instance of such courtliness on Updike's part: the occasion was Erica Jong's first novel, *Fear of Flying*, published in 1973 at the crest of the women's movement. Placing it in the tradition of *Catcher in the Rye* and *Portnoy's Complaint* as narrated by a "New York voice on the couch," Updike found that *Fear of Flying* "has class and sass, brightness and bite" and that "Containing all the cracked eggs of the feminist litany, her soufflé rises with a poet's afflatus." Later in the review, he turns to the back jacket flap in which "Mrs. Jong, with perfect teeth and cascading blond hair, is magnificently laughing." Whether or not *Fear of Flying* is a good novel — and I don't think it is — such a way of praising, whether the subject is Jong's prose or her vivid looks, surely grates. Admittedly such excess isn't found in Updike's praise of such other American women novelists as Joyce Carol Oates, Alice Adams, Ann Beattie, Cathleen Schine, and — most extensively — Anne Tyler. But still, he seems in writing about women writing to operate at less intensity, from a greater amused and tolerant distance, than he does when the novelist is a male whom he feels to be more part of the competition. You could argue that perhaps the most gifted of the above novelists, Anne Tyler, has clearly justified — and doubly benefited from — the sustained attention Updike has given to her novels as they have come out. You could also argue that there is something a little too faint-hearted in his occasional attempts to point out her limitations, as in this one from his review of her novel of 1985, *The Accidental Tourist:*

> If Anne Tyler strikes us as too benign, too swift to tack together shelter for her dolls, it may be that we have lost familiarity with the comedic spirit, the primal faith in natural resilience and the forces of renewal. . . . The constuctive, tinkering, inventive, systematic side of our selves is not enough; he who would save his life must lose it.

The reservation is hinted at only to be swallowed up by a little reminder of what "we" have supposedly lost faith in, followed by the suave "he who would save his life must lose it." This sort of grace-fulness is really indistinguishable from softness on the critic's part;

the potentially adverse judgment slides away into nothing much to bother about, as novel and novelist are affirmed.

How much of Anne Tyler's reputation is due to Updike's championing of her, one can't say; but his appreciations of novels written by this younger contemporary have a disinterested and freely given air about them. As a reviewer, his situation is altogether more simple, less potentially tricky, than when — as he has done three times — he receives a novel to deal with written by a Nobel prize winner who is among the living. To this may be added the fact — I assume it is agreed upon by most readers — that the novels in question, *Humboldt's Gift* (1975), *The Dean's December* (1982), and *The Theft* (1989), are by no means the best of Saul Bellow, a category defined by the earlier novels, from *The Victim* through *Mr. Sammler's Planet* and including most impressively *Seize the Day* and *Herzog*. One has to marvel at the skill with which Updike manages to praise and admire Bellow the novelist while making clear the unsatisfactoriness of the particular novel at hand. So he assesses Bellow's headlong style in *Humboldt's Gift* as "breezy and tough and not always grammatical," and finds his penchant for the "commaless series" ("black bread raw onion bourbon whiskey herring sausage cards billiards race horses and women") to constitute "a rather too determined exercise in relaxation." In this novel "effusion replaces conversation," as everyone ends up sounding like the protagonist, Charlie Citrine. But after all the just criticisms of the book, there is an *And yet* paragraph in which we are recalled to the great satisfactions Bellow still provides: "the scenes of Chicago justice as manipulated by woolly, cannibalistic lawyers and urbane Slavic judges (hilarious scenes, as devastating to the legal profession as anything in *Bleak House*); the barbed caricatures of Manhattan intelligentsia; the unfailingly tender sketches of old Chicago neighborhoods" — these are "evocations enlivened by love and alarm." Still, the final paragraph of the review doesn't shirk the duty of placing *Humboldt's Gift* in its relation to earlier Bellow, in particular to his first novel, *Dangling Man*, whose similarities to *Humboldt* Updike points out. But then the outcome of the comparison:

But after making one's way through the worldly mass of *Humboldt's Gift*, so rich in information and speculation, one wonders if, for Bellow's kind of dangling, rather than doing, man, the shorter length and implicative texture of the youthful book weren't better. . . . *Dangling Man*, though in snippets, merged earth and air, whereas *Humboldt's Gift*, washed up on our drear cultural shore like some large, magnificently glistening but beached creature from another element, dramatizes, in its agitated sluggishness, the body/mind split that is its deepest theme.

Bellow can't have been happy to read this (though he may have remembered his characterizing of Updike as a writer of "sensibility" merely), but it feels much less like a payback than a sympathetic and successful effort to enter Bellow's fiction and characterize it fully. The characterization, for all its adverse — in my view justified — criticisms of *Humboldt's Gift*, feels large-minded and sound, as does a moment at the end of Updike's adverse review of *The Dean's December*, Bellow's grayest and perhaps in the long run most forgettable novel. Without shirking, saying what's wrong with it, Updike makes a turn toward celebrating Bellow's enterprise as a writer:

Bellow believes in the soul; this is one of his links with the ancients, with the great books. At the same time, like those great books, he feels and conveys the authentic heaviness in which our spirits are entangled; he has displayed for thirty years an unsurpassedly active awareness of the corporeal, of the mortal, of human creatureliness in all its sexual and assertive variety. He is not just a very good writer, he is one of the rare writers who when we read them feel to be taking mimesis a layer or two deeper than it has gone before.

There has been no better statement than this of what he calls Bellow's "gift for the actual."

But it is Philip Roth, the contemporary novelist closest to him in years (Roth was born a year after Updike) and subject, who provokes Updike's most enlightening and engaged critical response.

Roth's *Goodbye Columbus* appeared the same year as *The Poorhouse Fair* and Updike's first collection of stories. From then on, the productivity of each kept pace with the other. Aside from a reference or two to *Portnoy's Complaint*, one of them in a piece about "orality" in modern fiction, Updike never reviewed Roth until *Zuckerman Unbound*, second of the Zuckerman trilogy, appeared in 1981. This short review was succeeded by a longer one of *The Anatomy Lesson* and the trilogy as a whole. He went on to review briefly Roth's autobiography, *The Facts*, and, at some length, *The Counterlife*, the novel that followed the trilogy; then after a mixed response to *Operation Shylock* (1993), said to have upset Roth, Updike ceased to review him, although he has made in passing a warm reference to *Sabbath's Theater*. My sense is that his criticism of Roth owes its liveliness and perception in part to the fact that it was in response to — as was not the case with Bellow — some of Roth's best work. Here was, and is, a fictional talent as quick and resourceful, as brilliant as Updike's is — in other words something to rise to when the occasion presented itself.

Rise to it he does in his full description and elaboration of Roth's art in *The Anatomy Lesson* and *The Counterlife*. Updike hazarded the suggestion, in reviewing *Zuckerman Unbound*, that after Roth's early excursions into realism (*Letting Go*), psychodrama (*Portnoy*), and fantasy (*The Great American Novel*) he has become "something of an exquisitist," "moving . . . among his by now highly polished themes with ever more expertness and care." No one else, to my knowledge, made this point about "later Roth," and Updike rose to encomium by saying that one of our most "intelligent and energetic" novelists had now become one of our most "scrupulous." If these seem adjectives Updike wouldn't mind having applied to himself, so his observation of Roth's paternal-familial theme, while wholly accurate, feels also not to characterize Roth only: "Roth has been preëminently a celebrant of a son's world. Who else has given us so many vivid, comical, shrewdly seen but above all lovingly preserved mothers and fathers in fiction? Or has so faithfully kept fresh as moral referent the sensations of childhood?" The "who else" can only be filled in with Updike's own name; still, his way of speaking as if it applied to Roth alone is discreet, a classy gesture.

The "exquisitist" has in the Zuckerman trilogy kept always in front of us, throughout Nathan's tribulations, the "moral referent" of childhood sensations, even as he writes the "ferocious, heartfelt book" that is *The Anatomy Lesson*. Like most reviewers of that novel, Updike has his reservations, which eventually surface near the review's end, as a *Yet* introduces his sense that of the three Zuckerman books this one is "the least objectified and coherent." What makes the qualification less than critically disabling to the novel is that it has been preceded by handsome admiration that rejects the easy notion of Roth having exhausted his material: on the contrary, "inflammations one might have thought long soothed burn hotter than ever; the central howl unrolls with a meditated savagery both fascinating and repellent, self-indulgent yet somehow sterling, adamant, pure in the style of high modernism, that bewitchment to all the art-stricken young of the Fifties." Comparisons, suggested by the novel, to Kafka and to Beckett follow. This is criticism at the top of its bent, fully *written* and making use of the range of "creative" description available, and by now more than well practiced, to Updike the writer of fiction. So that the spectacle is of powers exerting themselves aggressively to claim a similar power in the work of a contemporary, a rival — such a spectacle is rare, and highly satisfying in its performance.

Updike isn't unaware of what some critics of the Zuckerman books complained of — claustrophobia induced by obsessive concentration on the hero's plight. He notes that Zuckerman's "frantic, hilarious, anguished eloquence . . . leaves little air for any other characters to breathe." In fact those characters hardly exist except to display Roth's "great powers of mimicry." When he reviews *The Counterlife*, Updike's admiration for that novel is qualified slightly by the wish that Roth, now that he has stepped into metafiction (*The Counterlife* plays around with realism in its treatment of Nathan and his brother Henry), might trust himself as "simple realist" by way of doing even more with characters quite removed from "the claustral travail of a writer's self-impersonations." But mainly, as with the earlier review, Updike employs his own creative powers to bring out Roth's, noting how "the virtuoso imaginer rarely fal- ters; satisfying details of place and costume, astonishing diatribes, beautifully heard and knitted dialogues unfold in chapters impecca- bly shaped, packed, and smoothed." As with his earlier praise of Roth as celebrant of the son and his family, Updike employs the "No other writer" locution: "No other writer combines such a sur- face of colloquial relaxation and even dishevelment with such depth of mediating intelligence." This incisive point about Roth's work seems original to Updike's review. Indeed, on occasion one feels that Updike's sentences take him into exploratory characteri- zation of Roth's fiction that, previous to the sentence having been written, didn't exist in his conscious, critical mind. For example:

> Tirades, philippics, self-expositions: reading a Roth novel becomes like riding in an overheated club car, jostled this way and that by the clamorous, importunate crowd of talkers while glimpses of the outside world tantalizingly whip past the steamed-up windows. The train slackens momentum and clanks to a halt, and we press our forehead to the glass only to see that we already *were* in this station, an hour or two ago.

One imagines Roth reading this, wincing slightly at the comparison, but pleased too that his own effort has managed to stimulate such bold yet precise commentary on the part of one of his best readers.

The casual titles Updike has chosen to bestow on his five collec- tions of prose might be regarded by the credulous as a sign that he doesn't take the business of criticism all that seriously, even that he believes what Matthew Arnold, in "The Function of Criticism," said most people believed — that "the critical power is of lower rank than the creative." Yet in virtually the same breath, Arnold insisted that the business of the critical power was no less than "in all branches of knowledge, theology, philosophy, history, art, science, to see the object as in itself it really is." This seeing, for which another word is *disinterestedness* and for which the prime requisite is curiosity, is what Updike's decades of criticism testify to. No one could have kept at it that long, with that degree of commitment and with the display of pleasure obviously taken in the activity, had he not been, in the deepest sense, dead serious about its value. In his address to the intelligent lay reader, he is our best critic.

NINE

POET, MEMOIRIST

In a 1997 interview with TV's Charlie Rose, its occasion the publication of *Toward the End of Time*, Updike spoke of his recent literary projects as "packing my bag a little bit." A glance at his work from the past ten or so years shows what he is referring to: *Self-Consciousness*, his memoir of 1989, he describes as a preemptive strike at would-be biographers, by way of providing at least "the elements of an autobiography." With *Rabbit at Rest* (1990) the Angstrom tetralogy was complete, and in 1993 appeared *Collected Poems, 1953–1993*, four decades' worth of serious and light verse. "Well, why would you collect your poems unless you were getting ready to go on a journey," he remarked in the interview. Many of the stories in *Trust Me* (1987) and *The Afterlife* (1994) are told from the retrospective viewpoint of an aging man, some of whose circumstances bear similarities to Updike's. *In the Beauty of the Lilies* (1996) is a family chronicle pursued through four generations, and *Toward the End of Time* (1997), while ostensibly a novel set in the future, is remarkably backward-looking in much of its temper. *Bech at Bay* (1998) seemed to have wound up the fortunes of Henry Bech by awarding him the Nobel Prize although he has since reappeared in a story. So on a number of fronts, and with the millennium upon us, Updike's metaphor of packing his bag seems accurate. This chapter deals with his most overtly reminiscential later work: the previously uncollected poems written after 1985, when *Facing Nature*, his fourth book of verse, appeared; and

Self-Consciousness, a similarly poetic coming to terms with his past which its foreword calls "a specimen life, representative in its odd uniqueness of all the oddly unique lives in the world." In that foreword Updike writes that he will attempt to address his readers "in a mode of impersonal egoism." The oxymoronic aspiration is one also aspired to and attained by some of the strongest poems written contemporaneously with *Self-Consciousness*.

From the beginning of his career, of course, he had been a particularly retrospective writer, using again and again as the material for stories and novels his experience undergone not so many years previously as a Pennsylvania adolescent. We remember the "breakthrough" story — so he felt it to be — "The Happiest I've Been," in which, at its conclusion, John Nordholm's exultation at the wheel of the car that winter dawn on the Pennsylvania Turnpike is summarized as "a widespreading pride: Pennsylvania, your state — as if you had made your life." What distinguishes the retrospective note in Updike's poems, memoirs, and short fiction from the late 1980s and beyond is the sense that the "making" of a life has indeed been accomplished; that in its most essential respect life is over, done with, and whatever words get said about it won't alter that central fact. There is an analogous moment of such essential realization in Jarrell's poem "Aging," in which the poet's struggle "to find again, to make a life" suddenly turns in on itself with the following unanswerable question, prompted by remembering the seemingly endless moments of childhood:

> Did I not make in them
> Myself? The Grown One whose time shortens,
> Breath quickens, heart beats faster, till at last
> It catches, skips. . . .

Grow old along with me, the worst is yet to be.

This sense of life and the self having been thoroughly "made" is, in a writer as resourceful as Updike, a provocation to write compellingly about mortal thoughts. In the final paragraph of the second chapter of *Self-Consciousness*, "At War with My Skin," the writer's lifelong battle with psoriasis, fought especially in long sessions in the sun on various beaches, is used as the occasion to say a lot about the kind of life in which the battle has taken place. Despite his skin, he says, he has had his fun — "my children and women and volleyball games." "I have preened, I have lived," he almost uncomfortably boasts; then, thanks to his metothrexate state of 1980s curedness, looks forward to the following:

> Between now and the grave lies a long slide of forestallment,
> a slew of dutiful, dutifully paid-for maintenance routines in
> which dermatological makeshift joins periodontal work and
> prostate examinations on the crowded appointment calendar
> of dwindling days.

As for all those sessions in the sun — on Crane's Beach in Ipswich, at Martha's Vineyard, in the Caribbean — they have suddenly been used up: "For the first time in my life I own a house within walking distance of a beach, and I walk there scarcely three times a summer. Life suddenly seems too short to waste time lying in the sun."

Late Poems, 1988–93

How much the death of Updike's mother in 1989, at eighty-five, sharpened this sense of the shortness, in some ways the finished nature, of his own life can't be stated. My sense is that it did so enormously. Some lines about her from "Fall," a poem dated October 1989, show the son at a loss, even poetically, to deal with the dead woman who had fallen with a fatal heart attack and in so doing cut her eye:

> What corner or edge might have given the gash?
> I saw none, then saw her glasses, a circle and half
> of plastic frames, the one lens popped
> and skipped a foot away amid the dust.
> I picked it all up, and the little wool hat
> (it was getting to be fall) she wore for warmth,
> with a spot of dried blood on the blue threads.
> She seemed so very small in these her remnants.

These minute particulars mainly reveal the son's and poet's inability to imagine a "satisfying" close to this ultimate indignity. The poem's final two lines — "'Oh, Mama,' I said aloud, though I never called / her 'Mama,' 'I didn't take very good care of you'" — are deliberately, embarrassingly inadequate as a thing to say, as a way to end a poem about an ending.

"Fall" is, in an especially grim sense, an occasional poem, and Updike's verse, both serious and light, had always been occasional, stimulated by a bit of travel, a daughter's graduation, a personal moment in life's progress ("Upon the Last Day of His Forty-Ninth Year"). As with the casual titles given to his collections of critical reviews, the poems are deliberately low-key in their appeal to readerly expectations. This casualness feels carried over as well into the prosody (or lack of it) of individual specimens. Frost once said that in English verse there were really only two meters — strict and loose iambics. Updike's iambics, as in the lines about his mother quoted above, are at times about as loose as one can get. Written out as prose, they would sound wholly natural. Or consider the opening of "Back Bay," a leisurely description of shopping with his son for some clothes to make that son's birthday:

> My adult unemployed son and I
> (he composes electronic music)
> for his birthday traversed the Back Bay
> region of Boston, looking for suitable clothes
> as a present. A leather jacket, he thought,
> might be nice, but we had no idea where,
> at this outset of summer, such an item
> might be found.

Whatever happens of interest in this poem — and it goes on to describe an amusing and agreeable ramble — will have nothing to do with its prosody, which is relaxed to the point of dishevelment.

"Back Bay" dates from 1988 and like most of the later poems doesn't reveal any newly discovered passion for formal effects. Generally there is little rhyme, and the sonnet form is really little more than a convenient mold for getting some thoughts into a shape. One of the few rhyming sonnets, "Enemies of a House" only proves this rule:

> Dry rot intruding where the wood is wet;
>   hot sun that shrinks roof shingles so they leak
> and bakes pane-putty into crumbs; the pet
>   retriever at the frail screen door; the meek
> small mice who find their way between the walls
>   and gnaw improvements to their nests; mildew
> in the cellar; at the attic window, squalls;
>   loosening mortar; desiccated glue;
> ice backup over eaves; wood gutters full
>   of leaves each fall and catkins every spring;
>   salt air, whose soft persistent breath
> turns iron red, brass brown, and copper dull;
>   voracious ivy; frost heaves; splintering;
>   carpenter ants; adultery; drink; death.

The poem is a list, its items separated by semicolons, never making a completed sentence of itself yet indubitably finished, as the natural enemies turn — in that strong concluding line — into human ones (the movement from carpenter ants to adultery is especially effective). Here is, we might say, proof that Updike, should he put his mind to it, could write a sonnet that is both prosodically correct (but not quite — the eleventh line is a foot short) and adventurous. The enjambed lines make satisfying rhythmic events ("salt air, whose soft persistent breath / turns iron red, brass brown, and copper dull"), while exhibiting from line to line a lively observation and expertise about how a house is undermined. Yet the unpretentiousness of the list format, and the lack of any strong or varied tone in the speaking voice addressing us, keep the poem's temperature on the cool side, the felicity of domestic noticings as playful as it is serious.

"Enemies of a House" is one of a number of Updike post-1985 efforts in verse that, even for this candidly autobiographical writer, stand out as instances of retrospective bag-packing of a more intense and intimate sort than seen in previous poems. Most of these later

ones have less of a shaped quality than does "Enemies of a House,"
and they touch us rather through the accents of a voice confident
that it can assume a responsive audience: the voice, in other words,
of a poet, also a literary celebrity whose productions, especially in
fiction, are known and admired. "Perfection Wasted," another sonnet (this one unrhymed), could perhaps be spoken by anyone thinking about death, but is also the utterance of a writer whose performance has been refining and extending itself over decades:

> And another regrettable thing about death
> is the ceasing of your own brand of magic,
> which took a whole life to develop and market —
> the quips, the witticisms, the slant
> adjusted to a few, those loved ones nearest
> the lip of the stage, their soft faces blanched
> in the footlight glow, their laughter close to tears,
> their tears confused with their diamond earrings,
> their warm pooled breath in and out with your heartbeat,
> their response and your performance twinned.
> The jokes over the phone. The memories packed
> in the rapid-access file. The whole act.
> Who will do it again? That's it: no one;
> imitators and descendants aren't the same.

It begins out of nowhere, an afterthought perhaps, that takes on
substance as, like "Enemies of a House," a list expands and intensifies into a lifetime's gloss on the self as a performance — if not the
best act in town, still the only one "you" are capable of. And it turns
out to be a one-time thing, however long its run. The final line's
attempt to explain why "no one" is the only right answer to the
question "Who will do it again?" seems less than forceful or
inevitable, but its weakness doesn't matter all that much either,
since the work of the poem has accomplished itself.

In *A Midsummer Night's Dream* Theseus is allowed to be eloquent
about how lunatic, lover, and poet are "of imagination all compact,"
and how the poet's eye "in a fine frenzy rolling" glances from earth

to heaven and back, giving local habitation and name to the "forms of things unknown." Many of Updike's slight poems, their material packed into the loose sonnet form, give such local habitations, sometimes to things one might think beneath mention. Although we are used to surprises from Updike's Wordsworthian forays into the expression of "humble" (Wordsworth's adjective in his preface to *Lyrical Ballads*) life and materials, nothing has quite prepared us for some lines from "The Beautiful Bowel Movement," a hymn of praise to one of the humblest of such materials:

> this one,
> struck off in solitude one afternoon
> (that prairie stretch before the late light fails)
> with no distinct sensation, sweet or pained,
> or special inspiration or release,
> was yet a masterpiece: a flawless coil,
> unbroken, in the bowl, as if a potter
> who worked in this most frail, least grateful clay
> had set himself to shape a topaz vase.

I know no better instance of an artist's belief that form counts, that everything natural has its ideal or spiritual fulfillment. We are here to give praise, said Updike about our earthly purpose, and in his poems praise can be accorded the most earthly phenomena. Whether the humor implicit in writing such a lyric can prevent it from seeming grotesque is a matter of individual judgment.

But it is the poems about the sexual life, remembered and present, that are most daring and where the voice shaping the experience is most intimate and sincere. The latter word may seem an inappropriate one to use for a writer as tricky and playful as Updike, yet it seems a fair way to describe the quality of these poems. Two of them, "Mouse Sex" and "To a Dead Flame," are about adultery, and the precarious, revelatory nature of remembered moments. Both are written in very loose iambics indeed, crammed into unrhymed stanzas of no significantly determined length (eight lines, eleven lines) but suitable for the meditative exploration each poem leisurely makes. In "Mouse Sex" the man discovers a dead, poisoned mouse in his cellar, notices that it's a female ("her tiny neat vagina, / a pumpkin-seed-shaped break in the dulcet fur"), and is moved to recall another moment in which "the vagina's simplicity" was made apparent to him. This was when, in the midst of making love to his mistress, a sudden sound downstairs at her house ("her husband or the wind") turns his erection "inconvenient":

> We listened, our love-flushed faces an inch apart.
> The sound was not repeated. In the silence,
> as the house resumed its enclosing, she said,
> voice thickened and soft and distinct,
> "Put it in me." In my wild mind's eye I saw
> the vagina as a simple wanting, framed in fur,
> kept out of sight between the legs but always there,
> a gentle nagging, a moist accommodacy.

He does as commanded ("a man and not a mouse"), though the outcome is "less memorable" than "the urgent, imperiled invitation." He finds for the first time, he tells us, that "sex had an equitable basis," even in possible proximity to the husband-cat downstairs ("Her husband, that creep, / creeping about for all we knew"). Then in the next to last of six stanzas, the moment is apotheosized:

> Suppose that moment, frozen, were Heaven or Hell:
> our hearts would thump until the death of stars,
> the trees outside would stir their golden edges,
> the bed would squeak, the frightened inch
> between our skins would hold the headboard's grain,
> her brazen thighs would simply, frankly part,
> our eyes and breath would forever entertain
> our mutual inquisition. *Put it in.*

This imagined end of sexual inquiry, frozen into timelessness, is the climactic moment in the poem from which the final stanza falls away, as its closing lines — "We enter into one another; the universe / rises about us like a hostile house" — seem little more than a good try at closure. But again it doesn't matter: the frozen moment has been voiced with such unsettling conviction as to make questions of the poem's overall "unity" less than crucial.

In reading Updike's poetry one thinks of Frost's insistence on the speaking voice, the "sound of sense" at work on fact ("The fact is the sweetest dream that labor knows") and on things ("We love the things we love for what they are"). But there is a central matter on which, in their practice as poets, the two writers' approach to how much of the biographical self a poem may or should reveal is strikingly different. It is a question of how you measure, and Frost once addressed that question in a letter:

> Everybody knows something has to be kept back for pressure and to anybody puzzled to know what I would suggest that for a beginning it might as well be his friends, wife, children, and self. . . . Poetry is measured in more senses than one: it is measured feet but more important still it is a measured amount of all we could say an we would. We shall be judged finally by the delicacy of our feeling of where to stop short.[1]

Noting the roughness, the relative inattention with which Updike regards his "measured feet" — the extremely loose iambics, the slight rhythmic flaws or not fully sustained rhyme pattern — it is perhaps unsurprising that he is not concerned to follow Frost's caveat about keeping back such things as wife, children, and self (remember "The Beautiful Bowel Movement") and not interested in "stopping short," in measuring out "all we could say an we would."

For all their fictional changing of names, ages, places, Updike's novels and stories from the 1960s and beyond were still remarkably and unabashedly personal in the way so many of them fed off his own biography. In these late poems on sexual themes, there is an analogous inclination to display rather than conceal the younger self — this display conducted from the "made" vantage point of age. Like Yeats, he began to play the age card early; certainly by the time he reached his fifties he presented himself, and not just humorously, as "old." In the final chapter of *Self-Consciousness* his head is becoming "full of holes," and his watch cap, visible on the dust jacket of *Odd Jobs*, is now being worn, he tells us, "all winter, inside the house and out." In that same chapter he treats us to a moment of sudden happiness as he walks back from the mailbox, having fetched the *Globe* of a Sunday morning. Seven possibilities are listed as contributing to this feeling, one of them that he and his wife had just made love, "successfully all round, which at my age occasions some self-congratulation." This sort of confession is both winning and slightly embarrassing to the reader who can't resist the invitation to enter, just a bit, the self-consciousness of this writer, all fifty-seven years of him. Granted it is a more dramatic or melodramatic spectacle when the sixty-one-year-old Yeats begins "The Tower" by cursing "this caricature, / Decrepit age that has been tied to me / As to a dog's tail." But Updike is not averse to making capital out of instances of his own decrepitude.

"To a Dead Flame," for example, begins with addressing the woman ("Dear X") by cataloging some of the aspects of the speaker's present sorry physical state, with particular reference to his eyebrows ("jagged grey wands / have intermixed with the reddish-brown, and poke / up toward the sun and down into my eyes"), or his stiff neck, or his "furtive" potency — unlike the days when she would "smilingly" complain about it — or his white hair, or from time to time "that loose mouth / old people make, as if one's teeth don't fit." He tells "X" that she's well out of it, then realizes he doesn't believe this, for reasons that follow in the closing two stanzas of the poem:

> The world is still wonderful. Wisps of mist
> were floating off your old hill yesterday,
> the hill where you lived, in sight of the course
> where I played (badly) in a Senior Men's
> Four-Ball in the rain, each green a mirage.
> I thought of us, abed atop that hill,
> and of how I would race down through your woods

to my car, and back to my life, my heart
enormous with what I newly knew —
the color of you naked, the milk of your sighs —
through leaves washed to the glisten of fresh wounds.

Life has not been wholly made, wholly fixed, when such a memory
can occur of racing through the woods, enormous with new knowledge. But the memory quickly prompts a larger, more disenchanted
reflection:

What desperate youthful fools we were, afraid
of not getting our share, our prize in the race,
like jostling marathoners starting out,
clumsy but pulsingly full of blood.
You dropped out, but we all drop out, it seems.
You never met my jealous present wife;
she hates this poem. The living have it hard,
not living only in the mind, but in
the receding flesh. Old men must be allowed
their private murmuring, a prayer wheel
set spinning to confuse and stay the sun.

Picking up from his race back through the woods, after their sexual encounter, to "life," both the man and his "flame" are seen as but
two more jostling competitors in the marathon of life, "pulsingly full
of blood" and only to drop out at one or another stage along the
way. The writer, still running, without illusions, contemplates the
race he's not going to win and wonders (we may imagine) how to
complete the poem not too resonantly. He looks over his shoulder
at his present wife ("she hates this poem"), surely the wrong audience for such a letter to an old lover; then he looks, with a bit of a
wince, at the "receding flesh" inventoried in earlier stanzas, and
makes the unheroic complaint that "The living have it hard." He
may just barely echo T. S. Eliot's noble charge at the end of "East
Coker" — "Old men ought to be explorers / Here and there does not
matter" — but slides off into justifying the poem he's written as

merely a "private murmuring" that must be allowed: "a prayer wheel / set spinning to confuse and stay the sun," written by way of putting off that final sunset. And so it ends, in a way I can imagine someone calling sentimental, yet that seems to me not so, but rather strongly aware, in its blend of self-deprecation, passionate memory, and rueful philosophizing, of the possibilites for expressing human feeling in words. How many contemporary poets could render such an experience with as much clarity and sanity? The tendentious question needs support, and I find some of it in Alec Guinness's old-age diary, *My Name Escapes Me,* which contains the following entry: "Reread a number of poems from John Updike's collection, *Facing Nature.* He is provocative and stimulating. There can't be many better novelists alive and yet it is somehow surprising to realize what a good poet he is." In a number of the poems written after *Facing Nature* appeared, Updike surprises even more, through the confessional air that sets the prayer wheel spinning.

There is also something audacious in the frankness with which he writes about the diminished present, diminished for the aging man in certain ways, even as his books continue to pour out, his honors accumulate, his stature as eminent man of letters grow ever more established. One feels Updike has been emboldened by this combination of age and success into delivering himself, as from a great distance, of poetical reflections on the paradoxes, the vanities, the spectacle of life. As contrasted to the vivid presentation — in "Mouse Sex" and "To a Dead Flame" — of youthful erotic life, "clumsy but pulsingly full of blood," a sonnet about the present, "Elderly Sex," is, although not written with first-person directness and reference, still candid: "We are walking a slack tight wire, we / are engaged in unlikely acrobatics, / we are less frightened of the tiger than / of the possibility the cage is empty." He sums it up in these few words: "Nature used to do more."

Although the poems are arranged in the order in which they were completed, and although *Collected Poems* follows the 250 pages of "Serious" with 100 pages of "Light" verse, the final three poems in the "serious" section make a satisfying completion in the way they ask questions of or look bemusedly askance at what the writer has come to. Each is a sonnet; none attempts to make as much claim on us as do, at moments, "Mouse Sex" and "To a Dead Flame." If we remember that Updike's first volume of poetry was titled *The Carpentered Hen, And Other Tame Creatures*, these three final poems, written not long after he turned sixty, all feature the man for whom "nature used to do more," now tamed into an ironic reflector on the results of all he has done. "Upon Looking into Sylvia Plath's *Letters Home*" explores the difference, yet similarity, between two artists born the same year:

> Yes, this is how it was to have been born
> in 1932 — the loving parents
> everyone said loved you and you had to love;
> the believing having a wonderful life began
> with being good at school; the certainty
> that words would count; the diligence with postage,
> sending things out. . . .

After similarity is further established, three lines remind us of the difference, yet persist in asserting kinship: "You, dead at thirty, leaving blood-soaked poems / for all the anthologies, and I still wheezing, / my works overweight; and yet we feel twins." There follows "At the End of the Rainbow" in which our author, visiting a college, has completed his reading stint to much applause, signed copies of his books, checked out the smiling coeds, and is now alone in his motel room with things "all gone, endured. The square made bed. Hi-tech / alarm clock, digital. The john. The check." Having made up one's bed, one's life, it is time to lie in it: such are the rewards of having stayed in the literary race and almost won it.

Finally there is "Academy," a sonnet that, it may be, Updike decided to rhyme just to show, at the end of the collection, that he could have done it more often. The venue is clearly the American Academy of Arts and Letters in New York City, at a gathering of the members of which the speaker is one:

The shuffle up the stairs betrays our age:
sunk to polite senility our fire
and tense perfectionism, our curious rage
to excel, to exceed, to climb still higher.
Our battles were fought elsewhere; here, this peace
betrays and cheats us with a tame reward —
a klieg-lit stage and numbered chairs, an ease
of prize and praise that sets sheath to the sword.

The naked models, the Village gin, the wife
whose hot tears sped the novel to its end,
the radio that leaked distracting life
into the symphony's cerebral blend.
A struggle it was, and a dream; we wake
to bright bald honors. Tell us our mistake.

There is no answering voice, nor do we need one, since "Academy"
has said it all. Along with its accompanying poems it gives force and
meaning to the notion of Updike's *Collected Poems* as work not just
gathered together but as exhibiting overall — and especially in its
latter stages — an air of self-possession and calm that is yet the
opposite of tame.

The foregoing account has made no attempt to "place" that work
in the landscape of contemporary poetry. Updike seems to me very
much an anomaly and not really "in" that landscape at all. He is
without the postmodern stylistic individuality, eccentric and (to
me) unsatisfying, of a John Ashbery; but any affinities with the
"new formalist" concern for making sense in the well-made poem
are scarcely detectable. The question of whether these poems (I am
speaking especially of the late ones) could stand convincingly on
their own, without knowing that they are the creation of a conse-
quential writer of fiction who has displayed himself to us over
decades, is one I can't answer, since I'm unable and unwilling to
read them in such a pure, detached light. Although his verse shows
sympathetic affinities with that of his friend L. E. Sissman, about
whom he wrote with affection (Sissman died young, of Hodgkin's

disease), and though it shares a wry humor with a younger poet he has praised, Billy Collins, Updike as poet is strictly one of a kind and not the less valuable for that.

Self-Consciousness

Just a year before Updike published his memoirs, he wrote a short review of Philip Roth's *The Facts*, Roth's short, "novelist's autobiography" as his subtitle had it. In the review Updike said that Roth's account of his life would have been a thinner, watered-down version of the author's explosive novels were it not that he had summoned a major character from those novels, Nathan Zuckerman, to advise "Roth" about whether or not to publish the book. (In an epilogue Zuckerman tells "Roth" emphatically *no*, since the book was a "safe," false version of a much more violent and interesting life.) Updike found that this epilogue lifted autobiography "into the liberating uncertainties and revisionary cross-references of fiction," and he quotes with seeming approval Roth's insistence, in a *Paris Review* interview, that writing fiction is, like writing autobiography, a "transformation, through an elaborate impersonation, of a personal emergency into a public act." Although Updike chose the word *memoirs* to label his own exploration in self-consciousness, and although his book doesn't have the more or less chronological structure of Roth's, it is every bit as much a novelist's autobiography. And since Updike's sentences, as a rule, are at least as elaborately shaped and figured as Roth's, the novelist's way of writing autobiography, his style, will occupy the foreground, with "the facts" — Roth's ostensible main concern — being correspondingly shaped by that style. But what, one may ask, is the "elaborate impersonation" carried on in the six chapters of *Self-Consciousness?* How does Updike go about lifting a potentially thinner version of the life he has already so richly and frequently explored in his fiction into "liberating uncertainties"? And if there is no reason to apply the words he used about Roth's autobiography to his own, what better ones are there to employ?

Recall the main subjects taken up in turn by the six essays: the author revisits his hometown and takes us on a tour of it ("A Soft

Spring Night in Shillington"); he describes, with the fullness of an expert storyteller, his lifelong battle with psoriasis ("At War with My Skin"); in equal detail, he considers his fortunes as a stutterer and an asthmatic ("Getting the Words Out"); he explores, in the attempt to understand and also defend it, his qualified support for the American war in Vietnam ("On Not Being a Dove"), the chapter ending with a coda about his dental tortures; he composes a letter to his two African-American grandsons, the letter consisting mainly of tracing their filial descent from the paternal, Updike line ("A Letter to My Grandsons"); finally, he sets forth his inclinations and predilections toward religious matters of intimate and ultimate concern ("On Being a Self Forever"). What any first-time reader of the book is struck by is the amount of time devoted to portraying its author as a sufferer, a prey to bodily ills (skin, speech, lungs, teeth) and to social disapproval — familial and public — for his unenlightened stance on Vietnam. Can Updike really be wholly serious in dwelling at such length on what scarcely approaches the ills borne by the less fortunate? This writer is, after all, the first to admit that his life has been an extremely favored one ("I have preened, I have lived"). Isn't there something unnatural and ungracious, even dishonest, in adopting this perspective on the self as victim rather than master of circumstance?

We are dealing in part here with the habit of self-depreciation that the gentleman writer takes as second nature — in Updike's case the country boy from Pennsylvania showing himself as ultrasophisticated, even aristocratic, in his self-consciousness and his manner of displaying it. It is also a gesture of loyalty toward the question he asked in that earlier memoir, "The Dogwood Tree," about his own work; whether it is possible "to transcribe middleness" and think of it as a worthwhile task "in view of the suffering that violently colors the periphery and that at all moments threatens to move into the center." The answer given by *Self-Consciousness* is an unambiguous one: yes, it is both possible and worthwhile to transcribe middleness, to dwell at length on one's less-than-tragic ills. It may be even more worth doing when the larger "suffering" moves closer to the center, as it did in the

1960s. In the book's first chapter, one of many childhood phenomena recalled is "the ice plant up behind Philadelphia Avenue," water from which "disappeared down a grating with a twisting, golden tumult that in my tame landscape had a Wordsworthian resonance." Here, and again, tameness is insisted upon (compared, say, to the Lake District's mountains and cataracts) so that the prose expended on it can deliver a golden world, something like a tumult with mighty resonance. In an analogous manner, the afflictions of psoriasis and stuttering can be worked upon, through words, so as to make them reveal nothing less than one life's secret, under the conviction that if you write well enough about minute particulars you will be writing about everything, including the places where truth resides.

Especially in the first Shillington chapter, Updike is at pains to insist upon the "tame landscape" not of his hometown merely but of his own engagement, as a child, with life. He speaks of the delight with which, during a rain shower, he would visit the upturned furniture on the side porch where he could "crouch, happy almost to tears, as the rain drummed on the porch rail . . . and touched my wicker shelter." The phrase for this state, employed a number of times in *Self-Consciousness*, is "keeping out of harm's way." One of his early stories is titled "A Sense of Shelter" and on the side porch of the Shillington house, or leaning close to the "chill windowpane" as the raindrops pelted, or huddling under bushes and doorways, this sense "of being out of the rain, but *just* out" was achieved. (In *Rabbit Is Rich* Harry Angstrom is provided with similar feelings about rain.) Yet the long paragraph in which such "tame" instances of keeping out of harm's way are set forth is typical of much of the writing in these memoirs, in that by the end of the paragraph Updike has moved into very much bolder territory in the claims he makes for such an activity. He speaks of such — surely idealized — states as being opposite to "the burden of activity, of participation" in the world's welter, with its concomitant guilts and cruelties. By contrast,

> There was nothing cruel about crouching in a shelter and letting phenomena slide by: it was ecstasy. The essential self is

innocent, and when it tastes its own innocence knows that it lives forever. If we keep utterly still, we can suffer no wear and tear, and we will never die.

He will return to the matter of the self and its life in the book's final chapter; here in this fantasy that by keeping utterly still, out of harm's way, one will never die, the child is truly father to the man, at least to the man-as-writer of these memoirs.

In fact the "tame" character of Updike's subject matter is an opportunity for him, through the incorrigibly metaphorical figuredness of language, to create fantasies of an extravagance comparable to that occurring in the fiction, and we remember that *Self-Consciousness* comes at the end of a decade in which appeared, only a few years previously, *The Witches of Eastwick* and *Roger's Version*. With his psoriasis, for example, he imagines himself, while on one of his periodic visits to the Caribbean sun, becoming "clear," his unblemished white skin separating him from all the "unclear" people in the world. But there is always, very quickly, *And yet*:

> And yet, I self-consciously wondered, was not my sly strength, my insistent specialness, somehow linked to my psoriasis? Might it not be the horrible badge of whatever in me was worth honoring: the price, high but not impossibly so, I must pay for being me? Only psoriasis could have taken a very average little boy, and furthermore a boy who loved the average, the daily, the safely hidden, and made him into a prolific, adaptable, ruthless-enough writer. What was my creativity, my relentless need to produce, but a parody of my skin's embarrassing overproduction? Was not my thick literary skin, which shrugged off rejection slips and patronizing reviews by the sheaf, a superior version of my poor vulnerable own, and my shamelessness on the page a distraction from my real shame?

He continues in this vein, moving from one unanswerable, highly provocative question to another, until he interrogates his selfishness, his lack of sufficient "social conscience": "So wrapped up in my skin, so watchful of its day-to-day permutations, I have, it might be, too little concern to spare for the homeless, the disenfranchised, and the unfortunate who figure so largely in the inner passions of smooth-pelted liberals like my first wife." Here is one of the most outrageous evidences of Updike's thick skin, literary or otherwise, as the boy who wanted nothing more than to stay out of harm's way is suddenly transformed into a monster of self-regard, inviting political and social disapproval for the brazen reference to "smooth-pelted liberals like my first wife." It's a lot to blame on your skin, one might think, but it's also the way Updike's Emersonian relentlessness converts natural facts into spiritual fulfillments that are aimed to discompose not just his enemies but his readers as well. He smiles, and nods politely, gracefully, but he's playing hardball and for keeps.

So it seems like more than a compliant nod to the terminology of the Vietnam era for him to title the most controversial chapter of Self-Consciousness "On Not Being a Dove." In his quoted letter to the New York Times, by way of explaining an earlier response to a 1966 English questionaire that found its way into a volume, Authors Take Sides on Vietnam, Updike took the quite moderate position that "genuine elections" were needed for the South Vietnamese to express their will, and that until that will was expressed, he did not see "that we can abdicate our burdensome position in South Vietnam." The letter to the Times expressed, he admitted, his own quite "equivocal" position toward the war but also expressed at some length his difference from the doves: he refused to believe that the war was being prosecuted to maintain business prosperity, or that Lyndon Johnson was pursuing it out of "crazed stubbornness." Indeed he judged that "aesthetic distaste" for that president played too large a part in dovish proclamations. He suggested, however, that Johnson not run for president in 1968, and he held out the hope of a negotiated settlement, with the Vietcong a partner in achieving it (this was still 1967).

There is nothing "hawkish," in either tone or content, in Updike's public statements on Vietnam, and he made no more public statements on the subject after 1967. What got under his skin, if one may use that phrase, was the moral tone of left-liberal "dovish" assaults on the president, the government, the country. In the ensuing years he portrays himself as unable to stop talking, at home and in the company of what might have been "post-liberal socio-economic-cultural harmony," about the war; instead he is "beset, defending an underdog, my back to the wall in a world of rabid anti-establishment militants." He remembers in one such heated conversation, Philip Roth in a "calm and courteous tone" pointing out to him that he was the most aggressive person in the room. However much this was in fact the case and accurately remembered by the memoirist, the force gained by putting it all into words and sentences is only increased, as metaphorical possibilities and imaginative connections multiply themselves.

As with the chapter about his overproductive psoriasis and how thick-skinned his public, writerly self had become, "On Not Being a Dove" launches a series of questions, not to be answered, but the asking of which makes a case against himself — of whether, to put it crudely, he wasn't just too insulated, too selfish, especially when a matter such as Vietnam suggested there were issues to be risen to more compelling than those of personal convenience and temperament. Stung by Alfred Kazin's remark in reviewing *Couples* that Updike could brilliantly describe the adult world yet fail to convey its "depths and risks" — since as a writer he was "wholly literary," "the quickest of quick children" — he speaks back in nervous, defensive disbelief:

> Was I really so oddly isolated from adult depths? Had I in fact *too* successfully found a place for myself out of harm's way? Perhaps there *was* something too smooth in my rise and my style, something unthinkingly egocentric in my sopping up love and attention from my grandparents and parents and now my children, something that drained my immediate vicinity, and something distanced and cruel in my writing, with its vengeful element of "showing" people. . . .

Did in fact "the relentless domestic realism" of his fiction imply "self-exemption from normal intra-familial courtesy?" Was his "inner smoothness," under that roughened skin, "defective"?

This asks for it, by saying the worst you can say against yourself, but does so in hopes of forestalling those critics out there who were about to say it. In at least one case it may have had the effect rather of goading a reviewer to heights of vituperation to which he might otherwise not have risen. In perhaps the single most brutal instance of this — though for anyone except the recipient it offers some wicked wit — the leftist critic Fred Inglis (in *The Nation*) spoke of Updike's "famous jeweled style" as "more that of a writer to whom absolutely nothing has ever happened beyond his discovery that he liked playing with words."[2] Inglis went on to upbraid what he claims *Self-Consciousness* betrays: "a perfectly unconscious self made up of petty-minded vengefulness, high-pitched sanctimony, political silliness of a really worked-at variety and old-fashioned grandparental boringness that the kids no doubt are bound by duty to tolerate but that will surely tax others." Perhaps Inglis would have been this abusive all on his own, but Updike's preemptive strike at himself must have raised the ante. It is unlikely that a critic so temperamentally and politically alienated from his subject can be answered in any relevant way, but it should be registered that the "points" Updike makes against himself are not trivial ones and are not stage-managed so as to provoke the immediate correction, as who shall say, why *no*, your career, your style, are not at all "too smooth." After all it is the memoirist who is perceptive enough to bring up the possibility of "something distanced and cruel in my writing" — which having been said, quietly and pointedly, there is no way of taking back. In other words, *Self-Consciousness* is interestingly explorative of a writerly self.

Inglis's crack about the "grandparental boringness" of chapter 5, "A Letter to My Grandsons," shouldn't obscure the fact that however one judges that tone (and on one occasion I find it off-putting, when Updike refers to the grandsons' "dear little brown skins"), the chapter is an impressive genealogical hymn to father and grandfather especially, with a strongly located eastern-seaboard topography — New Jersey and Rhode Island as the main paternal preserves.

After the confessional and inquisitorial liveliness of "On Being a Dove," the movement into relative impersonality in this chapter is a suprising one that seems deliberately contrived to deny us whatever further revelations we might have hoped to be given concerning Updike's psyche. In other words, he is not about to write the sort of memoir that gathers in intensity toward some concentrated moment of truth: "memoirs," rather, contains the possibility of discontinuity or at least of modulating into a different key, in the case of chapter 5 a genealogical one.

The final modulation, in the last chapter — "On Being a Self Forever" — has a feel of ultimacy as it mixes Emersonian reflections about "the essential I" with the most homely details about the aging self of the memoirist who, as he puts it, is "near the end," and who, obedient to medical voices, has given up alchohol (in deference to the skin drugs he takes), cigarettes (deference to emphysema), and coffee (deference to high blood pressure). So he is left with nothing to do but continue to get the words out every day: "writing is my sole remaining vice," he announces rather proudly. What puts him even nearer the end is the approaching death of his mother, and the book turns in on itself as he moves from a philosophical consideration of death and the self, back into the Plowville farmhouse he is visiting once more, fresh from reading at a midwestern university (remember the late poem "At the End of the Rainbow"), planning to go on to Trenton, New Jersey, by way of researching what we have just read in the previous chapter about his father's family. That was the past; this brief visit to a mother who has been ill and whose days are clearly numbered is the present.

The ten pages about this visit seem to me matchless. He has taken his mother out to dinner, driven back with her through some sleety weather that makes navigation difficult (she fears they will hit a deer); now he reads in a book he has for review, then can't fall asleep, so lies awake hearing his mother breathe in another room:

> Now the dog heaves in its sleep, woofing at some dream-prey,
> its claws scratching on the soft old pine floorboards. Sleep will

not come for me. The house is too noisy, the bed clammy as though I am already dead. I cannot escape myself. The sleet, the fear that we will hit a deer keep revolving in me. My brain buzzes with selfish, scared thoughts. We fall asleep in selflessness, when our thoughts turn self-forgetful. Masturbation and prayer both attempt this; I feel too old for either. I feel forsaken, lost. But when I am not looking, perhaps when I am thinking of the dog's dreams or of the old roof-ball line at the playground, sleep does come. I awake in light, feeling as if my soul has a slight sore throat, my membranes still chafed by the fear of earthly existence.

Then he hears his mother and the dog "talking" downstairs; it has snowed during the night; he rises to shave and dress. It was only four decades before this year of 1987 when Peter Caldwell woke up for school, in the second chapter of *The Centaur*, and heard his mother and father talking about his father's suspected illness. This concurrence, or confusion, between fact and fiction is engaging, even exhilarating; but of course one feels it only by reading *Self-Consciousness* not in its own terms merely but, like the late poems, by harking back to earlier words, earlier times — to all the lost selves one is conscious of.

TEN

RABBIT RETIRED

A previous chapter, "Extravagant Fictions," which surveyed Updike's novels over the ten years from 1978 *(The Coup)* to 1988 *(S)*, notably omitted his longest and happiest — certainly his most celebrated — work from that period, *Rabbit Is Rich* (1981). The third volume in what would be the Angstrom tetralogy won all three of the big literary prizes for that year — the Pulitzer, the National (then called American) Book Award, and the National Book Critics' Circle; it also received the most unanimously approving critical response of any book Updike had published. Treating it here with its successor, *Rabbit at Rest* (1990), makes sense inasmuch as the two books are continuous, stylistically and tonally, in ways that distinguish them from both *Rabbit, Run* and *Rabbit Redux*. Their mood is comic-elegiac, their technique an extension of the "documentary" realism seen in Updike's earlier fiction, and their treatment of American society and culture — no longer the heated, contested, and overtly dangerous society it was in *Rabbit Redux* — is resigned and accepting, if ironically so. A lot of time seems to have passed, and suddenly it is too late to do much, if anything, about either society in the large or the individual life of one of its aging citizens. Rabbit rich and at rest: the words carry with them, when played out in the action of the novels, an acquiescent, helpless complicity with the world's ways and with human limitation generally.

Rabbit Is Rich

Rabbit, Run opens with the protagonist, "an unlikely rabbit," headed home from his boring job selling Magi-Peelers and stopping to watch, then play, basketball with a group of kids. This remembered glow of the game, recaptured in the brief scuffling on the court, makes Rabbit Angstrom's adult job life even more of a mockery than it already feels. In *Rabbit Redux* we are introduced again to him, now as "Harry" ("years have passed since anyone has called him Rabbit"), emerging with his father from the little printing plant where they work, "ghosts for an instant, blinking, until the outdoor light overcomes the look of constant indoor light clinging to them." The Angstroms, father and son, along with their accompanying workers, are part of the four o'clock "darkness" that "presses down early from the mountain that hangs above the stagnant city of Brewer." By contrast, and by way of setting the rather different tone of the later Angstrom books, Harry in the first paragraph of *Rabbit Is Rich* has become Rabbit again, at least to the narrator who presents him to us, looking out through the "summer-dusty windows of the Springer Motors display room watching the traffic go by on Route 111." It is mid-June of 1979, the time of the gasoline shortage, but Rabbit, peddling Toyotas at the lot once owned by his father-in-law, is jaunty, even as "The fucking world is running out of gas." His jauntiness, compared to his demeanor in the previous books, is built into a more humorous and playful narrative voice than heard previously:

> The fucking world is running out of gas. But they won't catch him, not yet, because there isn't a piece of junk on the road gets better mileage than his Toyotas, with lower service costs. Read *Consumer Reports*, April issue. That's all he has to tell the people when they come in. And come in they do, the people out there are getting frantic, they know the great American ride is ending.

With the gas crisis heating up,

> People are going wild, their dollars are going rotten, they shell

out like there's no tomorrow. He tells them, when they buy a Toyota, they're turning their dollars into yen. And they believe him. A hundred twelve units new and used moved in the first five months of 1979, with eight Corollas, five Coronas including a Luxury Edition Wagon, and that Celica that Charlie said looked like a Pimpmobile unloaded in these first three weeks of June already, at an average gross mark-up of eight hundred dollars per sale. Rabbit is rich.

The boldness of using a novel's title to conclude its opening paragraph — three brisk words coming after a heavy inventory of Toyota's finest — indicates the strongly voiced, flexible progression of this opening *tour de force*. Spoken by neither Rabbit nor Updike, but both at once, this is prose that's on the move and that, like Rabbit's sense of himself, behaves like something that won't be caught, at least "not yet." It has, I think, much to do with the ease most readers felt in responding positively to the novel's world.

In fact, from the beginning of the book Rabbit is caught by, caught up in his past, that past we've shared with him in the earlier novels. There are two epigraphs to *Rabbit Is Rich,* one of which, quoting from Sinclair Lewis's *Babbitt,* may invoke that writer as Updike's American predecessor in satiric realism, but is more likely there for the Rabbit-Babbitt connection. At least as telling is the other epigraph, three lines from the poem "A Rabbit as King of the Ghosts" by Updike's Reading kinsman, Wallace Stevens. In *Rabbit Is Rich* the protagonist is king of the ghostly dead, phantoms whose presence makes themselves powerfully felt:

> The dead, Jesus. They were multiplying, and they look up begging you to join them, promising it is all right, it is very soft down here. Pop, Mom, old man Springer, Jill, the baby called Becky for her little time, Tothero. Even John Wayne, the other day. The obituary page every day shows another stalk of a harvest endlessly rich, the faces of old teachers, customers, local celebrities like himself flashing for a moment and then going down. For the first time since childhood Rabbit is happy, simply, to be alive.

So Rabbit's happiness is fed significantly by the rich harvest of obituaries he can't avoid: "It gives him pleasure, makes Rabbit feel rich, to contemplate the world's wasting, to know that the earth is mortal too," he thinks to himself with particular reference to the vanished anthracite coal mines. Early in the novel, then, the word *rich* acquires nuance and surprise in its reach.

As does the notion, so potent in the first Angstrom novel, of Rabbit running. There running was, though always abortive, a bolt out of marriage, responsibility, society: like the late-night journey in the car that ends a few hours later back in Mt. Judge; or like Rabbit's return to his wife after their daughter is born, only to make another run; finally, at the book's end, a bolt away from the crowd of mourners at the gravesite of his dead child — "with an effortless gathering out of a kind of sweet panic growing lighter and quicker and quieter." Twenty-one years later, as he tells his coworker at Springer Motors, Charlie Stavros, he has taken up jogging, an activity unheroic in itself and made even more domesticated by its limits — around the block after supper a couple of times a week, so as to avoid listening to his wife and mother-in-law arguing. If, as he thinks chirpily in the opening paragraph, he's not yet running out of gas, neither is he running anywhere significant.

Some of the novel's most evocative writing is directed not at any projected launching out, but at the steady sameness of recurrence, the seasonal pattern coming around once more:

> The day is still golden outside, old gold now in Harry's lengthening life. He has seen summer come and go until its fading is one in his heart with its coming, though he cannot yet name the weeds that flower each in its turn through the season, or the insects that also in ordained sequence appear, eat, and perish. He knows that in June school ends and the playgrounds open, and the grass needs cutting again and again if one is a man, and if one is a child games can be played outdoors while the supper dishes tinkle in the mellow parental kitchens, and the moon is discovered looking over your shoulder out of a sky

still blue, and a silver blob of milkweed spittle has appeared
mysteriously on your knee. Good luck.

The real right place to be — where it all happens — is, in the words
of the song, back in your own backyard. There, swinging open the
gate and entering into his little vegetable garden, Harry "finds a
hundred memories, some vivid as photographs and meaningless,
snapped by the mind for reasons of its own, and others mere facts,
things he knows are true but has no snapshot for. Our lives fade
behind us before we die." Spotting a Japanese beetle on a bean plant
leaf, he "snaps the iridescent creature off. Die." Of course there is
nothing essentially different here — no change in the poetry Harry
is provided with to contemplate life — from the moment at the
playground with Nelson in *Rabbit, Run*, when "He feels the truth:
the thing that has left his life has left irrevocably; no search would
recover it." The same sense of irrevocableness, right down to the
remembered playground scene, is there in the backyard one above.
In the earlier playground passage "Nature" is said to be through with
us "when we make children for her . . . and we become, first inside,
and then outside, junk. Flower stalks." So here, we have the backyard weeds and insects that do their thing and die, snapped off like
the Japanese beetle from the bean plant leaf.

But what *Rabbit, Run* was relatively lacking in, *Rabbit Is Rich* has
in abundance: a comic life, often mordantly offered, that finds itself
in tandem with elegiac reflections on time passing. Similarities
between the hero's observations and those of Leopold Bloom were
observable in *Rabbit, Run*; now Rabbit — like Bloom, always curious
— wonders at the empty gasoline stations with shrouded pumps and
asks, sensibly, "Where did the shrouds come from? Some of them
quite smartly tailored, in squared-off crimson canvas. A new industry,
gas pump shrouds." At times the clever observation seems too clever
for Rabbit, indeed too clever for any of us, as when Harry tries to
pierce the mystery of some women living nearby who appear to be
lesbians and who do a lot of carpentry: "[He] had always meant to
ask them what it was like, and why. He can see not liking men, he

doesn't like them much himself, but why would you like women any better, if you were one? Especially women who hammer all the time, just like men." (The punch line here is a special bonus.)

Sex is also, now, an occasion for unheroic treatment, consonant with the aging of a marriage. In *Rabbit, Run* Janice's unwillingness to have sex with Rabbit shortly after Rebecca's birth causes him to leave home once more. In *Rabbit Redux* Janice and Harry's love-making, after she tells him about her lover Stavros and just prior to her leaving Harry to live with him, is desperate, intense, fused with the moon landing and the Vietnam War as seen on television: "her body a stretch of powdery sand, her mouth a loose black hole, her eyes holes with sparks in them, his own body a barren landscape lit by bombardment, silently exploding images." Now their erotic encounter at bedtime occurs as Rabbit is engaged in the most prosaic, though engrossing, of activities — reading the latest *Consumer Reports*. Janice comes to bed naked and kisses him openmouthed:

> He tastes Gallo, baloney, and toothpaste while his mind is still trying to sort out the virtues and failings of the great range of can openers put to the test over five close pages of print. The Sunbeam units were most successful at opening rectangular and dented cans and yet pierced coffee cans with such force that grains of coffee spewed out onto the counter.

The parade of facts continues, Harry persisting in his reading while his wife's tongue "like an eyeless eager eel intrudes and angers him." Her eagerness does finally result in an erection, but a bit of fellatio, so exciting to him in *Rabbit, Run*, now occasions something less than fulfillment — memories, rather, as he thinks about Ruth, of guilt and betrayal. Eventually, after Janice falls asleep, Rabbit, having moved inside her, comes to orgasm ("So who says he's running out of gas?"). Twenty pages later, catching sight of his wife's legs on the tennis court (she has good legs), he thinks a wholly inglorious thought in a wholly Rabbit-like mode: "Ought to try fucking her some night when they're both awake." It's a kind of thought for the day, the crudest of reflections seasoned as if with eminent good sense and, perhaps, an ironic twist to it.

As a compelling plot, *Rabbit Is Rich* has less to offer than *Rabbit Redux*, where Harry's increasing involvement with Jill and Skeeter and its disastrous denouement kept us turning pages. By contrast, *Rabbit Is Rich* moves along and about in a leisurely manner, from the Toyota lot, to Harry's golfing and socializing with the Harrisons and the Murketts at the Flying Eagle Club he joined (he lusts after Webb Murkett's wife, Cindy), to the arrival of Nelson with his girl-friend Melanie in tow, to the eventual arrival of Nelson's real part-ner Teresa ("Pru"), who is pregnant by him. There are preparations for the marriage, involving counseling by the gayish minister "Soupy" Campbell; there is the wedding itself with a reception afterward at the Angstroms. These events suggest the domestic atmosphere of the comedy, which makes excursions into "specialty" numbers, as when Harry and Janice buy gold (Kruggerands) and make love afterward, to them and to each other; or when the three couples (Murketts, Harrisons, Angstroms) have a night of sexual swapping on their vacation in the Caribbean. The episodic nature of the novel may be seen as appropriate to middle-age sprawl and to the semiconscious realization on Rabbit's part that there is no com-pelling, overarching narrative to his life — as there seemed to be, if he could but find "it," in *Rabbit, Run*.

Not that Harry has wholly given up the search for something more than the daily grind, even though that grind is now admittedly less tedious. There is a lovely stretch of writing, just over ten pages, in which Harry, Janice, and her mother Bessie spend a few weeks on an old-fashioned vacation at the Springer cottage in the Poconos where they go every August. Here food, sleep, and exercise "swell to a sumptuous importance," as "the kiss of morning fog through a rusted window screen" mingles with other sharply realized sensations:

> the blue jay switching stances on the porch rail; the smooth
> rose-veined rock holding shut the upstairs door that has lost its
> latch; the very texture of root-riddled mud and reeds where

the fresh cedar dock pilings have been driven: he feels love for each phenomenon and not for the first time in his life seeks to bring himself into harmony with the intertwining simplicities that uphold him, that were woven into him at birth. There must be a good way to live.

Here Updike's powers as an observer of elemental things serve well his hero's mute aspirations toward an essential life with all the distractions and complexities scraped off — the way all of us try to feel at our summer vacation cottage near the lake or on the river.

This attempt to bring about reformation and find the good way to live is about as successful as any such a summertime venture is likely to be. Rabbit "eases off on the gin and snacks" and gets serious about his jogging. But the solitude and opportunity for thought that running provides inevitably releases memories of his past and the mortality of things, as "the blue and gold of his new shoes flickering, [he] skims, above the earth, above the dead." A litany of names once again confirms him, as earlier, king of the ghosts; and the ghosts of vacations past surface too in an especially evocative passage where he remembers the Angstrom family's occasional, unsuccessful summer day trips to the Jersey shore,

the hours on poky roads in the old Model-A and then the mud-brown Chevy, his sister and mother adding to the heat the vapors of female exasperation, Pop dogged at the wheel, the back of his neck sweaty and scrawny and freckled while the flat little towns of New Jersey threw back at Harry distorted echoes of his own town, his own life, for which he was homesick after an hour. Town after town numbingly demonstrated to him that his life was a paltry thing, roughly duplicated by the millions in settings where houses and porches and trees mocking those in Mt. Judge fed the illusions of other little boys that their souls were central and important and invisibly cherished.

If this is felt to emanate less from Rabbit's past than from that of some Everychild, unhappy in the family car as it slowly traverses the pre-superhighway roads of the 1930s and 1940s, the effect is heightened rather than lessened. "There must be a good way to live," yet it didn't present itself back then, even as it is now still elusive.

The most powerful ghost in *Rabbit Is Rich* is finally tracked down when Rabbit gets up the courage, after a couple of abortive attempts, to visit his old lover, Ruth, with whom — twenty years previously — he lived briefly and who, he is convinced, may have borne him a child. This "child" turns up in the novel's early pages when a young woman and her boyfriend appear at the Toyota lot, looking at cars for sale. Rabbit takes them for a test drive, becoming increasingly certain that the girl, Annie, is his daughter and that Ruth — who was pregnant by him and from whom, at the end of *Rabbit, Run*, he ran away — failed to have the abortion she had planned to have. Ruth, now very fat and the widow of the man she says was father of her daughter, tells Rabbit where to get off, insisting that she aborted their child and refusing his offer of money to help her out. As he gets up to leave,

> She stands too, and having risen together their ghosts feel their inflated flesh fall away; the young man and woman who lived illicitly together one flight up on Summer Street, across from a big limestone church, stand close again, sequestered from the world, and as before the room is hers.

But there is no sentimental meeting of long-lost souls:

> "Listen," she hisses up at him, radiantly is his impression, her distorted face gleaming. "I wouldn't give you the satisfaction of that girl being yours if there was a million dollars at stake. I raised her. She and I put in a lot of time together here and where the fuck were you? . . . I've known where you were all these years and you didn't give a simple shit what had happened to me, or my kid, or *anything*."

Rabbit finds "something odd" about the phrase "my kid," but doesn't pursue it, and they part with the sense of some sort of truce having been attained. It is one of the moments where one feels the difference in weight it makes to have, in one's readerly head, the ghost of *Rabbit, Run*.

Updike contrived an odd and oddly satisfying way of ending each of the Rabbit books with a short word of one or two syllables, as if to acknowledge the combination of narrative informality and vernacular play, with the director's evident hand. In each novel the effect is that of blurring the distinction between what Rabbit "thinks" and what his creator puts on the soundtrack by way of a fadeout. At the end of *Rabbit Is Rich* the Angstroms have moved to a new house, free at last of Bessie Springer, and are visited by Bessie, Nelson, and Pru along with the newest Angstrom, Judith, a substitute for the daughter Rabbit failed to get Ruth to admit was his. He is sitting in his new den, watching the Superbowl, and hears the guests arrive; Janice leads her mother upstairs to show her around, and Harry thinks Pru has joined them, but is suddenly surprised:

> Teresa comes softly down the one step into his den and deposits into his lap what he has been waiting for. Oblong cocooned little visitor, the baby shows her profile blindly in the shuddering flashes of color jerking from the Sony, the tiny stitchless seam of the closed eyelid aslant, lips bubbled forward beneath the whorled nose as if in delicate disdain, she knows she's good. You can feel in the curve of the cranium she's feminine, that shows from the first day. Through all this she has pushed to be here, in his lap, his hands, a real presence hardly weighing anything but alive. Fortune's hostage, heart's desire, a granddaughter. His. Another nail in his coffin. His.

Of the four endings to the Rabbit books, this one — in its blend of delicate observation and dark reflection — is the most telling, indeed just about perfect.

Rabbit at Rest

The finale to *Rabbit Angstrom* is Updike's longest novel (512 pages), and not only culminates the career of his most fully imagined protagonist but stands as the writer's prime achievement in longer fiction, the book that somehow had been in the making all along and over the decades. This reader felt its genius directly upon publication, and surely that feeling had to do in part with its coming after Updike's novels from the 1980s. For *The Witches of Eastwick, Roger's Version,* and *S* — each of which has its distinct accomplishment and interest — feel special, slightly theatrical, and sometimes perverse when put up against the centrality and solidity of *Rabbit at Rest.* Chronologically as well as humanly, the novel seems most akin to the memoirs Updike published the previous year, since it is self-consciousness that Harry Angstrom, in all his incorrigible, reckless assertiveness, so movingly and memorably displays. And not Harry only: there is more of Updike in this book than in any of his previous ones, including *Self-Consciousness.*

Such a claim can be proved only along the pulses of particular readers, and readers whose pulses don't sustain such proof continue to exist, as they have since *Rabbit, Run.* When the Everyman edition of the tetralogy was published in 1993, Robert Kiely, an English professor at Harvard, having surveyed the whole, did not like what he found and asked what to him seemed the "unavoidable" question about these books: "Is it possible to sustain interest for 1,516 pages in an ignorant, insensitive, uneducated, self-pitying bigot of no particular talent, imagination, or intelligence?"[1] He added that if this description of the hero seems harsh, "it is, in fact, a fair description of Harry 'Rabbit' Angstrom." But only "fair" if one disregards Updike's sentences except to abstract from them a character who, on the basis of various utterances and prejudices, can be unambiguously named a slob. There is nothing new in this complaint, which, to the extent that it can be dealt with at all, has been dealt with more than once in these pages. Kiely's other main complaint — that "Harry and his ilk are clueless about the big social and political forces that are raging round them" — can probably best be met by looking into our own hearts (and those of our ilk) to ask how many clues we educated, sensitive ones possess about such forces, or how much more adept than Harry we are and have been at distinguishing significant events in the political and social passing parade from the latest phenomenon in Hollywood, TV, or professional basketball.

When, just before publication of the novel, Updike wrote a front-page piece for the *New York Times Book Review* titled "Why Rabbit Had to Go," he connected his hero's fate with the death of his own mother in 1989, not long after he had finished the first draft of his novel (amazingly, the long book was written in just under a year). In a clever formulation he called *Rabbit at Rest* "a depressed book about a depressed man, written by a depressed man."[2] That sentence didn't survive in the Everyman introduction to the tetralogy, but Updike admitted to feeding, shamelessly, medical and hospital details of his mother's last illness into the physical tribulations of his hero. Frequent visits to the Pennsylvania farm, as his mother's health declined, must have been crucial to animating, yet once more, the fictional Diamond County where the Rabbit books occur. The Florida territory, by contrast, is new and perhaps the book's great triumph of place; its first section, and part of the final, third section, derive from "research" conducted in the Gulf Coast area. Deleon, the city where Harry and Janice own a condo in Valhalla Village to which Harry returns for his last days, was named for Linda Hoyer's (Updike's mother's maiden and pen name) unfulfilled aspiration to write a novel about the "discoverer" of Florida. And the connection between Pennsylvania and Florida, which Harry enacts in his flight by car from the one to the other, was given body, Updike tells us, by his own driving and tracing the route from farm to Gulf Coast. At any rate the location of action has never been more fully and convincingly done than in this novel, appropriate for a book that wants to be about America, "the happiest fucking country the world has ever seen," thinks exultant Harry at the high moment of his Uncle Sam impersonation.

In response to the perception on some readers' part in *Rabbit at Rest* that he had made his hero more "lovable," Updike said that it had not been his intention to make him so, and in his introduction to *Rabbit Angstrom* he invoked Dostoyevsky's underground man as, like Rabbit, *"incorrigible,"* not about to accept good advice from

anyone, "taking direction from his personal, also incorrigible, God."
One thinks, as a single illustration out of many, of the moment
when, after Harry has suffered his first heart attack, then has had
angioplasty, his physician advises him that, were he in Harry's
"shoes," he would have a bypass, and soon — "You're just toying
with your life otherwise." After the doctor leaves Rabbit thinks to
himself, *"but you're not in my shoes. And what's life for but to toy
with?"* It has not been sufficiently noticed how much of the satisfaction from following the mind of an incorrigible character comes
from our being able to entertain, indeed to toy with, this kind of
subversive, irresponsible, "foolish" response to the notion of doing
what's best for us. "Whenever somebody tells me to do something
my instinct's always to do the opposite. It's got me into a lot of
trouble, but I've had a lot of fun," he tells his granddaughter Judy.
The analogy here is with the reader who, if Rabbit had always done
what he was supposed to have done — what was "best" for him —
would have had no novel of any interest to read.

Perhaps the most physically vivid and recurrent example of
Harry's incorrigibleness is in the realm of food, and Updike cleverly
plays the role of providing good advice for his hero to disregard by
quoting lines from Frederick Douglass in one of the book's
epigraphs: "Food to the indolent is poison, not sustenance." Five
pages into the novel, while waiting at the Deleon airport for
Nelson, Pru, and his two grandchildren to arrive for a visit, and
while Janice is using the bathroom, Harry buys and consumes a
Planter's Original Peanut Bar. The plan to share it with his grandchildren quickly evaporates in the rush of "sticky brittle stuff, the
caramelized sugar and corn syrup," and he eats it all, receiving "as
the candy settles . . . a sense of doom" that "claws around his heart."
Food as an irresistible poison is related to the sense of doom that
keeps descending on Harry — here in the airport, and later, remembering the Lockerbie aircraft disaster — and the heart is established
as our most vulnerable target. (Ted Weems's awful 1940s-revival
recording of "Heartaches," even then a golden oldie as Harry has
become, surfaces at one point in his consciousness.)

He remembers his old basketball coach Marty Tothero telling him, "when you get old you eat and eat and it's never the right food." Getting the right wrong food into Harry is a task Updike performs with relish, from Planter's Peanut Bars to the macadamia nuts that hold especially rich qualities for his taste: "A couple won't kill me," he reassures his old lover, Thelma Harrison, as "to be polite" he takes a few of them — "Nuggets, they are like small, lightweight nuggets with a fur of salt." Upon holding one of them in his mouth, it breaks into two halves, "the surface of the fissure as smooth to the tongue . . . as baby skin." And he proceeds to improve the tasteless diet cola he is sipping by grabbing a small handful of dry-roasted cashews ("The second worst thing for me"). After a golf game in Florida as part of a foursome, Rabbit eats eighty percent of the "wonderful array of nibbles" provided by Valhalla Village's Club Nineteen. His partner warns him about sodium, and Harry rejoins, "Yeah, but it's good for the soul." At dinner in the Mead Hall, Valhalla Village's dining room, he follows up his eye-of-round steak (rejecting the shellfish supposed to be "good" for the elderly as "filthy gluey unspeakable stuff") with pecan pie topped by a "big oozing dip of butter-pecan ice cream." At lunch, back in Brewer with Charlie Stavros, he is tempted by a desert of "cheesecake made from low-fat goat's milk topped with delicious creamed gooseberries." "It's your funeral," says Stavros. Perhaps the healthiest thing Harry ingests, aside from a low-cal broiled fish meal served up by his daughter-in-law Pru, are what he presumes to be pistachio nuts, bought from a machine at Deleon's Jungle Gardens, where he and Janice have taken the grandchildren. These presumed pistachio nuts turn out to be food for the birds — "Little brown things like rabbit turds" — that, admittedly, have a bitter taste but are probably not loaded with salt. Seldom has the poetry of "bad" food been more convincingly detailed than in *Rabbit at Rest*, and it is but one of the strands in the book's overall metaphorical, figural density.

As for the Florida scene, anyone who has put in time on the Gulf Coast in the Sarasota–Fort Meyers stretch has driven along Route 41, the Tamiami Trail, which Rabbit thinks, with total justification, "the most steadily depressing" of any road he has ever seen. It is of course the sort of vista Updike is expert at doing up, but the Florida section generally is filled with so much fresh observation and so many horribly apt touches that one reads it and winces at, for example, the reality of Deleon's retirement specimens:

> men with bankers' trim white haircuts and bankers' long grave withholding faces wearing Day-Glo yellow-green tank tops stenciled CORAL POINT or CAPTIVA ISLAND and tomato-red bicycle shorts and Bermudas patterned with like fried eggs and their permed and thick-middled women in these ridiculous one-piece exercise outfits like long flannel underwear in pink or blue, baby colors on Kewpie-doll shapes, their costumes advertising the eternal youth they have found. . . .

It is almost too perfect a target for presentation. There is as well the "mortuary calm" of Valhalla Village at 4 P.M. "though in fact most everybody behind these doors has contrived something to do in the afternoon, golf or tennis or a beauty-parlor appointment or a bus trip to the Everglades." This "mass-produced paradise" where his wife's inheritance has taken him, the corridors of Valhalla Village "floored in peach-colored carpet" and smelling of "air freshener, to mask the mildew that creeps into every closed space in Florida," is evoked not to "satirize" the life of elderly well-to-dos, but to make by contrast a case for the lively animus with which Rabbit, himself obsessed with his own dwindling life and its possibilities, exercises pointed observation and sardonic wit.

The sardonic backlashings at aging remind us that Rabbit, like the tetralogy, is winding down. The elegiac sense so strong in *Rabbit Is Rich* becomes even stronger here, particularly when, after his heart attack in Florida, he returns to Pennsylvania for what will be the last time. His rediscovery of the old Brewer–Mt. Judge neighborhood in the opening pages of part 2 ("PA") is especially poignant. As in *Rabbit Is Rich*, he likes to get out into his backyard at the end of the day, breaking off and burning old flower stalks and plants, and he feels peace

> when the light dims and the weeping cherry glows in the dusk,
> its florets like small pink bachelor buttons and the whole
> droop-branched womanly forgiving shape of it gathering to
> itself a neon pallor as the shadows lengthen and dampen; the
> earth's revolution advances a bit more and the scraps of sun-
> light linger longer under the April sky with its jet trails and icy
> horsetails. . . .

That note continues and extends itself to touch, once again, on the
scene late in *Rabbit, Run* when Rabbit takes his small son to the
playground and discovers that we are nothing but "Flower stalks."
This moment is now reprised with Rabbit in his yard at dusk:

> The cement pool is cracked but still holds water. Like himself,
> Rabbit thinks, turning toward his house with its lit windows
> that seem as far away and yet as strangely close as his parents'
> house used to when he was a kid playing. . . . Then as now,
> waking from twilit daydreams, he discovered himself nearer a
> shining presence than he thought, near enough for it to cast a
> golden shadow ahead of his steps across the yard; then it was
> his future, now it is his past.

A hard-nosed reader not inclined to be taken in by Updike's excursions into his own or his hero's childhood by way of contrasting the
diminished present might call this sentimental, even self-pitying
writing, as in the easy move from the cracked cement pool to the
cracking, still-functioning protagonist. But as Lionel Trilling once
asked challengingly, is self-pity not a human activity calling for
expression? As for sentimentality, the rich specificity of backyard
impressions and memories keeps us reading attentively and energet-
ically; there is nothing slack about this writing, whose imaginative
pressure is as high as any place in the tetralogy.

The book's *tour de force* is Harry's flight, in his car, back to Florida,
there to meet his heart's destiny. But there are other brilliant and
harrowing sequences, particularly his first heart attack in the
Sunfish, when he manages to get himself and his granddaughter

back safely to shore, there to collapse. The subsequent angioplasty, performed back in Pennsylvania, is scarily relayed, one of Updike's trademark jobs in doing the relevant medical research, then putting it into convincing sentences and paragraphs. There is also, depending on your sense of what is mainly funny or mainly tasteless, the scene in which the Toyota representative, Mr. Shimada, comes around to Springer Motors and announces to Harry that, because of Nelson's bad management (he has cooked the financial books to support his cocaine habit), his father has lost the franchise. Mr. Shimada delivers a sermon on the differences between little Japan and a big country like America, doing so in the accents of a caricature "Jap":

> In former times, in Japan, very simple things make men happy. Moonright on fish pond at certain moment. Cricket singing in bamboo grove. Very small things bring very great feering. Japan a rittle ireand country, must make do with very near nothing. Not rike endless China, nor rike U.S. No oiru wells, no great spaces. We have only our people, their disciprine.

Here of course we can't blame Harry for the racial stereotype, and if, like me, you don't mind it — indeed actively enjoy it — it may have something to do with having grown up, like Updike did, during the Second World War when, at least so all the movies declared, they really did "talk rike that."

Deprived then of the car lot, his job, largely of his wife (Janice has taken up real estate and become an active businessperson), and increasingly, it will be, of his health as the good effects of angioplasty wear off, what is there for Harry to do except to run? Updike of course has planned it all, but needs a precipitating event to make the bolt to Florida reasonably happen. This occurs at the end of the novel's second part, the night Harry comes home from the hospital after his "procedure," when he has a one-fling moment with his daughter-in-law, at whose house he is sleeping. (Nelson is away at drug rehab, and Janice, who doesn't want to miss her real estate class but feels guilty about leaving her husband alone his first night home, contrives the temporary lodging, thus making the coupling possible.) For some readers the event is simply too much to take — home from the hospital and making it with your daughter-in-law the same night. It can also be questioned as constituting merely a convenience, as precipitating event, for Harry's discrediting and disappearance (Pru eventually confesses to Janice what happened). Yet the event is carefully prepared for, even though it still comes as a shock. Although accompanied by rather melodramatic stage props — lightning flashes and thunder peals just before Pru, who has been sitting on Harry's bed, suddenly cries "*Shit*" and peels off her bathrobe and nightgown — this coming together feels inevitable, at least as figured in the language. Before supper Harry had been lying in bed, responding to the beginnings of rain on the window. He thinks back to the window screens of the Wilbur Street apartment he and Janice occupied in *Rabbit, Run*, "the kind you used to buy in hardware stores before combination storms made them obsolete":

> They never precisely fit, leaving splinters of light through which the mosquitoes and midges could crawl, but that wasn't the something tragic about them. Tragedy lay in a certain fil-tered summer breath they admitted, the glint of sun along seg-ments of the mesh, an overlooked fervor in their details — the bent screening, the sliding adjustable frame stamped with the manfacturer's name, the motionless molding of the window itself, like the bricks that all through Brewer loyally hold their pattern though the masons that laid them long ago are dead. Something tragic in matter itself, the way it keeps watch no matter how great our misery.

There is no sequence of sentences anywhere in the tetralogy that more evidently shows the disparity between Updike's five-dimensional perceptions and Rabbit's (presumably) more limited register of them. And it is bothersome, even debilitating for readers who can't "believe" in the protagonist who is given such musings ("Tragedy lay in a certain filtered summer breath"). I know no way to resolve this problem, if it's felt as one; certainly not by claiming that Harry in his postoperative state has become incredibly sensitive to the contours of nature — although one of the first things he becomes aware of, on his return from Florida, is the beauty of trees on both sides of a street in Brewer (Bradford pears, Janice tells him, that the city is planting everywhere). But the focus in the window-screen passage on the "motionless molding" of the window. and the comparison of it to the bricks of Brewer that "loyally" hold their pattern over the years, belongs to Updike's poetic realm, the one he tapped early on in "The Dogwood Tree" when he spoke of the "wordless reassurance" that "things are pressing to give" — "like a brick wall or a small stone." Now the emphasis on the "tragic" in matter reflects the thirty years that have elapsed between that early memoir and *Rabbit at Rest*.

Something "tragic" in matter, then, turns out to be something tragic in human life. As Harry is lying in the hospital recovering from the angioplasty, he thinks "fondly of those dead bricklayers" who were so ingenious in the "festive pattern of recess and protrusion, diagonal and upright" as they did their roof work up there on the scaffold:

> Lying here thinking of all the bricks that have been piled up and knocked down and piled up again on the snug square streets that lift toward Mt. Judge, he tries to view his life as a brick of sorts, set in place with a slap in 1933 and hardening ever since, just one life in rows and walls and blocks of lives.

Yet though he finds satisfaction in such an overview, it doesn't last, and he soon begins to feel once again that — in a nice verbal stroke — "he is the heart of the universe." In other words, I am and am not a brick; am and am not just one more example of tragic matter. So perhaps the decision to sleep with Pru — or her decision to let him do so — is less a matter of decision, the conscious choice by a moral agent, than something as irresponsible, natural, inevitable as the lightning and thunder that precede it, or the concluding description of Pru's "pale wide-hipped nakedness in the dimmed room . . . lovely much as those pear trees in blossom along that block in Brewer last month were lovely, all his it had seemed, a piece of Paradise blundered upon, incredible." After such a glimpse, there is really no place for Harry to go except to Florida, the false paradise.

There, alone in his condo, prey to the inanities of TV and the silence of his nonringing phone, his heart begins "to talk to him," the signals of pain becoming more "hostile and deliberate, the knives of a strengthening enemy." He goes to the doctor and gets the same lecture he was given after his initial attack ("You ever eat any of this salty junk that comes in bags?" "Well — once in a great while"). He is advised to lose forty pounds, begin walking two or three miles every day, and, most importantly, develop what his doctor calls "a healthy interest in life. Get interested in something outside yourself, and your heart will stop talking to you." This has the ring of more good advice (we should all develop healthy interests in life, surely), but for the literary character whose self has been the unremitting focus of Updike's art for fifteen hundred pages, there is much built-in irony. Still, Rabbit does cut down on the bad food, does take substantial walks about Deleon, finds himself becoming interested in different neighborhoods — until one day he comes upon some black kids playing basketball on an outdoor court. One of the moving delights of the tetralogy, probably to be experienced fully only by a first-time reader of it, is the combination of surprise and absolute rightness that accrues from Rabbit's coming home, back to where it all started in the opening words of *Rabbit, Run*: "Boys are playing basketball around a telephone pole with a backboard bolted to it. Legs, shouts. The scrape and snap of Keds on loose alley pebbles seems to catapult their voices high into the moist March air blue above the wires." Back then Rabbit stopped to watch, then to shoot a few; thirty years later nothing has really changed: "A backboard and netless hoop lifted up on pipe legs preside at either end. A small pack of black boys are scrimmaging around one basket. Legs, shouts."

The final one-on-one basketball game he engages in with a young black man called Tiger is beyond praise, and I resist quoting except to note the wonderful touch of having Tiger marvel at Rabbit's successful deployment of the obsolete, two-handed set shot ("Man . . . that is pure horseshit"), then as Rabbit sinks his last basket and collapses to the ground, to have the shocked youth repeat, "Pure horseshit." Tiger feels a Rabbit-like impulse to flee, and after a deliberate few steps of walking, basketball under his arm, he breaks into a run. We are then treated to an aerial perspective of the fallen hero: "Seen from above, his limbs splayed and bent, Harry is as alone on the court as the sun in the sky, in its arena of clouds." In many ways this feels like the truest end of things, almost more than the subsequent, brief glimpse of him in the Deleon intensive care unit, visited by Nelson whose plea for him not to die almost constitutes a redeeming moment for the luckless boy. The one-word final sentence, existing at a level beyond or under words, is simply "Enough." We can't help reading it as among other things Updike's decision — on page 1,516 — that it is time to call a halt.

When *Harvard Magazine* published the earlier-mentioned dismissive account of Updike's tetralogy, a number of readers of both sexes wrote in Updike's defense (there were no — at least no published — defenses of the reviewer) from various perspectives. One of the strongest of these came from Warner Berthoff, a distinguished critic and historian of American literature, who provided a kind of sociological-cultural rationale for what Updike had done in these books. His letter read in part as follows:

> Through the whole series, the manifest ground or field of action has been the progressive breakdown of all the main traditional supports of ordinary life — church, marriage, schooling, community and family, occupational stability and satisfaction — and a resulting hollowness or emptiness in our common quotidian existence that leaves homeless and dangerously unanchored the deep human desire for integration, for some decent fusion of selfhood and living circumstance. As all Updike's writing acknowledges, the imperatives of this desire are ultimately religious, whatever reckless form they may take on.

And, he adds, "Updike has set this story in the world he knows best and has a birthright intimacy with, the world of small towns and small cities, economically decaying."[3]

At first glance, this claim may seem too systematically comprehensive, attributing more plan and foresight to Updike's extended improvisation on a man's life than could conceivably have been the case. But that Rabbit wouldn't think this way about himself, or that Updike's narrative resists incorporating, in explicit language, such large truths about American life, may be part of what makes for the solidity of *Rabbit Angstrom*. Most certainly Updike didn't begin *Rabbit, Run* with an analysis of American life as motive or goal; and even in the later novels, longer and more packed with names, dates, and media events, the "sociological" motives still takes very much a backseat to the story we follow. Indeed, it is not a question of what Updike might have intended but of what emerges when, stepping back from the tetralogy and trying to think of it as a whole, we look to draw out principles or assumptions that obtain about the American republic in its post-world-war journey toward destabilization and fragmentation.

Such words, used by me or Mr. Berthoff, are facile if not immediately grounded and qualified by the presence of what makes these books so much more, and so much more interesting, than sociological analysis. Berthoff alludes to that "more" when he says the "imperatives" behind Updike's effort are "ultimately religious, whatever reckless form they take on." In Harry Angstrom the recklessness is apparent, to the extent that some readers find him unpalatable as a character. But the more interesting recklessness is Updike the writer's, whose presentation of life, however it may be mined for social and cultural truths about the past four decades, is reckless in its lack of caution; in its willingness to court incorrectness in many forms, not just the political; in the sheer overkill of its fifteen hundred pages crammed with what some prudent, more cautious novelists would have omitted, pared down. Most important in contributing to the "reckless" form that any attempt to list sociological imperatives must necessarily leave out are the comic and satiric bits that characterize the novels, especially the last two of them. ("On the evening news half the commercials are for laxatives and the other half for hemorrhoid medicine, as if only assholes watch the news.") It is this last aspect that more than anything gives artistic life to the depiction and presentation of the mundane, the unextraordinary, the repeated.

Of course, and as usual, this is no more than Updike has said about himself, most trenchantly in *Self-Consciousness* when, alluding to his earlier remark that he had "a Pennsylvania thing to say," extended the saying: "I, who seemed to myself full of things to say, who had all of Shillington to say, Shillington and Pennsylvania and the whole mass of middling, hidden, troubled America to say." This remark is quoted by Elizabeth Hardwick in her appreciative review of the memoirs where she salutes the Rabbit novels as taking place "in a thick vegetation, crabgrass, and rotten dandelions pushing up over the lost basketball tournaments, the car lots, the aging elders, the songs and creaking beds, bad jobs, the growing and failing business of the lower-class and petit-bourgeois landscape."[4] With this list Hardwick expresses concretely, indeed novelistically, the impulse Berthoff rendered more abstractly. Together they seem intelligent and strongly felt responses to the ambitiousness of what Updike has done in *Rabbit Angstrom*; and they represent a more considered, though not more enthusiastic tribute, than occurred in a review of *Rabbit at Rest* by the English writer Jonathan Raban — "one of the very few modern novels in English (Bellow's *Herzog* is another) that one can set beside the work of Dickens, Thackeray, George Eliot, Joyce and not feel the draft."[5] Whether or not Raban would agree to extend the claim to the tetralogy as a whole, we may let it stand in its immoderate, even reckless, affection, as something memorably and, in this reader's judgment, truly said.

ELEVEN
P O S T - R A B B I T   E F F E C T S

This closing account of Updike's recent, post-Rabbit fiction aims to be tentative and inconclusive. After all, the writer shows no signs of abating his astonishing productivity, and to label, as does my chapter title, his work in the 1990s as "effects" may be merely glib. Surely it doesn't suggest how much creative life is to be found in the four novels, as well as the "quasi-novel" *Bech at Bay* (1998) and the short fiction contained in *The Afterlife* (1994) — to say nothing further of other nineties publications such as *Collected Poems* (1993) and the two massive collections of essays and criticism, *Odd Jobs* (1991) and *More Matter* (1999). But there is another reason, aside from recent additions to the rapidly increasing oeuvre, for abstaining from judgments etched in stone about work that has appeared, as it were, only yesterday. The reviewer of the individual volumes as they appear is called upon to judge them as firmly and unambiguously as possible; a writer completing an account of a literary career may occupy himself with describing its most recent trajectory and trying to make imaginative sense of it in relation to what came before. (I will say nothing here about the often-amusing *Bech at Bay*, nor about *Brazil*, published in 1994 — in my judgment his least successful, certainly least humorous novel.)[1]

What immediately preceded these books are the stocktaking memoirs, *Self-Consciousness*, and the last and best of the Rabbit books. As noted previously, Updike has spoken of "packing my bag a bit," by way of acknowledging the impulse behind his latest work. But that work, especially the novels and stories, is also a determined effort *not* to continue what has been already done, and well done, previously. The attempt is rather to make it new by way of experiment, to give readers what they weren't quite expecting to get and what, when they got it — compared to the well-prepared-for satisfactions of *Rabbit at Rest* — was unlooked for, often ambiguous in its impact.

Memories of the Ford Administration

A prime example of such an ambiguous product is the novel published two years after *Rabbit at Rest*. *Memories of the Ford Administration*, in its throwaway title and its clever jacket design — a composite face-montage of James Buchanan and Gerald Ford — as well as its teasing epigraphs, presents itself, as did novels from the previous decade like *The Witches of Eastwick* and *Roger's Version*, as a product of "wicked" Updike, playing fast and loose with the securely realistic convention that controls *Rabbit at Rest*. One of the epigraphs, from Rousseau's *Confessions*, offers the following apology: "I am well aware that the reader does not require information, but I, on the other hand, feel impelled to give it to him" — as if to say, my needs as a novelist are more significant than what you as a reader may think you do or don't require of fiction. Just as aggressively, in returning to the figure of Buchanan, on whom Updike lavished so much research and imaginative energy in the late 1960s (finally bringing out the play *Buchanan Dying* in 1974), he takes up once again a subject not at all enticing to most readerly curiosities.

This time the narrative is made complicated and double-faced by having it emanate from, in the first person singular, an academic historian who has for years been trying and failing to write a book about Buchanan. This professor, Alfred ("Alf") Clayton, has been asked by a journal titled *Retrospect* to give them his memories of the administration of Gerald Ford (1974–77). In his response Alf plunges us back to 1974 (the year of Updike's own separation from his first wife) soon after he left his wife and three children to take up bachelor residence in Adams, an industrial town across the river from Wayward Junior College in New Hampshire, a two-year college for women where Alf teaches. Alf gives us much more information than we require about famous people who died in 1974, lists the best-selling books and hit tunes of that time, and rehearses his sexual adventures with the woman for whom he left his wife, and with various more momentary female connections. In the witty excess of Alf's word-play, his antic sense of humor and generally aggressive address to the world, to the editors of *Retrospect* and to readers of the novel, we are reminded of earlier Updike mischief makers like Tom Marshfield in *A Month of Sundays* (published the year after *Buchanan Dying)* or Roger Lambert in *Roger's Version*, characters with more than a bit of the rascal in them. Updike's narrative moves us, often abruptly and without transition, from one of Alf's twenty-year-old memories — such as temporarily moving back to the marital nest when his mother visits from Florida — to Buchanan's response to the death of Ann Coleman, the women to whom he had been engaged before she broke it off. In other words, slabs of "ancient" and more recent history are juxtaposed, enabling us to make thematic and psychological connections between characters and periods of time, at the same time as that very activity of making meaningful, "true" statements about the past is called into question.

Indeed everything in this book is surrounded by invisible quotation marks, with the recognition that anything said or stated could really, with reason, have been said or stated another way. Alf informs the editors of *Retrospect* that he is attempting "to work into the fabric of reconstruction the indeterminancy of events." This indeterminacy is expressed in the fabric of Updike's novel by imagining alternative ways in which the story of Buchanan's life could be told, and by frequent employment in italicized prose of sentences in which other, earlier writers (historians, diarists, journalists) have come to terms with that life. These evidences complement Alf Clayton's humorously cynical, imperfect attempts to reconstruct the tone and temper, the "facts" of the Ford years. In a typical passage from his Buchanan manuscript Alf worries the question of whether there was in fact "ever an actual afternoon" in which Buchanan met Grace Hubley and spent time with her instead of paying a call on his fiancée, this neglect precipitating their estrangement. Sentences from historical accounts are interrupted by bracketed interpolations referring us to earlier "bracketed disclaimers"; ellipses in the quoted account are, Alf assures us (in brackets) "not mine." Everything is up for grabs, and it's no wonder Alf can't get his book written.

Yet turning to the recent past and consulting his personal memory is scarcely more comforting: "For that matter," he asks the editors of *Retrospect,* "was there ever a Ford Administration? Evidence for its existence seems to be scanty." He has looked up lists of hit songs from the years 1974–76 and can't recall any of the tunes, nor has he read any of the nonfiction best-sellers from those years, nor has he watched the top TV shows, having had no TV in his bachelor digs at that time. His own past, in other words, seems as difficult reliably to connect with larger public facts as does his hero Buchanan's. As a further indication of the unreliability of things, Updike had the clever idea of tapping into academic deconstruction, its prevalence and trendiness in the 1970s and 1980s providing a metaphor for the instabilities, the slippages and gaps between language and the world to which language was presumed to refer. Alf is contemptuous of and satirizes the "anti-canon deconstructionist chic, which flattened everything eloquent, beautiful, and awesome to propaganda baled for the trashman." But he is also its prey, unable to put his own or his hero's life together in dependable terms. Overall the novel exhibits a frenetic and skittering playfulness that is just this side of confusion and breakdown. Updike of course holds it all together through the artful maze of his narrative.

The least original aspect of *Memories of the Ford Administration* is the account of Alf's complaints about his wife, Norma ("The Queen of Disorder"), and his ups and downs with his mistress Genevieve ("The Perfect Wife"). The capitalized, ironic reference is a way of devaluing both women as people to be taken seriously and sympathetically, and in that way *Memories* is wholly continuous with the satirical surface of *A Month of Sundays.* But something different is apparent in the treatment of Buchanan, more especially in Updike's entering the suffering mind of Ann Coleman on the night she dies of an overdose of laudanum. Here the novel attains an imaginative dimension as powerful as the "Pennsylvania" family portraits, like the grandmother in *Pigeon Feathers*, or the Updike men, father and grandfather in the genealogical chapter of *Self-Consciousness*. Ann, stricken with chills and fevers, puts herself to bed in the Philadelphia bedroom of her sister's house, but feels "trapped in her own skull, a closed oval chamber maddeningly echoing with images she could not control or organize." The doctor is summoned, gives her a dose of laudanum, says that it may be repeated once, but warns against anything further. Ann sleeps, then wakes, takes another draft of the elixir, but the images echoing in her mind will not abate. In a single paragraph her mind ranges from God, to the early death of her sister and brothers, to lines from Byron's haunting and desolate poem "Darkness," to Christ's agony on the cross, to the rebellion effected by John Adams, Washington, and Tom Paine, to Adam and Eve and the darkness their trespass purchased. The fifteen or so pages that carry the suffering woman to her death are grippingly effective in making us realize the tumult of Ann Coleman's agony; it is of course quite impossible (and unnecessary) to imagine them originating in the cocky, embattled Alf Clayton, Updike's representative, who lacks the depth of historical and novelistic imagination with which his creator is endowed.

But this episode's very power serves to point up by contrast the relative dryness of much of the later sections on Buchanan. Or so it seems to a reader like myself, without either the professional historian's or the fascinated novelist's investment in (say) Buchanan's 1820 conversation with Andrew Jackson about presidential politics, or Buchanan's ambassadorial doings in Russia, or his relation to pre–Civil War events as president. The record is easier to follow than it was in the unchronological, dreamlike sequences of *Buchanan Dying*. But the words from Rousseau's epigraph begin to ring in our ears: there is indeed a surfeit of "information" relative to our needs, though not to the novelist's. In the final third of the book, for example, the pages on Buchanan clearly outnumber the ones devoted to Alf, whose own story of the end of his affair with Genevive and his return to Norma seems of little consequence. And there is nothing approaching the human vividness of the Ann Coleman section in the final block of Buchanan material, consisting of a sequence of fifty pages contrived to break the back of any but the most determinedly captivated reader. It is a commonplace that most novels have trouble in their later reaches but here the trouble seems located in what looks like a misjudgment or overestimation on Updike's part of our staying power, perhaps of his own as well.

Displaying his usual good sense about his own work, Updike was interviewed by Dick Cavett on the publication of *Memories* and said he found it a hard book to describe, with its "two-level operation."[2] He had been long interested in the man as the only bachelor president, the only president from Pennsylvania, the president that history neglected, but he admitted it was hard to justify why he did the "monstrous thing" of writing a novel with so much historical baggage; perhaps simply because "I've been carrying Buchanan around with me for years, and I had to get rid of him." In that same interview, Cavett asks him whether he (Cavett) was wrong to feel a sense of evanescence, of nostalgia for a time past, permeating *Memories*. Updike assures him that no, he was right to feel this, and that neither history nor memory "can really bring back the past"; thus that there was a kind of "mourning" to the novel's atmosphere. Although we get plenty of that "mourning" sense of things in the stories Updike was writing at the time, frequently with an aging man as protagonist, it is there in *Memories* also. At the end of the novel Alf is confused about the time, the place, and the woman (was it Norma, was it Genevieve?) that made up a remembered skiing occasion, and he signs off to his *Retrospect* readers by noting that their "provocative query seems to have delivered me into darkness. The more I think about the Ford Administration, the more it seems I remember nothing." The strategy here, on the novelist's part, is to have his protagonist fail to remember (unlike Proust's Marcel), to remember "nothing," while in fact the novelist is remembering all of it. In his recent story "How Was It, Really?" (*New Yorker*, May 17, 1999), a similar strategy is at work, the divorced and remarried man trying and failing, he tells us, to remember what it was like — that first marriage, those four children, those endless parties: "It frightens me," he confesses to his daughter, "how little I remember." But his creator is not similarly forgetful.

In the Beauty of the Lilies

The long novel of almost five hundred pages that appeared in 1996 is told from some distance, the teller's voice able to remember and encompass with full confidence four generations of an American family, traced over the course of this century. *In the Beauty of the Lilies* is a four-section narrative beginning in Paterson, New Jersey, in 1910 with Clarence Wilmot, a Presbyterian minister, experiencing a loss of faith; it concludes in 1990 with the death of his great-grandson in a shoot-out with federal authorities at the Lower Branch Temple compound in Colorado. The two middle sections focus on Clarence's third child, Teddy, who moves from his father's Paterson to Basingstoke, an imaginary town in Delaware where he marries a young woman named Emily. Their daughter, Esther (Essie), grows up to become a Hollywood movie star, taking the name Alma DeMott. The novel's title, from Julia Ward Howe's "Battle Hymn of the Republic," sets the American tonality and also registers Updike's conviction, voiced in *Self-Consciousness*, that he had something to say, not just about Shillington, Pennsylvania, but about "the whole mass of middling, hidden, troubled America." He had heard, he writes,

> things in my two childhood homes, as my parents' giant faces revolved and spoke, achieving utterance under some terrible pressure of American disappointment, that would take a lifetime to sort out, particularize, and extol with the proper dark beauty. *In the beauty of the lilies Christ was born across the sea* — this odd and uplifting line . . . seemed to me, as I set out, to summarize what I had to say about America. . . .

All of his books, he imagined, would contribute to this "continental *magnum opus*," but it's likely that *Lilies* was conceived of as playing an important part in the contribution.

By way of explaining the "distance" in the narrative of *Lilies*, Updike suggested it might be due to the "God's-eye perspective" with which the generations are viewed.[3] In his note to the Franklin Library edition he writes, perhaps too coyly, that God was the hero of the chronicle and that "I invited Him in, to be a character in my tale, and if He declined, with characteristic modern modesty, to make his presence felt unambiguously, at least there is a space in this chronicle plainly reserved for Him, a pocket in human nature that nothing else will fill."[4] Whatever can be said or not said about that "pocket" the narrative God in this novel, even while sustaining a disinterested loftiness, enjoys putting together the large and the small, juxtaposing or placing in immediate sequence public events of the sort that newspapers take account of, with intimate personal experiences and changes. An instance of such practice opens the novel, as the "Clarence" section begins not with the minister's sudden loss of faith, but with a motion picture being made in Paterson by D. W. Griffith (*The Call to Arms*) starring Mary Pickford who, on this day at the end of spring 1910, "sweltered" on horseback and, overcome by the heat, fainted. Immediately we move to the minister's study:

> At the moment when Mary Pickford fainted, the Reverend Clarence Arthur Wilmot, down in the rectory of the Fourth Presbyterian Church at the corner of Straight Street and Broadway, felt the last particles of his faith leave him. The sensation was distinct — a visceral surrender, a set of dark sparkling bubbles escaping upward.

One is reminded of Pope's lines from *An Essay on Man* in which the God's-eye perspective is memorably described:

> Who sees with equal eye, as God of all,
> A hero perish, or a sparrow fall,
> Atoms or systems into ruin hurl'd
> And now a bubble burst, and now a world.

It is a seeing with equal eye that constitutes the narrative of *Lilies* and brings with it at the verbal level an absolute assurance in the power of language to express anything and everything, without ambiguity. Keats's "negative capability" — the capacity to rest in doubts and uncertainties he saw as the mark of the supreme (Shakespearean) poet — is far from the capability aspired to and demonstrated in this the most spacious and leisurely of Updike's novels.

What are the liabilities of eschewing novelistic negative capability in favor of God's-eye certainty? In dealing with Updike's works generally I have also attempted to deal with what seem to me the work's liveliest, or most potentially damaging criticisms. One of the most recent is James Wood's, who in *The Broken Estate*, his collection of essays on literature and belief, has denigrated Updike's powers as a convincing "theological writer" in his novels.[5] Or rather, and unlike Herman Melville, Updike is too tranquilly theological, rather than disturbedly metaphysical, in his portrayal of doubt, absence, the loss of faith. This means, Wood argues, that by the same token his portrayal of belief, of fullness, of presence, is also unconvincing. Updike is an "oddly calm Barthian" because he accepts too placidly the world's particularity as not a proof of God's existence, but a consoling substitute for it. Wood presents a new version of the old complaint about Updike's articulateness, saying that any possible moment of absence, of despair, is too quickly filled up with gorgeous writing. So that — and Wood uses it as an example — when the Reverend Wilmot loses his faith that day in 1910, the presentation of this loss is inadequate. Clarence surveys the old religious-philosophical books in his study — Bunyan, Calvin, Thomas à Kempis — and thinks that they "were ignorant but not pathetic in the way of the attempts of the century just now departed to cope with God's inexorable recession: the gallant poems of Tennyson and Longfellow, phrasing doubt in the lingering hymnal music." Is this Wilmot's language or Updike's, Wood asks rhetorically, certain that not only is it the latter's but that the Wilmot character is thereby deprived of exhibiting any real loss of faith. It is Updike who reviews, as if for the *New Yorker*, Clarence's apostasy, rather than presenting it truly from within. The very use of a phrase like "God's inexorable recession," says Wood, is a tip-off that the novelist is scarcely disturbed by what has happened, since he is all too much in command of putting it into words. In Melville (in *Moby-Dick* especially) the anguished narrative refusal to rest content for long in any one metaphor is exciting and authentic, since it is testimony to Melville's religious seriousness, his wrestle with matters of belief and unbelief, presence and absence; thus Melville's engagement with reality is "existential." In Updike the lack of authentic drama is a measure of timidity and complacence, a refusal to take religious matters as seriously as Wood wants them to be taken.

I am prepared to agree that the treatment of Clarence's loss of faith ("God's inexorable recession"), indeed of any event in *Lilies*, is presented in an undramatic rather than "existential" manner. But such presentation is the result of a narrative decision that in no way devalues the experience presented. Of course one may prefer observing the dramatic ambiguity of unresolved struggle in a character seen up close to the cooler, more impersonal treatment provided by a novelist who is not himself falling upon the thorns of unbelief but engaged rather in patiently constructing a panoramic novel of large proportions. The novel form has many routes toward truth, and *Lilies* in its untroubled though not unsympathetic proceedings is one way of telling a truth. The panoramic aspiration, comparable to nothing in earlier Updike novels, is embodied in the deal of research that clearly went into the book: an afterword lists a number of people and books that have been useful to the writer. In *Lilies* we have listed for thanks accounts of the Paterson Silk Strike of 1913, a bicentennial history of Delaware, books on film and on religious cults, and a novel by Updike's younger contemporary, Brett Easton Ellis. Updike even goes so far as to thank a greenhouse gardener's companion (Teddy Wilmot's Basingstoke sweetheart and wife first works in her father's greenhouse). But the novelist's decision to confess so clearly his indebtednesses has not prevented him from being criticized for too dutifully or mechanically splicing them into the narrative, especially in the Hollywood section. Again, this way of distancing, with its slightly artificial taste of large events looking over a character's shoulder at each moment, may count against a sense of dramatic immediacy in events of which the outcome is uncertain. For example, from the very moment in section 4 when Clark joins the Lower Branch Temple and acquires a new name ("Esau"), we know what the outcome will be — that it will bear the imprint of the Waco, Texas, disaster. But as with the distanced presentation of character, this undramatic inevitability (eventually the place is going to blow up) is the consequence of a certain kind of narrative, rather than a black mark against it. After all, the story we read with a truly open sense of possibility — of something happening or maybe not happening, perhaps this way, perhaps that — is a story read only once, for the first time. *Hamlet* reread, *Moby-Dick* reread will not hold out the possibility that the prince kills Claudius in act 3 or that the *Pequod* and its crew of merry men survive the white whale and live happily ever after in New Bedford. This is not to deny that, compared to the Rabbit novels or to less realistic works like *The Coup* or *Memories of the Ford Administration*, *Lilies* feels more straight-ahead and also foreclosed, even on a first reading. But if one accepts the convention of storytelling the novel follows, the problem of giving assent to the narrative is not really a problem.

This is not, I hope, to dismiss cavalierly James Wood's criticism of Updike for not being exercised enough by "the tremors of faith." A really exercised novel, which dealt dramatically with those tremors — as did Updike's early story "Pigeon Feathers" — could not be written with the continuously accomplished ease that permeates every passage of *Lilies*. Wood's way of being dissatisfied with a writer he admits to be "one of the few theologically literate novelists" is to compare Updike disadvantageously with Melville, a truly "metaphysical" writer, and to link Updike with Hawthorne as only a "theological" one who, in Hawthorne's case, couldn't understand Melville's suffering. Perhaps not, but to be "only" a theological novelist, and like Hawthorne to boot, seems scarcely to signal failure on Updike's part. If, as he suggests, *Lilies* presents a God's-eye perspective on things, then *theological* is not an inappropriate label for both Updike and his precursor. In his preface to *The House of the Seven Gables* Hawthorne says that he has provided his romance with a moral — "the truth, namely, that the wrong-doing of one generation lives into the successive ones, and, divesting itself of every temporary advantage, becomes a pure and uncontrollable mischief." A similarly God's-eye perspective is characteristic of the narrative voice of that novel, given to expressing itself as follows:

> Nevertheless, if we look through all the heroic fortunes of mankind, we shall find this same entanglement of something mean and trivial with whatever is noblest in joy or sorrow. Life is made up of marble and mud. And without all the deeper trust in a comprehensive sympathy above us, we might hence be led to suspect the insult of a sneer, as well as an immitigable frown, on the iron countenance of fate.

Perhaps this address is more urbane than God-like, and it addresses the reader directly — as *Lilies* does not — to comment on the "moral" to be found in the work in progress. But it is equally undisturbed by the materials, the situation and characters, with which it works. Metaphysical tremors touch neither Hawthorne's nor Updike's impeccable narrative surfaces.

Is there a moral to the generational saga that is *In the Beauty of the Lilies*? There are certainly all sorts of thematic connections to be made among its four sections. The centrality of the movies, from Clarence's postministerial fascination with them, through his son's attendance at them, to his granddaughter's starring in them, and his great-grandson's ill-fated role in a real-life one, is plain enough. Yet as soon as one formulates what the narrative doesn't explicitly say — that belief in the movies has replaced belief in God — the formulation sounds banal and probably untrue. Hawthorne's formulations about the "entanglement" of the trivial with the noble, of joy with sorrow, and of how the "wrong-doing" of one generation lives on, in different ways, through successive ones, have universal force; but only by a feat of abstraction can they be said to emerge from the particular American lives surveyed in *Lilies*. I don't think, in other words, that this is a novel one reads by moving from its lively sur-face to intuit depths, deep meanings; nor does its arresting title, either while reading, or after the novel is read, yield further inter-pretive rewards. Even though the time spanned is far greater than in any other fiction of Updike's, the reader doesn't have the sense, cumulatively, of going anywhere; in fact for both characters and readers, the situation is that described by Santayana's often-quoted maxim about how those who don't understand the past are con-demned to repeat it. If that seemed to be the "moral" emerging from *Memories of the Ford Administration*, it shows up again here, with this improvement on Santayana — that no one can understand the past, therefore everyone is condemned to repeat it. Of course it all depends on what is meant by "understand"; Updike gives us in this novel a pretty skeptical take, as far as his characters go, on the suc-cess of such a historical activity.

By speaking, with reference to *Lilies*, of its distanced narrative address, of its undramatic rather than dramatic technique of pres-entation, and of its lack of overall development — in the sense of an action being progressively explored and complicated — I run the risk of dwelling on what the book *doesn't* do, doesn't manifest. But the risk is worth it if the singularity of this novel, when compared to Updike's others, may be suggested. Its weight is static rather than dynamic, and its particular four-part form is such that, to judge from the responses of reviewers and readers, it invites discussion in terms of these separate parts. There is, however, no consensus on which of the parts excels or which falls short of credible assent. Some admire the treatment of Clarence's apostasy in section 1, or Clark/Esau's violent end in the final section. One reviewer praised the Alma DeMott/Hollywood story as most vividly alive with particularities, while another found that section too heavily laid-on with movie lore. I myself incline toward the relatively quiet section 2, Teddy's adolescence in Basingstoke and his courtship of the greenhouse owner's daughter with a deformed foot. But such disagreement is worth noting only because it didn't, indeed couldn't occur with earlier Updike novels, none of which has this absolute breakup into four nearly equal sections, each named for its central character.

Finally, and to further distinguish *Lilies* from Updike's other novels: it is the easiest one to read page by page, to "follow" without encountering resistance and playful impediments to easy access (as in *Roger's Version*), or lyric densities as found in the Rabbit books and *Of the Farm*. In writing about this novel, I am aware that I've quoted little from it, indeed have not been tempted to quote from it — a critical state completely unlike my usual one vis-à-vis an Updike fiction. Despite the large differences in situation and character among Clarence and Teddy, Alma and Clark, they share the fact of a narrative procedure that evenly and uninterruptedly tells their stories to a close; thus their individual voices don't sound all that different — again an observation about the novel that might, but should not, be construed as a point against it. The "point" is that *Lilies* is a much odder, much more experimental book than it appears at first glance. Its terms are so grand that it invites, positively courts, the judgment that it is a failure. Yet what would "success" look like, given the desire to write, in the language of the novel's dust jacket, "one saga, one wandering tapestry thread of the American Century"? There is no answer to the question, but it may help to measure just what Updike did accomplish in this book.

Toward the End of Time

Early in this chapter I hazarded that judgments etched in stone might be resisted when dealing with a writer's most recent work, published only yesterday. I had in mind most especially the provocative and disturbing, "futuristic" novel that appeared in the fall of 1997 and drew decidedly mixed responses from reviewers. *Publishers Weekly* pronounced *Toward the End of Time* a book "that has all the hallmarks of a classic"; while Michiko Kakutani wondered, in the *Times*, how a distinguished writer could produce such a "lousy" book. Interviewed by Charlie Rose, Updike admitted that it was a "strange" novel and that after the third-person, distanced, historical *Lilies*, he wanted to "write about a period when nobody knew what happened and also a somewhat more intimate novel, first-person narrative." If *Lilies* stayed within historical periods, extended as they were, its successor would push all limits, observe no boundaries. Accordingly the book is set in 2020 and narrated by a sixty-six-year-old retired investment counselor, writing (as it were) the journal of a year, from a comfortable house on the North Shore where he lives with his second wife, Gloria, and within proximity (they are clustered in the Route 128 area) to numerous children and grandchildren. This may sound cozy and domestic, but nothing could be farther from the case, since Ben Turnbull's imagination is haunted and plagued by intimations of mortality.

These feelings are not, significantly, a result of what has happened to the larger world since Ben's sympathies with "current events" are, to say the least, limited. In that larger world the United States has been devastated by a nuclear exchange with China (America won, but at great cost); the national economy has collapsed; oceans and lands are depleted; the federal government has ceased to exist. In Massachusetts the state currency ("Welders," named after a former governor) has replaced dollars. Mexico, neutral in the war, has become a land of opportunity for young Americans who sneak across its border. As an agent of protection, FedEx is replacing the more or less nonexistent local police (you don't see them supervising road repairs anymore, Ben notes amusingly). Underfoot are voracious inorganic manifestations called metallobioforms, or more familiarly, "trinkets." Overhead from time to time is visible a mysterious "circular intrusion" or "torus" floating above the clouds, perhaps from another galaxy. Time's arrow, a figure frequently evoked in the novel, points "toward an entropy when all seas will have broken down all rocks and there is not a whisper, a subatomic stir, of surge." In short, the world of 2020 is a "dwindled, senile" world, moving toward the end of time.

Like that larger, if dwindled, world, Ben Turnbull's personal sense of things is shrunken; on the novel's first page he compares himself to a "patient with a dwindling appetite" and he wakes at night stricken by dread: "my professional usefulness over, my wife more of a disciplinarian than a comfort, my body a swamp in whose simmering depths a fatal infirmity must be brewing." And so it is, in that most manly of glands, the prostate. Ben's voice has its ancestors in first-person Updike narrators like Tom Marshfield in *A Month of Sundays* and Roger Lambert in *Roger's Version*. And although he operates at a more coldly sophisticated level of disdain than Harry Angstrom, there is a shared, often aggrieved sense of maleness, especially of marriage, described by Ben as "a mental game of thrust and parry played on the edge of the grave." But *Toward the End of Time* is no straightforward realistic chronicle of aging and decline. For as Ben more than once remarks, nature refuses to stand still and so does Updike's narrative, whose main principle is metamorphosis, enacting what an epigraph from Martin Gardner calls "the endlessly forking chains" of possibility. Such branchings are sometimes blatant and dreamlike, as when in the opening section "The Deer," first of five alliterated sections (The Deer, The Dollhouse, The Deal, The Deaths, The Dahlia), the doe that persists in eating Gloria's euonymus hedge, thus maddening Gloria though not Ben, becomes a young prostitute named Deirdre who replaces Gloria in Ben's bed until one day she disappears and the wife returns. Deirdre is a fantasy, "a branching not existent in the palpable universe," but also as real as anything in a novel that juxtaposes ancient historical sequences of man's aggressive violence (Egyptian tomb-robbers, the destruction of a ninth-century monastic order) with the mindless preyings of parts of nature upon other parts — "Nature, which would consume my life as carelessly and relentlessly as it would a dung beetle," says Ben.

There are many other recurrent concerns in Ben's life and thoughts: his boyhood in a depressed western Massachusetts town; his memories of his first wife Perdita and his guilt at neglecting their children, now slightly assuaged by the presence of grandchildren; and rounds of golf with a couple of old pals: "Give up golf? I love those men. They alone forgive me for my warts and stiffnesses, my tainted breath and protruding nostril-hairs, my tremors and white-capped skin cancers. My golf companions too are descending into deterioration, and trying to put a good face on it. . . ." There are Updike-inspired satiric vignettes, strongly tinged with disgust, of phenomena such as shopping malls that scarcely need a futuristic venue since we're familiar with them already:

> Young couples, tattooed and punctured visibly and invisibly, with studiously brutal haircuts, strolled hand in hand as if in a garish park of the purely unnatural, so deeply at home here it would not have surprised me if, with a clash of nostril studs and a spattering of hair dye, boy and girl had turned and begun to copulate. Malls have become a public habitat soaked in slovenly intimacy; its customers step naturally from huddling around televison in their living rooms to cruising these boulevards of superfluity, where fluorescent-lit shops press forward temptations ranging from yogurt-coated peanuts to electric-powered treadmills.

Although these are our malls, we never thought to speak of them as "boulevards of superfluity." Ben's Thoreau-like investment in minutely describing the changing days and seasons is one side of a coin, the other side of which contains malls, the "tourist traps" of Boston's Quincy Market, and the "hideous" look of patients at the waiting room of Massachusetts General Ambulatory Care Center. Even as Ben claims to be "conscious as my days dwindle of how poorly I have observed the world," a reader's powers are consistently and invigoratingly taxed to keep up with the rich observation contained on almost every page of the novel.

In fact, Ben's confession about how poorly he has observed the world provokes him into some follow-up observations, one of which in particular elicited scoffings from reviewers like James Wood who felt that observation was being carried to a ludicrous plane: "Sitting on the toilet yesterday, I suddenly saw as if for the first time the miraculous knit of the Jockey underpants stretched across my knees." Is this patently absurd, an example of Updike's superfluity — the bankruptcy of a baroque style expending itself on nothing? But the jockey shorts' "miraculous knit" is further investigated:

Tiny needles, functioning in cunning clusters at inhuman speeds, had contrived to entangle tiny white threads with perfect regularity to form this comfortably pliable, lightweight, and slightly elastic fabric. Engineers had planned and refined generations of machines, giant looms deploying batteries of hooked needles scarcely thicker than a hair yet containing moving parts, minuscule springs and latches, to duplicate mechanically the intricate action of patient human hands.

The passage concludes with praise of "such wonders of fabrication" that are "no less deserving of praise than those of that blind weaver, Nature." *Homo faber*. Of course the "miraculous knit of the Jockey underpants" taken by itself sounds pretty silly and self-regarding to the nth degree. But what comes after it, a hardworking and ingenious attempt to put into words how the product gets made (compare Robert Pinsky's excellent poem "Shirt"), is satisfyingly vigorous. In addition, it's reasonable to think of this excursion — one of many in the novel — as Ben Turnbull the diarist writing to himself, indeed talking back to himself by proving that perhaps he hasn't observed the world so poorly after all. There is humorous life, indeed slyness, in his show-offy attempt — quite a successful one, it seems to these eyes — to keep oneself going, the retired businessman not at all retiring from his pursuit of fabricated utterances.

Such humor, often of a dark character, pervades the novel, and many reviewers and readers seem to have missed it.[6] Or simply have not been amused, or have decided that a novel that is "misogynistic" — a novel in which Ben engages in numerous unuplifting fantasies about his wife, his lover-whore Deirdre, a teenage girl who resides for a time in a hut on the property, a daughter-in-law, and others — must be responded to with moral disgust as the product of "a narcissistic and dirty-minded man" (Kakutani). One can of course, in good lit-critical style, distinguish author from protagonist, and Updike in his Franklin edition note to the novel has made such an attempt, pointing out all sorts of respects in which he and Ben Turnbull are biographically dissimilar. But as with the novelist's relation to Rabbit Angstrom as well as his other heroes, Updike's willingness to endow his man with extravagant bursts of negative female-directed rhetoric pulls us up short. Ben talking to Deirdre can sound sometimes like Henry Miller ("I whispered into her ear how I wanted before I died to pump a ton of jism into her, into her mouth, into her little puckered asshole, into her huge warm cosmic cunt") or like a post-Schopenhaurian generalizer about the species:

> Our mothers wipe our bottoms and praise our first babbled words, our nurses at the finale tidy up and maternally murmur amid the mess of our dying, but the women who out of whatever motive swallow our seed through one of their holes deliver the acceptance that matters. They drink our groins' milky tears.

Probably no argument, however ingenious, is likely to convince anyone repelled by this sort of all-stops-out writing, and Kakutani compares, as a similarly disgusting character, Roth's protagonist in *Sabbath's Theater*. But the sexual bias, in its immoderacy, is continuous with that lavished on the weave of Turnbull's underpants, or the tawdry proliferation of malls, or the exaggerated attention paid to each morning's new slant of light on the euonymus bush. We may lay such reflections to Turnbull's inner agitations, but also, surely, to Updike's calculatedly overheated and mischievous way with words — his indulged temptation to say things that are over the line, too much by half, and that don't emanate from the "nice," fastidious, elegantly polite man of letters we meet within other contexts. He himself notes that he turned sixty-five a few months before *Toward the End of Time* was published. Is it too far-fetched to think of one of Yeats's Crazy Jane poems, written when Yeats was about the same age as Updike, in which the Bishop tells Jane to live in "a heavenly mansion" rather than in the "foul sty" she still inhabits? To which Jane/Yeats memorably replies:

> 'Fair and foul are near of kin,
> And fair needs foul,' I cried.
> 'My friends are gone, but that's a truth

Nor grave nor bed denied,
Learned in bodily lowliness
And in the heart's pride.'

Ben Turnbull might well be uncomfortable with such high — or low — heroic affirmations, but I doubt he would want to contradict the truth of the declaration that fair needs foul. In any case, this "need" makes itself evident in Updike's performance, by turns frantic and docile yet always composed, that marks this "strange" novel.

Late Stories; *The Afterlife*

To conclude this journey through Updike's writings with his recent short fiction is to usher him out in the form some readers find him most at home in, most in powerful control. That control, that power, was not gradually acquired over decades; after all, "The Happiest I've Been," "Pigeon Feathers," and the stories with composite titles ("The Blessed Man of Boston . . .," "Packed Dirt . . .") that came at the beginning of his career were not to be improved on. His high level of performance in the short story was quickly taken for granted, thus less argued about than the novels, which often engaged readers in more provocative ways — as with *Toward the End of Time*. In that novel and some of its predecessors, the "nice" or responsibly adult narrator was pushed aside in favor of more aggressive, bothersome figures who enjoy not monitoring their expressiveness. By contrast the stories are invariably told by and are usually about a presence in whose hands we put ourselves with confidence. *Trust Me*, says the title of the collection he published in 1987, and we do. The voice will not pull any rugs out from under us.

Trust Me and *The Afterlife* contain forty-four stories, and further ones continue to appear in the *New Yorker*. In *Problems* (1979) there were a number of stories, published around the time of Updike's divorce and remarriage, which showed a man — variously called Fraser or Ferguson or Ferris or Farnham — whose domestic circumstances to some extent paralleled Updike's own; in *Trust Me* three stories about men named Foster or Fegley or Fulham continue the game. In each of them the man seems a vaguely good-hearted, slightly bemused fellow, helping his former wife and their children clean out the attic by throwing away old disused board games; or trying to come to terms with his son's artistic predilections as a maker of mobiles; or — in the charming story "The Wallet" — working himself into a severe state of nerves over a check that hasn't arrived in the mail, and a misplaced wallet eventually recovered by a grandchild. As Fulham squeezes the found wallet, his "beloved bent book of leather," he feels "very grandpaternal, fragile and wise and ready to die." Many of the stories in *The Afterlife*, not just the ones about Ferris or Fredericks, Fogel or Fanshawe, feature an aging man who feels, dimly, that something is missing, that — Fanshawe thinks in "Playing with Dynamite," remembering the beginning of a sexual affair — "Things used to be more substantial." In "Short Easter" Fogel, nearing retirement, spends an Easter day that coincides with the arrival of Daylight Saving; thus an hour is lost. This loss, along with his perceived absentmindedness, memories of the unsatisfying quality of childhood Easter-egg hunts, and the prospect of brunch at a neighbor's house, add to the holiday gloom. His wife accuses him of becoming "doddery," suggests a brisk hour of yard work, cleaning out last year's leaves from the forsythia. But the teeth of the bamboo rake keep breaking, and before you know it Fogel is meditating, Ben Turnbull–like, on the futility of all this pulling of weeds, since, he thinks portentously, "All labor was tied to human life, life as pointless as that of any new little jade-green weed already joyously sprouting beneath the damp-blackened leaves." After the brunch, after gin and tomato juice and the "crushing accumulation" of social politenesses, he takes a nap — something he doesn't usually like to do — in his younger son's old bedroom, with posters of European cars and rock stars still marking the walls. Waking to a parched mouth and some dribble on the pillow, he has lost track of time, doesn't hear his wife anywhere, is suddenly chilled by a "curve of terror" in his abdomen. He takes an inventory:

> His eyes checked the items of the room — shiny posters, vacant
> fireplace, light plug, bookcase of abandoned schoolbooks, rack

of obsolete cassettes, stolen NO PARKING sign, stuffed rabbit
wearing a vest — one by one. Everything seemed still in place,
yet something was immensely missing.

Just how "immensely missing" the mundane accumulation of familiar details can make the lost man feel is the burden of these stories,
carried through details that in their banality are absolutely telling
and inescapable.

The relationship in "Short Easter" between immensely missing
one's past, figured through the absence of children who have fled
the nest, and feeling, as in "The Wallet," "fragile and wise and ready
to die" scarcely needs underlining. It is these complementary states
of being that animate the two most powerful stories in *The Afterlife*,
each of them ranking with the best Updike ever wrote. One of
them, "The Journey to the Dead," is more conventionally a story,
with a protagonist named Fredericks who observes the slide into
death of a female college friend of his former wife. The other, "A
Sandstone Farmhouse," which brings back Joey Robinson from *Of
the Farm*, is, though told in the third person, so patently an account
of Updike's mother's death and his consequent closing down of her
house that it may serve here as a last word on the most central person and subject of his literary career.

In "The Journey to the Dead" Arlene Quint asks Martin
Fredericks to drive her to the hospital, thinking that a ride from him
will be easier than a taxi and counseling him, with some humor,
"None of your sudden stops and starts." Arlene has experienced a
recent "cancer scare," and is evidently undergoing further treatment. Fredericks had recently encountered her, also divorced, at a
party in a Boston apartment, high up and looking out on the city,
"amber and platinum and blurred dabs of neon red" creating a
slightly surreal effect. Though seemingly happy to be free and single
again, Arlene is in fact, Fredericks realizes, "taken" and, glad on the
whole she has declined his offer to walk her home, he decides to let
her alone. But the subsequent call for a ride to the hospital brings
her back into his life, and after she is released he calls on her a few

times, mainly to talk about his former wife and learn things about her he hadn't known.

Rather than simply narrating the meetings and conversations between him and Arlene, conversations in which not much happens, the narrative moves out and enlarges itself, first through Fredericks's memory of another dying woman his own age, who after her breast cancer recurred gave a kind of farewell party for her friends. When Fredericks and his then wife drove onto the property, he was careful to avoid running over a garden hose; when he explained his concern to the hostess she replied, "Ach, the hose," and with a "sweeping, humorous gesture" said "Phooey to the hose!" Yet Fredericks moves it, trying to imagine

> how these appurtenances to our daily living, as patiently treasured and stored and coiled and repaired as if their usefulness were eternal, must look to someone whose death is imminent. The hose. The flowers. The abandoned trowel whose canary-yellow handle winks within weeds in the phlox border. The grass itself, and the sun and sky and trees like massive scuffed-up stage flats — phooey to them. Their value was about to undergo a revision so vast and crushing Fredericks could not imagine it.

But the writing here precisely imagines it, by way of preparing us for such a revision. He then thinks about how "the dying" live in a world much like our own, keeping on living, watching television: "No radical insights heightened their conversation, though Fredericks listened expectantly." A classics major in college, he recalled Odysseus's journey to Hades, Aeneas's to Avernus, and how the dead encountered there are wordless or "silly" or like "angry Dido," "*inimica*." And he recalls Gilgamesh to whom Utnapishtim says, "As for death, its time is hidden. The time of life is shown plain." Some of these words resurface in the remainder of the story, with deepening force. Fredericks's conversations with Arlene, preceding her final entry into the hospital, increasingly focus on his attempt to re-create his past with his ex-wife. Finally there comes a day when Arlene tells him she's "too tired and full of pills" to, as she puts it, "do Harriet for you today." Hanging up, Fredericks realizes what he has been asking her to "do" — "Harriet when young and that whole vast kingdom of the dead, including himself when young." He feels hot with embarrassment.

In the story's final scene Fredericks pays a last visit to Arlene, this time at the hospital after she has had a stroke. He is scared, doesn't want to visit her, but does, parks his car in the hospital garage, rides down in an elevator "through murky corridors of cement and tile," emerges into the "cavernous hospital lobby" with its "well-lit comings and goings, of immigrants arriving on a bustling shore." (Compare Philip Larkin's bleak poem, "The Building": "Humans, caught / On ground curiously neutral, homes and names / Suddenly in abeyance.") In *Toward the End of Time*, Ben Turnbull contemplated with distaste the "hideous" look of hospital patients at the ambulatory care center. Fredericks, visiting Hades, finds all his powers called forth to make that visit:

> He threaded his way through corridors milling with pale spectres — white-clad nurses in thick-soled shoes, doctors with cotton lab coats flapping, unconscious patients pushed on gurneys like boats with IV poles for masts, stricken visitors clinging to one another in family clumps and looking lost and pasty in the harsh fluorescent light.

Words from the *Odyssey*, in T. E. Lawrence's version, swim into his head: *"There beset me ten thousand seely ghosts, crying inhumanly."* Eventually he finds Arlene's room; as at the earlier party where he met her, it overlooks the city, the view of which is now dominated by "a great ugly iron bridge spotted with red rustproofing paint and crawling with cars." Though it's only the Charles River flowing under that bridge, we conjure up other, more classical streams of darkness and oblivion.

Arlene has lost her speech, is trying, evidently, to recover expression by using some alphabet cards provided her. Fredericks finds himself speaking much too loudly, as it were for both of them, while she tries to spell words he can't make out. Incredibly banal and inappropriate things pass his lips: "You have a terrific view," he says, and asks her when she will be going home. She points to the clock, then tries to find a card: "She held one up the wrong way around, and then with a grimace on the side of her mouth that was not dead she flipped it away. He remembered the gesture. *Phooey*." Seldom has such an undistinguished word carried as much emotional and dramatic freight. Fredericks babbles on about the hospital, about the crush in the elevator, and makes a Statue of Liberty gesture to designate the hospital aide holding up a tray full of coffee cups in that crush. It is to no avail, and he lowers his arm

> shamed by the shining unblinking fury of Arlene's eyes, one eye half shut. The dead hate us, and we hate the dead. *I went pale with fear, lest awful Persephone send me from Hades the Gorgon's head, that fabulous horror.*

He gets up, says he must "split," a word once sarcastically used in her presence. Again, to no avail: "Arlene unsmilingly stared. *None of your sudden stops and starts.* He promised, insincerely, to come again, and, like heroes before him, fled."

As with other stories of Updike, I have done little more than try to rehearse, while neglecting much, its main moments of imaginative power. Here they seem principally to lie in the interpolated moments of language from the narrator's memory ("No sudden stops and starts"; "Phooey") and the grand, assured cadences from classical texts ("There beset me ten thousand seely ghosts, crying inhumanly"). Both kinds of interpolations create frozen moments of elevated and chilling perspective. The wonderful archaic word *seely*, meaning anything from lucky or blessed to silly, defenseless, or miserable, is an adjective that comprehends not just the dead and the dying but all of us, especially Fredericks, who flees the scene as "heroes" have been wont to do. I don't know of any single story in Updike's work, or of another writer's, that more unflinchingly, and with something like human dignity, confronts us with our lot. It may be thought of as a sad postscript to the boy's final conviction when he buries the pigeons in "Pigeon Feathers" "that the God who lavished such craft upon these worthless birds would not destroy His whole Creation by refusing to let David live forever."

"It is because I believe in things and in people while I walked along these paths that the things and the people they made known to me are the only ones that I still take seriously and that still bring me joy." Proust's words from the "Combray" section of *Swann's Way* bring us to "A Sandstone Farmhouse," Updike's farewell to his mother, to Pennsylvania, to his youth. In *Of the Farm* we were introduced to Joey Robinson in the first person singular, and that novel, in which Joey's mother plays the central role, ends with son and mother circumspectly coming to terms with one another "in our old language, our only language, allusive and teasing, that with conspiratorial tact declared nothing and left the past apparently unrevised." Now the mother is dead, and although the son engages in no sweeping revision of the past, nor significantly alters the terms in which he see his mother, there is a felt pressure to find some last words not wholly allusive and teasing. So the story succeeds in doing, almost without our registering it. For while "A Sandstone Farmhouse" is artfully organized, that organization, compared to the allusions to Hades in "Journey to the Dead," doesn't call attention to itself. The shifts in perspective are made deftly and unobtrusively, but they have cumulative force and weight.

For example, it begins we know not quite when or where: "Joey's first glimpse of the house was cloudy in his memory, like an old photo mottled by mildew." It turns out that this was the glimpse of a twelve-year-old struggling not to be carsick ("his father's hand on the gearshift") as miles of Pennsylvania farm country pour past. Telephone poles dot the humanless landscape. Then the house comes into focus, that house whose presence will be increasingly and particularly realized in the story. By its second paragraph, Joey is thirteen and they have moved, leaving behind his much-loved brick city dwelling in order to realize his mother's dream of living again in the house where she was born. There is nothing in this material that Updike hasn't touched on more than once before — in the stories, in *Of the Farm,* in the memoirs. But Joey's presiding consciousness in "A Sandstone Farmhouse" is graver and more impersonal than was his lively, cleverly evasive and rather cocky presence in the earlier novel. By the story's third paragraph his focus has narrowed to a memorable tearing-down, with his father and grandfather, of a stone kitchen fireplace and its chimney that extended to the attic. He remembers himself and his grandfather carefully moving the stones out the attic window to be lowered on a makeshift pulley by his father. The stones accumulated into "a kind of mountain it became Joey's summer job to clear away":

> He learned a valuable lesson that first summer on the farm, while he turned fourteen: even if you manage to wrestle only one stone into the wheelbarrow and sweatily, staggeringly trundle it down to the swampy area this side of the spring-house, eventually the entire mountain will be taken away. On the same principle, an invisible giant, removing only one day at a time, will eventually dispose of an entire life.

In Updike's first novel, *The Poorhouse Fair,* the aged John Hook entertains the fantasy that the dead, including his son and daughter, had vanished out of carelessness: "that if like him they had taken each day of life as the day impossible to die on, and treated it carefully, they too would have lived without end and would have grown to have behind them an endless past." But this is not to be; the giant's claims will not be denied; it will "eventually dispose of an entire life." With an extra space after those words, we move to the story's center of attention: "When, over forty years after that summer of 1946, his mother died, and the at last uninhabited house yielded up its long-buried treasures, he came across a photograph of her at the age of ten, posing in front of the porch." We are then launched on an extended, vividly detailed portrait of the house and its former inhabitant. In a sense the story seems to tell itself, rather than emanating from a special consciousness with needs, with an agenda. Updike gets himself and gets Joey out of the main line of vision.

But not wholly, and at his mother's funeral, as he imagines her there in the cherrywood casket about to be interred, he is overtaken by an image of her as a young woman hurrying to catch the trolley car to her job at the department store downtown. He remembers her telling him, "Oh, how you'd run, and if you just missed it, there wouldn't be another for twenty minutes, and you wanted to cry." The memory does it, unleashing the floodgates. Men don't very often weep in Updike's fiction, and the only significant predecessor to Joey's tears is Richard Maple's at the supper table the night he tells his children about his impending separation from Joan. As on that occasion, the release in tears feels exhilarating to Joey:

> His tears came and kept coming, in a kind of triumph, a break-through, a torrent of empathy and pity for that lost young woman running past the Pennsylvania row houses, under the buttonwood trees, running to catch the trolley, the world of the Thirties shabby and solid around her, the porches, the blue mid-summer hydrangeas, this tiny well-dressed figure in her diminishing pocket of time, her future unknown, her death, her farm, far from her mind.

It's not only the tears that keep coming, but the writing, continuing for two pages with only a single paragraph break. The image of his mother running "was as potent, as fertile, as a classic advertisement, which endlessly taps something deep and needy within us." Here what is tapped finds expression in a sequence of images, pictures, and memories that succeed one another with urgent necessity. It is a wonderful moment in Updike's fiction and testifies of course to the absolute power of mother over son. At the very end of the sequence, Joey tells us that *this* — the mother running to catch the downtown trolley — is the mother he had loved, "before she betrayed him with the farm and its sandstone house." The confession could scarcely be put more explicitly and without qualification or teasing evasiveness.

More than once in Updike's writing the suggestion has surfaced of a sexual lack or misfit between the parents of the youthful protagonist. In the unpublished novel *Home* there is an account of the first night of a parental honeymoon in which things do not go at all well. But the "secret" comes closest to getting out in "The Sandstone Farmhouse," when Joey, visiting his mother at the farm shortly before her death, asks her, with reference to his father, "What didn't you like about him?" In answer she speaks of how her husband loved "Energetic little women" like her own mother, and declares that there was "no reason to marry me. I was *big*. It was a mistake, and we both knew it. . . . We knew it the first day of our honeymoon." Sensing his curiosity, she continues, "Oh Joey . . . don't ask. It was un*speak*able," and he, feeling he doesn't want to be this close to a revelation, responds to her "Maybe I *should* speak it" by heading out to the kitchen with an "Oh no, no thanks, that's all right." In the words from *Of the Farm*, the "conspiratorial tact" has left the past "apparently unrevised" — but not quite. The imminence of her death makes such pretenses just a little less compelling.

It is tempting to dwell on and quote from other particularities, so fully present in this story, of reducing the empty farmhouse "to its essence, removing every trace, even a rusty pencil sharpener screwed to a windowsill, of his life and the four lives that had ended." But as with so much else in Updike's work, the critic is left feeling superfluous, reduced to quoting and shaking his head admiringly at the rightness of things evoked, like that forlorn pencil sharpener, down to the last detail. We are put here in the world to give praise, to pay attention, is the way he once put it. In the final sentences of "A Sandstone Farmhouse," as Joey Robinson shuttles between his Manhattan apartment and the final weekend cleanups at the farm, he feels dislocated in Manhattan, "guilty, anxious, displaced." And in a formulation that rings with Updike's accent, a benediction, not without its ironic component, is bestowed upon this hero, "fled" from the scene as at the end of "Journey to the Dead": "He had always wanted to be where the action was, and what action there was, it turned out, had been back there."

That sentence would be an appropriate place to conclude this account of Updike's literary career. Yet the career is far from concluded: a forthcoming collection of short fiction, *Licks of Love*, includes "Rabbit Remembered," a novella with reflections on the departed hero by various friends and family members. And even as I write there has appeared *Gertrude and Claudius*, a novel which, combined with the further works to come, will render my own criticism dated. I shall say no more about *Gertrude and Claudius* than to cite it as a most striking example of his unpredictability and originality. He has engaged in previous historical and mythical reconstructions — *Buchanan Dying* and *Memories of the Ford Administration*; the "flashbacks" to remote periods in *Toward the End of Time*; the generational succession of *In the Beauty of the Lilies*. But one was unprepared for what this experienced writer, looking to bring out his first book of the new millennium, would turn his attention to: nothing less than the life led, before they began to act in Shakespeare's play, of the king, the queen, Hamlet, his dead father, and various supporting players. It sounds like a gimmicky idea, and in other hands might well have issued in nothing more. In the hands of this canny and resourceful constructor, the results, if not wholly unexpected, are further confirmation of literary genius.

But any reader who has reached this point is surely aware of my conviction that Updike is never less than an interesting writer, and at his best a major one. In giving space to strictures his work has received from critics like Frederick Crews and James Wood, I wanted to suggest that one of the marks of a major writer is the ability to provoke, and that if Updike hasn't quite elicited the degree of hostility accorded D. H. Lawrence or T. S. Eliot or — to move back a little — John Milton, he has nevertheless provoked some critics into impressive statements of his failings and limitations.

This capacity to irritate is of course connected to an unstoppable production of books and essays ("Has the bastard ever had an unpublished thought?") but also to something more revealing: the fearsome, seemingly effortless nature of his articulateness. In the preface to *Women in Love* Lawrence wrote that "any man of real individuality tries to know and to understand what is happening, even to himself, as he goes along. This struggle for verbal con-

sciousness should not be left out in art. It is a very great part of life."
Updike annoys some by appearing, in his authorial self, to leave out
that effort; the verbal consciousness exhibited by his narrators, his
characters, his own performance as poet or critic, is so fully developed, so fully *there*, that it seems to have been composed in advance
of the material on which it is exercised.

Yet it would be a mistake to sell short the struggle for verbal consciousness that has been his daily employment for so many years. In
the sonnet "Perfection Wasted," quoted earlier, he notes that "another
regrettable thing about death / is the ceasing of your own brand of
magic, / which took a whole life to develop and market." "The whole
act. / Who will do it again?" asks the poem, and the answer is, of
course, no one. Written in 1990, when Updike had been developing
and marketing his magic for four decades, the personal ring is unmis-
takable, and it is heard also five years later in a brief piece (later published in *More Matter*) titled "Updike and I" in imitation of an essay
by Borges. The piece investigates this phenomenon known as
"Updike": "I created Updike, out of the sticks and mud of my
Pennsylvania boyhood," the man tells us. He can hardly blame people
when they mistake him for that created figure, not realizing that
"Updike" works "only in the medium of the written word" and
involves himself in "pained exactions of language" that the more
worldly man, blundering swiftly through life, avoids. More and more
time, the man tells us, seems to be spent in "being Updike, that monster of whom my boyhood dreamed." But the real wear and tear
accrues around the inescapable dailiness of such an activity. The man
gets up in the morning, brushes his teeth, descends to the kitchen for
breakfast and to read the newspaper, postpones as long as he dares the
moment when he must head back upstairs "and face the room that
Updike has filled with his books, his papers, his trophies, his projects":

> The abundant clutter stifles me, yet I am helpless to clear away
> much of it. It would be a blasphemy. He has become a sacred
> reality to me. I gaze at his worn wooden desk, his boxes of dull
> pencils, his blank-faced word processor, with a religious fear.

332 Updike   America's Man of Letters

> Suppose, some day, he fails to show up? I would attempt to
> do his work, but no one would be fooled.

This then is the ambiguous reward for a lifetime of becoming
Updike, something we may presume the man lays claim to with disbelief perhaps, but with more than a touch of elation.

Introduction

1. Denis Donoghue, "The Zeal of a Man of Letters," *New York Times Book Review*, 18 September 1983, 1.

2. Gore Vidal, "Rabbit's Own Burrow," *Times Literary Supplement*, 26 April 1996, 3–7.

3. George J. Searles, ed., *Conversations with Philip Roth* (Jackson: University Press of Mississippi, 1992), 151.

4. Quoted by Dean Flower in his useful essay, "John Updike 1932 –" in *American Writers: A Collection of Literary Biographies*, Retrospective Supplement 1, eds. A. Walton Litz and Molly Weigel (New York: Charles Scribner's, 1998), 317–38.

Chapter 1: First Fruits

1. Throughout this book, quotations from Updike's poems are from *Collected Poems, 1953–1993*.

2. Whitney Balliett, "Writer's Writer," *New Yorker*, 7 February 1959, 138–42.

3. John Bayley, *The Short Story: Henry James to Elizabeth Bowen* (New York: St. Martin's, 1988), 7.

4. John Updike, "Franny and Zooey," in *Assorted Prose* (New York: Knopf, 1965), 234–39.

5. In *Close Imagining: An Introduction to Literature*, Bejamin DeMott has some useful reflections on the story's ending (New York: St. Martins Press, 1998, pp. 27–33).

6. John Updike, letter to the author, 5 July 1973.

7. ———, "How Does the Writer Imagine?" in *Odd Jobs* (New York: Knopf, 1991), 134–35.

Chapter 2: The Novelist Takes Off

1. John Updike, *Rabbit Angstrom: A Tetralogy* (New York: Everyman Library, 1995). All quotations from the four Rabbit novels will be from this edition.

2. John Thompson, "Other People's Affairs," *Partisan Review*, January–February 1961, 122.

3. Whitney Balliett, "The American Expression," *New Yorker*, 5 November 1960, 222.

4. Mary Gordon, *Good Boys and Dead Girls* (New York: Viking, 1991), 17–23.

5. Philip Stevick, "The Full Range of Updike's Prose," in *New Essays on* Rabbit, Run, ed. Stanley Trachtenberg (Cambridge: Cambridge University Press, 1993), 48.

6. In "Rabbit Revised," Randall H. Waldron discusses Updike's revisions in the text of *Rabbit, Run*, especially with reference to sex. *American Literature* 56 (March 1984), 51–67.

Chapter 3: The Pennsylvania Thing

1. He put it succinctly in an interview: "I realized that this was not going to be my first novel — it had too many traits of a first novel." James Plath, ed., *Conversations with John Updike* (Jackson: University Press of Mississippi, 1994), 47. Earlier at Harvard he had written two-thirds of a novel, putatively titled *Willow*, set in a town much like Shillington.

2. John Updike, *Picked-Up Pieces* (New York: Knopf, 1975), 498.

3. Robert M. Luscher, *John Updike: A Study of the Short Fiction* (New York: Twayne, 1993), 26.

4. *Odd Jobs*, 307.

5. Updike credits William Maxwell with suggesting that he flesh out the adolescent hero's story by supplying words about that hero's family and background. John Updike, *More Matter* (New York: Knopf, 1999), 781.

6. *Picked-Up Pieces*, 498–99.

7. Larry E. Taylor, *Pastoral and Anti-Pastoral Patterns in Updike's Fiction* (Carbondale: Southern Illinois University Press, 1971), 57.

8. Saul Bellow, "Recent American Fiction; A Lecture Presented under the Auspices of the Gertrude Clarke Whittall Poetry and Literature Fund" (Washington: Library of Congress, 1963), 6.

9. John Updike, *Hugging the Shore* (New York: Knopf, 1983), 851.

10. *Conversations with John Updike*, 35.

11. Renata Adler, "Arcadia, PA," *New Yorker*, 13 April 1963, 184.

12. Joyce Carol Oates, "Updike's American Comedies," *Modern Fiction Studies* 21 (fall 1975), 459.

13. I. A. Richards, *Practical Criticism* (New York: Harcourt Brace, 1929), 254.

14. *Conversations with John Updike*, 27.

15. *Picked-Up Pieces*, 82–83.

16. Charles Thomas Samuels, "The Question of Updike," *Kenyon Review* 28, no. 2, March 1966, 269.

17. Anthony Burgess, "Language, Myth and Mr. Updike," in *Critical Essays on John Updike*, ed. William R. Macnaughton (Boston: G. K. Hall, 1982), 58.

18. Alice and Kenneth Hamilton, *The Elements of John Updike* (Grand Rapids, Mich.: William E. Eerdmans, 1970), 190.

19. Donald J. Greiner, *John Updike's Novels* (Athens: Ohio University Press, 1984), 121–40.

20. Elizabeth Tallent, *Married Men and Magic Tricks: John Updike's Erotic Heroes* (Berkeley: Creative Arts Book Co., 1982), 29.

Chapter 4: Adultery and Its Consequences

1. John Updike, *Couples: A Short Story* (Cambridge: Halty Ferguson, 1976).

2. *Hugging the Shore*, 852.

3. Robert Martin Adams, "Without Risk," *New York Times Book Review*, 18 September 1966, 4–5.

4. *Hugging the Shore*, 856–58.

5. *Conversations with John Updike*, 134.

6. Brian Way, "The Case for the Defensive," *New Review* 4 (April 1977), 57.

7. *Picked-Up Pieces*, 519.

8. Brigid Brophy, "Love in the Garden State," *Harper's*, December 1976, 81.

9. David Thorburn, "Recent Novels: Realism Redux," *Yale Review* 66, no. 4 (summer 1977), 585.

10. *Picked-Up Pieces*, 504.

Chapter 5: Impersonations of Men in Trouble (1)

1. Richard Poirier: *The Performing Self* (New York: Oxford University Press, 1971), 27.

2. Cynthia Ozick, "Bech, Passing," in *John Updike*, edited by Harold

Bloom, Modern Critical Views (New York: Chelsea House, 1987), 127–38.

3. *Conversations with John Updike*, 81.

4. George Plimpton, ed., *Writers at Work: The Paris Review Interviews*, Seventh Series (New York: Viking, 1986), 274–75.

5. Christopher Ricks, "Flopsy Bunny," *New York Review of Books*, 16 December 1971, 8.

Chapter 6: Impersonations of Men in Trouble (2)

1. Blanche W. Gelfant, "Fiction Chronicle," *Hudson Review* 28, no. 2 (summer 1975), 313.

2. See especially James A. Schiff, *Updike's Version: Rewriting* The Scarlet Letter (Columbia: University of Missouri Press, 1992).

3. *Conversations with John Updike*, 75.

4. Luscher, *John Updike*, 120.

5. Quotations from the story are from *Problems*, rather than from the slightly different version in *Too Far To Go*.

Chapter 7: Extravagant Fictions

1. Frederick Crews, "Mr. Updike's Planet," *New York Review of Books*, 4 December 1986, 7–10, 12, 14.

2. My letter and Crews's reply are in the *New York Review of Books*, 12 February 1987, 41.

3. *Conversations with John Updike*, 179.

4. Joyce Carol Oates, "*The Coup* by John Updike," *New Republic*, 6 January 1979, 32–34.

5. Harold Bloom, ed., *John Updike*, 1–7.

6. Kathleen Verduin, "Sex, Nature, and Dualism in *The Witches of Eastwick*," *Modern Language Quarterly* 46 (September 1985), 295.

7. *Conversations with John Updike*, 263.

8. Verduin, 294.

9. In addition to James Schiff's book (note 2, chapter 7), see Donald Greiner, "Body and Soul: John Updike and *The Scarlet Letter*," *Journal of Modern Literature* 15 (spring 1989), 475–95; and Raymond Wilson III, "*Roger's Version*: Updike's Negative-Solid Model of *The Scarlet Letter*," *Modern Fiction Studies* 35 (summer 1989), 241–50.

10. *Odd Jobs*, 858.

11. John N. Duvall, "The Pleasure of Textual/Sexual Wrestling: Pornography and Heresy in *Roger's Version*." *Modern Fiction Studies* (spring 1991) , 81–95.

12. Mervyn Rothstein, "In S Updike Tries Woman's Viewpoint," *New York Times*, 2 March 1988, sec. C, p. 21.

13. Michiko Kakutani, "Updike's Struggle to Portray Women," *New York Times*, 5 May 1988, sec. C, p. 29.

14. "Updike can no more conceal his snobbery here than he can hide his male superiority throughout the book." Hope Hale Davis, "Distaff Doormat," *New Leader*, 18 April 1988, 20.

Chapter 8: The Critic and Reviewer

1. *Picked-Up Pieces*, 517.

2. Martin Amis, "Magnanimous in a Big Way," *New York Times Book Review*, 10 November 1991, 12.

3. Gore Vidal, *United States: Essays 1952–1992* (New York: Random House, 1993), 497.

4. *Odd Jobs*, 447.

5. *Hugging the Shore*, 73.

6. More recently in "Man of Secrets," Updike has reviewed Edwin Haviland Miller's biography of Hawthorne. *More Matter*, 499–509.

Chapter 9: Poet, Memoirist

1. Lawrance Thompson, ed., *Selected Letters of Robert Frost* (New York: Holt, 1964), 361.

2. Fred Inglis, "On Being a Dud," *Nation*, 10 July 1989, 59–61.

Chapter 10: Rabbit Retired

1. Robert Kiely, "Rabbit Reread," *Harvard Magazine*, July–August 1996, 26.

2. John Updike, "Why Rabbit Had to Go," *New York Times Book Review*, 5 August 1990, 24.

3. *Harvard Magazine*, September–October 1996, 10.

4. Elizabeth Hardwick, "Citizen Updike," in *Sight-Readings* (New York: Random House, 1998), 129.

5. Jonathan Raban, "Rabbit's Last Run," *Washington Post*, 30 September 1990, Book World, 1.

Chapter 11: Post-Rabbit Effects

1. For an intelligent and severe review of *Brazil*, see "Bungle in the Jungle," by Rand Richards Cooper, *Commonweal*, 8 April 1994, 18–20.

2. *Conversations with John Updike*, 229.

3. Letter to the author, 17 March 1996.

4. *More Matter*, 831.

5. James Wood, "John Updike's Complacent God," in *The Broken Estate: Essays on Literature and Belief* (New York: Random House, 1999), 195–202.

6. Though not Joyce Carol Oates, who with her usual perceptiveness about Updike's writing called the novel "a cheerily bleak black comedy." "Future Tense," *New Yorker*, 8 December 1997, 117.

Books and Monographs

Baker, Nicholson. *U and I: A True Story*. New York: Vintage Books, 1992.

Bayley, John. *The Short Story: Henry James to Elizabeth Bowen*. New York: St. Martin's, 1988.

Bloom, Harold, ed. *John Updike*. Modern Critical Views. New York: Chelsea House, 1987.

De Bellis, Jack. *John Updike: A Bibliography 1967–1993*. Westport, Conn: Greenwood Press, 1994.

Gordon, Mary. *Good Boys and Dead Girls*. New York: Viking, 1991.

Greiner, Donald J. *John Updike's Novels*. Athens: Ohio University Press, 1984.

Hamilton, Alice and Kenneth. *The Elements of John Updike*. Grand Rapids, Mich.: William E. Eerdmans, 1970.

Luscher, Robert M. *John Updike: A Study of the Short Fiction*. New York: Twayne, 1993.

Macnaughton, William R., ed. *Critical Essays on John Updike*. Boston: G. K. Hall, 1982.

Plath, James, ed. *Conversations with John Updike*. Jackson: University Press of Mississippi, 1994.

Schiff, James A. *John Updike Revisited*. New York: Twayne, 1998.

———. *Updike's Version: Rewriting* The Scarlet Letter. Columbia: University of Missouri Press, 1992.

Searles, George J., ed. *Conversations with Philip Roth*. Jackson: University Press of Mississippi, 1992.

Tallent, Elizabeth. *Married Men and Magic Tricks: John Updike's Erotic Heroes*. Berkeley: Creative Arts Book Co., 1982.

Taylor, C. Clarke. *John Updike: A Bibliography*. Kent, Ohio: Kent State University Press, 1968.

Taylor, Larry E. *Pastoral and Anti-Pastoral Patterns in Updike's Fiction*. Carbondale: Southern Illinois University Press, 1971.

Trachtenberg, Stanley, ed. *New Essays on* Rabbit, Run. Cambridge: Cambridge University Press, 1993.

Essays and Reviews

Adams, Robert Martin. "Without Risk." *New York Times Book Review*, 18 September 1996: 4–5.

Adler, Renata. "Arcadia, PA." *New Yorker*, 13 April 1963, 182–88.

Amis, Martin. "Magnanimous in a Big Way." *New York Times Book Review*, 10 November 1991, 12.

Balliett, Whitney. "Writer's Writer." *New Yorker*, 7 February 1959, 138–42.

———. "The American Expression." *New Yorker*, 5 November 1960, 222–24.

Bayley, John. *The Short Story: Henry James to Elizabeth Bowen*. New York: St. Martin's, 1988.

Bellow, Saul. "Recent American Fiction." Washington: Library of Congress, 1963.

Berthoff, Warner. *Harvard Magazine*, September–October 1996, 10.

Brophy, Brigid. "Love in the Garden State." *Harper's*, December 1976, 80–82.

Burgess, Anthony. "Language, Myth and Mr. Updike." In *Critical Essays on John Updike*, ed. William R. Macnaughton. Boston: G. K. Hall, 1982, 55–58.

Cooper, Rand Richards. "Bungle in the Jungle." *Commonweal*, 8 April 1994, 18–20.

Crews, Frederick. "Mr. Updike's Planet." *New York Review of Books*, 4 December 1986, 7–10, 12, 14.

Davis, Hope Hale. "Distaff Doormat." *New Leader*, 18 April 1988, 20–21.

Donoghue, Denis. "The Zeal of a Man of Letters." *New York Times Book Review*, 18 September 1983, 1.

Duvall, John N. "The Pleasure of Textual/Sexual Wrestling: Pornography and Heresy in Roger's Version." *Modern Fiction Studies* (spring 1991), 81–95.

Flower, Dean. "John Updike 1932–." In *American Writers: A Collection of*

Literary Biographies. Retrospective Supplement 1, eds. A Walton Litz and Molly Weigel. New York: Charles Scribner's, 1998.

Gelfant, Blanche W. "Fiction Chronicle." *Hudson Review* 28, no. 2 (summer 1975), 309–20.

Gordon, Mary. *Good Boys and Dead Girls*. New York: Viking, 1991.

Greiner, Donald J. "Body and Soul: John Updike and *The Scarlet Letter*." *Journal of Modern Literature* 15 (spring 1989), 475–95.

Hardwick, Elizabeth. "Citizen Updike." In *Sight-Readings*. New York: Random House, 1998, 115–31.

Inglis, Fred. "On Being a Dud." *Nation*, 10 July 1989, 59–61.

Kakutani, Michiko. "Updike's Struggle to Portray Women." *New York Times*, 5 May 1988, sec. C, p. 29.

Kiely, Robert. "Rabbit Reread." *Harvard Magazine*, July–August 1996, 26.

Oates, Joyce Carol. "Updike's American Comedies." *Modern Fiction Studies* 21 (fall 1975), 459–72.

———. "*The Coup* by John Updike." *New Republic*, 6 January 1979, 32–34.

———. "Future Tense." *New Yorker*, 8 December 1997, 116–17.

Ozick, Cynthia. "Bech, Passing." In *John Updike*, ed. Harold Bloom. Modern Critical Views. New York: Chelsea House, 1987, 127–38.

Poirier, Richard. *The Performing Self*. New York: Oxford University Press, 1971.

Raban, Jonathan. "Rabbit's Last Run." *Washington Post*, 30 September 1990, Book World, 1.

Richards, I. A. *Practical Criticism*. New York: Harcourt Brace, 1929.

Ricks, Christopher. "Flopsy Bunny." *New York Review of Books*, 16 December 1971, 7–9.

Rothstein, Mervyn. "In S Updike Tries Woman's Viewpoint." *New York Times*, 2 March 1988, sec. C, p. 21.

Samuels, Charles Thomas. "The Question of Updike." *Kenyon Review* 28, no. 2 (March 1966), 268–76.

Schiff, James A. *John Updike Revisited*. New York: Twayne, 1998.

———. *Updike's Version: Rewriting* The Scarlet Letter. Columbia: University of Missouri Press, 1992.

Searles, George J., ed. *Conversations with Philip Roth*. Jackson: University Press of Mississippi, 1992.

Stevick, Philip. "The Full Range of Updike's Prose." In *New Essays on Rabbit, Run*, ed. Stanley Trachtenberg. Cambridge: Cambridge University Press, 1993, 31–52.

Tallent, Elizabeth. *Married Men and Magic Tricks: John Updike's Erotic Heroes.* Berkeley: Creative Arts Book Co., 1982.

Taylor, Larry E. *Pastoral and Anti-Pastoral Patterns in Updike's Fiction.* Carbondale: Southern Illinois University Press, 1971.

Thompson, John. "Other People's Affairs." *Partisan Review,* January–February 1961, 117–24.

Thorburn, David. "Recent Novels: Realism Redux." *Yale Review* 66, no. 4 (summer 1977), 584–91.

Trachtenberg, Stanley, ed. *New Essays on Rabbit, Run.* Cambridge: Cambridge University Press, 1993.

Updike, John. "Why Rabbit Had to Go." *New York Times Book Review,* 5 August 1990, 1, 24–25.

Verduin, Kathleen. "Sex, Nature, and Dualism in *The Witches of Eastwick.*" *Modern Language Quarterly* 46 (September 1985): 293–315.

Vidal, Gore. "Rabbit's Own Burrow." *Times Literary Supplement,* 26 April 1996, 3–7.

———. *United States: Essays 1952–1992.* New York: Random House, 1993.

Waldron, Randall H. "Rabbit Revised." *American Literature* 56 (March 1984), 51–67.

Way, Brian. "The Case for the Defensive." *New Review* 4 (April 1977): 55–57.

Wilson, Raymond III. "*Roger's Version:* Updike's Negative-Solid Model of *The Scarlet Letter.*" *Modern Fiction Studies* 35 (summer 1989), 241–50.

Wood, James. "John Updike's Complacent God." In *The Broken Estate: Essays on Literature and Belief.* New York: Random House, 1999, 195–202.